ROYAL HISTORICAL SOCIETY

STUDIES IN HISTORY 74

PEACE THROUGH LAW

PEACE THROUGH LAW

BRITAIN AND
THE INTERNATIONAL COURT
IN THE 1920s

Lorna Lloyd

THE ROYAL HISTORICAL SOCIETY

THE BOYDELL PRESS

First published 1997

A Royal Historical Society publication
Published by The Boydell Press
an imprint of Boydell & Brewer Ltd
PO Box 9   Woodbridge   Suffolk IP12 3DF   UK
and of Boydell & Brewer Inc.
PO Box 41026   Rochester   NY 14604–4126   USA

ISBN 0 86193 235 8

ISSN 0269–2244

A catalogue record for this book is available
from the British Library

Library of Congress Cataloging-in-Publication Data
Lloyd, Lorna.
    Peace through law : Britain and the International Court in
the 1920s / Lorna Lloyd.
        p.   cm. – (Royal Historical Society studies in history, ISSN
0269-2244 ; 74)
    Includes bibliographical references and index.
    ISBN 0-86193-235-8 (hc : alk. paper)
    1. Permanent Court of International Justice. 2. League of
Nations–Great Britain. 3. Arbitration, International. 4. Pacific
settlement of international disputes. 5. Great Britain–Politics
and government-1910–1936. I. Title. II. Series: Royal
Historical Society studies in history ; no 74.
JX1971.5.L58   1997
341.5′52′094109042–dc21   96–46636

The paper used in this publication meets the minimum requirements
of American National Standard for Information Sciences –
Permanence of Paper for Printed Library Materials, ANSI Z39.48–1984

Printed in Great Britain by
St Edmundsbury Press Ltd, Bury St Edmunds, Suffolk

TO ALAN

Let us be grateful to women for taking an interest in the League of Nations. In politics as in art they are always 'mystic', that is to say, somewhat emotional, somewhat prone to veneration, and not unfrequently [sic.] they are taken in. Their superstitious respect for what they believe to be competence, their somewhat servile respect for anything that is suggestive of power, their love of eloquence, their taste for incidents and for intrigue: all these attractive characteristics add to their beauty. They dispel indifference; they diffuse emotion; they take sides; and one notices how, being less interested in ideas and facts than in men, they delightfully deem it their role and duty ever to be rewarding somebody.

– Robert de Traz, *The spirit of Geneva*, trans. Fried-Ann Kindler, London 1935, 33

Contents

The Society records its gratitude to the following whose generosity made possible the initiation of this series: The British Academy; The Pilgrim Trust; The Twenty-Seven Foundation; The United States Embassy's Bicentennial funds; The Wolfson Trust; several private donors. Publication of this volume was further assisted by a generous grant from the Scouloudi Foundation.

Acknowledgements

This book began as a PhD thesis submitted to the University of London. The (then) Social Science Research Council provided financial support when I was a research student; the University of Keele gave me the leave of absence which greatly facilitated the completion of this work. The CAWMites Fund made a grant towards preparing the manuscript for publication and a grant from the Scouloudi Foundation assisted the book's publication. I am very grateful to all of them.

I also much appreciate the expertise of the archivists and librarians who so readily helped me with my research. For permission to publish extracts from collections, I thank the following: the Bodleian Library and Mr Alexander Murray (for the Gilbert Murray papers); the British Library (for the Cecil papers and for permission to quote from the Balfour papers); the British Library of Political and Economic Science (for the Dalton and Passfield papers); Cambridge University Library (for the Baldwin papers); the Controller of Her Majesty's Stationery Office for Crown-copyright records in the India Office records and the Public Record Office; David Higham Associates for permission to quote from the Cadogan papers; the Earl of Balfour (for permission to quote from the Balfour papers); the Hon. Francis Noel-Baker (for permission to quote from the Noel-Baker papers); Professor Ann K. S. Lambton (for permission to quote from the Cecil papers); the Master, Fellows, and Scholars of Churchill College, Cambridge (for the Cadogan, Hankey and Noel-Baker collections); the United Nations Association (for the League of Nations Union papers); the United States National Archives (for Department of State papers); and the University of Birmingham (for the Austen Chamberlain papers). Dr Robert Holland, Dr Don Page and Dr Peter J. Yearwood kindly allowed me to quote from their doctoral theses. And the American Society of International Law gave me permission to reprint a revised version of chapter 1 which appeared in *The American Journal of International Law* lxxix (1985). I thank them all.

While the manuscript was awaiting publication, a Faculty Research Award from the Canadian government enabled me to do further research in the superb National Archives in Ottawa. I was agreeably pleased that the material in the Canadian Archives supports the thrust of the argument in this book. Where possible I have incorporated new information obtained in Ottawa.

For loving, loyal encouragement, I could not have asked for a better mum and dad. I am grateful to them and to my sister, Mrs Patricia Knight, who rendered invaluable practical assistance by cheerfully and uncomplainingly typing, retyping and formatting large chunks of the book. The late Professor G. L. Goodwin, the late Professor Sir James Fawcett and the late Professor F. S. Northedge gave me helpful advice on individual chapters. Other very useful comments and corrections on individual chapters came from Mrs Anna Ascher, Professor Martin David Dubin, Professor Sir Kenneth Keith, Ms Kathleen MacManus, Mr Tadashi Kuramatsu and Dr Peter J. Yearwood. I am most appreciative of their help.

Above all, however, the following three friends are those towards whom I am most indebted in respect of this book. Mr Nicholas Sims developed my understanding and interest in International Relations when I was an undergraduate at the London School of Economics and suggested that I go on to research. He was always encouraging and interested in my work, he gave me much-valued assistance at the final stage of the submission of my thesis, and he generally acted as a tonic to my spirits.

Without the late, the Rt Hon. the Lord Noel-Baker PC, this book would have been very much the poorer. He readily shared his memories of the quest that was so dear to his heart and of the period covered by the book. In so doing he greatly deepened my understanding of the people and issues that were involved.

Last, but not least, Professor Alan James suggested the subject to me and then, when I followed a somewhat different path from the one he had envisaged, was pleasingly enthusiastic about what I was doing. He was the kindest of companions and guides. When I was unsure of my way he gave me wise advice. When I felt desperate he kept me going with immense patience and good-humoured tolerance. And, while any errors are my own, his insistence on rigorous intellectual discipline at all times has left its invariably beneficial mark on me and my book. Accordingly, with deep gratitude and affection, I dedicate this book to Alan.

Lorna Lloyd

Abbreviations

Account by Cecil	Lord Robert Cecil to Arthur Henderson, 25 Sept. 1929, W 10270/21/98, *DBFP* vi, 442
Account by Hurst	'Account [by Cecil Hurst] of negotiations which took place at Geneva regarding the treatment of inter-imperial disputes', 21 Sept. 1929, PRO, W 9062/21/98 FO 371/14106
BED	British empire delegations
BLPES	London, British Library of Political and Economic Science
BM	British Museum
BMR	Belligerent maritime rights
Bodl. Lib.	Oxford, Bodleian Library
CCAC	Cambridge, Churchill College Archives Centre
CAS	League of Nations, Committee on Arbitration and Security of the Preparatory Commission for the Disarmament Conference (Nov. 1927–July 1928)
CAS, docs.	CAS, Memoranda on arbitration, security and the articles of the Covenant with annexes containing documents submitted to the Committee for consideration at its second session <C.S.S.10.>(1928.IX.3.)
CAS, third session	CAS, Report on third session (27 June–4 July 1928) [C.342.M.100.IX]<C.P.D.123> <C.A.S.75> (1928.IX.9)
CID	Committee of Imperial Defence
CID:BR first report	CID sub-committee on belligerent rights, first report 'The renewal of the arbitration treaties', 13 Feb. 1929, CP 40(29), Appendix 2 to *DBFP* vi
CID:BR second report	CID sub-committee on belligerent rights, second report 'Maritime belligerent rights', 6 Mar. 1929, BR 82(General 91/5), Appendix 3 to *DBFP* vi
CUL	Cambridge University Library
DBFP	*Documents on British foreign policy*, eds. W. N. Medlicott, D. Dakin and M. E. Lambert, ser. 1A, London 1966-75 (cited by volume and document number)
DCC	League of Nations Union, Disarmament campaign committee (Sept. 1927–Apr.1928)
DCJ	League of Nations, *Documents concerning the action taken by the Council of the League of Nations under Article 14 of the Covenant and the adoption by the Assembly of the Statute of the Permanent Court*, London 1920
DTMA	Draft Treaty of Mutual Assistance (1923)
Excom	League of Nations Union, executive committee
FRUS	*Papers relating to the foreign relations of the United States, 1927*, ii; *1928*, i, ii, Washington DC 1942, 1943

House of Commons *debs.*	*The parliamentary debates*, House of Commons, official report, fifth ser.
House of Lords *debs.*	*The parliamentary debates*, House of Lords, official report, fifth ser.
IASDC	League of Nations Union, International arbitration, security and disarmament committee (May 1928–June 1929)
ILP	Independent Labour Party
Legal advisers' memorandum	'Memorandum by the legal advisers of the Foreign Office respecting compulsory arbitration', 4 Mar. 1926, Annex to CP 257(26), *DBFP* ii, 68
LNA	Records of the League Assembly (cited with the number of the Assembly)
LNOJ	*League of Nations Official Journal*
LNU	League of Nations Union
NAC	Ottawa, National Archives of Canada
NCPW	National Council for the Prevention of War
PCIJ	Permanent Court of International Justice
PRO	London, Public Record Office
PVCJ	Advisory Committee of Jurists, *Procès-verbaux of the proceedings of the committee, The Hague, June 16–July 24 1920*, London 1921
TMC	Temporary Mixed Commission
UBL	Birmingham, University of Birmingham Library
USNA	Washington DC, United States National Archives

Introduction

The 'peace through law' movement in Britain in the 1920s appears to lend support to one popular caricature of British politics: that internationally, no less than domestically, Conservatives are hard-headed people who accept the ways of the world whereas Labourites are idealists who want to reshape things. For the idea that war could be expunged from international relations by, among other things, a grand adjudicatory scheme cut no obvious ice with the Conservatives. In left-wing circles, however, it had great appeal. Many Conservatives, it is true, did touch their deerstalkers in acknowledgement of the honourable hopes that lay behind the idea of peace through law, but that was all. Almost all socialists, on the other hand, genuinely endorsed the idea and really thought that it was essential for ushering in a warless world.

Much of the peace through law campaign in Britain came to be centred, in one way or another, on the Optional Clause of the Permanent Court of International Justice, which enabled states to accept the Court's compulsory jurisdiction. And this aspect of the campaign gave the caricature added substance. For whereas the Coalition and Conservative governments of the early 1920s showed no interest whatsoever in the Optional Clause, the Labour government of 1924 played a leading role in drafting the Geneva Protocol, under which signatories would have been obliged to accept the Optional Clause. But with that government's early fall the Protocol came to nothing. And, indeed, the Optional Clause may now have been doubly damned, for the new foreign secretary, Austen Chamberlain, was said to have entertained a particular antipathy towards it on account of its association with the Geneva Protocol.[1] During the next four-and-a-half years of Conservative rule much was heard in public and at the debates of the League of Nations in Geneva about the Optional Clause, but there was no sign that the Conservatives were changing their view.

Thus it is doubtful if the 1929 claim of Gilbert Murray, Regius Professor of Greek at Oxford University and a leader of the League of Nations Union, that the Conservative government had doggedly refused 'to accept the International Court'[2] would have been much contested. But the general election of that year led to the second Labour government, and within a few months Britain had accepted the Clause, the decision being announced at an occasion of relative flamboyance at Geneva. Here, surely, was a reflection of how, on the British political scene, light had triumphed over darkness. The new foreign secretary, Arthur Henderson, appeared to endorse this by saying that, on the Optional Clause, his view was 'diametrically opposed' to that of the previous government.[3] And a non-political source – the preface to a volume of *Documents*

[1] B. J. C. McKercher, *The second Baldwin government and the United States, 1924–1929: attitudes and diplomacy*, Cambridge 1984, 102n., 243.
[2] Francis West, *Gilbert Murray: a life*, Beckenham 1984, 202.
[3] Mary Agnes Hamilton, *Arthur Henderson*, London 1938, 284. Cf. Herbert Morrison's presidential

1

on British foreign policy – asserts that Labour's policy on the Optional Clause was one of the two major breaks which it introduced in 1929 into the general continuity of British foreign policy.[4]

Was it really so? It is noteworthy, and probably a reflection of the lack of credibility since 1945 of the idea of peace through law, that British policy on the Optional Clause in the 1920s seems to have been subjected to virtually no scholarly examination – notwithstanding the fact that at that time the Optional Clause was 'always with us'.[5] It is the purpose of this work to go some way towards filling that gap by mapping the path to signature. The book begins with the inclusion of the Optional Clause in the Statute of the Permanent Court of International Justice; looks at British policy towards it in the early 1920s, and, in particular, at the policy of the first Labour government; analyses the various pressures on the Conservative government between 1924 and 1929 – years which were supposedly barren so far as the government's attitude was concerned; and follows the second Labour government in its rush from success at the polls in May 1929 to that great moment of hope when Britain signed the Clause on 19 September.

address to the 1929 Labour Party conference: Labour Party, *Report of the 29th annual conference*, 1929, 150.
[4] M. E. Lambert, 'Preface' to *DBPF* iv, p. ix.
[5] C. A. W. Manning, *The policies of the British dominions in the League of Nations*, London 1932, 35.

PART ONE

STOP GO, 1920–1924

1

The Origins of the Optional Clause

The Permanent Court of International Justice (PCIJ) was established in 1922. Article 36, paragraph 2 of its Statute reads:

> The Members of the League of Nations and the States mentioned in the Annex to the Covenant may, either when signing or ratifying the Protocol to which the present Statute is adjoined, or at a later moment, declare that they recognise as compulsory *ipso facto* and without special agreement, in relation to any other Member or State accepting the same obligation, the jurisdiction of the Court in all or any of the classes of legal disputes concerning:
>
> (a) the interpretation of a treaty;
>
> (b) any question of international law;
>
> (c) the existence of any fact which, if established, would constitute a breach of an international obligation;
>
> (d) the nature and extent of the reparation to be made for the breach of an international obligation.[1]

States that wished to take advantage of the opportunity offered by this paragraph did so by signing a separate protocol which ran as follows:

> The undersigned, being duly authorised thereto, further declare, on behalf of their Government, that, from this date, they accept as compulsory *ipso facto* and without special Convention the jurisdiction of the Court in conformity with Article 36, paragraph 2, of the Statute of the Court, under the following conditions.[2]

This protocol was headed by the phrase 'Optional Clause'. In this way, Article 36, paragraph 2 itself came to be known as the Optional Clause. It was an appropriate terminology in that it gave states the *option* of accepting the compulsory jurisdiction of the Court, whether or not they attached reservations to it. This last possibility was envisaged by the third paragraph of Article 36, which stated:

> The declaration referred to above may be made unconditionally or on condition of reciprocity on the part of several or certain Members or States, or for a certain time.

The Optional Clause – as Article 36, paragraph 2, of the Court's Statute will henceforward be called – was introduced into the Statute of the Permanent Court at the first (1920) Assembly of the League of Nations. It was the result of a disagreement between those great powers (Britain, France, Italy and Japan)

---

[1] Statute of the Permanent Court of International Justice in 'Procès-verbal of the eleventh session of the Council, Geneva, November–December 1920': *LNOJ*, Jan.–Feb.1921, Annex 138a, 137.
[2] Optional Clause, ibid.

which refused to accept an international court possessing compulsory jurisdiction and the small powers, nearly all of which demanded compulsory jurisdiction. It emerged in the following manner.

The committee of jurists, June–July 1920

The Covenant of the League of Nations, which entered into force at the beginning of 1920,[3] provided for three principal organs. Firstly, the secretariat serviced the League under its first secretary-general, Sir Eric Drummond. Secondly, the Assembly contained representatives of all the members of the League. It could discuss 'any matter within the sphere of the League or affecting the peace of the world'. Its decisions, which required unanimity to enter into force,[4] were determined on the basis of one vote per League member. It was to be 'the general directing body of the League'.[5]

The third principal organ was the League Council which, according to the Covenant, was to contain five permanent members (the victorious great powers: the British Empire, the United States of America, France, Italy and Japan) and four non-permanent members periodically elected by the Assembly.[6] The defection of the United States left it with four permanent members until Germany was made a permanent member in 1926. As with the Assembly, each state had one vote on the Council and its decisions required unanimity.[7] The Council was, in effect, the executive of the League and represented the institutionalisation of the nineteenth-century Concert of Europe on a global scale. Apart from its primary role in the settlement of disputes, the Covenant assigned it specific responsibilities. One of these was the formulation of plans for an international court of justice, which were then to be presented to the Assembly.[8]

The League Council treated the establishment of the international court of justice as an urgent matter. At the second session of the Council in February 1920, Sir Eric Drummond nominated ten eminent jurists for membership of

[3] On 10 Jan. 1920 when the treaty of Versailles came into force.

[4] Apart from procedural matters, including the appointment of committees to investigate particular matters when a majority vote was required. A majority vote of the Assembly and the concurrence of the Council were required for a report on a dispute under Article 15 of the Covenant to have the same force as a unanimous report by the Council; for an increase in the non-permanent membership of the League Council; for the admission of new League members having permanent seats on the Council; and for the appointment of the secretary-general (other than the first, Sir Eric Drummond). A two-thirds majority was required for the admission of new members and for fixing the rules dealing with the election of non-permanent members of the Council. Amendments to the Covenant entered into force when ratified by the members of the Council and two-thirds of the members of the Assembly.

[5] League of Nations secretariat, *Ten years of world co-operation*, Geneva 1930, 11.

[6] The number of non-permanent members was increased to 6 in 1922 and 9 in 1926. The latter increase was accompanied by a change in the rules to allow for the re-election of non-permanent members, thereby creating a category known as 'semi-permanent members'. See below, 96–7, n. 28.

[7] Except on procedural issues, including the appointment of committees to investigate particular matters. Under Article 15 of the Covenant, the vote of a party to a dispute could not detract from an otherwise unanimous report. The Council could issue a majority report on a dispute, but this did not deprive members of 'the right to take such actions as they shall consider necessary for the maintenance of right and justice'.

[8] Under Article 14 of the Covenant.

an advisory committee of jurists which would produce a draft plan for the Court. The Council approved the list and although not all of those originally nominated were able to serve, the committee of jurists was able to meet at The Hague in the middle of June 1920.[9]

A little over a month later, after thirty-five meetings, the committee produced a draft Statute which, except for reservations on specific points, enjoyed the unanimous backing of all the jurists and provided for compulsory jurisdiction.[10] One of the reservations, however, concerned this matter. It came from Mineichiro Adatci of Japan, who was as unwavering in his opposition to compulsory jurisdiction as his colleagues were in its support. Adatci had intimated his uneasiness over this question at earlier meetings, but it was not until towards the end of the committee's work that he fully expounded his views to what he knew to be a body of men committed to compulsory jurisdiction. Appealing to the committee to be 'modest and practical', he argued that it would be contrary to the Covenant to grant such powers to the Court.[11]

The rest of the committee (including the British national, Lord Phillimore, who played a leading role in the committee's work) supported compulsory jurisdiction. This was partly because they believed that compulsory jurisdiction was a characteristic of a 'true' court and partly because, as lawyers, their thinking about an international organisation for peace had been conditioned by the Hague conferences of 1899 and 1907 and the predominantly legal approach that had been taken towards the problem of war before 1914. This had, to a great extent, focused upon the attempt to develop legal procedures for resolving disputes between states.

Towards the end of the nineteenth century, arbitration had become increasingly popular and a large number of arbitration treaties were negotiated. Clauses providing for arbitration were also inserted into a sizeable number of treaties. After the first Hague conference of 1899 had established the Permanent Court of Arbitration,[12] there were even more arbitration treaties negotiated and

---

[9] The Committee of Jurists finally contained five nationals of the great powers (USA, Britain, Japan, France and Italy), three nationals of former European neutrals (Norway, the Netherlands and Sweden), with the complement being made up by lawyers from Brazil and Belgium.

[10] The relevant articles (Articles 33 and 34) stated: Article 33: 'When a dispute has arisen between States and it has been found impossible to settle it by diplomatic means, and no agreement has been made to choose another jurisdiction, the party complaining may bring the case before the Court. The Court shall, first of all, decide whether the preceding conditions have been complied with; if so, it shall hear and determine the dispute according to the terms and within the limits of the next Article.' Article 34: 'Between States which are Members of the League of Nations, the Court shall have jurisdiction (and this without any special convention giving it jurisdiction) to hear and determine cases of a legal nature, concerning: a. The interpretation of a treaty; b. Any question of international law; c. The existence of any fact which, if established, would constitute a breach of an international obligation; d. The nature or extent of reparation to be made for the breach of an international obligation; e. The interpretation of a sentence passed by the Court. The Court shall also take cognisance of all disputes of any kind which may be submitted to it by a general or particular convention between the parties. In the event of a dispute as to whether a certain case comes within any of the categories above mentioned, the matter shall be settled by the decision of the Court.': Advisory Committee of Jurists, *Draft scheme of the Committee with reports to the Council of the League of Nations and resolutions by the Council relating to it*, London 1920, 12–13.

[11] PVCJ, twenty-fourth meeting, 14 July 1920, 541–3.

[12] The Permanent Court of Arbitration consisted of a bureau and a list of jurists who were available to act as arbitrators and whose governments had nominated them to serve in this capacity. The list was kept by the bureau at the Peace Palace at The Hague.

more arbitration clauses.[13] The second Hague conference of 1907 gave further momentum to the arbitration movement by recognising that certain types of disputes (notably those relating to the interpretation of treaties) should be submitted to arbitration.

In practice, states' obligations to arbitrate were very limited indeed because there was almost invariably a reservation of disputes involving third parties or involving 'honour, independence and vital interests'[14] – a phrase which enabled states to refuse arbitration whenever they saw fit. Similarly, although the United States was often seen as the standard-bearer in the arbitration movement, it actually ratified very few arbitration treaties because of the Senate's jealousy of its prerogative in foreign affairs.

However, the committee of jurists looked back to the progress which had been made in terms of the general acceptance of the desirability of compulsory arbitration and the rule of law in the pre-war years and through the Hague conferences. Two committee members – Elihu Root of the United States and Francis Hagerup of Norway – had attended the Hague conferences in an official capacity, and the chairman, Baron Descamps of Belgium, urged them to bear in mind that they were not confronted by a *tabula rasa*. Root had pointed out that Articles 12–14 of the Covenant of the League were vague and incomplete, but there was no official commentary on the Covenant that could clarify their meaning. Consequently, there was 'all the more reason why the Committee should take into consideration the work of the two Hague Conferences', which 'so strangely was forgotten in the drafting of the Covenant at Paris. The Committee was obliged to make good this omission'.[15] And this it did, urged on by those who managed, somehow, to interpret the 'spirit of the Covenant' as pointing in this direction.

However, there was a further reason why the committee believed that the court should have compulsory jurisdiction: its members envisaged a body which would not engage in arbitration as it had hitherto been understood, but in adjudication. The jurists on the committee believed that there were several important differences between arbitration and adjudication. Firstly, whereas arbitrators were chosen *ad hoc* by the parties to a dispute, judges belonged to an independent standing tribunal. Secondly, in arbitration the parties to a dispute had to agree on the law that the arbitrators were to apply. In adjudication, however, the court was bound by its statute which set out the rules on whose basis it was to operate, including the law to be applied in every case it heard. Thirdly, and most importantly, parties to arbitration had to set out in the *compromis* their agreement to arbitrate and the precise nature of the dispute. In adjudication, however, the court was seen as having the powers of compulsory jurisdiction whenever any party to a dispute took the matter to the court.

---

[13] For example, Nicolas Politis, the Greek diplomat and lawyer, calculated that between 1814 and 1914, arbitration had been extended by 70 special or compromissory clauses and 130 treaties; and that by 1914 there existed 139 arbitration treaties and 154 clauses were in operation between forty-seven states: *The new aspects of international law*, Washington 1928. See also J. Headlam-Morley 'Memorandum respecting the British government and arbitration: an historical review' (27 Jan. 1928), in his *Studies in diplomatic history*, London 1930. Headlam-Morley was the Foreign Office historical adviser.

[14] Subsequently referred to as the vital interests formula.

[15] *PVCJ*, eleventh meeting, 29 June 1920, 243.

'Arbitration means a combat before a combat', Loder had declared, whereas in a court, 'The gracious consent of the adversary is no longer required: one can do without him.'[16]

Britain's response to the draft Statute

The draft Statute of the Court reached Britain at the end of July 1920 with the recommendation from the British minister at The Hague that: 'The project now accepted is in all important respects that drawn up by Lord Phillimore and Mr. Root, and represents a complete victory for the Anglo-American point of view.'[17] However, this did not impress the British foreign secretary, Lord Curzon, who, after learning what was in the document, minuted: 'It would seem to me that Lord Phillimore or whoever represented us in framing this scheme must have been singularly oblivious to British interests.'[18] Sir Eyre Crowe (who became the permanent under secretary at the Foreign Office in November 1920) endorsed a proposal by Sir Cecil Hurst (the Foreign Office legal adviser), that a committee of eminent lawyers should examine the draft Statute. 'It certainly must be very closely examined by the best and sanest legal minds', he wrote.[19]

On 13 August a Cabinet committee was set up under the Lord Chancellor, Lord Birkenhead, to examine the draft Statute, but a breakdown in communications between the Foreign Office and the Cabinet secretariat, combined with the illness of Birkenhead, meant that decision-making was

---

[16] Memorandum by Loder, 'Unilateral summons or previous agreement', PVCJ, 249–51. His argument is elaborated in 'The Permanent Court of International Justice and compulsory jurisdiction', The British Year Book of International Law, 1921–2, ii, London 1921. In 1927 Lord Phillimore explained that there were three distinctions between a court of justice and arbitration. In arbitration, he said, states had to agree to arbitrate, agree to the compromis and agree to the arbitrators. In a court of justice, the court and the judges were established and 'the party complaining comes to the Court and says: "Bring my adversary before you that he may answer" ': House of Lords debs., 16 Nov. 1927, col. 107. It is important to recognise that the word 'arbitration' was used very loosely by lawyers and laymen throughout the 1920s. A strict definition of the term is provided in Article 15 of the Hague Convention for the Pacific Settlement of International Disputes of 1899 which states that: 'International arbitration has for its object the settlement of differences between States by judges of their own choice, and on the basis of a respect for law.' However, the term 'arbitration' was frequently treated as synonymous with adjudication. Thus, in the preparatory documents for the Committee of Jurists, the League's legal adviser, van Hamel, had thought it necessary to discuss whether Articles 12, 13 and 15 of the Covenant provided that the proposed court should be arbitral or arbitral and judicial. He concluded that the Covenant allowed for a judicial organ. This confusion may be due to the fact that the PCIJ, as established, did not have compulsory jurisdiction, and because of the novelty of the Court. People had not yet become used to distinguishing between the two procedures and there is sufficient similarity for the layperson to fail to perceive any difference. In addition, it was usual in the 1920s to use the term 'arbitration' to mean the pacific settlement of disputes by any means. Perhaps this is because the term had been inherited from pre-war attempts to develop the legal machinery for the pacific settlement of disputes or perhaps it was used simply because it was a convenient shorthand term for a less elegant and more awkward phrase. The latter explanation seems more likely. However, although there was little exactitude in terminology, it is nearly always clear how the term was being used.

[17] Despatch from Sir Ronald Graham, The Hague, No. 607, 24 July 1920, PRO, General 209523/203188 FO 371/4311.

[18] Minute, 5 Oct. 1920, PRO, W 512/241/98 FO 371/5480.

[19] Minute, 14 Aug. 1920, ibid.

deferred to the last moment – just before the League Council met to discuss the draft Statute in October 1920.

The British documents relating to the draft Statute are markedly hostile to the Court. Sir Eyre Crowe thought that 'expert opinion' held that the Permanent Court of Arbitration had 'everything that is practically required and practically valuable',[20] and the top legal advisers to the government (who were unconnected with the Foreign Office) held that the establishment of the proposed Court was not, at that time, desirable.

The objections to the PCIJ were heavily influenced by Britain's experience during the First World War. Her naval blockade of Germany had played a major role in the achievement of victory but had caused friction with the USA until 1917 (when America entered the war) and with the neutral states of Scandinavia and Holland throughout the war. Friction focused on the interpretation of belligerent maritime rights, that is the international law governing naval warfare. Britain had maintained 'high' belligerent maritime rights, an interpretation of the law that gave the British navy wide freedom of action. The neutral states, on the other hand, powerlessly argued for 'low' belligerent maritime rights or greater restrictions on the freedom of action of the navy of a belligerent state.[21] Sir Eyre Crowe's whole argument was based on looking at 'what might and would have happened in the time of our greatest national peril' – the Great War. Had the International Court existed during the war, he said, Britain would have then 'had to choose between losing the war or defying the International Court'.[22]

In addition to differences governing the laws of naval warfare, there was also believed to be a difference between the 'Anglo-Saxon' (i.e. Anglo-American) and the 'continental' (i.e. European) approach to international law. It was inevitable that the majority of judges on the Court would be 'continental' lawyers or would follow that school (for example, the Latin Americans). By virtue of sitting at The Hague they would be exposed to the 'pernicious influence of extreme German doctrines'. For, said Crowe, The Hague itself, and Dutch professors of international law were pro-German and anti-English.[23] Another fear, which was expressed by the law officers of the crown, was that the judges would inevitably divide on national lines. Finally, it was held that Britain could not commit future governments to execute the judgements of the Court. Some judgements could conceivably require parliamentary sanction which might not be forthcoming. Similarly, there was nothing to ensure that the other party to a dispute would comply with an adverse decision.[24]

By the time the ministerial conference met to consider the proposed Court on 18 October,[25] Britain was aware that the Italians and Japanese were opposed to

[20] Minute, 5 Oct. 1920, ibid.
[21] BMR will be fully discussed in ch. 6.
[22] Minute by Crowe, 2 Aug. 1920, PRO, General 20955/203188 FO 371/4311. As it was, Britain still faced outstanding claims from ex-neutrals and it was taken as axiomatic that if the Court had retrospective jurisdiction it would reverse British decisions and order Britain to pay heavy compensation. It was thus made clear that the Court should not have this jurisdiction and that its judgements should not constitute binding precedents.
[23] Ibid.
[24] Other objections were Britain's 'unhappy experience' of arbitration and the argument that as long as the United States was not a member of the Court, Britain should have nothing to do with it.
[25] That is a meeting (by which Prime Minister Lloyd George did not consider himself bound) of

compulsory jurisdiction and Arthur Balfour, who was to represent Britain at the imminent League Council meeting, had dismissed compulsory jurisdiction as a proposition that would hardly stand discussion. However, not only did the ministers decide to reject compulsory jurisdiction, but they also decided that 'the whole scheme should be referred back to the Drafting Committee to explore the practical difficulties'.[26]

Nevertheless, when the League Council met a few days later it did not reject the draft Statute. Presumably because of the widespread international support for the establishment of a court, Balfour thought that Britain should not appear to be obstructive. Accordingly, he tried to achieve his aims by less comprehensive means, and was successful. A few days later, Sir Cecil Hurst was able to report that: 'Mr. Balfour with great adroitness succeeded in eliminating, with the consent of his colleagues on the Council, all these objectionable features of the scheme.'[27]

Cecil Hurst, Dionisio Anzilotti (under secretary-general of the League) and Joost-Adrian van Hamel (director of the League's legal section) had jointly drafted the amendments which deprived the Court of its compulsory jurisdiction while the French representative, Léon Bourgeois, produced the report in which the Council explained its decisions regarding the Statute. The section of the report dealing with the Court's jurisdiction (which drew heavily on Britain's observations) argued that the inclusion of compulsory jurisdiction would have involved a modification of the Covenant and that it was inopportune to go further than the Covenant-makers had intended.[28] Amendments were also introduced with the explicit aim of preventing the Court from asserting authority in disputes involving prize, a subject which loomed large in British thinking about the Court.[29] These actions by the Council fulfilled its mandate

those cabinet ministers who might be interested in subjects on the agenda and whom he chose to invite.

[26] Minutes of conference of ministers, 18 Oct. 1920, PRO, W 1149/241/98 FO 371/5480.

[27] Memorandum by Hurst, 29 Oct. 1920, PRO, W 1504/241/98 FO 371/5480. The relevant articles now stated: Article 34: 'La compétence de la Cour est reglée par les articles 12, 13 et 14 du Pacte.' Article 35: 'Sans préjudice de la faculté conferée par l'article 12 du Pacte, aux parties à un litige de le soumettre soit à la procédure judiciaire ou arbitrale, soit à l'examen du conseil, la Cour connaîtra sans convention spéciale des litiges dont le règlement est confié à elle ou à la juridiction instituée par la Société des Nations, aux termes des traités en vigueur.': *DCJ*, Synopsis of amendments to the draft scheme, 41.

[28] For Balfour's argument that the drafters of the Covenant had deliberately intended that the proposed Court should not have the power of compulsory jurisdiction, see ibid. 38. Bourgeois's report contended that the draft Statute would have enabled the Court, rather than the League Council, to decide when diplomatic methods of settling a dispute had been exhausted and whether the dispute should go to the Court, the Council or some other international tribunal. Moreover, it could have done this before the Council had considered the dispute. But the Covenant had given freedom of choice to League members under Article 12. Furthermore, although the Council was not opposed to the actual idea of compulsory jurisdiction on questions of a judicial nature, several of its members had objected to the term 'any point of international law': Report adopted by the Council on 27 Oct. 1920, ibid. 46–7.

[29] Hurst had pointed out that the draft Statute 'produces in fact in an even balder manner all that the scheme for the creation of an international prize court would have achieved. That scheme . . . was rejected by Great Britain, and most people now think wisely rejected': Hurst to Hankey, 28 Sept. 1920, PRO, W 512/241/98 FO 371/5480. After the convention for an international prize court was opened for signature in 1907, it quickly became apparent that its ratification would be dependent upon which law the prize court would apply. Accordingly, the 1908 Declaration of

under Article 14 of the Covenant and the draft Statute was now submitted to the Assembly of the League.

The first Assembly of the League of Nations and the emergence of the Optional Clause

When the first Assembly met at Geneva in November–December 1920 it was immediately apparent that the great and small powers were sharply opposed over the question of the Court's competence. The attitude of the small powers in favour of compulsory jurisdiction was conditioned by the large number of lawyers who represented them in the Assembly, by the legalist approach to international relations of certain states (notably the Netherlands and the Scandinavian states), and by the widely-held belief that compulsory jurisdiction would be advantageous to small states. It was expected that the Court would redress the differences of power between the weak and the strong which had just been institutionalised in the League Council. An international court with compulsory jurisdiction would provide them with a forum where they could take their grievances against the strong and where the outcome would not be decided by the number of guns or economic power of a state. In other words, the small stood to gain what Britain stood to lose.

The Assembly delegated consideration of the draft Statute to the third (legal and constitutional) committee which was chaired by Léon Bourgeois, the Frenchman who had written the report for the Council the previous October. In turn, a small sub-committee of the third committee undertook the major task of examining in detail the draft Statute and the amendments which had been tabled.[30] Britain, France and Japan were soon revealed as opponents of compulsory jurisdiction; the Belgians, Portuguese and South Americans were proponents; and Greece, the Netherlands and Norway saw the necessity of accepting Bourgeois's injunction that they should 'calculate the limits of the possible'.[31] In due course, the sub-committee reported that compulsory jurisdiction could not be reinserted in the Statute because this would prevent the Assembly from obtaining the unanimity which was essential for the establishment of the Court.

London clarified the law of maritime warfare that was to be applied by the court. In 1910 a bill was introduced into parliament to provide for appeals to the international prize court but the bill was withdrawn. A second bill was passed by the Commons in 1911 but was rejected by the Lords. A provision was also added to the Statute to prevent the operation of the principle of *stare decisis*. The ministers conference in October 1920 had held that 'The scheme was detrimental to us as a sea Power since it would enable predominantly land Powers to build up a code of international law which would fetter the exercise of our sea power. Unless precaution was taken to prevent its application being made retrospective, it would even enable appeal to be made against the decisions of our prize courts in the late war.': PRO, W 1149/241/98 FO 371/5480. Although there was no question of Britain accepting compulsory adjudication, it was thought that the small states might use a system of precedent to put pressure on Britain.

[30] The sub-committee contained five members of the Committee of Jurists – Adatci (Japan), Fernandez (Brazil), Hagerup (Norway), Loder (Netherlands) and Ricci-Busatti (Italy) – and five others appointed by the bureau of the third committee – Doherty (Canada), Fromageot (France), Huber (Switzerland), Politis (Greece) and Hurst (Britain). Amendments that would have reintroduced compulsory jurisdiction had been submitted by Argentina, Colombia, Spain and Panama: *DCJ*, 43.

[31] Minutes of the first committee (constitutional questions), *The records of the first Assembly: meetings of committees 1920* (*LNA1* third committee), 280, 288–9.

One member of the third committee was unwilling to accept this outcome. Raoul Fernandez of Brazil, who had ardently championed compulsory jurisdiction in the committee of jurists, remained equally determined to get it now. At the same time, he was determined that the Assembly should assert its authority and aggrandise its power at the expense of the Council. Accordingly, he insisted that the Assembly should be able to discuss the amendments dealt with by the sub-committee. Hurst, Henri Fromageot of France, and Francis Hagerup of Norway vainly appealed to him not to try to amend the plan for the Court when it came before the plenary sessions. If he must, he could submit the amendments for a separate discussion during the plenary meetings. However, Fernandez insisted on his right to raise the matter in whichever way best suited him. He proposed, therefore, that the Assembly should approve the Statute of the Court subject to its ratification by the members. At the same time he proposed that the Assembly should approve an alternative Article 36 (the article relating to the competence of the Court, which did not provide for compulsory jurisdiction) which was practically identical to the compulsory jurisdiction proposal of the committee of jurists.[32] Then, when they deposited their ratifications to the protocol establishing the Court, the members of the Court would indicate which version of Article 36 they adhered to, that drawn up by the committee of jurists or that produced by the League Council at its October meeting.

Fernandez claimed that this scheme would reconcile the views of the advocates and opponents of compulsory jurisdiction. More specifically, he argued that it would meet the objections of the great powers that compulsory jurisdiction was beyond the scope of the Covenant inasmuch as his proposal would itself have 'the character of an amendment to the Covenant' (and would therefore require ratification).[33] However, unless he thought that the pressure of 'world public opinion' would shame all the great powers into accepting the alternative draft article, his proposal makes little sense. Had it gone through it would merely have led to the coexistence of two treaties which differed only in respect of one article.

Fernandez's proposal was considered by the sub-committee on 10 December. Other draft formulae for the Assembly resolution had been submitted by Fromageot of France, Max Huber of Switzerland and Arturo Ricci-Busatti of Italy. Whereas the latter had merely suggested a resolution giving the Assembly's approval of the establishment of the Court, Huber and Fromageot attempted to meet Fernandez's demands. Huber suggested that if necessary this should be by the introduction 'of a new annex to the Covenant which would provide for the co-existence of the two articles'. Fromageot, on the other hand, suggested that those who so wished should be allowed to accept the *additional optional obligation* of compulsory jurisdiction.[34]

---

[32] That is Article 34(1) of the draft Statute: see above n. 10; *LNAI* third committee, 298–301, 553.

[33] Legally-speaking, under Article 26 of the Covenant, any amendment to it required ratification by all the members of the Council and the majority of the members of the Assembly. Fernandez explained that his proposal would strengthen the authority of the Assembly *vis-à-vis* the Council since 'the risk of establishing a precedent dangerous to the authority of the Assembly would be avoided': ibid. 302.

[34] Ibid. 611–14.

The minutes of the meeting do not give any indication of its tone. They record that the sub-committee toyed with various combinations of the formulae before settling on the one that had been submitted by Fromageot. The formula that was to be inserted into the Statute of the Court was to constitute an *additional optional obligation* and not an amendment to the Covenant. It would be subject to reciprocity and states could specify the issues on which they accepted this obligation. Later that same day the third committee met as a whole and agreed on amendments to enable states to accept the obligation at any time after their acceptance of the Court's Statute, to impose time limits thereto, and to make it entirely clear that the Court could determine its own competence. They became paragraphs 2 and 3 of Article 36 of the Statute and were included in the form given at the beginning of this chapter. Thus the Optional Clause was born.[35]

In practical terms, the Optional Clause was scarcely different from Fernandez's alternative article. But Fernandez was bitterly disappointed. It was, he argued, 'inadmissible for a State to accept the principle of compulsory jurisdiction without knowing exactly towards whom it accepted such obligation'. On 13 December, when the Assembly discussed the Court, he pointed an accusing finger at the Council that had frustrated his hopes and declared that 'I was once enthusiastic; today I am barely confident. I am waiting.'[36] His disappointment and anger were echoed by most of the small states and all of the Latin Americans. 'A minority of delegations has once more paralysed the will of the majority', complained Lafontaine of Belgium.[37] 'You are promising us justice for tomorrow, but you are not giving it to us today' said Tamaya of Bolivia.[38] Loder of Holland warned the great powers: 'You are fighting against time, you will do so in vain.'[39]

Not all states expressed this anger. Hagerup of Norway, Demètre Negelescu of Rumania, Guiseppe Motta of Switzerland and Nicolas Politis of Greece recognised that they had to reach a consensus if they were to establish the Court and that the present proposal offered a springboard for the future. While acknowledging the significance of the occasion, *The Times* recorded that the proceedings were 'particularly dreary': the afternoon had been 'spent in a succession of unremarkable speeches by the delegates of smaller States',[40] and at least one delegate had addressed an almost empty hall. Balfour, the leader of the British delegation, and Bourgeois for France contented themselves with explaining that their states had always supported compulsory arbitration but that the Court had first to prove itself; in time, confidence in the Court would increase.

Finally, after almost six-and-three-quarter hours' debate, the Assembly passed a unanimous resolution approving the Statute of the Court for submission by the League Council to members of the League for ratification and Hymans, the Belgian president of the Assembly, dismissed it with the words 'we have accomplished a great work'.[41]

---

[35] Ibid. 312.
[36] *The records of the first Assembly. Plenary meetings*, 1920 (*LNA1* debs.), twentieth plenary, 13 Dec. 1920, 449.
[37] Ibid., 447.
[38] *LNA1* debs., twenty-first plenary, 13 Dec. 1920, 489.
[39] *LNA1* debs., twentieth plenary, 445.
[40] *The Times*, 14 Dec. 1920.
[41] Ibid.

The following day, 14 December, the Council approved the protocol of signature which had been prepared by the League secretariat. It was submitted to the Assembly on 17 December and made available for signature on that day and the next. Twenty-one League members signed the protocol and four of these also signed the Optional Clause at the Assembly.[42] Of these only Switzerland and Denmark had ratified the Optional Clause before the second Assembly opened in September 1921 (although, in the meantime, an additional three states had also adhered to the Clause).[43] By then a sufficient number of states had deposited their ratifications of the protocol establishing the Court for the Assembly to go ahead with electing the judges and for the establishment of the Court. By 15 February 1922, when the Court was formally opened, there had been thirty-one ratifications of the Statute and nine declarations accepting the Optional Clause had entered into force.[44] Ironically, Fernandez is generally credited as being the author of the Clause he so bitterly condemned.[45] And although Brazil had signed and ratified the Optional Clause before the Court opened, the Brazilian declaration stated that it would not come into effect until two permanent members of the League Council had ratified the Clause[46] – a condition which was not met until 5 February 1930 when Britain deposited its ratification of the Optional Clause.

Britain and the establishment of the PCIJ 1921-2

The Foreign Office had played no part in the negotiations over the Court Statute in December 1920. Its first news of the Assembly's sessions were gleaned from reports in *The Times*, and when the report of the third committee reached the Foreign Office on 22 December 1920, it made little sense since a finalised draft of the Statute was not available. Even when copies of the Assembly resolutions and the Statute of the Court did arrive, on

[42] Denmark, El Salvador, Portugal and Switzerland.

[43] Portugal ratified on 8 Oct. 1921 (the date of deposit of ratification of the protocol of signature) and El Salvador on 29 Aug. 1930 (the date of deposit of ratification of the protocol of signature). The states which had accepted the Optional Clause in 1921 before the second Assembly opened were the Netherlands on 6 Aug. 1921, Sweden on 16 Aug. 1921 and Bulgaria on 12 Aug. 1921 (the date of deposit of the ratification of the protocol of signature). Five additional states had signed but not ratified their declarations by the opening of the Assembly: Luxembourg, Liberia, Uruguay, Costa Rica and Finland. During the Assembly Haiti and Uruguay deposited ratifications of the Optional Clause (on 7 and 27 Sept. respectively).

[44] That is Bulgaria, Denmark, Haiti, the Netherlands, Norway, Portugal, Sweden, Switzerland and Uruguay. Seventeen states in all had signed the Optional Clause.

[45] See, for example, J. Wheeler-Bennett and M. Fanshaw, *Information on the World Court 1918–1928*, London 1929, 66; J. H. W. Verzijl, 'The system of the Optional Clause', *International Relations* i (1959), 585; Manley O. Hudson, *The Permanent Court of International Justice 1920-1942: a treatise*, New York 1943, 126.

[46] According to Fernandez, this was because: 'When I returned to my country, when I reported on our work and gave my Government my opinion, I said: I think it only right that by adhering to the clause concerning the compulsory jurisdiction of the Court, we should emphasise that, over and above the legal and political necessities, the great Powers which have a preponderating voice in establishing the composition of the Court are morally bound to set the example of submitting to its jurisdiction': League of Nations, Records of the sixth Assembly, plenary meetings, text of the debates, *LNOJ*, special supplement no. 33, 1925, eleventh plenary, 15 Sept. 1925, 84.

1 January 1921, the Foreign Office was still unable to take action since it did not know whether Britain and the dominions had signed. That they had done so was only known on receipt of a telegram from Drummond on 13 January.[47] By then Britain's lack of enthusiasm for the Court had apparently turned into a policy of procrastination. 'Continue policy of masterly inactivity',[48] suggested Villiers, the head of the Foreign Office department dealing with League affairs.

The ratification of Britain's adhesion to the protocol of signature of the Statute of the Court was considered by the Cabinet on 18 February. The Admiralty made sure that its still strong fears about belligerent maritime rights were fully taken into account by circulating a memorandum explaining that:

> The Admiralty have been watching with anxiety the sudden development of this Permanent Court. Unless the British view is openly stated and the functions of the Court strictly limited, some of the principal methods by which our Sea Power is exercised may be seriously jeopardised, if not, indeed nullified.[49]

However, as Birkenhead (the Lord Chancellor) pointed out, belligerent maritime rights were not jeopardised and there were no other valid objections to the establishment of the Court since Britain was not bound by the Optional Clause. The Attorney General, Sir Gordon Hewart, had already advised that Britain should 'absolutely refuse' to consent to compulsory jurisdiction[50] and, at the request of the Admiralty, this was explicitly stated. This being so, the Cabinet decided that 'the British Government had really no alternative but to ratify the Protocol'.[51] That, as far as the Cabinet was concerned, was that.

Approval of the wording which the treaty department suggested for ratifying the protocol was given in March 1921 and forwarded to the India and Colonial Offices for approval by the dominions and India.[52] Distance and lack of any effective machinery for co-ordinating imperial policy (in addition to the inexperience of the British dominions in international affairs) meant that there was a delay in obtaining the necessary agreement. By mid-April

---

[47] In November 1919, to the chagrin of Curzon and the Foreign Office, the Cabinet had decided that all League communications should go via a central office attached to the Cabinet, and the Foreign Office was deemed to be concerned only 'in a primary or secondary way'. This led to confusion in British policy towards the League and the PCIJ, one feature of which was that relevant papers were sometimes received too late for effective action to be taken (and were then received in too great a quantity). In October 1920, Hankey had a Foreign Office official seconded to the cabinet secretariat and claimed that this satisfied the Foreign Office and made for efficiency, but Foreign Office irritation continued until the fall of Lloyd George in October 1922. With his large secretariat threatened by the axe of the incoming prime minister, Bonar Law, Hankey decided immediately to return League business to the Foreign Office and thereby save expense. Lloyd George's personal interest in foreign policy did not extend to the PCIJ and the 'eclipse' of the Foreign Office had little impact on British policy towards the PCIJ.

[48] Minute, 15 Jan. 1921, PRO, W 573/22/98 FO 371/7033.

[49] Memorandum by the First Lord of the Admiralty (Lord Lee of Fareham), secret, 29 Jan. 1921, PRO, CP 2507 CAB 24/119.

[50] Memorandum by the attorney general (Sir Gordon Hewart), 3 Jan. 1921, PRO, W 291/22/98 FO 371/7033.

[51] Minutes of Cabinet meeting, 18 Feb. 1921, PRO, CAB 8(21), W 2008/22/98 FO 371/7033.

[52] Although the treaty department had submitted a draft based on the 'usual procedure' of the king making one ratification on behalf of the whole empire, the developing stature of the dominions meant that it was no longer possible to assume that they would automatically agree.

16

only New Zealand had assented to Britain's ratifying on its behalf the protocol of signature of the Statute, but a month later Australia, South Africa and India had all assented to ratification of the protocol. Canadian assent was slower in arriving because it was necessary to pass a bill of ratification through its parliament and this did not happen until the end of June.

In the meantime, in April 1921, President Harding of the United States had finally come out against joining the League. Until then Harding had maintained an ambiguous attitude which led Curzon to comment that he had 'no mind on the matter at all or rather that he had several minds which changed from day to day'.[53] This was a serious blow to Britain whose Foreign Office had envisaged the League as a kind of co-operative organisation under Anglo-American tutelage. The League was now fast becoming a liability and the establishment of the Court would serve to buttress it. The US decision did not, of course, prevent the USA from joining the PCIJ, but it was an obvious straw in the wind.

The previous year Crowe, who was now permanent under secretary (the most senior Foreign Office official), had warned that American past practice with regard to arbitration indicated that America could be no more trusted to adhere to the Court than to the League; the United States had always been inclined towards rhetorical flights of fancy about international courts and compulsory arbitration before 'blandly explaining that the constitution of America was so peculiar as to require that all the obligations specially binding upon other countries must be modified in favour of the United States'.[54] Together with Sir Gordon Hewart, the Attorney General, he had warned that while an international court would 'always present grave risks' to Britain, it should not even be looked at if America was not a member since the predominance of continental judges would lead to differing codes of international law growing up on different sides of the Atlantic.[55]

Crowe now called for an urgent reconsideration of British League policy. 'At present', he wrote, 'we are mechanically drifting in our hitherto accepted policy of developing the League in the vague expectation of America coming in.' It was now imperative to avoid any further commitment to the League and, as a first step, to scrutinise the PCIJ. He, himself, would 'do everything possible to delay ratification' of the Statute.[56] Curzon, the foreign secretary, had little interest in the subject of the League and declared, after reading 'all the papers', that he was 'left completely in doubt as to what is being done or what will be the result and whether we are to acquiesce, expedite or retard'.[57] Consequently he was given an explanatory minute which came down in favour of ratification because the government had given its word to both Houses of Parliament. In reply to a steady stream of questions it had repeatedly said that arrangements for ratifying the protocol of signature of the

[53] Minute, 29 Oct. 1920, PRO, A 8945/1054/45 FO 371/4590, cited in Peter J. Yearwood, 'The Foreign Office and the guarantee of peace through the League of Nations, 1916–1925', unpubl. DPhil diss. Sussex 1980, 284.

[54] Minute, 5 Oct. 1920, PRO, W 512/241/98 FO 371/5480.

[55] Memorandum by Crowe, 14 Oct. 1920, PRO, W 933/241/98 FO 371/5480; memorandum by Hewart (attorney general), 28 Sept. 1920, PRO, CP 1905 CAB 24/112.

[56] Memorandum, 20 May 1921, PRO, W 5895/22/98 FO 371/7034.

[57] Minute, 23 May 1921, ibid.

Statute of the Court were in hand and that it was engaged in consultation with the dominions.[58]

Crowe took this point but argued that a delaying policy would enable Britain to respond to events and, in particular, to the negative American policy towards the League:

> Apart from advertising the League and its clamorous votaries, there is no need to hurry on with the setting up of the international court, and if we can gain another years time by spinning out consultation with the Dominions and retarding ratification, I think we should do so.[59]

Curzon agreed to take the PCIJ to the Cabinet once more although he himself seems to have thought that it was a fruitless exercise and that it was too late to alter course. 'We are deeply committed', he said, 'and public opinion (which is seldom well-informed) undoubtedly favours the setting up of the Court.'[60]

In due course the Cabinet confirmed its decision and further decided that the dominions be urged to ratify soon. The latter were now the only obstacle to British ratification and Curzon was eager to press them and be done with the Court 'about which I am always having to make speeches in the House of Lords'.[61] At the League Council meeting in June, when one representative after another explained the steps his country was taking to deposit its ratification (and the Italians deposited theirs with a flourish), the British representative made firm the British commitment. The only reason why Britain had not yet deposited its ratification was, he said, its desire to act conjointly with the dominions.

This announcement was naturally 'received with the greatest possible gratification' by the other members of the Council.[62] The expected ratification by the Canadian Senate was duly received and with this, the last dominion's approval, Britain could go ahead. On 4 August 1921 the ratifications of Britain, India and the dominions were deposited with the League secretariat.

Britain and the PCIJ 1922-4

The political manoeuverings that accompanied the election of the judges to the court at the second Assembly in September 1921 confirmed Britain's belief that it had been wise to prevent the Court having compulsory jurisdiction. Hurst

[58] Other arguments for establishing the PCIJ were that failure to do so would be a severe blow to the League; the dominions would probably not follow Britain in such a course; and that British public opinion wanted to see the Court set up. On the other hand, and in addition to Crowe's arguments against ratification, there were some 'farsighted' people who thought that the burden of the PCIJ on the budget of the League would have an even more deleterious effect than the absence of the USA.
[59] Minute, 28 May 1921, PRO, W 5895/22/98 FO 371/7034. Crowe believed that it would be possible to delay action for a year as he was under the misapprehension that 5 June was the cut-off date for depositing ratifications of the protocol of signature as well as being the cut-off date for nominating judges. However, the requisite 24 ratifications were so slow in reaching Geneva that both deadlines were extended to the opening of the second Assembly.
[60] Ibid.
[61] Minute, 15 June 1921, PRO, W 6443/22/98 FO 371/7035.
[62] Note by Mr. Fisher on the Geneva Council meeting, 29 June 1921, PRO, CP 3101, W 7190/7190/98 FO 371/7060.

reported that the result was 'as good as could be expected' given 'the poor list of candidates',[63] but Crowe took a dim view of the prospects for the functioning of the Court. Just as the election of the judges had 'proceeded on purely political grounds', so it was to be expected that 'their eventual judgements will always be the result of political considerations, and not of the impartial application of judicial principles'. 'The story is unedifying and the result bizarre', concluded Curzon.[64] Hurst's account of the muddled circumstances surrounding the formal opening of the Court in February 1922 and of the extent to which English was not spoken by the judges,[65] gave Crowe another occasion to fulminate against the Court: 'This whole new Court is the fad of the internationalist and peacemongering busybodies', he minuted. 'Altogether the prospects of the smooth working of the new institution, and its furthering the cause of justice are not bright.' And the foreign secretary added that, in his view, 'Clearly trouble is brewing.'[66]

It happened that on several occasions over the next few years Britain was a party to proceedings before the Court, but on no occasion did the Foreign Office find that its earlier apprehensions were confirmed. There was no debate or consternation about two requests for advisory opinions[67] on questions of nationality and the delimitation of frontiers in eastern Europe.[68] Britain was party to the first request for a judgement by the Court in the *Wimbledon* case[69] in 1923, and there were no doubts that recourse to the Court was the best procedure for handling this dispute concerning the interpretation of the peace settlement. In *The Tunis Nationality Decrees* case of 1923[70] Britain was able to

---

[63] Hurst to Crowe, 15 Sept. 1921, PRO, W 1008/22/98 FO 371/7036. He reported that: 'The Court only contains three men who have judicial experience [a criterion to which the Foreign Office had attached primary importance]. It is made up of three judges, three legal advisers and five professors. I think I can safely prophesy that it will be completely dominated by Lord Finlay [of Great Britain] and Loder [of the Netherlands] assisted by a vast fund of information which Moore [of the USA] will provide and troubled with a certain amount of obstructiveness from Anzilotti [of Italy] and Huber [of Switzerland]. I doubt if the rest will count.'

[64] Minutes by Crowe and Curzon, 21 and 22 Sept. 1921, ibid.

[65] Hurst to Crowe, 15 Feb. 1922, PRO, W 1743/505/98 FO 371/8319. The majority of judges spoke only French, and Yovanovitch, a deputy judge, knew neither French nor English. Britain regarded a command of English as important for ensuring that Anglo-Saxon legal thinking would be taken into account by the judges.

[66] Minutes, 4 Mar. 1922, ibid.

[67] That is, the request by the Council or the Assembly of the League for the views of the Court on legal questions. After public hearings, the Court deliberated *in camera*. Its opinion was delivered in open court.

[68] These were the 1923 advisory opinions on the acquisition of Polish nationality and the delimitation of the Polish–Czechoslovakian frontier.

[69] It arose out of the interpretation of Article 380 of the treaty of Versailles and resulted from the refusal by the director of the Kiel Canal to allow the passage of the SS *Wimbledon* (a British ship chartered by a French company) to deliver armaments to the Polish naval base at Danzig. Britain, Italy and Japan contended that this violated the treaty of Versailles and in January 1923 they took it to the Court under Article 386 of the same treaty. The Court found by a majority of 8 to 3 in favour of the applicants.

[70] The dispute arose out of the decrees issued at the end of 1921 in the French Protectorate of Tunis by the *Bey* (the local ruler) and the French President. Their effect was to confer French nationality on a large number of British, Italian and Greek nationals who were resident in Tunisia. This meant that the British subjects (primarily of Maltese stock) were called up for national service. Those who resisted were imprisoned. In March 1922 the French authorities refused to grant fishing licences to Maltese fishermen unless, by the ninth of that month, they had accepted French nationality. Foreign

make use of the Court to get France to agree to settle the dispute.[71] Moreover, on this occasion Britain had every reason to be satisfied with the judges since the French judge supported the British contention that the dispute did not involve a question which was solely within French jurisdiction.[72]

However, this favourable experience of the Court does not in any way appear to have affected Britain's policy towards its jurisdiction. On no occasion between 1921 and the end of 1923 was the question of accepting the Optional Clause reconsidered by the British government. None the less, the Clause was not completely dormant in British politics during this period, as the proposal to accept the Optional Clause was raised from time to time within the Labour Party and the unexpected formation of the first Labour government in January 1924 made it a live issue in British foreign policy.

Office opinion was unanimous that Britain could not neglect the interests of its subjects and that it was morally and legally sound to maintain that they were British.

[71] Hurst initially advised that Britain's best course would be to demand arbitration under the Anglo-French arbitration treaty of 1903 as this procedure would enable either side to back down without losing face. On second thoughts he suggested that going to the PCIJ would be cheaper and it would enable Britain to act in conjunction with the Greeks and Italians who also had an interest in the matter. Then, together with Malkin (the assistant legal adviser), he recommended that the dispute be referred to the League Council which could then refer it to the PCIJ for an advisory opinion. The French had initially ignored British diplomatic protests and their formal reply, in August 1922, led Britain to place the dispute on the agenda of the Council. Once Britain had done this the French attitude was transformed. Balfour and Bourgeois agreed to resolve the dispute in a friendly manner but Paris remained sensitive and fearful of giving the appearance of having backed down. Lengthy negotiations requiring all Hurst's diplomatic skills produced agreement with France that the League Council should ask the PCIJ for an advisory opinion under Article 15(8) of the Covenant as to whether the dispute was, as the French contended, solely a matter of domestic jurisdiction. If the Court ruled that it was not a domestic matter, they would submit it to the court for adjudication. This procedure was adopted in a joint Anglo-French resolution and the following February the Court gave its opinion that the question of the Nationality Decrees was not a domestic matter. As it happened, it was unnecessary for the Court to go on to consider the merits of the case as the French were willing to come to a satisfactory agreement with Britain that British subjects 'up to and including the second generation born in Tunis' were entitled to decline French nationality as were all British nationals born in Tunis before 8 Nov. 1921 (the date on which the nationality decrees were issued).

[72] Interestingly, the lack of calibre of the judges (from the British point of view) was seen as advantageous to Britain. Although the judges 'certainly do not appear a very imposing body', said Malkin, Lord Finlay, the British judge, was so much better than his fellow judges 'that they were instinctively impelled to follow his lead'. This meant, he continued, that the Court was possibly a better bet than had been anticipated a couple of months earlier: Minute, 24 Apr. 1922, PRO, T 3725/224/317 FO 372/1846.

2

The Labour Party and the Optional Clause, 1920–September 1924

The place of arbitration in Labour's foreign policy

Before the First World War the Labour Party had no coherent foreign policy. Such ideas as were held about war were similar to, if not identical with, those of the radical liberals and non-conformists who made up the bulk of the peace movement, with a resultant emphasis on arbitration and disarmament. When Wilson's idea for a League of Nations gained widespread general support towards the end of the Great War, it was therefore natural for socialists to think in terms of a League which promoted disarmament and arbitration. No doubt it was for this reason that they were 'the most wholehearted supporters of the drive for world organization'.[1] But, given that the party had continued to devote its attention to domestic matters (such as the effect of the war on the working class) and to developments within the international socialist movement (especially after the Bolshevik revolution), ideas about the relationship between law and peace often remained hazy and the proposed new organisation was generally thought of in the context of the pre-war Hague conferences.

At the end of the war, however, a number of upper- and upper-middle class, Oxbridge-educated, former Liberals joined the Labour Party. Some, like Charles Trevelyan and Arthur Ponsonby, were drawn to the Labour Party as a result of their co-operation with the pacifists of the Independent Labour Party (ILP)[2] during the war. Others, like E. D. Morel and Norman Angell joined because Labour ideals most closely accorded with popular contemporary views about the best way of avoiding future wars. Generally speaking, while old Labour hands continued to be preoccupied by domestic matters, the recruits' primary political interest was foreign affairs. They not only clarified Labour thinking in this area but effectively took over the job of developing a foreign policy (and were, for this reason, known as the 'foreign legion').[3]

So far as the League was concerned, their efforts resulted in a pro-League foreign policy which accorded with radical liberal principles. This was a

[1] H. R. Winkler, *The League of Nations movement in Great Britain 1914–1919*, New Brunswick, NJ 1952, 259.
[2] The ILP was formed in 1893 and was one of the founding bodies of the Labour Representation Committee in 1900. It was affiliated to the Labour Party but held its own conferences, sponsored its own candidates for parliament and maintained its own, more radical policies. After disaffiliation from the Labour Party in 1932 it markedly declined in strength.
[3] The term was coined by George Young in *The reform of diplomacy*, 3, cited in W. P. Maddox, *Foreign relations in British Labour politics*, Cambridge, Mass. 1934, 74. Their contribution is fully discussed in Catherine Ann Cline, *Recruits to Labour: the British Labour Party 1914–1931*: New York 1963. See also H. R. Winkler, 'The emergence of a Labour foreign policy in Great Britain 1918–1929', *Journal of Modern History*, xxviii (1956).

considerable achievement since the Labour Party as a whole had been very disappointed by the League which actually emerged from the peace negotiations.[4] Particularly relevant in this connection were its objections to Article 10 of the Covenant, which had a central place in the League scheme for collective security.[5] And two other articles of the Covenant which were integral to the League's collective security scheme – Articles 11 and 16 – were also disliked by two important factions within the party – the pacifists and the pacificists – because of the possibility that they might involve the use of military force. The pacifist group, which included E. D. Morel and Arthur Ponsonby, together with a number of former Liberals, held that 'all war is *always wrong* and should never be resorted to, whatever the consequences of abstaining from fighting'.[6] Pacifists would not, therefore, accept military sanctions under any circumstances. On the other hand, the pacificists, who included Helen Swanwick and Noel Buxton, held that 'war, though *sometimes necessary*, is always an irrational and inhumane way to solve disputes, and that its prevention should always be an over-riding political priority'.[7] Pacificists might not, therefore, accept military sanctions under certain circumstances – for example, if they were used to uphold the *status quo* against Germany.

If, however, Labour rejected collective security, its claim that it could form a responsible government would be damaged and the party might lose votes in an election. For if a Labour government were to say that it would not support League sanctions it would appear to be backtracking on an important aspect of British foreign policy. The 'foreign legion' got around this dilemma by glossing over the collective security aspect of the League and by emphasising that part of the Covenant which had to do with pacification and peace-building. This approach was endorsed by Henderson and Clynes, both of them leading party members of the traditional type who had also been early advocates of the League idea.[8] Additionally, they had a leading role in the formulation of the party's foreign policy. Thus their acceptance of the 'legion's' scheme resulted in it becoming a part of Labour's official international policy.

[4] It was seen as too closely linked to the detested peace treaties; the exclusion of the ex-enemies and allied hostility to Soviet Russia made it look like an alliance of victors; its mandates system was suspected of being a fig leaf for imperialism; it was not within its remit to tackle what Labour saw as vital economic questions such as the international distribution of raw materials; and it was insufficiently democratic – socialists had envisaged as its central organ an international parliament of the peoples of the world.
[5] The objection to Article 10 lay in the fact that in Labour eyes its guarantee of territorial integrity seemingly confirmed fears that the League was intended to uphold an unjust *status quo* which had been imposed by a brutal peace settlement.
[6] Martin Ceadel, *Pacifism in Britain 1914–1945: the defining of a faith*, Oxford 1980, 3.
[7] Ibid. Ceadel says the term 'pacificist' was coined by A. J. P. Taylor (*The trouble makers: dissent over foreign policy 1792–1939*, London 1957, 51 n. 5) but see Rose MacCaulay, *Non-combatants and others*, London 1986 (first publ. 1916), 14.
[8] Henderson was a member of the Council of the League of Nations Union and had moved the December 1917 resolution which committed Labour to supporting a League of Nations. Clynes was invited to join the LNU's executive committee in 1919 although he does not appear to have played an active role in the organisation until the middle of 1921. In 1921 Clynes moved the TUC resolution calling for the reorganisation of the League in order that it might provide for 'the adequate democratic representation of all nations', but in so doing he asked his hearers to 'deal with the world as you find it' and not to suspect those who, like himself, were interested in developing the existing League: *Report of the proceedings of the fifty-third annual Trades Union Congress*, Cardiff, 7 Sept. 1921, 278. See also Clynes to House of Commons, 21 July 1919, House of Commons *debs.*, 960.

What Labour's resulting policy towards the League was based on was the belief that there would be no real threat to peace until Germany eventually rose up against the peace settlement. This was not an immediate likelihood since the victors of the Great War had disarmed Germany and given themselves a more or less free hand in their dealings with that country. They were morally obliged to make at least a move in the direction of disarmament,[9] and it was possible to argue that if they did so and Britain pursued a foreign policy of peace, appeasement and reconciliation, the wrongs of Versailles could be undone. Germany would then have no need to rearm and could be rehabilitated into international society through membership of the League. Through Article 19 of the Covenant[10] – the provision for peaceful change – the *status quo* could be made just and Article 10 would lose its sinister ring. By perfecting the machinery of peace there would be no need to use the machinery of war. In the words of Arthur Henderson: 'We hoped that if the nations used arbitration there would be no need for sanctions'.[11] This clearly pointed to the use of the PCIJ for the settlement of disputes, and hence to the Optional Clause.

There were thus two important reasons why the Labour Party looked with favour on the idea which was represented by the Optional Clause and attached so much importance to it in the 1920s. The first and most important reason was that it was a contemporary manifestation of the principle of arbitration which was a long-standing socialist principle as well as one that was dear to the 'foreign legion'. The second reason was tactical in that emphasis on the Optional Clause served to unite the party behind the League and enabled it to dodge facing up to the implications of collective security. Eventually, in the 1930s, this last issue could no longer be evaded. But in the 1920s, and despite the inconsistencies in its foreign policy,[12] it was able to get away with a League policy of building peace rather than applying sanctions. Thus, when the party formed a government in 1924, it not surprisingly reopened the question of Britain's attitude to the Optional Clause.

[9] The Peace treaty had asserted that German disarmament made possible 'the general limitation of the armaments of all nations' and this had been reiterated in the allied response to German protests in 1919. Germany argued that general disarmament was a legal obligation, the allies that it was of a moral nature. Article 8 of the Covenant provided for the formulation of plans for 'the reduction of national armaments to the lowest point consistent with national safety and the enforcement by common action of international obligations'.

[10] Article 19 stated: 'The Assembly may from time to time advise the reconsideration by Members of the League of Treaties which have become inapplicable and the consideration of international conditions whose continuance might endanger the peace of the world.'

[11] House of Commons *debs.*, 24 Mar. 1925, 295, quoted in W. Tucker, *The attitude of the British Labour Party towards European and collective security problems*, Geneva 1950, 107.

[12] For example, party conferences continued to support the ILP in its advocacy of a 'general strike' against war. In 1926 it passed, without debate, a motion proposed by Fenner Brockway and seconded by Arthur Ponsonby, calling on the workers to make it clear to their governments that 'they will meet any threat of war, so-called defensive or offensive, by organising general resistance, including the refusal to bear arms, to produce armaments, or to render any material assistance': Labour Party, *Report of the twenty-sixth annual conference, 1926*, 256. See also ILP, *Report of the annual conference held at Leicester, April 1927*, 7; C. Brand, *The British Labour Party: a short history*, London 1965, 110. Cf. Labour Party, *Report of the twenty-second annual conference, 1922*, 200–4. There were also problems when pacifists held ministerial office: Gilbert Murray described Lord Parmoor's speech to the fifth (1924) Assembly as 'pure pacifism from beginning to end' and he had to dash round trying to soothe perturbed delegates, one of whom described Parmoor as '*un fanatique d'un autre monde*': Murray to Cecil, 5 Sept. 1924, BM, Cecil papers, Add. MS 51132.

The first Labour government: MacDonald's decision in favour of the Optional Clause, January–August 1924

Much to the astonishment of its leadership, the Labour Party found itself forming a government after Baldwin had called a snap election over the issue of protection in December 1923. In the new parliament no party had an absolute majority.[13] Baldwin immediately proffered his resignation but the king insisted that he should only resign after being defeated in parliament. This duly took place six days after the new parliament had met in January and Ramsay MacDonald subsequently accepted the king's invitation to form a government. Because of his vanity, his sense of superiority to his colleagues, his desire to avoid giving the office to anyone else, and his genuine interest in international relations, MacDonald decided to combine the foreign secretaryship with the premiership. It was a mistake for which he paid by, it has been said, nearly killing himself with overwork,[14] and he was unable to keep command over foreign policy. MacDonald's Lord President of the Council – the seventy-two-year-old Lord Parmoor – was given responsibility for League affairs, and was thus thrust into a prominent position in League policy. However, he carried little political weight and was regarded in the Foreign Office 'as a cuckoo in the nest' or 'a strange animal who had found his way within a sacred enclosure'.[15] His merits (or, in the eyes of many English League enthusiasts, his demerits) in executing British League policy need not be dwelt on, for the significant point is that both he and Ponsonby, MacDonald's under secretary, were pacifists and were thus personally opposed to the military implications of collective security. But they were both strongly committed to disarmament and peace through law.[16]

Within a week of coming to power, MacDonald asked the Foreign Office to render advice on the Optional Clause and he was given a memorandum by Villiers, the head of the western (League of Nations) department, summarising the gist of the papers relating to the 1920 discussions on the jurisdiction of the Court.[17] In so doing the Foreign Office was clearly unaware of the significance of arbitration to Labour for, as Villiers explained, his memorandum was based on the assumption that 'the reasons against accepting compulsory jurisdiction remain as weighty and unanswerable in 1924 as they

---

13 The election was held on 6 Dec. 1923. Although the Conservative total share of the votes fell by only 0.1% it lost 87 seats and the Labour Party gained 49. The Conservatives won 258 seats, the Liberals 159 seats and the Labour Party 191 seats.

14 Conversation with Philip Noel-Baker, 23 Nov. 1975; MacDonald to Gilbert Murray, 19 Nov. 1924; MacDonald to Lady Mary Murray, 20 Dec. 1924, Bodl. Lib., Murray papers. This strain was compounded by his social rounds with Lady Londonderry.

15 Lord Parmoor, A retrospect: looking back over a life of more than eighty years, London 1936, 197.

16 Although in March 1918 Parmoor had moved, in the House of Lords, a resolution which called for the creation of both a League and an international tribunal 'whose orders shall be enforceable by an adequate sanction', he was already expressing the hope that it would be unnecessary to apply such a sanction: House of Lords debs., 476–9. Before joining the Labour government in 1924, Parmoor made it clear to MacDonald that 'I . . . do not share [Cecil's] views as to the guarantee of mutual defence . . . of using force . . . I hold the . . . view . . . that the League cannot be regarded as a superstate and ought to exercise its functions by appealing to public opinion. This is fundamental': Parmoor to MacDonald, 6 Jan. 1924, MacDonald papers, PRO 30/69/6/26[R].

17 That is the memoranda by Crowe, the Lord Chancellor and the law officers of the crown together with the Cabinet conclusion of October 1920: See above, 10–11.

were in 1920'.[18] It was believed in the Foreign Office that MacDonald's interest in the Clause was due to its merits having been urged on Ponsonby by Goldsworthy Lowes Dickinson (the Cambridge academic who had played a leading role in the war-time League of Nations Society and was now a member of the 'foreign legion'). However, MacDonald's interest in adjudication was not new. In 1917 he had called for an international court of arbitration to 'adjudicate' disputes when they arose. Moreover, the party was calling on the government to act. In March 1924, the party's influential advisory committee on international questions recommended that Labour's commitment to 'arbitration' should be made firm by acceptance of the Optional Clause,[19] and there was a steady stream of increasingly urgent questions from backbench MPs belonging to each of the three main political parties. These were dismissed by the Foreign Office with increasing evidence of irritation at the MPs' persistence in making what were regarded as rash requests.[20] But in June complacency within the Foreign Office was shaken and the pros and cons of the Optional Clause were debated for the first time since 1920 when the legal adviser, Sir Cecil Hurst, said that he had changed his mind and was in favour of accepting the Clause. He now held that because of the functioning of the League, 'as regards peace time disputes Britain would gain a little by accepting the obligatory jurisdiction, and that as regards disputes arising out of future wars there is no serious risk in accepting it'.[21] In other words, Hurst no longer thought that accepting the Optional Clause would threaten Britain's belligerent maritime rights (BMR), a danger which had been forcefully argued by Crowe in 1920 and the Admiralty in 1921.[22] Hurst had come to this conclusion – which was not shared by Malkin, the assistant legal adviser – only when he had sat down with the latter to write a new memorandum on the Optional Clause for MacDonald. By late spring, and being still unable to reach agreement, the two legal advisers decided to submit separate memoranda in which each set out the arguments as he saw them.

Malkin, who voiced the general consensus of opinion, held that the 'real question' was 'how far the certainty (for this is what it would really amount to) of

---

[18] Minute, 18 Mar.1924, PRO, W 2286/338/98 FO 371/10573.

[19] See PRO, W 2855/338/98 FO 371/10573. The name of the advisory committee changed slightly several times during the twenties. In 1924, for example, it was known as the advisory committee on international affairs but it is most commonly referred to by the name given in the text. For a discussion of the influence of the committee see Leonard Woolf, An autobiography, ii, London 1980 (first publ. in 5 vols, 1964–9), 365; Winkler, 'Emergence of Labour foreign policy', 254–5; Maddox, Foreign relations, 99–103. However, there may have been some justification for the Foreign Office view since Ponsonby was bemoaning his chief's deafness to party views and expressing doubts as to whether MacDonald even read the memoranda prepared by the advisory committee: Norman Angell, After all, London 1951, 239–40.

[20] For example, replies to parliamentary questions were drafted on the assumption that 'none of the Great Powers has accepted the Clause and it is very doubtful whether any of them will do so': Minute by C. W. Orde (first secretary in the western department), 15 Feb. 1924, PRO, W 1261/338/98 FO 371/10573. When preparing yet another reply to a question from the Liberal, John Harris, Ivone Kirkpatrick (second secretary in the western department) commented that Harris was 'exceedingly importunate. He asks this question almost every week. He seems unable to realise that H.M.G. cannot be expected to make a decision in a moment; indeed, it would be the height of rashness to do so. The matter is one which may vitally affect our national safety': Minute, 21 June 1924, PRO, W 5236/338/98 FO 371/10573.

[21] Memorandum by Hurst, 18 June 1924, PRO, W 5045/338/98 FO 371/10573.

[22] See above, 10, 16.

having to submit our action to the decision of an international court would hamper a British government in taking measures [i.e. the exercise of BMR] which they may consider legitimate in the circumstances of the time'. In such matters, he thought, the judges of the PCIJ would tend to 'apply the rules which they will find in the text books', rules which were 'based . . . entirely on the experience of the past' rather than

> endeavour to discover what should be regarded as the applicable rules of international law in the circumstances of the present . . .. If . . . we have to take up and argue any apparently well-founded complaints against belligerent action, we may find ourselves committed to rules which are no longer applicable, and which might be extremely injurious, or even fatal, to ourselves if we found ourselves subsequently at war.

The existence of the League made no difference since he held that any consideration of the League system of collective security must 'partake to a considerable extent of the nature of conjecture'.

So far as peace-time was concerned, Malkin thought that neither the advantages nor the disadvantages of accepting the Optional Clause would be great. Britain could generally obtain an arbitration if she wanted it in any of the cases covered by the Optional Clause but an open-ended commitment would be a nuisance:

> [A]s it may fairly be said that in such matters honesty is the policy of the British Government, such cases would probably be ones where we really had a strong case, and ought to be fairly certain of winning, if the court could be depended upon; though at the same time it is unfair, and in cases where colonial Governments are concerned, sometimes very inconvenient, that we should be put to the trouble and expense of an arbitration where the other side really have no case.[23]

Hurst, who completed his memorandum almost a month after Malkin but presented it to MacDonald at the same time and in the one file, did not share Malkin's apprehension concerning the legal validity of Britain's interpretation of BMR and the inevitability of the PCIJ ruling against Britain. It was, Hurst argued, easy to exaggerate the danger: naval struggles were rare and what happened in one war was no guide as to what might happen in the next. Although British actions in the First World War might appear to constitute startling developments, he himself doubted whether any of them were inconsistent with the old principles, 'and if they were not', he continued, 'there [was] no reason to assume that an international court would have condemned them'. None the less he accepted that there might be a 'serious risk' for Britain if it did not make a reservation covering disputes arising out of the war and that in any case the Admiralty would be alarmed and would oppose any suggestion that there should be no such safeguard. He accordingly suggested the reservation of disputes arising out of events preceding the date of signature. It would be both a reasonable condition and defensible on the ground that the government could not be expected to undertake any such responsibility in respect of the actions of its predecessors.

He did not, however, think that Britain would face any dangers from disputes arising out of the future exercise of belligerent measures because of the advent of

23 Memorandum, 21 May 1924, PRO, W 5045/338/98 FO 371/10573.

collective security through the League of Nations. In the past, the check on belligerent excesses had been the fear that a neutral state might join the enemy. If there were any neutrals during future wars, he thought that they would only be likely to protest on questions of fact which were involved in the decisions of prize courts. If this occurred, 'it is improbable that the court at The Hague would uphold the protests, or would condemn as inconsistent with international law, measures which were taken with the concurrence of the League'. Moreover, he argued, 'an unforeseen result of the working of the Covenant' was that in future states could not go to war without complying with the Covenant. If a neutral wanted to go to war to defend its rights it would first have to take its complaint to the League Council under Article 15 of the Covenant. Therefore, a well-advised state would obtain the League's approval for any contemplated measures to defend its rights the minute that the necessity of these measures could be urged. In this way, the reasonableness of a belligerent's action would come before the League at one stage or another. Thus it was that Hurst held that the balance of advantage lay in favour of accepting the compulsory jurisdiction of the Court. 'I doubt', he said,

> whether there has ever been a case in the last 50 years in which a British Government has deliberately acted in a manner which it knew to be contrary to the rules of international law as understood in this country. Consequently, where a dispute has arisen and has bid fair to be troublesome, resort to arbitration is welcomed as the best way out of what may develop into a tiresome situation.

The condition of reciprocity meant that any risks which Britain ran in accepting the Optional Clause were likely to be small. On the other hand, there were small, but positive advantages in being able to take another state to the Court, and he recommended that Britain should begin by accepting the Optional Clause for five years.[24]

Hurst's memorandum sparked off further Foreign Office memoranda supporting Malkin's viewpoint and underlining the fact that the Optional Clause was judged by its impact on Britain's exercise of BMR. Kirkpatrick, a second secretary in the western department, argued that when Malkin's memorandum was read in conjunction with that which Sir Eyre Crowe had written in 1920, the case against signature was irrefutable. Crowe's first reaction was simply to minute his agreement with Malkin. But since MacDonald gave no indication whether he had been persuaded by the arguments against the Optional Clause and made no minutes on the memoranda, it was possible that he might still be toying with the idea of accepting it.[25] Crowe was therefore spurred into writing another memorandum condemning the Optional Clause.

After emphasising that the acceptance of the Optional Clause would be a deliberate reversal of a decision which the Cabinet had taken in 1920 on the advice of the Lord Chancellor and the law officers of the crown, Crowe

---

[24] Memorandum by Hurst, 18 June 1924, PRO, W 5045/338/98 FO 371/10573.

[25] There is no statement or remark by MacDonald before the end of July to show which way his mind was turning. But it was characteristic of him to prevaricate and avoid making a firm commitment to anything. His Foreign Office advisers would have been extremely shortsighted if they had ignored the possibility that MacDonald's 'facility for dancing round the mulberry bush' (Philip Snowden, *An autobiography*, i, London 1934, 218) might result in acceptance of the Optional Clause.

explained that there were additional objections which had not been expressed in the legal advisers' memoranda. It was remarkable, he said, that neither Hurst nor Malkin had 'seriously discussed' the danger that political pressures might determine judgements. There was also the difficulty of binding the country to unforeseeable future commitments, as no constitutional government could bind its successors to pass legislation which might be required to execute a judgement. It was a difficulty which could arise in Great Britain as well as in other countries and it could be counted on 'almost with certainty' in the case of the United States. He disagreed with Hurst's implicit assumption that Britain would only want to refuse to arbitrate disputes arising out of a war. This was not so, he argued, citing the Newfoundland fisheries settlement which had formed part of the agreements constituting the Anglo-French Entente of 1904. In 1908 France had sought to reject this settlement by disputing the interpretation of its wording but fortunately for Britain the claim had not been pressed. Had it been pressed, Britain would have had to refuse arbitration on the grounds that a vital interest of the empire was involved.

He did not see how Hurst could have so changed his mind since 1920 when he had recognised the danger to which Britain would be exposed in accepting compulsory arbitration in disputes involving BMR. By proposing the reservation of disputes arising out of the late war being submitted to 'compulsory arbitration', Hurst showed that his former objections had not lost all their force. If Britain could not afford to run the risk of submitting those disputes to 'arbitration', how could it be seriously maintained that such risk would be negligible in all future wars? Crowe was not much impressed by Hurst's faith in the League. The risks were 'too grave to be neglected on any such merely speculative grounds, as to which, to say the least, profound differences of opinion are permissible'. In his inimitable style he dismissed the motivation which drew many Labourites to support the Optional Clause:

> Those who advocate it do so largely, if not exclusively, on purely theoretical and abstract sentimental grounds. In their eyes arbitration all round and in all circumstances is a panacea for all ills. The claim is surely exaggerated . . . . the various parties who in all countries have written the battle-cry of compulsory arbitration in international affairs on their banners, offer as a rule determined resistance to compulsory arbitration in their own home affairs, such for instance as trade union disputes . . . . no evidence has so far been adduced by anybody that the introduction of unrestricted compulsory arbitration in international disputes would meet any really felt need. We have all the existing advantages and facilities of the League of Nations to deal with grave international conflicts. Of course it yet remains to see the League machinery tested in a real and important crisis. But if that machinery should prove inadequate to meet such a crisis, the introduction of fresh guarantees for settling by arbitration deep-seated conflicts that might otherwise lead to war, will hardly advance matters, but may rather increase the feeling of scepticism with which all such paper guarantees are still regarded in many quarters. There is a strong conviction, widely held, that there is nothing to gain from unnecessarily hurrying the pace of further development, and that the pacifist energies would be better spent on fostering and spreading what in modern jargon is called the will to peace, rather than on concentrating on the erection of more machinery for dealing with hypothetical problems.[26]

[26] Memorandum respecting compulsory arbitration, 13 July 1924, PRO, W 6063/338/98 FO 371/10573.

A few days later a memorandum appeared from Lord Haldane, the Lord Chancellor. 'A valuable quarry'[27] for MacDonald because of his Cabinet experience and the prestige which he gave the government, Haldane had had the pick of government appointments and had chosen the Lord Chancellorship with the proviso that he should concentrate on reforming the Lord Chancellor's department and that he should have the chairmanship of the Committee of Imperial Defence, whose secretary, Hankey, was his friend. In the matter of the Optional Clause he was sympathetic to the Admiralty's viewpoint and expressed his concern at the implications that accepting the Clause might have on the rulings of Britain's prize courts. However, the emphasis of the memorandum was not on BMR but on the problem of getting the dominions to give their assent. This was because he held that '[i]n substance the constitution of our empire is not unitary, and it is perilous for the Imperial Government to proceed as if it were. We have to secure the assent of the Dominions and of India at every step'. In this respect, he said, Britain faced a difficulty which was analogous to, although not the same as, that facing the United States where the president dared not enter into undertakings unless he could be sure of having Congressional approval. It would be 'perilous to give an undertaking which, under a Constitution which is in substance non-unitary, we cannot be sure of being able to fulfil'. At the 'present stage of the Constitution of our Empire' it would be safer to avoid going further than Article 13 of the Covenant and to avoid the likelihood of 'keen controversy' arising as a result of accepting the principle of compulsory jurisdiction before the idea had had time to 'mature fully and to become familiar to our own people'.[28]

Haldane's argument did not satisfy MacDonald who now commented for the first time on the advice he was being given: 'we ought to go further than the legalist correctness of the L[ord] C[hancellor]'s valuable note [which] if published as our complete view and decision, would be regarded as a serious slap in the face for arbitration'. At the same time, MacDonald gave the first sign that he was definitely moving in the direction of the Optional Clause: by directing that the dominions be told that the British government wished to consider it 'sympathetically', and that he would like their comments without delay.[29] The dominions' comments were not, however, received before the fifth (1924) Assembly, where MacDonald spoke in favour of the Optional Clause. At this point the question of the Optional Clause cannot be discussed in isolation from other issues, especially the pacification of Europe. It is, therefore, necessary to turn briefly to the most recent attempt in the League to remove war from international relations: the Draft Treaty of Mutual Assistance.

The Draft Treaty of Mutual Assistance

The Draft Treaty of Mutual Assistance (DTMA) had evolved out of the League's work on disarmament. In 1921 the League had established the Temporary Mixed Commission (TMC) to consider the question and to prepare plans for

---

27 Richard Lyman, The first Labour government 1924, London 1957, 100.
28 Memorandum, 21 July 1924, PRO, W 6062/338/98 FO 371/10573.
29 Minute, 29 July 1924, ibid.

disarmament. In March 1922 the TMC was enlarged and Robert Cecil became a member of it. Cecil had then sought, through the commission, to gain acceptance of his view that the key to stability and peace in Europe lay in a general agreement which assuaged French insecurity. This meant recognising that a link existed between disarmament and security: France and other continental countries would only reduce their armaments if they could be sure of effective support from other countries to compensate for their weakened military position. This could be achieved through a treaty of mutual guarantee which would be drawn up by the League but would not actually form part of the Covenant. In 1922 Cecil's principles were accepted by the Assembly when it approved Cecil's famous 'Resolution XIV' which led in the following year to the DTMA.[30]

The main provisions of the DTMA were the determination of aggression as an international crime and the obligation on signatories to go to the defence of any other signatory facing aggression – providing that state had conformed to the treaty's disarmament provisions. The treaty was to be open to all states. The League Council was to determine whether aggression had taken place and what consequential action was to be taken – deciding on the sanctions to be imposed and the contribution to be made by any country (with the exception that military help would be intra-continental only), and appointing a commander-in-chief. Other articles allowed for 'complementary' defensive agreements made by two or more parties for their mutual defence and suggested the creation of demilitarized zones between countries to prevent a sudden attack. Finally, the treaty gave general suggestions as to how disarmament might be achieved.

The fourth (1923) Assembly, to which the Draft Treaty had been submitted, sent it to League members for their comments. The task of sending the British reply fell to MacDonald, but he did not regard it as having any urgency and it was not discussed by the Committee of Imperial Defence (CID)[31] until the beginning of April 1924. The CID decided to reject it and in May it was rejected by the Cabinet.

Cecil and Drummond blamed the rejection of the DTMA on the influence which officials wielded over MacDonald. Certainly it had been disliked in Whitehall, particularly because of the breadth of the general guarantee, the provisions regarding military sanctions and the probability of the French demanding further security while stalling on disarmament. And it was also the case that Hankey and Crowe – the officials whom Cecil had picked out as opponents of the League – were its fiercest critics.

The explanatory memorandum in which the CID rejected the treaty was very similar to one of Hankey's memoranda, and the official letter of rejection was

---

[30] For a clear and concise summary of the evolution of the DTMA see League of Nations secretariat, *Ten years of world co-operation*, Geneva 1930, 49-65.

[31] The CID was established on a temporary basis in 1902 after the Boer war had shown the need for planning and co-ordinating the empire's defence forces. It was made permanent in 1904 with its own secretariat. The prime minister was formally chairman of the committee which consisted of the cabinet ministers concerned with defence, military leaders and key civil servants. It had no executive power but it exerted considerable influence. From 1912 its secretary was Maurice Hankey who also became secretary to the Cabinet in 1916. During the First World War its meetings were suspended and its functions taken over by other committees and the War Cabinet. It had resumed full, regular meetings in 1922.

based upon Whitehall criticisms. But the DTMA was not rejected just because of those criticisms. The Labour Party's advisory committee on international questions had been doubtful about it, wanting British ratification to be conditional on certain amendments, and it was also criticised by the Union of Democratic Control and the parliamentary party.[32] The sanctions provision had been an anathema to Parmoor,[33] and MacDonald himself became involved in the matter, vetting the letter of rejection to the secretary-general and redrafting sections of it.

The preparation of the letter took place in a leisurely way because it was widely thought that an outright rejection of the treaty, without having anything to offer in its place would have unfortunate consequences for European security. Accordingly, during June and for most of July, MacDonald collected a variety of views as to the best course to follow. In this process he found that a number of people were thinking along lines which encouraged his liking for the Optional Clause, and therefore tended to counter the advice he was receiving from Crowe, Malkin and Haldane. Thus, when the letter rejecting the DTMA was sent on 5 July, MacDonald and Parmoor included in the last paragraph a statement of the government's desire to strengthen the Court.[34]

Within the Foreign Office there was an isolated proposal, endorsed by Villiers (the head of the western department) that the Covenant be strengthened so that

[32] A sizeable minority of the advisory committee (5 out of 13) had, however, voted in favour of a completely new treaty which would contain a binding commitment to submit all disputes to peaceful settlement: W. Gillie to MacDonald, 16 May 1924, MacDonald papers, PRO 30/69/1/31. The UDC held that 'The problem with which civilised mankind is faced is the problem of substituting processes of arbitration and law for self-destruction through war.' The Parliamentary Labour Party objected to 'its key provisions for separate treaties of "defensive" alliance as tending to re-establish those sectional agreements between the Powers which led to the War of 1914': H. S. Lindsay to MacDonald, 4 July 1924, ibid. 30/69/1/182.

[33] According to Noel-Baker, Parmoor played the major role in the rejection of the DTMA because of MacDonald's overwork: Conversation with Noel-Baker, 27 June 1976. See also House of Lords debs., 24 July 1924, 974, 980-3.

[34] This aroused the indignation of the Admiralty which had complained at the alteration of an earlier, Admiralty-approved draft. 'Reference to the International Court was at present optional', explained Beatty, the First Sea Lord, 'and it might be taken to imply that in future reference might be compulsory.' In this connection he pointed out that when referring to the PCIJ in the House of Lords, Lord Parmoor had stated that 'personally I should like to see that system made compulsory'. Under these circumstances the Admiralty were inclined to be anxious. His anxiety arose out of a passing reference in Parmoor's speech explaining the government's rejection of the DTMA and Haldane had replied that he had recently written a memorandum arguing that such a step was impossible and 'there was no cause for anxiety': CID, 187th meeting, 28 July 1924, MacDonald papers, PRO 30/69/1/115; House of Lords debs., 24 July 1924, 966-7. The British government's letter of rejection held that 'the guarantee afforded by the draft treaty is so precarious that no responsible Government will feel justified in consenting to any material reduction of its armaments'. Indeed, the scrupulous execution of the obligations of the treaty would actually lead to an increase in armaments. The reply then 'went on to criticize "the proposal to superimpose on a general treaty a system of partial treaties between groups of countries", and to protest against the "undesirable extension of the functions of the Council of the League" which the treaty appeared to involve. "The Council would become an executive body with very large powers, instead of an advisory body" ': Arnold Toynbee, Survey of international affairs, 1924, London 1925, 32. The government had accordingly decided that the DTMA 'holds out no serious prospect of advantage sufficient to compensate the world for the immense complication of international relations which it would create, the uncertainty of the practical effects of its clauses, and the consequent difficulty of conducting national policy': reply of the British government to the secretary-general of the League of Nations, 5 July 1924, PRO, W 4724/134/98 FO 371/10568.

the aggressor in a violent conflict – upon whom League sanctions should fall – could be determined by asking which side had refused arbitration.[35]

Meanwhile, on the other side of the Atlantic, the Shotwell committee was likewise suggesting that the aggressor in any dispute should be 'the party who refused to submit to the arbitration [sic] of the Permanent Court'.[36] Both proposals accorded with Labour Party thinking.

Because of a personal grudge, MacDonald would not have anything to do with the League of Nations Union (LNU).[37] However, he was willing to receive advice from the League secretariat and in June he was told by the secretary-general, Drummond, that on a recent visit to Scandinavia he had found two subjects uppermost in people's minds: the importance of MacDonald attending the League Assembly and the desirability of Britain accepting the Optional Clause. Drummond urged that if MacDonald did not accept the Optional Clause he should at least negotiate arbitration treaties.[38] When a copy of Drummond's letter was shown to Parmoor at a meeting of the League Council, the Lord President immediately wrote to MacDonald that although he understood that the Foreign Office was 'not prepared' to sign the Optional Clause, he was 'strongly in favour of it'. He thought that 'it would not only be a real gesture in favour of a League of Nations policy, but that no other proposal would go so far to promote the real interest of disarmament'.[39] MacDonald did not comment, but the following month he asked for a memorandum from Arthur Salter, a British member of the League secretariat, who had been making a particular

[35] See minute by Villiers, 26 Aug. 1924, PRO, W 7431/134/98 FO 371/10569. Cf. minute by Wellesley (second assistant under secretary), 28 Aug. 1924, ibid. During the Assembly, Harold Nicolson, a member of the central department, suggested that a British commitment to French security be couched in a more general League commitment in which arbitration would play an important role: Minute, 9 Sept. 1924, PRO, C 14272/2048/18 FO 371/9819. Nicolson's proposal was endorsed by Miles Lampson, counsellor in charge. I am grateful to Dr P.J. Yearwood for drawing my attention to these examples of Foreign Office thinking. However, as he points out, the League probably did not play a significant role in the thinking of the central department.

[36] An unsigned, undated memorandum among MacDonald's papers emphasises the link between his speech to the Assembly on 4 Sept. and the Shotwell committee's proposal: 'Memorandum on the creation of the Geneva Protocol': PRO 30/69/8/139. This link is also emphasised by Philip Noel-Baker: The Geneva Protocol, London 1925, 18–19. See also telegram from Felkin, Institute of Politics, Williamstown, Maryland, to Arthur Salter, 2 Aug. 1924, PRO, FO 800/400. The Shotwell committee – consisting of General Bliss (one of the US delegates to the Paris peace conference), David Hunter Miller (Woodrow Wilson's legal adviser at Paris) and Professor Shotwell of Columbia University – brought their proposals for outlawing aggressive war to Geneva but these were never thrashed out in a League committee: Alfred Zimmern, The League of Nations and the rule of law, 1918–1935, London 1936, 387–9.

[37] His grudge against the LNU arose out of what MacDonald took to be a personal slight in 1920 and its gist was thus summarised by Murray many years later. During the Great War Ramsay MacDonald had been 'such a pronounced pacifist that our committee asked Henderson and Thomas instead and left MacDonald out. I regretted personally the omission of MacDonald but I think the decision of the committee was probably right. My memory, however, still echoes with his angry words: "I will never, never forgive the League of Nations Union" ': Gilbert Murray, The League of Nations movement: some recollections of the early days (David Davies Memorial Institute, Annual memorial lecture, April 1955), 6. MacDonald was true to his word. He was the only leader of a major political party who did not become an honorary president of the Union and he told his secretary not to bring him any LNU papers.

[38] Drummond to MacDonald, 7 June 1924, MacDonald papers, PRO 30/69/1/200.

[39] Parmoor to MacDonald, 10 June 1924, PRO, Private Office correspondence on the League of Nations, PRO 800/400.

study of the securities for peace and the methods of achieving these securities. And, towards the end of August, Drummond sent MacDonald a detailed plan for strengthening the League. Both Salter and Drummond suggested that the Optional Clause be fully considered.[40]

By now, insofar as he ever decided anything, MacDonald had decided in favour of the Optional Clause, but he did not show his hand until he went to the Assembly in September. This was because he was, as he put it, 'frying other fish' (being preoccupied with the London conference on reparations which took place at the beginning of August), and because he wanted to try pursuing the larger policy 'before attempting the more circumscribed one' of accepting the Optional Clause.[41]

After his triumph with the acceptance of the Dawes plan on reparations, MacDonald went to Lossiemouth to relax briefly before setting off for Geneva. It is unlikely that he gave much, if any, attention to the Optional Clause during August; and the caveats with which he hedged his declaration in favour of the Optional Clause were no doubt partly due to his not having fully thought out his policy and partly due to his own innate caution and an awareness of the influential opposition against any move to accept compulsory adjudication. None the less, his decision was a significant indication of the strength of Labour's commitment to the Clause and, as the next chapter will show, his speech to the Assembly brought the Optional Clause firmly to the centre of the League's attempt to build peace and also firmly entrenched it as one of the Labour Party's immediate foreign policy aims.

[40] See Selby to Salter, 30 July 1924, and memorandum by 'a Frenchman and a Dutchman', 23 Aug. 1924, sent by Drummond to Selby, ibid.
[41] House of Commons *debs.*, 24 Nov. 1924, 2106–7.

3

The Fifth (1924) Assembly of the League of Nations and British Policy

Labour's approach at the fifth Assembly

Years later, Paul-Boncour recalled that 'A Genève on disait "l'année du *Protocole*", comme pour les grands vins',[1] and many years later still, Philip Noel-Baker said that if he could relive six weeks of his life, he would choose the fifth Assembly.[2] The air of the Assembly was full of determination to make peace and the time for it seemed propitious, for at last Europe seemed to be on the road to pacification. There were no major crises, such as Corfu, which had bedevilled the preceding Assembly; the problems of German reparations seemed solved; and Anglo-French tension, which had been aggravated by the French invasion of the Ruhr, had eased. The attendance at the Assembly of the socialist and Radical socialist leaders of Britain and France, MacDonald and Herriot, seemed proof that they were going to grapple seriously with the problems of peace, and it also served to upgrade the Assembly as their presence acted as a magnet on the leaders of other states.[3] As the Assembly opened Murray jubilantly told Cecil that

> The prominent fact is the change in public opinion and expectation. The French are transformed. Hymans, Beneš and Motta and the others are talking freely of Compulsory Arbitration; not merely the Optional Clause but complete Arbitration for all cases. Beneš told me last night that he wd [sic] sign such a treaty tomorrow. Also young de Jouvenal says definitely that the Fench [sic] delegation will agree to that if they can have security . . . There is an immense state of expectation and a feeling that MacDonald and Herriot will perform some miracle.[4]

MacDonald had, however, gone to Geneva tired and unprepared. As Murray reported further to Cecil, 'He came strange to the atmosphere and was inclined to think that not much could be done here except have a talk and arrange for a conference.'[5] His speech was hurriedly thrown together in consultation with Murray and Parmoor and, when at last MacDonald delivered it, he 'had a great

---

[1] 'At Geneva they spoke of the "year of the Protocol" in the same way as one speaks about vintage wine years': J. Paul-Boncour, *Entre deux guerres: souvenirs sur la IIIe République: les lendemains de la victoire 1919–1934*, Paris 1945, 152.

[2] Conversation with Noel-Baker, 3 July 1981.

[3] Eleven other foreign ministers attended the Assembly. In 1922, of the 48 states represented, 18.8% of delegations were headed by premiers or foreign ministers; for 1923 the figure was 12% of 50 states; for 1924 43.1% of 51 states: Felix Morley, *The society of nations*, Washington 1932, 580, cited in A. Bargman, 'The role of the Assembly of the League of Nations in the pacific settlement of disputes', unpubl. PhD diss. London 1952, 304–5.

[4] Murray to Cecil, 4 Sept. 1924, BM, Cecil papers, Add. MS 51132. Murray was a member of the British delegation to the Assembly.

[5] Ibid.

success on rising . . . and rather less sitting down'.[6] But he did, at least, announce that it was 'the desire of the British Government to sign undertakings like the Optional Clause' and his remarks concerning arbitration appealed to the audience. Warning the Assembly against the dangers of armaments and the futility of trying to guarantee security by military might, he turned to the central role of arbitration in a peaceful world. 'I am in favour of arbitration', he said. 'I see nothing else for the world. If we cannot devise a proper system of arbitration, then do not let us fool ourselves that we are going to have peace . . .. Justice must be allowed to speak before passion. That is arbitration. (*Hear, hear.*)' MacDonald added that it was through arbitration that the League could, at last, determine an aggressor, as was required by the League's collective security system: 'The test is, Are you willing to arbitrate? The test is, Are you willing to explain?' In keeping with the ambiguities of these remarks MacDonald was careful to avoid any firm commitment to either arbitration or the Optional Clause. But he had given the British delegation a sufficiently clear lead for it to advance on both fronts at the Assembly subject to the proviso that it should not bind Britain there and then.[7]

The next day Herriot took up where MacDonald had left off in a speech which was finely tuned to the Assembly and frequently interrupted by applause. Having expressed his gratification at MacDonald's remarks on arbitration (which were, he said, in accordance with French tradition and which he had been urging on MacDonald when they met in June) and, having taken care to underline the priority of French security, he won '[r]enewed and prolonged applause' as he declared that 'henceforth the aggressor will be the party which refuses arbitration'. 'Arbitration, as my friend Mr. MacDonald has said, is justice without passion', he continued,

> In that I recognise the nobility of his mind . . . [but as] Pascal said – and his words should, I think, serve as a watchword for the League of Nations – 'Justice without might is impotent. Might without justice is tyranny . . .. We must . . . mate justice with might and to that end we must ensure that what is just is mighty and that what is mighty is just.' (*Applause.*)[8]

Between them, MacDonald and Herriot had set the tone of the Assembly and a joint resolution which they submitted led directly to the Geneva Protocol of which the acceptance of the Optional Clause was an integral part. It happened in the following way.

[6] However, said Murray, 'in reaction as it were, against this slight coolness, his admirers raised a third [sic] and everyone joined in': Murray to Cecil, 5 Sept. 1924, ibid. MacDonald had offended French and Polish susceptibilities and, according to Madariaga, his style was inappropriate to the occasion: See Salvador de Madariaga, *Morning without noon: memoirs*, Farnborough 1973, 54–5.
[7] League of Nations, Records of the fifth Assembly, plenary meetings, text of the debates, *LNOJ*, special supplement no. 23, 1924 (*LNA5 debs.*), sixth plenary, 4 Sept. 1924, 43–4. MacDonald explained that it was necessary to 'devise more successfully than we have done hitherto the courts that are to operate under a system of arbitration', and to explore more fully the matters which should be referred to courts and the nature of the obligations upon states that went to arbitration. There were doubts about whether the Optional Clause operated in war-time as well as in peace-time and he wanted to know how far his government could go. To this end the Assembly should establish a commission which would examine the Optional Clause very carefully 'with a view to its being placed before this Assembly in a somewhat more accurate, expanded and more definite form than it now is'.
[8] *LNA5 debs.*, eighth plenary, 5 Sept. 1924, 52–3.

That evening, 5 September, following a visit from the journalist, Wickham Steed, MacDonald visited Beneš (whose room was on the floor below that of MacDonald in the Hotel Beau Rivage) and asked the Czech to sound out the French on a resolution which MacDonald proposed to submit to the Assembly. Beneš took it to the Hotel des Bergues and showed it to Paul-Boncour who undertook to show it to the rest of the French delegation. In the early hours of Saturday 6 September Herriot accepted the resolution and, at a private luncheon, the two leaders made verbal changes and MacDonald agreed that it should be presented as a joint Anglo-French resolution.[9] That afternoon the Assembly adopted, by a unanimous vote, the following resolution which served as the basis of the ensuing discussions:

The Assembly,
   Noting the declarations of the Governments represented, observes with satisfaction that they contain the basis of an understanding tending to establish a secure peace,
   Decides as follows:
   With a view to reconciling in the new proposals the divergence between certain points of view which have been expressed and, when agreement has been reached, to enable an international conference upon armaments to be summoned by the League of Nations at the earliest possible moment:
   (1) The Third Committee is requested to consider the material dealing with security and the reduction of armaments, particularly the observations of the Governments of the draft Treaty of Mutual Assistance prepared in pursuance of Resolution XIV of the third Assembly and other plans prepared and presented to the Secretary-General since the publication of the draft Treaty, and to examine the obligations contained in the Covenant of the League in relation to the guarantees of security which a resort to arbitration and a reduction of armaments may require.
   (2) The First Committee is requested:
   (a) To consider, in view of possible amendments, the articles in the Covenant relating to the settlement of disputes:
   (b) To examine within what limits the terms of Article 36, paragraph 2, of the Statute establishing the Permanent Court of International Justice might be rendered more precise and thereby facilitate the more general acceptance of the clause:
   And thus strengthen the solidarity and security of the nations of the world by settling by pacific means all disputes which may arise between States.[10]

By the end of the Assembly this resolution had resulted in the drafting of the Protocol for the Pacific Settlement of International Disputes which became known as the Geneva Protocol. Since the subsequent discussion will concentrate solely on that part of the Protocol which is relevant to the Optional Clause, it is necessary first to explain very briefly how this aspect of the Protocol emerged and also to give a general outline of the whole Protocol.

[9] Conversation with Noel-Baker, 3 July 1981. On the emergence of the resolution see P. J. Yearwood, 'The Foreign Office and the guarantee of peace through the League of Nations', unpubl. DPhil diss. Sussex 1980, 400; MacDonald diary entry, 21 Sept. 1924, PRO 30/69/8/1; David Marquand, *Ramsay MacDonald*, London 1977, 354.
[10] *LNA5* debs., eleventh plenary, 6 Sept. 1924, 77.

The Geneva Protocol

When the first and third committees set about their respective tasks of examining arbitration and the Optional Clause on the one hand and security and disarmament on the other, it was discovered that the principles were interdependent and Beneš of Czechoslovakia undertook to draft a protocol on this basis. Thenceforward the work on the Protocol proceeded apace. A committee of twelve under the chairmanship of Beneš and fired by a determination to succeed worked long into the night. It combined the proposals and amendments emanating from the first and third committees until, on 29 September, the Protocol was at last complete.

What the Protocol proposed was the creation of a 'system for the pacific settlement of *all disputes* which might arise. In other words . . . a system of arbitration from which no international dispute, whether legal or political, could escape'.[11] It was to operate as follows. A definite solution was to be binding on the parties by one means or another for every dispute of whatever kind. Therefore, it was necessary that there should be no possibility of deadlock: for every situation provision had to be made for an obligatory, pacific method of settlement. All justiciable disputes would be resolved by a decision of the PCIJ and, accordingly, all signatories of the Protocol who had not already accepted the Optional Clause would have to do so within a month of accepting the Protocol. For disputes which were not justiciable, a settlement was in the first instance to be sought through the mediation and conciliation of the Council. If the Council failed to secure a settlement, resort had to be had to arbitration (in the strict sense of the term) unless all the parties preferred a political decision by the Council. Every solution reached by any of the methods indicated was to be binding upon the parties who undertook to execute it in good faith. If any party failed to carry out a solution so arrived at, the Council was to propose what practical co-operative measures the signatories were to take to induce the recalcitrant state to fulfil its obligations.

If any state did not submit disputes as outlined above, or did not carry out a solution so arrived at, and its actions threatened world peace, it would be declared an aggressor. The signatories were then automatically obliged to assist the attacked state but it would be for the League Council to authorise sanctions and states could make reservations as to the employment of land forces. The Council could receive individual or collective undertakings as to the military sanctions to be provided. These would become operative once the Council had decided by a majority vote that aggression had taken place and it was for the Council to propose the emergency measures which were to be taken. The whole

---

[11] *Arbitration, security and reduction of armaments. General report submitted to the fifth Assembly on behalf of the first and third committees by M. Politis (Greece) rapporteur for the first committee and M. Beneš (Czechoslovakia) rapporteur for the third committee.* (The Beneš–Politis report.) The design of the system had drawn heavily on the Anglo-French expression of support for arbitration (in the widest sense). This support had been echoed so much that Limburg of the Netherlands was not wildly exaggerating when he told the first committee that 'The alpha and omega of all the speeches [in the Assembly] had been compulsory arbitration [in the widest sense of the term]': League of Nations, Minutes of the first committee (constitutional and legal questions), *LNOJ*, special supplement no. 24, Geneva, 1924 (*LNA5* first committee), third meeting, 20.

Protocol would become operative following the successful conclusion of a disarmament conference which was planned for June 1925.[12]

The Optional Clause and the drafting of the Geneva Protocol: initial steps in the first committee

Returning to the proceedings of the Assembly and the work of the first committee, it should be noted first that the committee's task of examining the provisions of the Covenant relating to the pacific settlement of disputes rapidly developed into a system of compulsory arbitration in the widest sense of the term. However, it is the discussions on the committee's second task – that of examining whether the Optional Clause could be rendered more precise – that influenced the development of Britain's policy on the Optional Clause and which therefore merits attention.

In preparing for these discussions, Hurst held that it was important that Britain should have a clear line on the Clause, since it was the British prime minister who had instigated the discussions on the matter and in so doing had indicated his wish to accept it. Hurst thought that the real question for Britain was BMR. Although earlier that year (in June) he had argued that such a reservation was unnecessary for future disputes but that it would be a wise precaution to make a reservation covering disputes arising out of the First World War, the criticisms which had been made of his proposal and the possibility of public outcry led him to suggest now that it would be necessary to include a general reservation covering all disputes arising out of BMR. Britain could not, he maintained, argue that BMR were already excluded from the Optional Clause,[13] and it would be inadvisable to make a specific reservation on the subject lest Britain be exposed to the criticism of only being willing to accept 'arbitration' when this accorded with British interests. Instead he proposed a reservation of 'any dispute arising out of action taken in accordance with the covenant or with the concurrence or at the request of the Council of the League'. The line of argument to be taken in justifying the reservation was broadly similar to that which he had developed in June. In any future war Britain would be fighting in support of the Covenant and would accordingly have the body of the League on its side. In these circumstances compulsory arbitration 'i.e. between allies, is out of place'. It was possible that there could arise disputes as to the legality of naval operations taken at the request of the League, on the authority of the Council, and in order to enforce the provisions of the Covenant. But it would be unreasonable and illogical for Britain to be exposed to the risk of having to sustain single-handedly 'before one organ of the League [the PCIJ], measures which she has taken with the concurrence or at the

---

[12] For a fuller account see Noel-Baker, *The Geneva Protocol* and David Hunter Miller, *The Geneva Protocol*, New York 1925.

[13] In the past Britain had submitted disputes involving the exercise of BMR to arbitration 'with sufficient frequency to make people very sceptical as to the genuineness of any such argument if we now put it forward'. 'Another and stronger reason' was that Britain had rejected the draft Statute of the Court in 1920 because it would not have prevented the adjudication of questions involving BMR.

request of another organ of the League [the Council]'. Put this way, he thought it would be difficult for anybody to oppose the resolution.[14]

Parmoor, who had succeeded MacDonald as leader of the British delegation, gave his approval. When Hurst explained to the first committee that his country needed to reserve from the operation of the Optional Clause disputes arising out of measures taken on behalf of the League, his speech was on the whole well-received. The outcome of the discussions in the first committee was most satisfactory for Britain as it was quickly decided that it was unnecessary to amend the Optional Clause because the way it was worded allowed states to attach to their acceptance of it any reservations they wanted. It was also held that it would be undesirable to amend it because this would jeopardise the position of the seventeen states which had signed. However, if Britain had few difficulties with the first committee as a whole, the same did not apply to its relations with the dominions.

Dominion consultation: first steps

Until Hurst explained Britain's Optional Clause policy to the first committee, the dominions had played no part in the evolution of that policy. It was only at a specially-summoned meeting of the British empire delegations (BED) a few hours before Hurst made his statement to the first committee that the dominions were consulted. In effect, this was also the first time that they were informed of recent developments in British thinking. Although MacDonald had asked that a memorandum on the Optional Clause be despatched to the dominions at the end of July, a failure of communications in Whitehall meant that it was not until 6 September – the day after MacDonald had made his speech to the Assembly – that the despatch on the Optional Clause was finally sent.[15] And it was not until the day before the BED met that the British delegation circulated copies of the Optional Clause papers to its Commonwealth colleagues. It is not, therefore, surprising that the dominions were cautious and reserved when they finally met. The Australian and New Zealand representatives automatically reacted with suspicion of the dangers the Optional Clause posed to the exercise of BMR, given that they were almost completely dependent upon the British navy for their defence. However, Hurst assured them that there would be very careful consideration before any steps were taken and that retrospective action relating to the exercise of naval power during the late war would be reserved. The dominions could not commit their governments without consultation, but it was agreed that Hurst should go ahead with his statement to the first committee and that a joint telegram should be drafted and sent to the Commonwealth governments in the light of the committee discussions.[16]

However, a week passed before Britain summoned another BED meeting for 17 September – the day after Beneš had produced the first draft of the Protocol in which he had provided for the acceptance of the Optional Clause. As the dominions saw it, they had been left in the dark while negotiations took place in

[14] Memorandum on compulsory arbitration, 10 Sept. 1924, PRO, W 7830/338/98 FO 371/10573.
[15] See above, 29. PRO, W 6062/338/98 FO 411/1, W 8679/27/98 FO 371/11069.
[16] Summary of proceedings of third meeting of British empire delegations (BED), 11 Sept. 1924, PRO, W 7830/338/98 FO 371/10573.

closed sessions of a sub-committee of the first committee.[17] It was a stormy meeting, the dominions giving full vent to their anger and frustration. Accusing the British of lack of candour, Sir James Allen of New Zealand (normally a completely malleable but also a very conservative dominion) complained about the delayed receipt of the Optional Clause memorandum and the absence of the promised meeting to draft the joint Commonwealth telegram.[18] They were, he said, 'being too hurried over matters which were too vital to be done in a hurry' (an opinion seconded by Sir Edgar Walton of South Africa, who 'expressed some anxiety as to whether we were not going too fast . . .. In his opinion this preparatory work was largely premature'). All in all, he said, there was a general lack of consultation (an opinion seconded by Sir Joseph Cook of Australia who blamed it on the infrequency of the meetings of the BED and who explained that it was difficult to know what was going on because so much work was proceeding in sub-committees).[19]

The British could not ignore or dismiss these complaints. As later events were to show, Sir Littleton Groom was not making an empty threat when he warned that 'There was grave danger in Great Britain signing a protocol to which the Dominions could not agree'.[20] Certainly the Colonial Office was alarmed at this threat to imperial unity when news of dominion disquiet leaked into the press, and it persuaded the Foreign Office to send the dominions a soothing message from MacDonald.[21] And when the Irish Attorney General quitted Geneva, leaving Hurst the sole Commonwealth representative on the important fifth sub-committee, Hurst arranged for the remaining work to be done in full meetings of the first committee. In taking these steps Britain was not simply pandering to querulous colonials, for the emerging Geneva Protocol (and its requirement that signatories accept the Optional Clause) touched on two vital interests of Australia and New Zealand: the exercise of BMR and their 'white' immigration policies.

Imperial problems I: the defence of the empire

As the Protocol emerged there was considerable disquiet amongst Australians and New Zealanders about its possibly dangerous implications for British sea power. Both delegations made these apprehensions plain, but it was unnecessary for them to press the point as the Admiralty had begun taking steps to try to limit the course of the negotiations.

---

[17] This was the fifth sub-committee of the first committee whose members included Hurst and O'Byrne of the Irish Free State. The Irish Free State delegation did not, however, attend the BED meetings. The first committee adjourned from 12 to 24 Sept. The third committee likewise entrusted the working out of its proposals for security and disarmament to a sub-committee known as the fourth sub-committee of the third committee. The third committee was adjourned between 13 and 22 Sept.

[18] This was because Hurst, who was under pressure, had assumed that a draft telegram by the Australian, Sir Littleton Groom, would express the dominion point of view.

[19] Summary of proceedings of fourth BED meeting, 17 Sept. 1924, PRO, W 8980/134/98 FO 371/10571.

[20] Ibid.

[21] See Sir H. Lambert (Colonial Office) to Tyrrell, 23 Sept. 1924, PRO, W 8226/134/98 FO 371/10570; summary of proceedings of the ninth BED meeting, 28 Sept. 1924, W 8897/134/98 FO 371/10571. Imperial unity is fully discussed in chapter 7.

The speed of developments at Geneva had outstripped the receipt in London of communications from the British delegation so that Whitehall gleaned its knowledge of Assembly proceedings from reports in newspapers which were hostile to and deliberately misrepresented the emerging Protocol.[22] During the third week of September this had produced a 'naval scare' over the extent to which the British navy was being committed to the service of the League. The sanctions aspect of the 'naval scare' need not be considered here, but it is worth noting that Gilbert Murray attributed it, in part, to the interpretation given to Hurst's argument in the first committee about the reservation Britain needed to attach to the Optional Clause.[23] And steps which the Admiralty took over the Optional Clause question demonstrated how perturbed it was about the implications of the Optional Clause for the exercise of BMR.

The slowness with which London was kept informed of the work of the fifth Assembly was particularly marked with regard to the first committee. On 14 September, Lord Parmoor sent a despatch to London summarising the 'considerable progress' which had been made on the Optional Clause.[24] Unfortunately, the accompanying memorandum in which Hurst had set out the line which he followed in the first committee was inexplicably missing from the despatch. It was therefore held up in the western department until a copy of the memorandum was received on 20 September. By then Britain had further committed itself to the Optional Clause by putting forward proposals (aimed at filling the 'gap' in Article 15 of the Covenant) which confirmed Article 1 of Beneš's draft Protocol requiring signatories to accept the Optional Clause.

Three days later the Foreign Office still knew nothing officially of the proceedings of the first committee when a telegram was received from Lord Parmoor saying that the discussion on the inclusion of the Optional Clause in the Protocol had taken place (and was therefore at an end). He had, he said, made it clear that its acceptance by Britain would be subject to the reservation suggested by Hurst and he asked whether any further reservations would be required.[25] The Foreign Office replied that it would be necessary to reserve past naval action, and that Britain should not be bound by the Optional Clause if the Protocol fell through.[26] The Admiralty reacted sharply to these communications. A stiff letter was sent to the Foreign Office complaining that it had not been consulted on the reply to Parmoor's request for advice on the Optional Clause. Alex Flint, the permanent assistant

---

[22] This particularly applied to *The Times*: Cecil to Murray, private, 25 Sept. 1927, BM, Cecil papers, Add. MS 51132; Gwendolen Carter, *The Commonwealth and international security: the role of the dominions 1918-1939*, Westport, Conn. 1971 (first publ. 1947), 118-19. The British delegation believed that these were intended to weaken the government in view of the likelihood of an imminent election.

[23] 'i.e. we reserve cases where our fleet acting according to our own laws but not perhaps according to that of the Court'. Murray went on to explain that the other source of the scare was 'the obvious proposal that, if nations made reserves about Article 16 [of the Covenant] GB might say she w[oul]d act with her fleet but not with her army. Otherwise there is nothing in it': Murray to Cecil, 19 Sept. 1924, BM, Cecil papers, Add. MS 51132.

[24] PRO, W 7830/338/98 FO 371/10573.

[25] Telegram from Parmoor, urgent, 22 Sept. 1924, PRO, W 8062/134/98 FO 371/10570.

[26] Telegram to Parmoor, 25 Sept. 1924, ibid.

secretary at the Admiralty, asserted that neither the Optional Clause nor compulsory arbitration should be accepted with regard to disputes arising during a war and involving BMR whether or not they arose out of measures taken on behalf of the League. Also, neither the PCIJ, nor any other body, should have the power to give retrospective rulings on matters which might impose any liability on Britain.[27]

The Foreign Office, unlike the Admiralty, deemed it wisest to say nothing and wait to see how things turned out. It was felt that there was little point in pressing the Admiralty's demands on the British delegation since other states would probably look suspiciously on such far-reaching reservations. The delegation would, in any case, probably say that such a posture would 'stultify the attitude which they had adopted from the very beginning with regard to compulsory arbitration',[28] and would 'entail throwing the whole Protocol into the melting pot'.[29]

MacDonald, who had by now returned to London after fleeing from the Assembly back to 'dear quiet Lossiemouth', was sufficiently impressed by the Admiralty's objections to instruct Parmoor that Hurst's Optional Clause reservation was insufficient and that it was essential to reserve from compulsory arbitration and compulsory adjudication 'all wars *not forbidden* by the Covenant or protocol'.[30] However, he merely transmitted the summary of Admiralty views (which the Admiralty had wanted sent to Geneva as instructions). And, although he acceded to the request from the First Lord of the Admiralty, Chelmsford, to send a naval expert to advise Parmoor and Henderson, he also made it plain that this was an Admiralty initiative and that the adviser would be at their disposal as they saw fit.[31]

MacDonald also acceded to another Admiralty demand: that an urgent Cabinet meeting be held on the grounds that the Admiralty's views had not been fully taken into account at Geneva and that the Protocol should not be signed until the navy's arguments had been fully considered by the government. On 29 September, the day that the Protocol was completed, the Cabinet decided to instruct Parmoor that if he were unable to avoid signing the Protocol, he should make it perfectly clear that he was only recommending it to the government.[32] This Parmoor had been doing all along.

---

[27] See Alex Flint (Admiralty) to Foreign Office, confidential, 25 Sept. 1924, PRO, W 8232/134/98; Admiralty to Foreign Office, 26 Sept. 1924, W 8271/134/98; memorandum by Chelmsford (First Lord of the Admiralty), 27 Sept. 1924, CP 456(24), W 8493/134/98 FO 371/10570.

[28] Minute by Campbell, 26 Sept. 1924, and undated minute by Orde, PRO, W 8232/134/98 FO 371/10570.

[29] Minute by Campbell, 27 Sept. 1924, PRO, W 8271/134/98 FO 371/10570. See also minutes by Campbell and Tyrrell, 23 Sept. 1924, W 8013/134/98 FO 371/10570.

[30] Telegram from MacDonald to Parmoor, 26 Sept. 1924, PRO, W 8232/134/98 FO 411/1.

[31] Telegram from MacDonald to Parmoor, no. 88, 26 Sept. 1924, ibid. The naval expert, Captain A. D. P. R. Pound (director of plans for the Admiralty), was sent to Geneva on 27 September. See also Chelmsford to MacDonald, 26 Sept. 1924, ibid; Stephen Roskill, *Naval policy between the wars*, i: *The period of Anglo-American antagonism 1919-1929*, New York 1968, 430; Hugh Dalton diary entry, 4 Dec. 1928, BLPES, Dalton papers, vol. 10; Konni Zilliacus, *The mirror of the past: lest it reflect the future*, London 1944, 280n.

[32] PRO, CAB 21(54), W 8943/134/98 FO 371/10570.

Imperial problems II: the Japanese amendment

Meanwhile, at the same time as the Admiralty had been fighting for its freedom to exercise BMR, the proceedings at Geneva had been temporarily brought to a standstill over a specifically antipodean interest. This was when the Japanese introduced an amendment which Australia and New Zealand interpreted as being aimed at their 'white' immigration policy (a policy which, by preventing the immigration of Asians in general, and the Japanese in particular, maintained Anglo-Saxon predominance in these dominions). Although Australia and New Zealand held that their immigration laws were matters within their domestic jurisdiction and that they were accordingly no business of the League, they were concerned lest any discussion of them by the League might threaten this claim.[33] In the last week of the Assembly Japan proposed amendments to the Protocol which were aimed precisely in this direction.

The suggestion was that Article 5 should be amended so that the Council could recommend a solution for disputes involving domestic jurisdiction. This met with little public opposition in the first committee, although the Australian delegation later reported that the proposal 'raised serious doubts in the minds of several delegations as to whether it would not have the effect of setting up the Council as an appellate tribunal from decisions of the Court and thereby make possible interference in domestic affairs'.[34] Sir Littleton Groom, who was receiving frequent telegrams from Bruce about the necessity of preventing any possibility of 'white Australia' being taken to an international body, had been lobbying his fellow Commonwealth delegates and had emphatically stated in the BED that Australia would not accept 'compulsory arbitration' unless matters involving domestic jurisdiction were specifically excluded.[35]

Because of the importance of maintaining imperial unity in the matter of the Protocol, and because Lord Parmoor shared Australia's objections to the Japanese amendment,[36] the British delegation did its best to meet Australian demands without sacrificing the goal for which it was striving. As soon as the Japanese had tabled their amendment, Hurst had obtained an adjournment of the first committee so that he could consult the BED which subsequently instructed him to prepare an alternative to the Japanese amendment.

The following day Adatci, the Japanese delegate, dismissed the proposal which Hurst put forward and tabled a modified amendment of his own – an

---

[33] If successfully challenged they might, they feared, have difficulty resisting Japanese demands which emphasised the relative 'underpopulation' of New Zealand and Australia. Under Article 15.8 of the Covenant, the Council determined whether a subject was a matter of domestic jurisdiction but Article 5 of the Protocol transferred this decision to the PCIJ.

[34] Report of Australian delegation to the fifth Assembly, quoted in Carter, *Commonwealth and international security*, 115.

[35] Sir Littleton Groom to 6th BED meeting, 20 Sept. 1924, PRO, W 8897/134/98 FO 371/10571.

[36] Parmoor was the only member of the British delegation to object to the Japanese amendment. He opposed it because he judged it by its objective – immigration – rather than seeing it in the context of the Protocol as a whole. Henderson thought the Protocol should 'cover the whole ground'; Murray thought the Japanese wished 'to preserve the existing duty of the League and to appease feelings on both sides in the event of a dispute arising'; and Hurst pointed out that the proposal had been put forward 'very nicely and skilfully' and that it had the support of the whole of the first committee: Telegram from the British delegation to MacDonald, 26 Sept. 1924 (letter, 29 Sept. 1924), PRO, W 8311/134/98 FO 371/10571; MacDonald papers, PRO 30/69/1/200.

amendment that would have given the Council the duty of trying to find a settlement to a dispute which fell within the domestic jurisdiction of a state. If this were not accepted, he said, he would press for an alternative amendment (to Article 10 of the Protocol) whereby a state would not be condemned as an aggressor if it resorted to war after a dispute had been declared to involve a matter of domestic jurisdiction. When Hurst made no move, Groom – who was chairman of the first committee – vacated the chair to oppose Adatci and by the end of the meeting the future of the Protocol was in jeopardy since Groom made it clear that the Australian parliament would rather 'reject the whole protocol' than accept the Japanese amendments.[37]

There followed two days of flurried discussions while the fate of the Protocol hung in the balance. The outcome was the Hurst-Scialoja-Loucheur amendments which Hurst had drafted to meet the Australian demands in conjunction with the Italian and French legal advisers.[38] By now, however, Groom had received a telegram from Bruce instructing him to stand firm.[39] That night Groom was personally persuaded that Australia's position under the Protocol would be no worse in respect of immigration than it was under the Covenant, but he refused to be rushed into accepting the proposal. In the BED the following morning there was 'some very straight speaking',[40] and Groom warned Britain that his government had almost been pushed too far in agreeing to follow Britain's policy on the Optional Clause, quite apart from the additional obligations which the Protocol would involve.[41] The BED split, with Canada and India supporting the compromise amendments and South Africa and New Zealand siding with Australia. Later, at a private meeting in Groom's room, New Zealand, South Africa and Australia reluctantly concluded that they had to accept the most recent amendment or accept responsibility for wrecking the Protocol.[42] Thus, when the first committee met for the last time, the Protocol was completed with the committee's approval of the compromise Hurst-Loucheur-Scialoja amendments. But the British Commonwealth countries sounded a warning note

[37] See summary of proceedings of eighth BED meeting, 26 Sept. 1924, and note by Hurst, 27 Sept. 1924, PRO, W 8073/134/98 FO 371/10570 and W 8340/134/98 FO 371/10571. See also Littleton Groom's remarks to the first committee shortly after the BED meeting (i.e. the ninth meeting of the first committee). New Zealand shared Australia's views but was content for the most part to let Australia do battle on its behalf. South Africa held that a decision by the PCIJ that a dispute was within the domestic jurisdiction of states should be treated as final in removing it from the international agenda and India was concerned at the implications for its 'complex structure of some 500 autonomous states'.

[38] This involved adding a sentence to Article 5 of the Protocol allowing the Council or the Assembly to consider, under Article 11 of the Covenant, a situation falling within the domestic jurisdiction of a state. An amendment was also made to Article 10 of the Protocol which defined an aggressor. A state would only be presumed to be an aggressor if hostilities broke out over a dispute which an international tribunal had declared to be solely within the domestic jurisdiction of the attacked state if the dispute had not previously been submitted to the League Council or Assembly under Article 11 of the Covenant.

[39] See W. J. Hudson, *Australia and the League of Nations*, Sydney 1980, 53-4. Hudson, however, oversimplifies Groom's position.

[40] According to Groom and quoted in Carter, *Commonwealth and international security*, 116.

[41] Summary of proceedings of eleventh BED meeting, 30 Sept. 1924, PRO, W 8897/134/98 FO 371/10571.

[42] Carter, *Commonwealth and international security*, 116.

when giving their approval. Both Groom and Hofmeyr refused to commit their governments, as did Hurst who also attempted to soothe dominion anxieties by contending that the Protocol did not infringe state sovereignty.[43]

With the completion of the Protocol, the Assembly prepared to indulge in rejoicing in view of the fact that, at last, man had been able to agree on a plan which would 'make war impossible . . . kill it . . . annihilate it'.[44] Amidst the jubilations Lord Parmoor's closing speech to the Assembly jarred on the ear. Just as MacDonald had earlier had the ill-luck to be followed by Herriot, Parmoor had the misfortune to follow Briand. Not only was the Frenchman a gifted orator, but he also committed France to the Protocol then and there. And as evidence of good faith he made a declaration accepting the Optional Clause,[45] a step which his country would in any event be obliged to take on ratifying the Protocol. Parmoor, by contrast, seemed chiefly concerned to answer his critics at home, and repeated the point that Britain was not bound to accept the Protocol.[46] Dandurand, who was the only dominion delegate to participate in the closing sessions, also threw some cold water on the proceedings. He said that his country firmly believed in arbitration and that he thought it would accept the Optional Clause. But Canada was apprehensive of collective security, as he went on to explain in his celebrated 'fire-proof house' remarks.[47] All he would promise was that his country would examine the Protocol 'with the fullest sympathy'.

The Protocol was submitted to the Assembly on 1 October and on 2 October it was adopted in a solemn roll-call vote, after which it was immediately signed by fourteen states (and ratified by one – Czechoslovakia). At the same time the Assembly approved another resolution calling on states to accept the Optional Clause, which was 'sufficiently wide to permit States to adhere . . . with the reservations which they regard as indispensable'.[48] The tasks of the Assembly were now completed and the delegates went home.

---

[43] LNA5 first committee, thirteenth meeting, 30 Sept. 1924, 87–90, and fifth Assembly, Report of the British delegates relating to the Protocol for the Pacific Settlement of International Disputes, 1 Nov. 1924, London 1924, Misc. no. 21 (Command paper 2289). The Beneš–Politis report said that the amendments would make the application of the domestic jurisdiction reservation 'more flexible' but Politis, the rapporteur for the first committee, also held that the Protocol 'in no way derogates from the rule of Article 15, paragraph 8, of the Covenant, which protects national sovereignty'.
[44] Beneš–Politis report.
[45] The French declaration on the Optional Clause fell through when the Protocol was not ratified. Briand received '[l]oud, prolonged and unanimous applause' and 'was congratulated by many of his colleagues' as he returned to his seat. Parmoor had risen to 'unanimous applause' and received simply '[a]pplause' at the end of his speech. Even Scialoja, whose country, Italy, had been the most obstructive member of the Assembly, received '[p]rolonged applause' and 'was congratulated by many of his colleagues' as he sat down: LNA5 debs., twenty-sixth plenary, 1 Oct. 1924, 204–6.
[46] Ibid. 204–5.
[47] '[I]n this Association of Mutual Insurance against fire, the risks assumed by the different States are not equal[.] We live in a fire-proof house, far from inflammable materials. A vast ocean separates us from Europe': LNA5 debs., twenty-eighth plenary, 2 Oct. 1924, 222. Cf. Dandurand to sixth BED meeting, 20 Sept. 1924, PRO, W 8897/134/98 FO 371/10571.
[48] LNA5 debs., twenty-eighth plenary, 225.

The rejection of the Protocol

Hardly had the ink dried on the Protocol than the Labour government was defeated in the House of Commons in a vote of censure on 6 October. At MacDonald's request the general election was held on 29 October and the formation of the second Baldwin administration on 4 November doomed the Protocol. It was Britain's attitude to the Protocol which determined whether or not it would come into force, and the new Conservative government was opposed to it.[49]

MacDonald had put the Protocol into cold storage for the duration of the election campaign and one of the first acts of the incoming foreign secretary, Austen Chamberlain, was to confirm MacDonald's reference of the Protocol to the CID (to which Balfour was added for the consideration of this subject). Following two CID meetings in December 1924, a small sub-committee (dominated by Maurice Hankey and Sir Eyre Crowe) examined the Protocol in detail. It was decided, after two more CID meetings in February 1925, that the Protocol should be rejected. This was, in fact, a foregone conclusion, given the hostility which the Conservatives had manifested since the Assembly, and given that at the first CID meeting it was clear that no-one would defend the Protocol.[50] However, until he announced the rejection of the Protocol to the League in March 1925, Chamberlain would give no public indication of British policy and maintained a posture which he described as 'sapient as an owl and nearly as intelligible'.[51]

The deliberations within the British government which led to the rejection of the Protocol produced a number of strong attacks on the Optional Clause and the principle of compulsory arbitration. The Admiralty was the first into the fray with a memorandum written by Lord Chelmsford on 27 October, just before leaving office. One of his objections to the Protocol was the Japanese amendment which made it 'not improbable' that the dominions cherishing 'white' immigration policies would reject the Protocol. Imperial unity was vital in defence[52] and he urged that no action should be taken towards signing the Protocol unless it were known that all the dominions would sign. Another objection was the fact that its arbitration provisions would prevent the USA from signing it 'for two or three decades at least' because of the refusal of the American Senate to accept all but the most limited arbitral commitments.[53]

---

[49] For the Protocol to come into effect it had to be ratified by three permanent members of the Council (i.e. three out of France, Britain, Japan and Italy) and, even then, it would not enter into force until the successful conclusion of the proposed disarmament conference. Diplomatic soundings revealed that France could not afford not to show enthusiasm but did not regard the Protocol as a satisfactory substitute for a defence pact. The Japanese were hostile while Mussolini regarded it with utter distaste but was unwilling to incur any opprobrium by taking a lead in rejecting the Protocol.

[50] CID 190th meeting, 4 Dec. 1924, PRO, CAB 2/4. However, Robert Cecil was unwilling to express a final opinion at that stage and he urged the committee not to take too hasty a decision.

[51] Minute, 2 Dec. 1924, PRO, Chamberlain papers, FO 800/256.

[52] It must be borne in mind that this was before the Locarno treaties had led Britain to accept, in theory, the possibility of the dominions keeping out of a European war in which Britain was involved.

[53] In this he let America speak for itself by annexing a letter written in March 1923 by Secretary of State Hughes to President Harding. The letter, which summarised the failure of successive presidents to obtain Senate approval of arbitration agreements, concluded that 'it would seem to be entirely clear that until the Senate changes its attitude it would be a waste of effort for the President to

The Admiralty's views were also set out in a memorandum which was produced by the Joint Chiefs of Staff of the Armed Services on polling day, 29 October. They demanded that the question of reservations to the Optional Clause be referred to the departments and to the CID 'to ensure that the position of this country is fully safeguarded'. And they held that 'the operation of compulsory arbitration as regards Maritime Belligerent Rights must be eliminated beyond a shadow of doubt'. Hurst's proposed reservation of disputes arising out of measures taken on behalf of the League was inadequate. This was because it was not possible to be certain that the Council would prevent Britain's exercise of BMR being taken to court even if it upheld defensive measures taken by Britain in response to an act of aggression.[54]

Within the Foreign Office, Ronald Campbell (a senior member of the western department) had completed a detailed examination of the Protocol by mid-November. His memorandum, which Crowe commended to Chamberlain and which came to be treated as the Foreign Office line on the Protocol, rejected its provisions for compulsory arbitration[55] and dismissed as inadequate Hurst's proposed Optional Clause reservation. Perhaps of greater importance, however, was a lengthy minute which Crowe himself submitted to Chamberlain. It drew from the foreign secretary the awed comment that 'I feel it almost impertinent to say how able and powerful I think your paper',[56] and was commended to the CID by Curzon as 'an exceedingly powerful statement of the case' against the Geneva Protocol.[57] There were, said Crowe, two salient features which had to be considered: compulsory arbitration and sanctions (of which only the former is relevant to this discussion). The first way in which the Protocol extended the former principle was through the requirement to accept the Optional Clause. This had, '[so] far as can be gathered', been 'the outcome of a British initiative', but this step had been explicitly rejected in October 1920. It had been raised anew and discussed once more by the Foreign Office in July when, he said,

---

attempt to negotiate treaties with other powers providing for an obligatory jurisdiction of the scope stated [in the Optional Clause]'. Another objection was that the USA (which like Australia and New Zealand had a racist immigration policy) was 'extremely sensitive' on matters such as immigration and the Monroe Doctrine (which it contended fell within its domestic jurisdiction): memorandum by Chelmsford, 27 Oct. 1924, PRO, CP 478(24) CAB 24/168 and CID-541 CAB 4/12.

[54] These objections were made to paragraph 7 of Article 4 of the Protocol but they also apply to the Optional Clause. This Article, which was inserted at the behest of Britain, provided the same reservation to compulsory arbitration under the Protocol as Hurst had suggested for the Optional Clause, *viz*: 'The provisions of the present article [relating to arbitration and judicial settlement] do not apply to the settlement of disputes which arise as the result of measures of war taken by one or more signatory States in agreement with the Council or the Assembly.' Other occasions which the Admiralty held were not covered by the reservation were when there was a civil war and when Britain took measures in circumstances where both parties to a dispute were aggressors under the terms of Article 10 of the Protocol.

[55] The arguments against compulsory arbitration were that non-justiciable disputes were not suitable for arbitration; the exclusion of the Peace treaties from the scope of compulsory arbitration (which was not stated in the Protocol but was in the Beneš–Politis report) would render sacrosanct the territorial *status quo* in Europe; that the Japanese amendment could only reinforce the Council's power to intervene in matters of domestic jurisdiction; and that the Protocol could well have a dangerous effect on Britain's position in Egypt: memorandum by Campbell, 17 Nov. 1924, PRO, CID 540-B CAB 4/12.

[56] Minute, 23 Nov. 1924, PRO, W 9974/134/98 FO 371/10571.

[57] CID, 190th meeting, 4 Dec. 1924, PRO, CAB 2/4.

MacDonald had referred the matter to Haldane who had confirmed 'the adverse opinion expressed in the Foreign Office'. No actual decision was taken but the case had already been 'so fully and clearly stated' that it was sufficient to attach various papers that had been produced in 1920 and earlier that year in response to MacDonald's request for advice.[58]

The second extension of the principle of obligatory arbitration was the procedure laid down in Article 4 of the Protocol under which, if the parties to a dispute could not be induced to accept arbitration, the Council could consider the dispute and, by a unanimous report (excluding the disputants), impose a settlement. If it were unable to reach unanimity, the Council was to refer the dispute to arbitrators. It appeared to be admitted that this procedure could be applied to cases which had not hitherto been considered suitable for arbitration. But, said Crowe, compulsory arbitration was not only incompatible with past British practice, but was utterly inappropriate for matters involving vital interests. And he had to hand a topical example – Britain's position in Egypt and the Sudan. Although Britain had granted independence to Egypt in February 1922, it had done so subject to substantial reservations, namely:

(a) The security of the communications of the British Empire in Egypt;

(b) The defence of Egypt against all foreign aggression or interference, direct or indirect;

(c) The protection of foreign interests in Egypt and the protection of minorities;

(d) The Sudan.[59]

This was a significant limitation on Egypt's freedom and was naturally resented in that country. In August Crowe had warned that one of the first cases for compulsory arbitration with which Britain would be confronted would be the demand that Britain remove its troops from Egypt and hand over the Sudan. When, in October, Hurst had given his view that Britain's position in Egypt was legally untenable, Crowe had replied that 'whatever Sir C. Hurst might think', British imperial interests might 'reluctantly' force Britain to deny Egypt 'the unconditional status of an independent state'. And if this were the only practical way to avoid being driven out of the Sudan, or being declared the 'aggressor' under the Protocol by refusing to 'allow some "neutral" arbitrators to declare that we must leave the Sudan, then I feel sure the British Parliament, no less than the Dominions would not hesitate to adopt that method'.[60]

In his memorandum on the Protocol Crowe now argued that:

> there are questions to which arbitration is not applicable. There are issues so deeply interwoven with national history, tradition and sentiment that no foreign tribunal can be trusted truly to understand and appreciate what is at stake. How often have we seen that even the most learned and acute foreign jurists are absolutely incapable of grasping the fundamental ideas underlying the principles of law on which the edifice of justice is built up in England and in America. With equal if not greater force does

[58] Minute by Crowe, 'The Geneva Protocol', 17 Nov. 1924, PRO, W 9974/134/98 FO 371/10571. Also CID 538–B CAB 4/12.

[59] See Arnold J. Toynbee, *Survey of international affairs, 1925*, I: *The Islamic world*, London 1927, 195. See also below, 126.

[60] Minute, 17 Oct. 1924, PRO, W 8945/134/98 FO 371/10571.

this apply to what Bismarck called the imponderabilia of political psychology. Where such issues are at stake, it is merely provocative to demand in advance blind submission to a body of foreign lawyers by no means all of high reputation, or to some other unknown and unspecified persons. The obligation may be subscribed in the expectation that the actual case may not arise. But when thereafter the case does arise, natural forces will assert themselves, and paper guarantees will vanish into thin air. It is hiding one's head in the sand to be blind to this. Is it either safe or proper to enter into engagements which are not reconcilable with the real world of facts?[61]

When the CID met at the beginning of December the Optional Clause and compulsory arbitration were but one section of Maurice Hankey's 'catalogue of objections directed against every section' of the Protocol which he set out in a summary for the CID of the 'voluminous papers' before it.[62] And in his opening remarks, Curzon (the Lord President of the Council and chairman of the CID) said of the Optional Clause that

> doubts have been raised in the various Departmental Papers; first, as to the probable impartiality and competence of the Court; secondly, as to the risks and perils that may be involved in this system; thirdly, as to the attitude which the Dominions may be expected to take up towards it; fourthly, as to the willingness or unwillingness of the British Parliament, and equally also of the Dominion Parliaments, to accept the decisions of the Permanent Court thus referred to on questions, for instance, such as that which has been disturbing us during the past few weeks, namely, our position in Egypt, our status in the Sudan, and the provisions to be adopted for the security of the Suez Canal; fifthly, Sir Eyre Crowe . . . argues, and I think demonstrates, that these particular proposals are quite incompatible with British practice as it has hitherto existed; sixthly, there seems to be a general consensus that these particular proposals, whatever their intrinsic merits, would greatly incense the United States of America, and are foreign from every conception of arbitration as it presents itself to them; lastly, Sir Maurice Hankey points out . . . that the machinery which it is proposed to set up for this purpose of compulsory arbitration overlaps and in some cases appears to clash rather sharply with the machinery set up by the Washington Conference between two and three years ago.[63]

Two weeks later the whole matter of the Protocol was taken up for detailed examination by a sub-committee.[64] It began with the issue of compulsory arbitration on the grounds that this constituted the first main section of the Protocol against which criticisms had been levelled (the other objectionable aspect being sanctions) and also to benefit from the presence of Hurst who was due to leave London the following day. There is no suggestion in the summary that any consideration was given to signing the Optional Clause, which appears to have been dealt with as part and parcel of the Protocol's arbitral provisions. Nor is there any indication of Hurst having put forward arguments in support of a move in this direction. Compulsory arbitration *per se* was immediately

---

[61] Minute, 'The Geneva Protocol', 17 Nov. 1924.

[62] Arbitration, security and disarmament. Synopsis prepared by the secretary, 2 Dec. 1924, secret, PRO, CID ID/G/17 CAB 16/56.

[63] CID 190th meeting, 4 Dec. 1924, PRO, CAB 2/4.

[64] Its members were Hankey (in the chair), Crowe, Sir Henry Lambert (acting permanent under secretary, Colonial Office) and Arthur Hirtzel (under secretary, India Office). Representatives of the Treasury, Board of Trade and the services attended when sanctions were discussed. Hurst attended five of the meetings.

dismissed and, since the sub-committee could not think of any satisfactory alternatives, it was decided that it was 'evident in the first place that Article 3' of the Protocol – the Optional Clause – 'could not be accepted'. Neither could the other arbitral provisions be accepted, even though it was recognised 'that if the clauses dealing with compulsory arbitration were deleted from the Protocol the very keystone of the structure would be removed and it would fall to the ground'.[65]

Throughout these discussions there was, however, one voice in favour of compulsory arbitration and the Optional Clause: that of Robert Cecil. Baldwin had reluctantly included Cecil in the Cabinet as Chancellor of the Duchy of Lancaster and Cecil was Chamberlain's Foreign Office subordinate with responsibility for League affairs. It seems that it was through the Protocol that Cecil began to incline towards the Optional Clause. When Hankey produced a detailed memorandum arguing that the Protocol represented a move towards the French conception of a League which would have included 'compulsory arbitration in an extreme form', he sent a copy to Cecil.[66] Cecil was willing to accept that this had been so in 1919, and the records of the Paris peace conference, together with Cecil's own diary, confirm that he had strongly resisted American attempts to require League members, in the last resort, to submit disputes to arbitration. But Cecil was critical of Hankey's assumption that since a proposal on the lines of the Protocol had once been rejected, it ought not to be considered again. Although Cecil later regarded the Protocol as 'a serious mistake' and did not think it as good as his own DTMA,[67] he supported it because he thought it would further disarmament, because it had widespread European support and because it approached the issue of the pacification and security of Europe in a desirably overall way. And in supporting the Protocol Cecil had to accept compulsory arbitration. He explained the way in which his mind was working in a note to Chamberlain. If, as Cecil believed, disarmament was essential for peace, the first step was to get nations to accept the principle which had long been accepted among individuals in Britain: 'that a man may not try and right his wrongs by violence even though the provocation is extreme'. The compulsory arbitration provisions in the Protocol would not, in practice, be considerable and they 'would mean that we should only do what we thought right when the occasion arose'.[68]

Cecil's views did not, however, cut much ice with Chamberlain who had authorised Crowe to tell the CID sub-committee that the arbitration provisions of the Protocol (including the Optional Clause) were, like sanctions, 'of such an impossible nature that they should be ruled out'.[69] Perhaps it was the strength of opposition to compulsory arbitration that led Cecil to make the strange suggestion that Britain should accept compulsory arbitration while 'holding

[65] GP (24) 1st consultation, 18 Dec. 1924, PRO, CAB 16/56.

[66] 'Geneva Protocol', note by the secretary, 23 Dec. 1924, (circulated 8 Jan. 1925), PRO, CID 558-B CAB 21/289. See also GP (24) 2nd Consultation, 19 Dec. 1924, PRO, CAB 16/56.

[67] Viscount Cecil, A great experiment: an autobiography, London 1941, 159, and memorandum sent by Cecil to Baldwin on 22 Mar. 1925, BM, Cecil papers, Add. MS 51080.

[68] 'Note on the Geneva Protocol', sent by Cecil to Chamberlain on 17 Nov. 1924, UBL, Chamberlain papers, AC 51/44. See also memorandum by Cecil, 23 Feb. 1925, BM, Cecil papers, Add. MS 51103.

[69] Crowe to GP (24) 1st consultation, 18 Dec. 1924.

ourselves at liberty to refuse to be bound by an award resulting from such an arbitration if that reward were unacceptable to us'[70] – a proposal that was rightly rejected as likely 'to bring arbitration into contempt'.[71] But the seed had been planted in Cecil's mind. He went along with the decision to reject the Protocol. But when this was done in what he thought was a disastrous manner using language that seemed 'harsh, and even insolent',[72] he urged Baldwin to make a gesture that would demonstrate that British policy was still governed by the principles of the League: namely, to drop a hint that Britain would make 'a properly guarded adhesion' to the Optional Clause.[73] This was one of Cecil's more unrealistic suggestions for, by the end of December 1924, it was obvious that Britain's policy on the Optional Clause was not to sign it.

For the time being, therefore, Britain's steps along the path towards the Optional Clause had been arrested by the same objections as had been raised against the Clause in 1920, and with the same lack of discussion as to whether there was anything to be said in its favour. But the matter had not been entirely taken back to the starting point, for at home two people of importance had changed their minds. Hurst's careful consideration of the question had made him believe that acceptance of the Clause would be advantageous to Britain; and Cecil had been led by the Geneva Protocol to begin thinking that acceptance of the Optional Clause might help pave the way to disarmament. Abroad, the actions of the first Labour government at the fifth Assembly had given the Optional Clause greater international prominence and identified it as a potentially important contribution to the building of a peaceful world. Thus the Optional Clause was now on both the international and domestic agenda. Moreover, additional developments occurred during the next four years which meant that the government could not lightly brush the issue to one side. Britain came under increasing pressure to reconsider its policy on the Clause, and as a result the new Conservative administration found itself being impelled towards taking a different line to that of the Coalition and Conservative governments of the early 1920s.

---

[70] Ibid. Cecil had privately made this suggestion to Hankey.
[71] Ibid.
[72] Cecil to Salisbury, 30 Mar.1925, BM, Cecil papers, Add. MS 51085.
[73] Memorandum sent by Cecil to Baldwin on 22 Mar. 1925. See also Cecil to Baldwin, 16 Mar. 1925, BM, Cecil papers, Add. MS 51080.

PART TWO

SLOW BUT STEADY, 1925–1929

4

The League of Nations Union
and British Policy

During the second half of the 1920s, the British government was under strong domestic pressure to sign the Optional Clause. This was very largely due to the activity of the League of Nations Union (LNU), which at this time was a strong and apparently influential pressure group. It had a very large membership, clear support from many sections of British society (including all of the main political parties), and seemed to have the ear of the government. Thus, although arbitration had for long been dear to the left and to all sections of the British peace movement, the LNU became far and away the chief agency through which public support for the Optional Clause was mobilised and expressed during the period of Conservative government from 1924 to 1929. The LNU's efforts meant that the question of Britain's acceptance of the Clause was for a while quite high on the political agenda. However, its considerable work had but a minimal effect on the course of British policy.

The League of Nations Union

The League of Nations Union represented the expression of a basic principle on which the League had been founded: the belief that democratic public opinion could have a beneficial effect on foreign policy and that it could persuade governments to uphold the League. As the Union put it:

> No great world movement is possible without the impetus behind it of the great masses of population; no great moral material sanction can lie in the hands of the League unless placed there by the will of the people, for in the last resort it is they who must enforce the law of the League, and it is the knowledge of the existence of that will, both in their own people and elsewhere, which will restrain unscrupulous Governments from international crime.[1]

And, as the Union saw it, its job was

> to lend power to the League's elbow, to foster the growth of its influence and prestige; to win for it the wholehearted support of British public opinion, and so ultimately of the British Government, and to stimulate the creation abroad of similar voluntary societies working for the League of Nations.[2]

[1] LNU pamphlet, *The works and needs of the League of Nations Union*, Feb. 1921, CCAC, Noel-Baker papers.
[2] *Headway*, June 1923, quoted in Ernest Bramsted, 'Apostles of collective security: the LNU and its functions', *Australian Journal of Politics and History* xiii (1967), 348. The LNU was organised as follows. Formally-speaking, the general council held final responsibility for all LNU activities. It was democratically elected and had representatives from all branches at its twice-yearly meetings which

For the Union to carry out this task it was necessary for it to become a mass organisation. In 1918, when the League of Nations Society and the League of Free Nations Association merged, it had only 3,841 members, but many of these were members of the British elite who lent the LNU authority and standing. They were able to bring into its committees leading figures from every walk of life. They gave it a sound organisational basis and were able to provide the necessary planning and direction for recruiting enough general support to justify LNU claims to speak on behalf of the public. They also set about the task of public education regarding the League. Undoubtedly, all this activity reflected the dedication to peace of the LNU's leading figures. Gilbert Murray, for example, the Australian-born Regius Professor of Greek at Oxford University, who tirelessly strove to save 'our wounded liberal civilisation';[3] and Lord Robert Cecil, who had played a key role in creating the League, and who worked continuously and selflessly at developing and encouraging the expression of that public opinion on which he believed the success of the League depended. Murray, Cecil and the Union's numerous speakers articulated the aspirations of many, as can be seen from the Union's membership figures. With the aid of zealous recruiters and frequent membership drives, the Union rapidly increased in size. By 1919 it had 10,000 members. Within a year this number had increased sevenfold and by May 1921 it had risen to 101,000. As early as 1923 it was sufficiently large for Arthur Balfour to believe that 'at certain moments' it could wield 'considerable electoral power' and that it was 'regarded by an ignorant British public as the British representative – so to speak – of the League of Nations'.[4] In 1925 the granting of a Royal Charter[5] confirmed its standing as

were generally held in June and December. In practice this general council was too unwieldy and met too infrequently to exercise effective control over all LNU activities. Policy formation devolved upon the executive committee, an elected body of about forty members which had the power to co-opt other members. In addition there was a management committee which looked after the day-to-day running of the Union. The management committee was made up of members of the executive committee. As the work of the LNU expanded, it was no longer possible for the management committee to get through all its work. In 1928, therefore, the name of the management committee was changed to the management and general purposes committee. It was to consist of all members of the executive committee and was charged with completing any unfinished business of the executive committee, but it was made quite clear that any matter of policy was the province of the executive. This was underlined by giving the chairman and vice-chairman of the executive committee the same positions on the management committee. There was a phalanx of further committees covering such matters as women's organisations, editorials (for *Headway*), parliament, religious organisations, education and labour organisations. As with the management committee, the names of some of these committees changed over time. Finally, there were sub-committees dealing with specific aspects of the League's work such as mandates, armaments and amendments to the Covenant. The secretary of the LNU from 1920 to 1938 was Maxwell Garnett who headed a secretariat of more than 100 full, part-time and voluntary workers.

[3] Gilbert Murray, *The League of Nations movement: some recollections of its early days*, London 1955, 12.
[4] Balfour to Cecil, 4 June 1923, BM, Cecil papers, Add. MS 51071.
[5] Under the Royal Charter the Union's objectives were: '1. To secure the wholehearted acceptance by the British people of the League of Nations as the guardian of international right, the organ of international co-operation, the final arbiter in international differences, and the supreme instrument for removing injustices which may threaten the world; 2. To foster mutual understanding, goodwill, and habits of co-operation and fair dealing between the peoples of different countries; 3. To advocate the full development of the League of Nations so as to bring about such a world organisation as will guarantee the freedom of nations, act as a trustee and guardian of backward races and underdeveloped territories, maintain international order, and finally liberate mankind from war and the effects of war.': Gilbert Murray, *From the League to the UN*, London 1948, 198.

did the acceptance of honorary positions by most leading politicians and every prime minister (except Ramsay MacDonald).[6] By the end of 1928 it had almost 750,000 members and 2,767 branches – although less than one third of the membership had paid the current subscription.[7]

It might seem reasonable to suggest that when such a body took up the Optional Clause and campaigned vigorously for its acceptance, the government would find it difficult to withstand the pressure, especially since one of the government's arguments against such a step was based upon public opinion. Such a scenario might be thought all the more likely since the inter-war period has sometimes been seen as the one time when public opinion did play a role in foreign policy making. In a different context – Canada – it has been argued that the LNU's equivalent society 'created the public opinion which persuaded Skelton and King to begin discussions at the diplomatic level on the Optional Clause'.[8] If the comparatively weak Canadian League of Nations Society could have so influenced policy then arguably the much stronger British Union should have had a greater impact.

Yet this was not so. It will be argued in chapter 7 that the above quotation exaggerates the significance of Canadian public opinion,[9] and it will be argued here that the LNU did not influence British policy on the Optional Clause. From 1925 to 1927 its attempt at gentle persuasion – passing resolutions in support of the Optional Clause and politely forwarding them to the government – was completely ineffective. But when it tried to campaign for the Clause and to mount an open, public debate, it soon deemed it prudent to back down. This was because the Optional Clause was a political issue and therefore impossible to advocate in a way which was not seen as a criticism of government policy. The government interpreted the campaign as one of opposition and, believing that the Union was being used by its political opponents to score party goals, attacked it. Thus the only way in which the Union could clear itself of the charges of partisanship was to stop the campaign. The Union was never able to resolve the conflict between its non-political standing and its desire to advocate policies which were seen as partisan. The Optional Clause campaign provides a graphic example of this problem and, in so doing, demonstrates why the LNU was unable to influence the government's policy on this matter.

The LNU and the Optional Clause 1922–5

In the early years the LNU focused almost completely on disarmament as the path to peace. Everything else was secondary to this, the major task, which preoccupied it. In May 1922, when the general council formally endorsed the

---

[6] See above, 32, n. 37.
[7] LNU membership figures were calculated on the basis of the total number of people who had ever joined, who had not resigned and were not known to have died. The paid-up figure was always much lower. Thus, in July 1928 only 201,864 were paid-up members. In March 1933 LNU membership topped a million but under 400,000 of these were paid-up. The paid-up membership reached its peak of 406,868 in 1931.
[8] Donald Page, 'Canadians and the League of Nations before the Manchurian crisis', unpubl. PhD diss. Toronto 1972, 313.
[9] See below, 175, n. 69.

recommendation that Britain should accept the Optional Clause, it was simply genuflecting towards a hallowed tenet of the peace movement. When, in 1923, a barrister, F. N. Keen (who had, as a member of the war-time League of Nations Society, advocated a court with full powers of compulsory jurisdiction) sounded out Cecil about submitting a memorandum on the Optional Clause to the LNU executive committee, the latter replied:

> Personally I am of Balfour's opinion. I think it would be rash to try to give to the Court a compulsory jurisdiction in disputes in which the Great Powers were involved. It is after all rather a strong order to ask a British statesman to submit compulsorily any disputes involving it may be [sic] the prosperity of many millions of British subjects to a Court whose competence is yet a matter of anticipation. I believe that to hurry matters in this direction will risk considerable delay eventually and perhaps failure of the whole scheme. It is not as though the peace of the whole world were directly involved, for the jurisdiction of the Court is at present confined to matters of a minor character.[10]

Keen accepted Cecil's argument that caution was advisable, but he disagreed with the substance of Cecil's letter. How, he asked, could Britain expect other states to submit grave disputes to the League Council if Britain itself were unwilling to submit purely legal disputes to jurists at The Hague? The argument about the 'minor character' of disputes submitted to the Court cut both ways: 'While it suggests that such matters would be less likely to lead to war, it also tends to minimize the seriousness of bringing them under compulsory jurisdiction.'[11] Very shortly after this, Keen's memorandum together with a memorandum written on the same subject by an LNU official, was considered by the executive which simply decided to publish them in the LNU monthly journal, *Headway*.

The low priority attached to the Optional Clause was further illustrated in the general election at the end of 1923. At that time it was common practice for organisations to send questionnaires to parliamentary candidates to elicit their views on topics with which the organisations were particularly concerned. This practice was adopted by the LNU and the questionnaire which it sent to local branches only included the Optional Clause amongst questions which were 'for branches to adopt or not as may seem best'.[12]

The first Labour government and the Geneva Protocol produced a dramatic change. Arbitration (in the widest sense) had been 'rediscovered' and elevated. Two leading LNU members, Murray and Noel-Baker, had made a significant contribution to the Protocol and the parliamentary questionnaire for the 1924 general election reflected arbitration's new status. The general council also congratulated the fifth Assembly for 'the great advance towards permanent peace achieved by the general recognition that arbitration, security and disarmament go hand in hand'.[13]

The rejection of the Protocol in March 1925 did not by any means reduce the appeal of the ideas which it embodied. From now on some links were almost

10 Cecil to Keen, 22 Jan. 1923, BM, Cecil papers, Add. MS 51163.
11 Keen to Cecil, 26 Jan. 1923, ibid.
12 Excom minute 891 and Annexes A and B, 15 Nov. 1923, BLPES, LNU II.5.
13 General council, 18 Nov. 1924, C.13 Records of Welsh national council of the LNU, quoted in Donald S. Birn, *The League of Nations Union 1918–1945*, Oxford 1981, 57.

always perceived between the three principles of the Protocol. Each of them could still be advocated separately and varying degrees of emphasis could from time to time be placed on each one of them. But at a deeper level they were seen to have an essential connection. Disarmament was still the main goal but the other two principles, although secondary, were thought to be vital both substantively and tactically: security was the sugar coating for the French to accept disarmament; arbitration was the domestic, English rule of law translated to the international scene.

In the spring of 1925, Philip Noel-Baker (who had recently become Professor of International Relations at the London School of Economics) produced a lengthy memorandum on the Optional Clause. A lawyer by training, Noel-Baker had emphasised the importance of an international court when he had acted as Cecil's assistant at the end of the war, and he had been promoting the Optional Clause from the time that the PCIJ had been established. He now took the opportunity to argue that the fifth Assembly had thrown the whole question of the Optional Clause into 'strong relief' and that Canada's positive attitude towards it,[14] had made it a 'question of vital importance' for the Commonwealth. The question facing Britain was simple: 'Shall we or shall we not agree that the highest judicial authority in the world shall be entrusted with the duty of defining and determining our legal rights and obligations?' The answer was equally simple: 'When the question is put like this it is difficult to see what valid ground of principle there can be for refusing to give to the Court such obligatory jurisdiction. Nor on practical grounds is there greater objection than there is in principle.' Three-fifths of the members of the League had 'accepted the Optional Clause in principle'; Italy was 'credibly reported' as having been on the verge of signing before Mussolini's march on Rome; Germany and France had a good number of arbitration treaties. Britain would be lagging behind the world if it did not sign.

The greatest barrier to accepting arbitration and adjudication – belligerent maritime rights (BMR) – would be reserved. But even this was not the question of the hour. What was needed in international relations was a court to prevent war, not to regulate its conduct. Were Britain to accept the Optional Clause, its example would no doubt lead to a general acceptance of the Optional Clause in international society; it would 'produce an immediate and invaluable effect upon the general atmosphere'; and, such was the speed with which international law was developing, that 'within a reasonable time an overwhelming majority of international disputes will be capable of settlement on the basis of legal rights and obligations'.[15]

Noel-Baker's argument fell on fertile soil for, as has been seen, the Geneva Protocol had led Cecil to alter his views on the Optional Clause and to begin suggesting within the government that Britain should seriously consider accepting it.

[14] See below, 163.
[15] 'Memorandum on the obligatory jurisdiction of the PCIJ', 15 May 1925, CCAC, Noel-Baker papers.

The failure of gentle persuasion 1925–7

The elevation of the Optional Clause to an important place in LNU policy was confirmed in the summer of 1925 when the LNU council issued its first appeal to the government to accept the Optional Clause at once. For the next one-and-a-half years the LNU attempted to use gentle persuasion to get the government to sign – that is by passing resolutions and appealing to the government in a manner calculated to avoid any offence. It was the obvious first course. The Optional Clause was not yet a major issue and the government and the Union wanted to be on good terms with one another. Chamberlain recognised the importance of the Union as a pressure group. Cecil, with his leading position in both the Union and the government, continued to hope that in this way he could achieve harmony between the policies which the Union advocated and those which the government adopted.

Good relations were on the whole successfully maintained. But there were problems and Chamberlain was suspicious of the Union. Chamberlain had good ground for some complaints in 1925. For example, he was invited to a Birmingham LNU meeting at which a resolution was on the agenda (and more or less assured of passage) supporting the Geneva Protocol. A typewritten circular which certainly misrepresented the government's policy was circulated in connection with an 'Arbitration Petition' which was being organised by the National Council for the Prevention of War (NCPW)[16] with the assistance of the LNU. The Union responded quickly to Chamberlain's protest by bringing the deviant branch into line and repudiating the circular. And it was also the case that complainants were not limited to Chamberlain: Cecil, too, threatened to resign over what he took to be a slight on his honour in an article in *Headway*.[17]

There was, however, one disagreement that summer which clearly indicated the delicacy of the relationship between the LNU and the government and was a harbinger of the way in which Chamberlain would react to anything more than the gentlest persuasion. In August, Major John Hills, the Conservative vice-chairman of the LNU's executive committee, sent Chamberlain an executive committee resolution suggesting that the British delegation to the forthcoming Assembly should contain representatives from all three major political parties. Chamberlain exploded angrily. The incidents about which he had earlier complained were blown up out of all proportion and blamed on the Union's leaders. He would not tolerate any attempts by the Union to dictate to the government and he threatened to resign from the Union. 'Is not the League, or its Committee, acting beyond its proper duties', he asked, 'when it advocates the specific solution of a particular difficulty to which it knows the Government

---

[16] The NCPW was the name used by the National Peace Council between 1923 and 1930. It had been established in London in 1908 to provide a forum for consultation and discussion between the representatives of voluntary organisations with a common interest in the problems of peace. The offending circular, which was headed 'Arbitration or war', repeated, out of context, remarks that Chamberlain had made in the House of Commons and implied that signing the petition would strengthen the hands of the government in its League policy.

[17] Ignoring the doctrine of collective responsibility, the article had criticised Cecil for supporting aspects of the government's policy with which he did not agree personally: Cecil to Murray, 18 Nov. 1925, BM, Cecil papers, Add. MS 51132.

of the day is opposed?'[18] But while Chamberlain saw the proper role of the LNU as handmaiden to the government, and anything more as subversive of the parliamentary system, the LNU could not comply. As Hills explained to Chamberlain after three-weeks deliberation:

> The Union is entirely non-party. It supports the Government. It always tries to support the Government and if it had to differ it would do so with reluctance; and if it has differed in the past it has never (so far as I know) attacked the Government.

> That I take is its province. You consider that it is acting beyond its proper duties when it advocates the specific solution of a particular difficulty to which it knows the Government of to-day is opposed. I do ask you to consider what would be its position if it followed your formula. It would never be able to advocate anything to which the government of the day was opposed. It would become the organ, not of the League, but of the government. You object to the Union suggesting to the Government an alteration in the composition of the British delegation [to the Assembly]. If it cannot make such a suggestion it can do nothing. It would be powerless. You would require the League of Nations Union to support whatever composition was selected by the Foreign Secretary of the day, be he you or be he a member of another party. Surely this can never be the duty of a body formed to support the League. It would fail in its duty and would be an organisation which no self-respecting person would think it worth while to join if it had to refrain from criticism of every action of every government. I trust I do not misrepresent you, but this seems to me the implication of your argument.

> Is not the duty of bodies consisting of members of different parties something as follows:–

> They should always try to act with the government of the day. They should search for reasons for support, and should never take a carping attitude. If they have to differ, they should try first the method of private suggestion. Suggestion is not opposition. If suggestion fails, they should again consider whether the point at issue is so vital that a body consisting of all parties must oppose a government which some of them support politically. This is the very last resort; and in the case of the Union has never arisen.[19]

Chamberlain did not reply and the Union pursued the method of private suggestion but with no result apart from a statement of government policy which was obtained that summer in the following manner.

In August 1925, the LNU's collaboration with the NCPW resulted in a petition containing 500,000 signatures and calling on the government: 'with the sixth Assembly of the League of Nations in view . . . to accept forthwith the principle of arbitration in all international disputes and as a first step, to sign at once the [Optional] Clause'. Chamberlain's reply to James Hudson (the Labour MP for Huddersfield, a member of the LNU executive and secretary of the NCPW) who had presented the petition, was subsequently published and became the 'standard' answer of the government to any enquiries about its willingness to accept the Optional Clause.

The reply began by distinguishing between those situations in which a dispute was likely to lead to war and those in which war was unlikely. With regard to the

---

[18] Chamberlain to Hills, 5 Aug. 1925, Bodl. Lib., Murray papers.
[19] Hills to Chamberlain, 26 Aug. 1925, UBL, Chamberlain papers, AC 52/464. See also PRO, FO 800/258.

former situation, Britain was already bound to submit such disputes either to the League Council or to arbitration (in the widest sense) under Article 15 of the Covenant. Britain had no desire to escape this obligation but if it accepted the Optional Clause it would lose the option of having a dispute settled by the Council rather than the PCIJ. Since the whole object of the Covenant was the pacific settlement of disputes there could be no objection to the procedure which involved the Council rather than the Court.

With regard to situations in which a dispute was unlikely to lead to war, the reply stated that no country had done more than Britain to further the settlement of appropriate disputes by arbitration. Britain already had many arbitration agreements which all included the safeguard of the vital interests formula. Article 13 of the Covenant obliged Britain to submit to arbitration such disputes as were 'generally suitable' for this procedure. By accepting the Optional Clause and/or going for the currently popular 'all-in' arbitration treaties, Britain would be agreeing in advance to submit to adjudication or arbitration every dispute including those which might not lead to war but which, might none the less, touch upon vital interests, honour or independence.

There was, then, no reason to accept the Optional Clause for either category of disputes and there were two further objections to the Optional Clause. Firstly, successive governments had concluded that it would be unwise since the constitution of the Commonwealth required the dominions to assent to such a step; and, secondly, it was unwise for Britain to accept an unqualified commitment which it might be impossible to meet (and which might then be conducive of an unsolvable dispute). The letter concluded by saying that Chamberlain hoped that arbitration would 'steadily grow in favour'.[20]

A fortnight after the publication of Chamberlain's letter to Hudson, Gilbert Murray replied to it in the *Manchester Guardian*. Writing in his capacity as chairman of the LNU executive committee, Murray began by saying that the petition had merely asked the British government 'to follow the example of 23 other members of the League, including France and Belgium',[21] in accepting a clause whose object was:

> to facilitate the reign of law and mutual confidence among members of the League so that even the smaller members may rest assured that they will receive their legal rights and will not be exposed as soon as they have a difference of opinion with a Great Power to the danger of intimidation or chicanery.

With regard to the situations posited in Chamberlain's letter to Hudson, Murray held that simply by virtue of its might, a great power would be considerably advantaged. In a dispute 'likely to lead to rupture' it would probably be able to prevent a unanimously adverse decision by the League Council and in a dispute which was 'unlikely to lead to a rupture' it could sit tight and ignore the small power *ad infinitum*.

[20] C. W. Orde (on behalf of Chamberlain) to Hudson, 4 Sept. 1925. Initially marked 'confidential', Chamberlain later approved its publication and it appeared in *The Times* on 26 Sept.
[21] Strictly speaking, this was inaccurate. By that date, 23 states had signed but only 14 of these declarations were in force by Oct. 1925. The Belgian declaration had not yet been ratified while the French declaration was later replaced by a different declaration which was ratified.

The need for Commonwealth consent and the problem of BMR were 'old and well-known herrings'. Although the Locarno agreements had wrought a change in war-time conditions, the British government could easily consult the dominions; once Britain made up its mind the dominions would probably follow. All in all: 'The advantages on which the Foreign Office sets store are undesirable. The mischief is that they are unjust.'[22]

The government and the Union having thus stated their views, neither side took its differences any further. The Optional Clause was now a firm part of LNU policy. It was a matter of course for the general council to pass resolutions in favour of the Optional Clause and compulsory arbitration and individual branches continued to take initiatives in support of the clause. Throughout 1926 the Union took pains to avoid any clashes with the government and to emphasise its formal support for government policy. The absence of records to the contrary in Foreign Office files and the private papers of Cecil, Murray and Chamberlain suggest that relations were amicable enough from the government's point of view although there remained a whiff of suspicion about the Union and its activities.

As 1926 drew to a close and 1927 opened, the extent to which government and Union were seeking a harmonious co-existence can be seen in a meeting between them. At the end of December Hills had sent Chamberlain the latest resolutions which had just been passed by the general council together with a carefully-worded letter. Many of the resolutions were, he explained, in conformity with government policy; others were 'suggestions which may not be without value'; and there were also 'some criticisms, the frank character of which you will, I know, appreciate, since the spirit in which they are made is altogether constructive'.[23]

One of the important resolutions was that which Hills had moved from the chair, on behalf of the executive committee, urging the importance of the government signing the Optional Clause as a first step towards compulsory arbitration in all disputes. Hills recognised that Chamberlain had not been able to agree to the Optional Clause on a former occasion but he pointed out that the Union had proposed that Britain should attach to its acceptance of the Clause 'the very important condition' of reservations compatible with the Clause and that in this way Britain could reserve cases involving BMR pending the satisfactory codification of maritime law.[24]

While hoping that Hills was not under the misapprehension that the questions covered by the LNU resolutions had not loomed very large in the last couple of years, the western department of the Foreign Office thought there was little to be gained by going into them with him. It recommended that Chamberlain send a reply saying that the resolutions would certainly be most carefully considered and their subject-matter would continue to receive the government's earnest attention. Chamberlain, however, decided to write privately to Hills explaining his fear that such a letter might be considered 'insufficient and therefore unfriendly' but that a more detailed and 'necessarily . . . more argumentative' reply 'would only anger without convincing'. Rather

[22] *Manchester Guardian*, 9 Oct. 1925; Bod. Lib., Murray papers.
[23] Hills to Chamberlain, 30 Dec. 1926, PRO, W 56/56/98 FO 371/12660.
[24] Ibid.

than choosing, as he put it, between Scylla and Charybdis, he suggested that he receive a deputation from the general council and that he make a reasoned statement for publication.[25] Hills responded enthusiastically. Perhaps Chamberlain could reply for the present that the resolutions would receive 'careful attention etc.' and go on to say that in June he would welcome the opportunity of addressing the next general council in order to explain what he was doing and thinking. Chamberlain would have a 'tremendous reception' and he would thereby 'capture the hearts of the Union'.[26] This, however, clashed with Chamberlain's plans. He therefore agreed to what, from the LNU's point of view, was the next best course, that of receiving a deputation from the executive in February. During the two-hour meeting, cordiality was the key-note. Chamberlain prefaced his remarks by recalling that when he became foreign secretary

> I think I was somewhat suspect to the League of Nations Union, who were perhaps prone to think I was by temperament rather hostile to an experiment on so great a scale and about which such high hopes were cherished in certain quarters. I frankly confess that I had my doubts, though I also cherished my hopes.[27]

Be that as it may, he was now a supporter of the League and he looked forwards to its gradual extension. Murray, as leader of the deputation, took pains to emphasise the Union's full appreciation of the contribution which Chamberlain was making to the League and to explain that its resolutions urging policies which were not those of the government were 'not expressions of opposition, but merely expressions of differences of opinion that are almost bound to arise between thoughtful people engaged in the same general cause'.[28]

With regard to the Optional Clause, Chamberlain pointed out that Britain's record made it 'one of the most active practisers of arbitration'. However, he went on to say that it was not possible to accept compulsory jurisdiction because of the difficulties over BMR; the need for imperial unity; the problem of being unable to guarantee that legislation which might be required in pursuance of a judgement would be passed by parliament; and to refer the deputation to the other problems set out in the 1925 letter to Hudson.[29] He also raised a new objection – omitted from the printed minutes of the meeting – which was that the Court was international and, as such, did not operate in the manner of English courts. The Union's suggestion of attaching reservations to the Clause was turned into an objection. Chamberlain did 'not much like signatures with reservations' for, given that almost every signatory attached its own reservations, it would be difficult for Britain to know what obligations it would be entering into on accepting the Optional Clause.[30]

In replying to Chamberlain, Hills said that they realised the force of all that the foreign secretary had said, but he asked whether it was not the case that

---

[25] Chamberlain to Hills, 6 Jan. 1927, ibid.
[26] Hills to Chamberlain, 10 Jan. 1927, ibid.
[27] Transcript from the notes of Treasury reporters of a deputation to the secretary of state from the LNU on 22 Feb. 1927, PRO, W 1773/56/98 FO 371/12660. See also Bodl. Lib., Murray papers.
[28] Ibid.
[29] See above, 61-2.
[30] 'Transcript from the notes of Treasury reporters', PRO, W 1173/56/98. Cf. Cushendun (Cecil's successor) speaking to the House of Lords a year later: House of Lords debs., 8 Feb. 1928, 72-3.

whenever the British empire ratified the Clause it was out of the question that it should do so unconditionally in that it would be necessary to safeguard BMR? He quite agreed that it would be pointless to make reservations so sweeping as to render the obligation meaningless, but surely the time was approaching 'when we shall know so well what . . . [our] reservations must be, that we should sign'?[31]

In retrospect the February 1927 meeting was a turning point. It was the last amicable meeting between Chamberlain and the LNU for over a year. It sums up the most that could be achieved by the Union through gentle persuasion and polite private suggestion. It could have good relations with the foreign secretary and be treated by him with a courtesy beyond that which his Foreign Office advisers deemed necessary. But that was all. The Union's leaders, however, were becoming fed up with the government's refusal to listen to their arguments. They could see that if they continued in their present course of politely asking the government to accept the Optional Clause in the name of peace and justice, they could expect the government to continue replying that it sympathised with the Union's sentiments but it could not accept the Clause on account of the national interests at stake. On the other hand, Chamberlain had made it quite plain that if the Union tried to do anything else, he would react fiercely. Cecil's resignation from the government in August 1927 removed most of the leadership's doubts about the necessity of avoiding a conflict with the government over the Optional Clause and they found themselves driven into the position which Hills had outlined two years earlier.

'The very last resort': the movement into a period of conflict

For as long as Cecil remained in the government there was no likelihood of a serious clash with the Union. In 1923 he had told the Union that he had accepted the offer of a ministerial appointment 'because I think that I can be of more use to the League of Nations inside than out, and I have made it quite clear to the Prime Minister . . . that it was only on those terms that I could consent to become a member of his Government'.[32] As long as Cecil followed this course, the Union which he in effect controlled was committed to supporting this line. But Cecil was never really sure that he was doing the right thing. He was never happy in the second Baldwin government and thoughts of resignation were never far from his mind.

He accepted the limited, secondary role which Chamberlain assigned him in League policy. He did his best to execute British policy loyally and he 'felt horribly mean' to find himself 'heartily' agreeing with Paul-Boncour's criticism of Britain at the sixth (1925) Assembly.[33] In 1926 he was persuaded not to resign over the crisis regarding the membership of the League Council but he found himself feeling more and more isolated from his party. Apart from Halifax and his brother, Salisbury, he regarded the members of the Cabinet as either 'middle class monsters' or 'pure Party politicians'[34] who not only 'reject[ed] in their

[31] Ibid.
[32] Excom minute 704, 31 May 1923, BLPES, LNU II.5.
[33] See below, 92. Cecil to Irwin, 29 Sept. 1927, BM, Cecil papers, Add. MS 51084.
[34] Cecil to Irwin, private and confidential, 16 Dec. 1926, ibid.

hearts the League of Nations, but they did not propose to take any step for getting rid of war'.[35]

In the spring of 1927 he was again on the verge of resignation when, as he saw it, the obdurately obstructive attitude of the armed forces (and particularly the Admiralty) had forced him to put forward in the League's Preparatory Commission for the Disarmament Conference 'fatuous propositions'[36] which were 'difficult to reconcile with any serious desire for . . . success'.[37] Overworked, frustrated and, as he admitted, 'more or less a wreck'[38] through nervous exhaustion, he left a letter in Chamberlain's room informing him of his intention of to resign over the foreign secretary's conduct of business. The immediate crisis passed when Chamberlain persuaded Cecil not to go through with it by threatening to resign himself. Under doctor's orders Cecil took things easy for the next couple of months but the breakdown of the Coolidge naval conference that summer was the final straw for him. Despite his 'most earnestly expressed protests'[39] the government had taken a course which he believed led to the failure of the talks and which he felt unable to defend.

Cecil believed there was now no question about his isolation and lack of influence in the Cabinet and that the time had come to fulfil his pledge to the LNU. Whereas for him, he explained, 'disarmament was the most important public question of the day',[40] the Cabinet as a whole 'did not think it mattered very much'[41] and would support Churchill when he and Cecil disagreed over disarmament.[42] So Cecil turned his attention to trying to promote his foreign policy objectives outside the government and through the LNU. He had resigned, he said, 'in order to get full freedom to advocate the cause of disarmament, in which the ultimate judge and sovereign power is public opinion'.[43] His years of frustration and his desperation when he resigned made his cause all the more urgent. When his sister chided him for his 'gloomy view of now or never',[44] Cecil explained that he always had in his mind the failure of Castlereagh's plans. Cecil had hoped to get rid of war by disarmament but now he felt that

> as long as this Government is in office there will be no determined lead in that direction from here or I think any other country which is really ready to take the matter up whole-heartedly. As Boncour used to say to me repeatedly at Geneva, it was only he and I who were in earnest about disarmament. On the other hand, *I do think*

[35] Viscount Cecil, *A great experiment: an autobiography*, London 1941, 189. Cf. idem, *All the way*, London 1949, 175-6, 191.
[36] Cecil to Irwin, 29 Sept.
[37] Cecil to Baldwin, 9 Aug. 1927. This was his first resignation letter which he was persuaded to tone down for publication: UBL, Chamberlain papers, AC 54/28. It is printed as Appendix 2 to Cecil, *Great experiment*.
[38] Ibid. 184.
[39] Cecil to House of Lords, 1 Nov. 1927, House of Lords *debs.*, 93.
[40] Cecil's public resignation letter to Baldwin, 9 Aug. 1927, UBL, Chamberlain papers, AC 54/28.
[41] House of Lords *debs.*, 16 Nov. 1927, 88.
[42] Cecil to Irwin, 29 Sept. 1927, BM, Cecil papers, Add. MS 51084. For a sympathetic account of Cecil's frustrations as a minister and the events leading up to his resignation see Dick Richardson, *The evolution of British disarmament policy in the 1920s*, London 1989.
[43] Editorial, *Manchester Guardian*, 10 Sept. 1927.
[44] Lady Gwendolyn Cecil to Cecil, 2 Feb. 1928, BM, Cecil papers, Add. MS 51166.

we might do something about arbitration; and to establish arbitration is a step towards disestablishing war.[45]

This was an important change of emphasis. Until then the Union's support for the Optional Clause had been completely subordinated to disarmament. Now, however, while disarmament remained the vital ultimate goal, the Optional Clause became the immediate goal. It was seen as necessary for disarmament, it was an important step towards building what was then called the 'peace mentality', and it was something which could be done at once.

It was explained as follows in an important editorial in the *Manchester Guardian* following a meeting between Cecil and C. P. Scott, the newspaper's editor. Until then the LNU's policy had been to support Locarno in the hope that the Locarno system would gradually be extended in the direction of the Geneva Protocol. The Union had now lost faith in that approach and the only practical step towards peace which could be taken at the moment would be in the direction of the pacific settlement of disputes. It was clearly impractical to resurrect the Geneva Protocol for immediate adoption, but the government could take the initiative of accepting the Optional Clause and declaring its willingness to sign 'all-in' arbitration treaties. Such a move, it was held, would 'constitute a first and very considerable instalment of a policy aiming at security based on arbitration which is itself the only possible foundation for disarmament and peace'.[46] Just as a later prime minister was alleged to have talked of resolving Britain's economic problems 'at a stroke',[47] so too did Cecil then speak of the comparative simplicity of accepting the Optional Clause – by a 'mere motion'[48] as opposed to the more difficult process of negotiating arbitration treaties. Cecil also thought that a campaign on the Optional Clause had a chance of succeeding. He understood that the government's decision against signature was not one of principle but was because the government thought that the time to sign had not yet arrived. The Union would show the government that the British public thought that the time had come.

The launching and organisation of the LNU campaign

Cecil resigned from the government in August 1927 and at the beginning of September the LNU's executive committee declared its 'unabated confidence' in him; that it shared his contention that the reduction and limitation of armaments was essential for peace; and that this, in turn, could only be achieved by extending the principle of arbitration and by states 'pooling' their security in the League of Nations.[49] This was endorsed by an extraordinary meeting of the

---

[45] Cecil to Lady Gwendolyn Cecil, 24 Feb. 1928, ibid. (emphasis added).
[46] Editorial, *Manchester Guardian*, 10 Sept. 1927; Scott papers cited in Birn, *League of Nations Union*, 70. Cf. Cecil to House of Lords, 15 Feb. 1928, House of Lords *debs.*, 106–7.
[47] 'This would, at a stroke, reduce the rise in prices, increase productivity and reduce unemployment': Extract from a Conservative Central Office press release and attributed by *The Times* to Edward Heath during the 1970 election campaign which brought Heath the premiership. Quoted in D. Butler and A. Sloman, *British political facts 1900–1979*, 5th edn, London 1980, 254.
[48] Cecil to Lord Balfour of Burleigh, 2 Jan. 1928, BM, Cecil papers, Add. MS 51166.
[49] Excom minute 95, 8 Sept. 1927, BLPES, LNU II.8.

LNU general council on 21 October when it launched the LNU's disarmament and arbitration campaign. Despite its nomenclature the campaign was very much concerned with the Optional Clause. General disarmament and general arbitration of disputes (in the widest sense of the term) represented the ultimate desired goal but the Optional Clause was the immediate goal.

The LNU campaign got swiftly off the ground. This was because the preparatory work for a large-scale campaign had been undertaken the preceding winter, before the Union had accepted the idea of campaigning in such a way. In November 1926 a reduction of armaments committee had been set up at a meeting between two members of the executive (Major Hills – the then chairman – and Philip Noel-Baker) and two members of the secretariat (Garnett and Epstein). Since disarmament was so high on the LNU agenda, it was a reasonable step to take and in line with the Union's creation of committees to cover every aspect of League activity. However, under the exuberant leadership of Philip Noel-Baker, the nine-member committee prepared for a large-scale disarmament campaign at an estimated cost of £1,000 for the winter, rising to £2,000 if it were to continue its activities into the summer of 1928. The LNU was to produce specially-written pamphlets and provide speakers for special study circles which were to be set up all over the country to arrange public demonstrations. An LNU office would be devoted to writing articles for provincial newspapers and making contact with leading journalists. Leading members of the LNU would write letters to the quality press. Mrs Oliver Strachey (a member of the executive and a writer and campaigner for women's rights) would devote herself to liaising with members of both houses of parliament, arranging deputations to MPs and organising the despatch of 'spontaneous' letters to MPs and leading politicians. She was to be given a room in LNU headquarters and would have a secretary. There she would compile an index recording the attitudes of MPs towards disarmament and this would enable the establishment of a parliamentary committee. There would be a pamphlet for businessmen and liaison with houses of commerce. Finally, the LNU would itself produce and distribute a fully thought-out and practical proposal for disarmament.

Cecil's resignation and his decision to use the Union to demonstrate to the government that the British public was behind the policies he had unsuccessfully advocated as a Cabinet minister provided the vital fillip which threw the energies of the Union behind the ambitious plans. The reduction of armaments committee became the nerve centre of the campaign under a new name – the disarmament campaign committee (DCC). The campaign itself was frequently referred to as the disarmament campaign although it is important to re-emphasise that, while disarmament had not been downgraded in importance, the immediate focus of the campaign was the Optional Clause.

The newly-named disarmament campaign committee was given a status reflecting the LNU council's endorsement of the proposal to throw the weight of the LNU behind the campaign. It was chaired by Gilbert Murray (as chairman of the executive); its size was increased to thirteen; it had its own secretariat (which rose to ten full-time officials); and it had its own rented offices in Grosvenor Crescent. In practice the conduct of the campaign fell into the hands of Cecil, Murray, Noel-Baker, Mrs Strachey and Will Arnold-Forster (who had been contracted from the NCPW to act as the campaign's organising secretary). It had its own distinctive blue notepaper and its financial appeals were made on its own behalf and not the LNU's.

Throw-away leaflets, pamphlets and posters were an important part of the campaign. By the end of 1927 there were eight 'throw-away' leaflets and four more had been approved by the middle of January. Twelve different posters on the theme of disarmament in general were printed and, in addition to the Union's important pamphlet on the Optional Clause which will be discussed below, there were further pamphlets on such issues as 'the freedom of the seas' and 'unemployment and disarmament'. There was a special pamphlet for the Co-operative Union (which lent its full support to the campaign) and another one elaborating on the Caxton Hall resolutions of October 1927. Another method was door-to-door petitioning. Pamphlets (with LNU membership appeals enclosed) were delivered to homes and a week later an LNU member went round knocking on doors for subscriptions. This could produce dramatic results: in one area a simple door-to-door canvass of 1,200 houses doubled the membership of the local LNU branch from 400 to 800. Many proposals for the campaign were forthcoming, perhaps the most delightful being the suggestion that song-sheets be printed for Sunday evening meetings in public cinemas. After one or two brief speeches by, say, undergraduates, the audience would enliven the occasion by communal singing. This was, however, rejected as was the idea of petitioning on a national scale (petitioning being regarded as outdated and less effective than letters to MPs).

The main thrust of the campaign consisted of public meetings. Cecil was most in demand as a speaker but, as he obviously could not accept every invitation, a list of 'first-rank' speakers was compiled and the DCC carefully co-ordinated their travels. Cecil, who devoted himself tirelessly to the campaign from an office in DCC headquarters, held himself available to talk to DCC speakers. There was a national 'speakers conference' in London in January 1928 as well as regional 'speakers conferences' and 'speakers classes' in university LNU branches.

The first week for which a tally was kept of the number of 'disarmament campaign' meetings was armistice week, when there were 226 'large meetings' and, in the early months of 1928, the campaign seemed a spectacular success. At the beginning of February Cecil addressed an overflow meeting in Glasgow which brought in 600 new members and at which a large number of people signed pledges to work for disarmament.[50] Headquarters were subsequently informed that it was hoped to obtain a million such promises in the west of Scotland. Large numbers of signatures were also obtained in Colchester and Oxford, and additional forms had to be printed to meet the demand from university branches. By mid-March over 100,000 of these had been sent out.

In February 1928 Cecil testified to the House of Lords that he had

> never addressed meetings at all comparable with the meetings I have addressed during the last three or four months. That has nothing to do with what I have said to them

---

[50] As a means of winning 'new and active supporters of the [c]ampaign' the DCC had adopted Cecil's suggestion that anyone who was unwilling to join the LNU should be invited to sign a promise to 'undertake to do my utmost by all constitutional means to forward the policy of international Arbitration and Disarmament'.

. . ... the temper, the size and the enthusiasm of the meetings are quite different from what they were on this same kind of topic a few years ago.[51]

One peer after another rose to agree. The Liberal former Lord Chancellor, Buckmaster, said there was no doubting 'the enthusiasm or unanimity' of the last LNU meeting he had addressed;[52] Viscount Astor, the former Conservative MP and chairman of the directors of the *Observer*, said that his experience of 'a considerable number of audiences in different parts of the country' showed that 'public opinion is becoming increasingly ready and anxious to take any and every step to substitute alternative means of settling disputes in place of war'.[53] And Phillimore, the British member of the 1920 committee of jurists, had

> no hesitation in saying that all those with whom I have to deal are in favour of the Optional Clause, and it is not I who push it on my people, it is my people who push it on me, and who will not endure its not being brought forward and pressed upon every occasion.[54]

The LNU's case

The case which the LNU presented in favour of signing the Optional Clause is best exemplified by a formidable forty-three-page pamphlet which appeared early in 1928.[55] Carefully and intelligently written, the pamphlet avoided the simplicity which bedevilled the pages of the LNU's monthly journal, *Headway*. It had no inaccuracies (although the truth was sometimes a little stretched)[56] and all references were carefully footnoted. Its emphasis on the League's and states' willingness to uphold legal obligations was characteristic of the era and of the nation.

The pamphlet began by explaining what the Optional Clause was; said it was necessary because the word 'generally' in Article 13 of the Covenant limited states' obligations to arbitrate disputes (its omission would have implied an obligation to accept compulsory arbitration); and explained that with regard to legal disputes it closed the 'gap in the Covenant' that allowed war under certain circumstances. It also explained that the clause had resulted from the refusal of Britain and France to accept compulsory adjudication in 1920. A list was given of the 27 states which had signed the Clause and the signatures which had not been ratified were asterisked. The pamphlet then identified and examined nine

[51] House of Lords *debs.*, 15 Feb. 1928, 116-17.
[52] Ibid. 139.
[53] Ibid. 142-3.
[54] Ibid. 143.
[55] LNU pamphlet, *The Optional Clause*, 1928. Unless otherwise stated all quotations in this section are taken from this pamphlet.
[56] The number of states which had accepted the Optional Clause was overstated by counting the number of signatures rather than the number of declarations in force. The assertion that the intention of the Optional Clause was to close the 'gap in the Covenant' in Article 15.7 (whereby when the members of the Council who were not parties to a dispute were unable to agree on a unanimous report, the members of the League were entitled to go to war after the 'cooling off' period provided for in Article 12.1) was going a bit far. The gap had hardly been mentioned before the fifth (1924) Assembly: F. P. Walters, *A history of the League of Nations*, London 1969 (first publ. in 2 vols 1952), 271.

arguments which had been put forward by the government against the Optional Clause.[57]

The first argument was 'MIGHT versus RIGHT': that on major issues it was better to fight than submit to the judgement of a third party. This was 'utterly false [and] wholly contrary to those principles upon which civilised international relations must be based'. Britain had pioneered arbitration, had been its supporter and, because of its far-flung empire, was 'in some respects the most vulnerable of all nations'.

The second argument was entitled 'THE IRRESPONSIBLE PUBLIC': that the public could not be counted on to support the submission of important legal decisions to adjudication 'even within the admitted sphere of law'. The counter-argument was divided into two parts: general considerations and matters of vital interest. The LNU held that if this second proposition were true there was 'all the more reason for giving a clear lead to public opinion' and if the government did not do so the LNU would. But the LNU doubted the validity of the proposition and believed that the law-abiding British had a better respect for, and understanding of, the law than had other nations. Many of them had declared their support for the Optional Clause and, although they might not understand the technicalities, they understood the principle so that the government could carry with it the country and parliament.

With regard to matters such as the Suez Canal, which were of vital interest, an unscrupulous press might kindle public passions as things stood. But it was 'almost inconceivable' that this would succeed if the disputants had agreed 'in advance, in cold blood' to submit such a matter to court. If there were a danger of becoming blinded by passion there was 'all the more reason for putting up a handrail for our guidance now, whilst we can still see to do so'. The important point was to make it clear in advance where Britain stood rather than simply telling other states to 'trust us always to do the right thing'.

The third argument was that of 'THE IRRESPONSIBLE PARLIAMENT': parliament might refuse to accept an adverse judicial award. But, if this argument were valid, it would cut at the root of every important treaty obligation such as the Covenant and it was 'high time that we recognised how extremely precarious must be the obligations incurred at Locarno'. However, the LNU held that no arbitration had yet led to war, that Britain was not 'in the habit of dishonouring its bond', and the loyal acceptance of an adverse award was infinitely preferable to war. Two analogies were drawn: of the individual in domestic society who refused to accept the jurisdiction of a court, and of football: 'Even a football crowd accepts the decision of the referee.'

---

[57] The sources used in the pamphlet were: (1) 'a speech delivered by . . . Hurst in the third commission of the sixth [1925] Assembly' (i.e. Hurst's statement to the first committee: see below, 94). (2) A 'letter from the Foreign Office to Colonel Spender Clay, M.P., published in *The Times*, September 26, 1925' (the LNU is here confusing Chamberlain's letter to Hudson with an earlier letter sent to Spender Clay in the spring of 1925: see PRO, W 3849/27/98 FO 371/11069). (3) The speech by Locker-Lampson (under secretary of state at the Foreign Office) to the House of Commons on 11 July 1927. (4) The speech by Chamberlain to the House of Commons on 24 Nov. 1927 (in which Chamberlain had referred to Haldane's memorandum for MacDonald; see below, 77). (5) Cushenden's speech to the House of Lords on 16 Nov. 1927 (see below 79, n. 89). (6) Britain's Jan. 1928 reply to the League Committee on Arbitration and Security (see below, 111–3). (7) The views the dominions expressed at Geneva.

The fourth argument was that of 'THE IRRESPONSIBLE FOREIGNER': acceptance of the Optional Clause did not allow Britain to distinguish between states with which it was willing and not willing to arbitrate. The first criticism of this was made by another domestic analogy. 'This seems a curious and unfortunate attitude', it was argued. 'In civil life we do not refuse to accept the rule of law simply because we regard some of our fellow-citizens as lawless.' The second criticism was of the government's avowed preference for bilateral treaties. This was inconsistent with the League principle that peace was the concern of all, and the Optional Clause was simpler and speedier than the 1,540 such treaties which would be required to bind all League members.

The fifth argument was that of 'THE INDEPENDENT DOMINIONS': the problem of obtaining their assent and the importance of the doctrine of *inter-se*. Attention was also drawn to the 1926 imperial conference agreement that no Commonwealth country would sign without further consultation. There were four aspects of this argument. Firstly, if Britain led the way the dominions and India would follow. Canada and the Irish Free State were willing to sign, there were indications that South Africa might be willing, and Australia and New Zealand had always been the dominions most willing to leave 'the broad issues of imperial foreign policy' to Britain. Secondly, there was the possibility that it might create difficulties between the dominions. This might happen if there were an attempt to take an intra-Commonwealth dispute to the Court, but it could be circumvented by including a reservation similar to that whereby Belgium reserved disputes for which the parties had agreed to another method of settlement. Chamberlain had also suggested that there might be the danger of one dominion being willing to arbitrate and another unwilling. For what it was worth, this was seen as an argument in favour of signing. Thirdly, the LNU denied the possibility of maintaining the complete diplomatic unity of the empire. This had already been demonstrated by the Locarno treaties. If Britain could accept a commitment to go to war without assured dominion support, 'it can hardly be wrong to undertake the immeasurably lesser risk of accepting legal judgement in legal disputes without assurance of the Dominion's [sic] concurrence'. Finally, reference was made to the analogy between the constitution of the empire and that of the USA, an analogy which Haldane had drawn in 1924 and which Chamberlain made public. This was that just as the President had to win Congressional approval for all foreign policy commitments and every single arbitration, so too did Britain need the agreement of the dominions. The LNU held that 'this curious constitutional difficulty' had 'no analogy in the constitution of the British Empire'.[58]

The sixth argument against the Optional Clause was that it was unnecessary with regard to 'DISPUTES "LIKELY TO LEAD TO RUPTURE" ' since Britain had already committed itself to the pacific settlement of disputes through the League Covenant. The LNU insinuated that because Britain had not mentioned it in the 1928 memorandum for the League Committee on Arbitration and Security, it had '[p]erhaps . . . been abandoned as fallacious'. Whether or not this was so:

> The Covenant does not ensure that all disputes 'likely to lead to a rupture' shall be 'the subject of pacific *settlement*'. It only ensures that they shall be the subject of

[58] *Inter-se*, the 1926 imperial conference and the views of the dominions are fully discussed in chapter 7.

pacific *procedure*. That famous 'gap in the Covenant' cannot be ignored . . .. instead of its making 'no difference' whether we sign the Clause or not, it makes just all the difference between retaining and renouncing the right in certain circumstances to resort to war for the decision of a legal dispute . . .. If the gap were not real the Optional Clause would not have been made, and the fifth Assembly would not have passed a unanimous resolution recommending signature.

The seventh argument was with regard to 'DISPUTES NOT LIKELY TO LEAD TO RUPTURE'. Following on from the last argument, it was held that if the government had renounced the right of private war (i.e. war which was not conducted on behalf of the League), it would not be difficult to make the same renunciation with regard to less serious disputes:

If rupture is unlikely that must surely be either because the parties are *too rational* to fight – in which case there can be no objection to accepting the judgement of reason; or else that one of the parties is *too weak* to fight – in which case the need for the law's protection of the weak is manifest.

The eighth argument led on from the sixth and seventh: it was about the 'HONOUR OR VITAL INTERESTS' reservation which was found in every pre-war arbitral agreement but not in Britain's 1919 treaty with Uruguay or the League Covenant. This formula drove a 'wide breach . . . right through the principle of arbitration' because, by including this reservation, 'a State destroys any assurance that it can be relied upon to accept the rule of law in legal issues'. The LNU held that there were strong objections to the reservation. Before the war the Kaiser had approved von Bülow's endorsement of this reservation as enabling Germany to resist all calls for arbitration, and if Britain insisted on it, it would 'keep open a gap of undefined extent' and would be 'incompatible with the principle for which the Optional Clause stands'.

It was 'an irony of history that Great Britain, of all countries, should now be keeping alive that old formula. No country has in the past done so much to discredit it'. The *Alabama* arbitration, the *Dogger Bank* case, the delimitation of the Canadian–American border were all evidence that an arbitral award or an agreement was preferable to fighting. The risks involved in accepting the Optional Clause

are in fact incomparably less than the risks of modern war or the risks of maintaining a deadlock. We believe that the reservation concerning honour and vital interests makes a fatal breach in the principle of arbitration, creating that kind of uncertainty which is one of the most fruitful sources of international distrust, and that it should be wholly renounced.

The ninth argument against the Optional Clause was the 'VAGUENESS OF THE CLAUSE' itself. But any significant ambiguities could be clarified by making a declaration or reservation when the Optional Clause was accepted. In any case it was held that not only was there a greater body of international law than was commonly supposed, but also that there was an advantage in its not being rigidly codified. To illustrate this, an analogy was drawn with English law in the reign of Edward II and from which 'the great structure of the English Common Law has been raised by judicial decisions'.

The pamphlet finally considered the question of reservations. Many people thought it best that there should be no reservations save that of reciprocity, but there were two reservations which Britain could make 'without injury to the principle of the Clause'. The first was that which had been suggested in the argument concerning the dominions: a reservation similar to that whereby Germany and Belgium excluded disputes for which the parties had agreed on another method of pacific settlement. (This would enable the Commonwealth to maintain the Judicial Committee of the Privy Council as the body dealing with inter-imperial disputes.) The second reservation was of 'disputes concerning the rules of naval war'.[59] In conclusion, the pamphlet held that: 'Our country, which was a pioneer of the principle of Arbitration, cannot now be among the first to accept the rule of law within the admitted sphere of law. Let us ensure that it shall not be among the very last.'

In preparing this pamphlet, as in most aspects of the campaign, the LNU did what it could to avoid being unnecessarily provocative to the government although exaggeration and simplification occasionally crept in. At the same time, however, it was careful to give no ground because an important issue was at stake and the Union wanted its pamphlet to provide the basis for a full debate on the merits of the Optional Clause. And, although the leadership was aware that there might be difficulties with the government – on 31 October Cecil had confided to Murray his fear that 'we may easily be driven' into taking 'a more or less hostile attitude to the Government'[60] – it did what it could to prevent conflict. The 'Notes for Speakers' which had initially been drafted by Norman Angell, were subjected to 'considerable discussion' before the job of producing another draft was given to Cecil and leading representatives of the main political parties – Murray, Hills and George Barnes. And even then the rewritten draft was only adopted after further 'considerable discussion'.[61] Similarly, the resolution to be passed by campaign meetings was the product of lengthy talks and a working group. Speakers were instructed to minimise differences with the government and branches were urged 'to ensure the non-Party character of the LNU' when establishing their local campaign committees.[62]

The government's response

Likewise, the government did not relish a quarrel with the Union. Cecil's resignation was an embarrassment not only within Britain and at Geneva. It had occurred at a low point in Anglo-American relations and could contribute to the further deterioration of that relationship by adding fuel to American criticisms of British policy.[63] It was also half-way through the government's term of office. If the campaign lasted long it would form part of the background to the next general election and, although the evidence is patchy, it seems clear that the Foreign Office ministers, at least, were alive to this consideration.

[59] Alternatively, Britain could reserve 'disputes concerning the rules of naval war *when we were acting on the League's behalf*' on the grounds that 'This would be a logical corollary of applying the Union's policy of all inclusive pacific settlement and renunciation of war.'
[60] Cecil to Murray, 31 Oct. 1927, Bodl. Lib., Murray papers.
[61] Excom minutes 225, 20 Oct. 1927; 239, 3 Nov. 1927; 252(b), 17 Nov. 1927, BLPES, LNU II.8.
[62] LNU document S.G. 1818, 8 Sept. 1927, Bodl. Lib., Murray papers; *The Times*, 8 Nov. 1927; LNU, DCC, minute 53, 8 Nov. and minute 60, 15 Nov. 1927, BLPES, LNU IV.52.
[63] See below, 133.

There is very little material on the LNU campaign in either the Foreign Office records or Chamberlain's private papers so that it is impossible to know exactly how the government responded in private to the LNU campaign. But such material as survives suggests that at first barely any attention was paid to it.

At the beginning of October 1927 British policy on the Optional Clause was, in fact, reviewed because of the establishment of the League Committee on Arbitration and Security and the adverse criticism Britain had encountered at the League Assembly.[64] Throughout September the *Manchester Guardian* had carried a lively discussion of the small states' attempts to resurrect the Geneva Protocol.[65] Ramsay MacDonald and Gilbert Murray had joined in the debate with letters in support of the Protocol but the Foreign Office officials who examined their arguments dismissed them as unfounded.[66] There is no indication that the government was bothered by the *Manchester Guardian's* evident sympathy for Robert Cecil's viewpoint: it was in response to criticisms made at Geneva, not at home, that British policy, including the Optional Clause, was examined by Ronald Campbell, a senior member of the western department. However, in respect of the Optional Clause, all Campbell did was to dig out the various memoranda which had been given to MacDonald in 1924, saying that it was 'impossible[ ] to add to the arguments contained in those documents'.[67] He had then summarised what had happened in 1926 when the Optional Clause was reconsidered by the government and discussed at the imperial conference which had agreed that no member of the Commonwealth would take action on the Clause without first bringing it up for further discussion. There was no reason, he continued, to believe that any of the dominions had changed their views, nothing had happened in the last year to cause Britain to modify its policy, and he drew the comforting conclusion that '[t]here seems in short every reason to maintain our attitude'.[68] This was the general line which Chamberlain and Cushendun, Cecil's successor, adopted in public although subsequent chapters will show that both men were changing their minds about the Clause for reasons other than the LNU campaign.

During November the government appears to have remained unconcerned about the LNU campaign, perhaps sharing the view of the editor of *The Times* that the campaign had been taken up by an opposition which was 'depressed by the general dullness of the season'.[69] There is no record in the Foreign Office files of the major debate which took place in the House of Lords in November 1927 and there are no briefing papers for Foreign Office ministers. However, there does remain one briefing paper prepared for Samuel Hoare, the secretary of state for Air, to use in a debate with MacDonald at the Cambridge Union. It was said that the criticisms which had been levelled against the government

[64] See below, 99, 108–111.

[65] See below, 98–9, 102–5.

[66] See *Manchester Guardian*, 14 Sept. 1927 and undated notes by Ivone Kirkpatrick and Ronald Campbell attached to 'Arbitration, security and disarmament', memorandum by Campbell, 8 Oct. 1927, PRO, W 11899/61/98, in *DBFP* iv, 211.

[67] 'General survey' (n.d.), annex 3 to Campbell memorandum, 8 Oct. 1927. For the memoranda submitted to MacDonald see above, 24–9. Crowe's Nov. 1924 minute (see above, 47–9) was attached to the annex dealing with Murray's letter which appeared in the *Manchester Guardian* on 14 Sept. 1927.

[68] 'General survey', annex 3 to Campbell memorandum, 8 Oct. 1927.

[69] Editorial, 'Peace and propaganda', 14 Nov. 1927.

were based on misrepresentations but there was no comment on the LNU campaign. It simply explained why the government could not comply with the Union's request on the Optional Clause and said that it was 'gratifying' that, on the whole, the Union approved of the government's policy.[70]

Another indication of the government's seeming complacency was its response to a request made by the chairman of an LNU district council. The correspondent said he had 'considerable misgivings' that, with many 'geese' in the Union, the campaign might degenerate into an attempt to discredit the government and direct public attention 'towards an impossible policy'. But his request for 'ammunition' with which to defend the government's policy was met by simply sending him a copy of the 'standard' 1925 letter to Hudson.[71]

There were, however, indications that a conflict was brewing. At the beginning of November the compiler of *The Times* 'Political Notes' warned that there was a 'real danger' that the LNU campaign 'may quickly degenerate into an anti-Government demonstration'.[72] Cecil tried to scotch the suggestion by privately approaching *The Times* writer who consequently reported a few days later that the LNU was going to invite more Conservatives to rally round.[73] But then Cecil acted as if he were intent on a confrontation. On 16 November there was a debate in the House of Lords on a motion which Parmoor introduced in favour of the Geneva Protocol. After Parmoor had spoken, Cushendun – Cecil's successor – rose to give his maiden speech to the House of Lords, a speech in which he devoted a considerable amount of time to explaining why the government could not accept the Optional Clause.[74] Cecil was the next to speak. After giving Cushendun the customary welcome to the upper chamber, Cecil at once launched into a detailed explanation of his reasons for resigning from the government. In so doing, he wiped out the moderation of his much toned-down resignation letter which, even as it stood, constituted a slap in the face for the government and a condemnation of its policy on disarmament and the League.[75] Balfour, who followed Cecil, rose, he said, with 'very great reluctance' at apparently being 'brought into some kind of collision' with his kinsman and long-standing political colleague. But he was 'wholly unable to understand' how Cecil had come to adopt his 'extreme course'. The only explanation that Balfour could surmise was that 'the inevitable differences of opinion' between colleagues, 'differences in themselves small' had accumulated

---

[70] The briefing paper, which was prepared by Cadogan, was not read by Chamberlain: Hoare to Chamberlain, 17 Nov. 1927; notes by Cadogan, 10 Nov. 1927; minute by Cadogan, 22 Nov. 1927; undated minute by Chamberlain, PRO, W 11024/61/98 FO 371/12676.

[71] See Sir Theodore Morison (chairman of Tyne District LNU Council and principal of Armstrong College, Newcastle-upon-Tyne) to Chamberlain, 2 Nov. 1927; undated minute by Cadogan; Chamberlain to Morison 4 Nov. 1927; minute by Kirkpatrick, 8 Nov. 1927, PRO, W 10373/56/98 FO 371/12660.

[72] 'Political notes', 2 Nov. 1927. This was because it was held that the leading LNU speakers were either prominent Liberals or Labour people. The only Conservatives were 'apparently' the Lords Lytton and Cecil. The methods of the campaign were also conducive to an anti-government tendency.

[73] However, the writer held that the Conservatives would still be disadvantaged because opposition spokesmen had more spare time: 'Political notes', *The Times*, 4 Nov. 1927.

[74] See House of Lords *debs.*, 16 Nov. 1927, 77–83.

[75] See ibid. 85–94.

to a point at which, were it not disrespectful, Balfour would say that 'his temper gave way'.[76]

This was welcome grist to the mill of the Opposition which capitalised on it a few days later in a House of Commons debate, while the government played it down. However, Chamberlain then scored a valuable point against the Opposition by quoting at length from Haldane's 1924 memorandum – on the grounds that Haldane had stated the problem facing the empire 'so lucidly, so clearly, and so temperately' and that it represented the same view as was held by his advisers.[77] MacDonald was furious, complaining that Chamberlain had committed a 'gross violation of our unwritten constitution' by making public the contents of a confidential paper. But Chamberlain had obtained Haldane's permission and there was nothing MacDonald could do about it.[78]

Both parliamentary debates illustrated an important point which was not fully appreciated by the LNU and which explains the development of the quarrel between the government and the Union. In November 1927 the question of Britain signing the Optional Clause was a matter which clearly fell into the realm of party politics. It was the Labour Party which championed the immediate acceptance of the Optional Clause and the most that Duff Cooper (a member of both the government and the LNU executive, who was actively involved in the LNU campaign) could say was that he favoured arbitration but that it was necessary to make sure the empire marched in step. Given that the arguments used by the Labour Party in its advocacy of the Optional Clause were similar to those used by the LNU, and given that the government had been conditioned to seeing public debate on the subject in a party political context, the government was predisposed to look for signs of partisanship in the LNU campaign. It is difficult, if not impossible, to see how the LNU could have avoided the pitfall of party politics. It was, in short, riding for a fall.

Before the year was out the Conservative Party had supplied its speakers with a warning against 'A Campaign of Mis-representation' by a partisan LNU.[79] It availed little for Cecil to point out that the LNU executive contained fourteen Conservatives, nine Labour supporters, twenty Liberals and four or five whose politics were unknown to him; that there was nothing in the LNU's official policy to which the Conservatives need take exception; that there was no party prejudice in the speeches of 'those who are really entitled to speak for the Union'; and that it was entirely the fault of the Conservatives if certain branches had fallen into non-Conservative hands.[80] It was widely accepted in

---

76 Ibid. 94–5.
77 House of Commons *debs.*, 24 Nov. 1927, 2107–8. See also Locker-Lampson to House of Commons, 11 July 1927, House of Commons *debs.*, 1886–7. On Haldane's memorandum see above, 29.
78 See MacDonald to Chamberlain, 29 Nov., 2 Dec. 1927; Chamberlain to MacDonald, 1 Dec. 1927; Selby to Haldane and Haldane to Selby, 24 Nov. 1927; Chamberlain to Haldane and Haldane to Chamberlain, 2 Dec. 1927, PRO, Chamberlain papers, FO 800/261. See also Dudley Sommer, *Haldane of Cloan: his life and times*, London 1960, 419–23.
79 This was the heading of a section in the party's *Hints to speakers*. It was illustrated with quotations from *Headway* and the LNU's *Notes for speakers*.
80 Cecil to J. C. C. Davidson (chairman of the Conservative Party, a close friend of Baldwin and Baldwin's private secretary), 30 Dec. 1927, UBL, Chamberlain papers, AC 55/57. However, the executive committee recognised that there were some breaches of the non-partisan line.

Tory circles that Cecil was 'quite unable to appreciate the anti-government bias which permeates the activities of the League of Nations Union'.[81]

However, Chamberlain's initial reaction was not to lash out angrily as might have been expected from his behaviour in 1925. As a colleague of Cecil he had managed to prevail on him to resign more moderately than might have been the case. And, being advised by Conservative Central Office that the LNU executive was 'very sensitive to criticism',[82] he first tried privately to persuade the Union to stop the campaign. It was inappropriate, he told Murray, to try to force the government's hand. It was not the LNU's job to advocate policies which the government had already considered and rejected and it would be a disservice to both the LNU and the League to persist in such an attempt.[83] But Cecil had gone too far down the road to turn back, and as Murray told Chamberlain, the LNU believed that an important principle was at stake:

> The difference between us is really based on a difference as to the help or harm done to the League by the support of an interested and informed public opinion. Without such public opinion, I hardly see how the League can possibly succeed in its tasks, and it was in this belief that the Union was formed.[84]

And they were poles apart on the Optional Clause as can be seen from a private exchange between Cecil and J. W. Headlam-Morley, the Foreign Office historical adviser.

Following remarks which Cecil had made about the *Alabama* arbitration, Headlam-Morley obtained Chamberlain's permission to send Cecil a lengthy memorandum on Britain's historical experience of arbitration. Cecil's copy of the memorandum is littered with such comments as: 'This is quite inaccurate', 'Pooh!', '!!', 'This is not so. It was the reference to arbitration that mattered – not the terms of the submission', 'The writer here assumes the function of a prophet', 'This only shows that as we all know the civilisation of the U.S.A. is in some respects elementary!!' and, finally, on the second to last paragraph, 'A glimpse of truth'.[85] His reply to Headlam-Morley was more moderate. He was, he said, unconvinced. Headlam-Morley assumed 'that the only question is whether in any particular case it would or would not be justifiable for us to go to arbitration'. However, Cecil thought: 'The real proposition is that the general acceptance of Arbitration would be so large a step towards establishing peace that the possibility of our suffering in this or that particular case is not really a comparable consideration.'[86] Thus the stage was set for an open conflict between the government and the LNU.

---

[81] Pemberton Wicks (political secretary, Conservative Central Office) to Chamberlain, 4 Jan. 1928, UBL, Chamberlain papers, AC 55/57. See also AC 55/509.

[82] Ibid.

[83] Chamberlain to Murray, 11 Jan. 1928, UBL, Chamberlain papers, AC 55/385. See also Chamberlain to Murray, 28 Jan. 1928, AC 55/387.

[84] Murray to Chamberlain, 13 Jan. 1928 UBL, Chamberlain papers, AC 55/386. See also Murray to Chamberlain, 6 Jan. 1928, AC 55/384.

[85] See BM, Cecil papers, Add. MS 51127.

[86] Cecil to Headlam-Morley, 9 Mar. 1928, BM, Cecil papers, MS 51099. See also Headlam-Morley to Cecil, 7 June 1928, L 3136/2688/402, ibid. Headlam-Morley's 'Memorandum respecting the British government and arbitration: an historical review' (27 Jan. 1928) is printed in his *Studies in diplomatic history*.

The battle joined and the retreat of the LNU

In February 1928 the government launched its attack on the LNU. The occasion was a speech by Cushendun to the Lords during the debate on Cecil's motion that 'this House hopes that His Majesty's Government will press forward a policy of international disarmament and will, after consulting the Dominions, accept . . .. the Optional Clause.'[87] After Cecil's opening speech, Cushendun rose. This was, he said, the fourth time (in a little over four months) that he had had to rehearse the government's case. This he did. He then vehemently attacked the LNU for 'acting with impropriety when it presses its adherents to support this particular policy of my noble friend [Cecil]. I do not think my noble friend is entitled to use the League of Nations Union as a means of putting forward his own particular policy.' Cecil was not, Cushendun thought, a better 'League-ite' than he, who reckoned he had belonged to the Union from the beginning. Cushendun had always understood that the LNU's object was 'to inform public opinion with regard to the League of Nations, to popularise it, and to convince people of its necessity and of the good it can do in the world'. Under 'the compelling and persuasive influence' of Cecil and a few others, the public

> may be prepared at public meetings at present to throw up their hats for the Optional Clause, but I feel certain that on very slight reflection and a little more mature consideration of all the pros and cons of the case public opinion, which is very fickle, may turn round and rend those who first of all misled it . . .. we are entirely in accord . . . in pressing on . . . the policy of international disarmament, [but] I cannot hold out any hopes that, at any rate in the immediate future, we shall change the policy of the Government, which has been consistent, not merely during the tenure of the present Government, but from 1920 up to the present time. It would be a very unwise step to go beyond the system of arbitration to which experience has made us accustomed and take what is something in the nature of a leap in the dark by signing the Optional Clause.[88]

Unfortunately for the government, Cushendun's mastery of the subject of the Optional Clause had not greatly improved since he had first had to justify government policy the previous November.[89] He revealed an ignorance of facts which, while understandable, cast doubts on the merits of his whole argument, especially given that it was delivered to a chamber which included men with great expertise on the subject. Having said that the Court's original draft Statute had provided for compulsory adjudication, he continued:

---

[87] House of Lords *debs.*, 15 Feb. 1928, 104–5.
[88] Ibid. 133–4.
[89] During the debate in the Lords on 16 Nov. he had made the curious remark that signing the Optional Clause would mean signing away the necessary safeguard that was included in 'almost all our Arbitration Treaties': 'the hitherto accepted saving clause as to vital interests, honour and independence'. This was made use of in the LNU pamphlet on the Optional Clause where it was pointed out that the sole arbitration treaty concluded by Britain since the First World War – with Uruguay – had not contained this reservation. Cushendun's remark may be explained in part by his having been thrown in at the deep end by having to make a major speech on the Optional Clause in his first address to the Lords. It may also have been due to his having misunderstood a badly-worded section in a memorandum by Ronald Campbell: see Campbell memorandum, 8 Oct. 1927, annex 3. Unfamiliarity with the subject probably also explains his somewhat confused remarks about Article 13 of the Covenant: See House of Lords *debs.*, 16 Nov. 1927, 80–1.

Cushenden: 'Why was it not left in a compulsory form? It was amended by the Assembly of the League itself. The Assembly after, no doubt, very full consideration and discussion, came to the conclusion that a compulsory clause might prevent people joining the League.'

Cecil: 'No.'

Cushendun: 'I do not know what the reason was, and I do not much care, but the fact remains that the compulsory nature of the Clause was removed and the Optional Clause as we now know put in its place. Therefore, that is the policy of the League.'[90]

Cecil had been ready for Cushendun's attack and had mustered his forces. One after another of the noble Lords supported Cecil. Buckmaster complained that Cushendun's speech had been largely devoted to universal arbitration, which was not the question at hand, just as the government had not been requested to submit all the country's vital interests to arbitration (as Cushendun had suggested). Phillimore complained that the first half of the speech had been devoted to explaining why the Optional Clause was unnecessary, the second half to explaining that Britain was fearful of submitting disputes to the PCIJ unless it were certain of having its own way. And, as has already been seen, Phillimore, Astor and Buckmaster testified with Cecil that the general public was keen to sign the Clause.[91]

Only Salisbury, who was left to wind up the debate on behalf of the government, supported Cushendun. In doing so he emphasised that most speakers, belonging as they did to the legal profession, had taken 'too professional a view of this question'. Their speeches might mislead the hearer into thinking that the PCIJ was comparable to a British court, but the judges of the PCIJ had to cope with a law which was 'almost chaotic' in many parts. In time of crisis the public might not be willing to fulfil Britain's obligations and the government could not risk great national disasters which might arise from acting as it was being asked to act.[92] No vote was taken and the motion was withdrawn at the end of the debate but the government had been bettered in argument by the supporters of the Optional Clause. However, in the now-open conflict between the government and the Union, it was not – as the Union had intended – the merits of the Optional Clause which became the central issue, but the role of the Union.

Three days after the debate in the Lords, *The Times* joined battle on behalf of the government. A letter from Vice-Admiral Aubrey Smith, who had spent four years as the British naval expert on the League's Permanent Advisory Commission, was prominently featured on the centre page and made the subject of an editorial. Aubrey Smith had written to complain about an address which Philip Noel-Baker had given in the church of St Mary-le-Bow. Noel-Baker had, he said, grossly simplified the question of disarmament by brushing aside the technical difficulties. He had made dubious statements about 'war-mongers . . . shrieking . . . across the Atlantic' and about Anglo-American relations being at their lowest point for fifty years. Such statements served no useful purpose; a pulpit was 'strangely inappropriate' for them; and he wondered if subscribers to

---

[90] Ibid. 15 Feb. 1928, 132.
[91] See ibid. 137–8, 146, and see above, 70.
[92] Ibid. 150–3.

LNU funds realised 'the partisan nature of the propaganda which is being employed in their name'?[93] The editorial stated that Smith had 'expresse[d] in vigorous language the misgivings . . . felt by many friends of the League at the recent activities of the so-called League of Nations Union'. It endorsed Smith's criticism of Noel-Baker for 'making partisan statements against the Government from the pulpits of the Established Church'; it endorsed the criticism of Noel-Baker's comments on the state of Anglo-American relations; and it endorsed Chamberlain's and Cushendun's complaints about the LNU's attempts to force upon the government a policy which it knew was unacceptable to it:

> If such utterances were isolated they would not be worth mentioning. But unfortunately this kind of thing is being dinned into the ears of uninformed audiences all over the country; and the propaganda often assumes a thoroughly mischievous character . . .. many of the trained speakers of the Union make a point of extolling every country but their own, and imply that in Great Britain alone is good will lacking – a grotesque travesty of the truth.[94]

The battle being joined, issue after issue of *The Times* carried letters which did not debate the pros and cons of the Optional Clause, but the pros and cons of the LNU campaign: whether the Union was criticising, opposing or standing aloof from the government; whether or not it spoke for the public as a whole or for a political party. Try as they might to avoid being consciously partisan, the LNU leaders were accused of being unconsciously partisan. For, said an editorial in February, 'Strong party men, speaking or writing on behalf of the Union, may perhaps inevitably find their arguments coloured by their party attitude. PROFESSOR GILBERT MURRAY, for instance'.[95]

The gulf between the LNU and the government widened and their quarrel became sharper. A few days after he had been named in the editorial, Murray wrote complaining that 'a certain section of the Conservative Press' was, by 'daily pinpricks', actually trying to drive the Union into the arms of the opposition.[96] In private he wrote that with Cushendun 'blocking and practically betraying the cause of arbitration and disarmament', it was 'rather difficult to translate that belief into a positive statement of policy which shall have no criticism in it'.[97]

Looking back, Cecil said that his only amazement was that the campaign had been so moderate.[98] He complained to Lord Queenborough, the LNU treasurer and leading Conservative politician, that the Conservatives had 'become so sensitive to any criticism . . . that they instantly conclude that anyone venturing to criticise it in any way does so purely from Party motives'.[99] And he complained to Murray that he was finding the LNU's disagreement with the

---

93 *The Times*, 18 Feb. 1928. Noel-Baker replied to these accusations (and others which Smith had made) in a letter published on 21 Feb.
94 Editorial, 'The League and the "Union" ', 18 Feb. 1928.
95 Editorial, 'The peace temper', 27 Feb. 1928.
96 *The Times*, 1 Mar. 1928.
97 Murray to Cecil, 9 Apr. 1928, Bodl. Lib., Murray papers.
98 Cecil, *Great experiment*, 193.
99 Cecil to Queenborough, 29 Mar. 1928, BM, Cecil papers, Add. MS 51166.

government too polite, its non-partisan platform too restrictive for him to say what he really thought.[100]

Letters continued to appear in the press and the climax of the quarrel came in April when Cushendun made a thinly-veiled threat to resign from the LNU. On 14 April *The Times* published a letter from a Mr B. C. Allen of Salcombe, Kent. 'Probably ninety per cent of the members of the Union have joined it', he wrote, 'not because they wish to teach the Cabinet its business, but because they have a horror of unnecessary war and are therefore anxious to support the League of Nations.' Two days later a letter from Cushendun appeared. Allen was 'probably not far wrong', said Cushendun, for he had received letters from branch secretaries and other active LNU members 'to show that this attitude of the [LNU] Council is causing a good deal of dissatisfaction'. It was wrong for a professedly non-partisan body which included among its honorary presidents two members of the Cabinet, to agitate 'in favour of a policy which has been rejected, not only by the Government, but by the Imperial Conference'. The Union might continue to do useful work but it would be a pity if it persisted in the present endeavour 'to teach the Cabinet its business' for this might make it 'impossible for the Prime Minister and his colleagues and supporters to remain members of the Union'.

Cecil replied the following day, 17 April. He outlined the resolutions which had been passed by the special meeting of the LNU council in October and again at its regular meeting in December; he pointed out that the Clause was favoured by some dominions; he corrected Cushendun with regard to the 1926 imperial conference which was 'certainly not opposed to the Optional Clause in itself, though it accepted the view pressed upon it by the home Government'; he said it was right for the LNU to continue advocating the Optional Clause while taking precautions to ensure against partisanship; and, finally, he thought it would be regrettable if Cushendun dissociated himself from the LNU because of disagreement on this point.

For all this, the antagonists still conducted their quarrel in the manner of English gentlemen. Thus, when Cushendun read that he had supposedly emphasised his 'bitter clash' with Cecil in a speech, he immediately disclaimed this in a letter to Cecil:

> The local reporter of the 'Daily News', evidently disconcerted because I gave him no material for fanning a flame, came up to me and asked – 'Are you going to pursue your quarrel with Lord Cecil'? 'Quarrel'? I replied. 'I have no quarrel with Lord Cecil'. 'Well, are you going to reply to his letter in The Times'? [i.e. 17 April] 'Certainly not', I answered, 'I have expressed my point of view, and I have nothing more I want to say, there is nothing whatever in the nature of a quarrel between Lord Cecil and myself.' He thereupon must have gone straight away and telegraphed to his paper his account of a great 'clash' between you and me, and, without reporting my speech, wrested a single half-sentence from it in support of his false statement that my speech had 'emphasised' this 'clash'.[101]

Meanwhile the LNU was doing its own heart-searching about the campaign. Although the immediate issue was the Optional Clause, branches had been

[100] Cecil to Murray, 3 Mar. 1928, Bodl Lib., Murray papers. See also Birn, *League of Nations Union*, 72.
[101] Cushendun to Cecil, 23 Apr. 1928, BM, Cecil papers, Add. MS 51166.

encouraged to hold meetings on the general issue of 'disarmament' which was in keeping with the name of the campaign (the campaign for international disarmament and arbitration). This represented the ultimate goal which was being sought and could also be widely interpreted to cover all related issues. In early March the campaign committee noted with dismay that there had been a decline in the number of such meetings. The reason was probably saturation. Many branches had 'had' their meeting on 'disarmament' and were looking for a new subject. The committee fell back on the obvious solution. In addition to this first, general, meeting, branches could be encouraged to hold three more on the questions which had been identified as the necessary partners of peace: disarmament *per se*, arbitration (including the Optional Clause), and security. It worked and the number of meetings returned to a satisfactory level. However, this did not hide the fact that support for the campaign was patchy and some areas were inefficient and/or disinterested.

Financial difficulties were also looming. Initially a few large donations had been obtained as a result of a letter which Cecil sent asking 'special friends to contribute to the disarmament campaign'.[102] At the end of November 1927 the balance was very healthy. Total receipts were just over £1,700, total expenditure just over £630. Further donations were smaller. There were the odd fifty or ten pounds but most money now came from collections made at disarmament meetings and were in the region of three to four pounds. The sale of 'peace and goodwill' Christmas/New Year cards further boosted the campaign's funds, but by the beginning of February 1928 the campaign had incurred liabilities in excess of its income. None the less, the committee decided 'to go ahead energetically with the issue of the publications necessary for the effective prosecution of the Campaign'.[103] Cecil signed fresh appeals to individuals and March receipts jumped from their usual fifty or sixty pounds to £646. By the end of April the committee had exhausted both the special DCC fund and sums that had been pledged over several years by David Davies and Sir Daniel Stevenson.

By now, however, members of the executive were vexed at the way in which the campaign had developed and there were further difficulties with the secretariat due to Maxwell Garnett's personal opposition to the campaign.[104] It was possible that the campaign was affecting the LNU membership drive. Over the last three months the increase in membership had been 'substantially less' than for corresponding periods in the previous two years. And, although only six resignations had been reported to headquarters, it was probable that there had been others. In March Cecil had won the committee's agreement to a memorandum in which he argued that occasional criticism of the government was inevitable; that it did not in itself indicate partisan opposition; and that if the Labour and Liberal Parties were using the same arguments as the LNU in their attacks on the government, 'How can that be prevented? Is the Union to drop its long-continued advocacy of a policy the moment any political party in

---

102 DCC minute 6, 30 Sept. 1927, BLPES, LNU IV.52.
103 DCC minute 143, 7 Feb. 1928, BLPES, LNU IV.37.
104 Garnett believed that the LNU was falling prey to the Communists in respect of disarmament and tried to oppose this. Whatever his merits 'Garnett overstepped the limits of what an official of the Union should have allowed himself to do and opposed the Executive's policy in many ways': Noel-Baker to the author, 27 Apr. 1982. In May, Murray won the executive's agreement to a proposal that the role of Union staff should be purely secretarial.

opposition supports it? . . .. [If so it] might well be regarded as showing that the Union was allowing party considerations to affect its policy.' The only course was to be scrupulous: to have 'someone outside party politics' – like a mayor or a bishop – to chair meetings and to have a three-party committee scrutinise all leaflets.[105]

Such arguments, however, hardly approached the nub of the question from the conventional Conservative point of view and Major Hills presented the executive with a motion that the disarmament and arbitration campaign should cease on 21 April – exactly six months after it had been launched and the time when Arnold-Forster's six-month contract as organising secretary expired. On Cecil's suggestion the proposal was referred to a 'committee of six' under Murray's chairmanship. After a 'frank and informal interchange of views on the whole subject referred to them' the committee recommended that the campaign be wound up. This was because the present difficulties were 'in danger of being exaggerated owing to special and temporary circumstances', namely Cecil's resignation (with which most LNU'ers 'presumably' agreed) and the likelihood of providing opposition parties with ammunition against the government in the run-up to the general election.[106]

As Hills had recommended, the expiry of Arnold-Forster's contract was taken as the point for terminating the campaign. The disarmament committee was to be renamed the international arbitration, security and disarmament committee (IASDC) and was to campaign no more: its task would be to advise the executive on these matters and to supervise the public presentation of Union policy as set out in the resolutions of the executive. Steps to improve the Union's relations with the Conservative Party were also taken (such as including a recently-published collection of Chamberlain's speeches on the 'special list of books' and printing on the cover of the 'Notes for Speakers' a reminder of the importance of avoiding party politics and presenting LNU policy in a positive and constructive way). Hudson and Lumley were both able to tell the executive of conversations with Chamberlain aimed at 'thawing relations' and Hills reported the prime minister's willingness to receive a deputation.[107]

Public reconciliation took place on 29 June when Baldwin and Chamberlain received a deputation headed by Cecil and Murray. After Murray had explained that the Union had sought the meeting in order to discuss the government's policy on arbitration (i.e. the Optional Clause), Chamberlain restated the government's policy on the matter and Baldwin said he would do all he could to keep the League out of party politics.[108] The period of open conflict was at an end.

---

[105] DCC minute 158, 29 Mar. 1928 and memorandum by Cecil, 'The LNU and disarmament', 23 Mar. 1928, annex SG 216 OA, BLPES, LNU IV.37.
[106] Chairman's report of a committee of six, 30 Apr. 1928, BLPES, LNU II.9.
[107] Excom minute 105, 3 May 1928, ibid.
[108] The Times, 30 June 1928.

The aftermath of the campaign

Of course, suspicion did not die overnight, nor did it ever completely fade. For example, letters criticising the Union continued to appear in *The Times* during the summer of 1928. But both government and Union wanted to keep their relationship on an even keel. In October the prime minister was the principal speaker at the LNU's tenth anniversary celebration and the government treated the occasion as an opportunity to show willing and put across its point of view in much the same way as Hills had suggested that Chamberlain could have done in June 1927. Baldwin warned the Union against allowing itself to be manipulated for party political purposes, but he also took account of the Union's hopes for peace through law. In the draft speech which Anthony Eden (parliamentary private secretary to Chamberlain) had prepared, disarmament and arbitration were included because they 'always appeal to the zealots of the League of Nations Union'.[109] Cushendun, who was filling in for Chamberlain while the latter was recovering from illness, queried the advisability of using 'superlatives in praise of the Court',[110] but the prime minister, in fact, went further than the Foreign Office draft in commending the PCIJ and was 'received with prolonged cheers'.[111]

In the meantime, the successor to the disarmament campaign committee, the IASDC, had continued to provide speakers for a large number of meetings on arbitration and disarmament and the Foreign Office continued to receive expressions of support for the Optional Clause. When, in July, an MP asked the government to produce a white paper elaborating the reasons for its attitude to the Clause, there was a feeling that this might be a good idea. But it was clear that Cecil had far from convinced the Foreign Office that the public even understood what the Clause meant. 'Branches of the League of Nations Union pass resolutions about the clause, which are sent here written often in the most illiterate handwriting and from obscure villages', said one official. 'I cannot help feeling that if some simple statement in plain language were issued a great deal of the present ill-informed agitation might be stopped.' Such a statement could, he thought, take the form of setting out the text of the Clause 'and continue with the substance – indeed almost the actual text – of our [1925] letter to Mr. Hudson'.[112] However, on the advice of Hurst and Malkin this suggestion was not taken up. Given that the proposed Anglo-American arbitration treaty, which was then being considered, did not exclude vital interests, Malkin thought it uncertain whether it would now be possible to use a good deal of the material in the Hudson letter. Hurst shared this concern but thought that there was no need for a white paper given that the government had recently expressed its views in its statement to the League's Arbitration and Security Committee; since the arguments were not identical to those of 1925, the Hudson letter was now obsolete.[113] Thus government policy was not further elaborated and by the end

---

[109] Note for the prime minister, 8 Aug. 1928, PRO, W 10530/10363/98 FO 371/13402.

[110] Undated minute (? Oct. 1928) on the margin of the draft speech in ibid.

[111] See ibid. and *The Times*, 27 Oct. 1928.

[112] Minute by P. M. Broadmead (a clerk in the western department), 12 July 1928, PRO, W 6746/309/98 FO 371/13391.

[113] Minutes by Malkin and Hurst, 14, 16 July 1928, ibid. On the government's memorandum for the Arbitration and Security Committee see below, 111-113.

of the year the Optional Clause was unquestionably back in the court of party politics. It was high on the agenda of the Labour Party, whose MPs pitted their wits against the government in trying to ask awkward questions at every opportunity, while ministers either referred them to earlier statements or gave non-committal replies.

The general election of 1929

Although the Labour Party was promoting the Optional Clause, this was not because of the LNU campaign. In fact, the campaigning of the LNU left no mark on the 1929 election, and the Optional Clause did not figure as an election issue. What the campaign did show was that among public figures support for the League had become widespread. No doubt this reflected the fact that people in general were in favour of the idea of peace and that the League was seen as connected with this goal. And although it is not possible to show that this had any connection with the LNU campaign, public figures also avowed their support for the principles of peace while generally avoiding saying exactly what they meant. But it was unemployment, not foreign policy, that dominated the election and it is difficult to say whether attitudes to the League affected votes (although the Labour Party, for reasons unconnected with the previous year's campaign, made the acceptance of the Optional Clause a foreign policy priority). The election campaign also underlined the fact that the LNU's place was on the sidelines of politics and that the focus of policy debate was between political parties. It also further demonstrated what the LNU could and could not achieve as a campaigning body.

At the beginning of November 1928 the LNU executive established a general election sub-committee. However, its members – Cecil, R. S. Hudson, Leif Jones and Noel-Baker – were key members of the IASDC and they organised the LNU's election work through the latter organ as it had a degree of independence from the watchful eyes of the executive and finance committees: this was a reflection of the fact that the IASDC had its own funds which kept it afloat until the end of 1929. The programme which they adopted for the election was based on a 'statement of policy' which had been carefully considered at length and subjected to several redraftings within the executive committee to ensure that it would be free from party political taint and contribute to the election of pro-League MPs. As approved by the December 1928 general council, it was very close to the 'memorial' which the executive had approved earlier in the year for the autumn and winter activities of the IASDC. It claimed that the Kellogg pact had wrought such 'a fundamental change in international relations' that it was imperative to find alternatives to war for the settlement of disputes. Accordingly, the Optional Clause should be signed forthwith.

On Cecil's suggestion, the IASDC decided to solicit the views of party leaders on the 'statement of policy' and that this should also be done by every branch in respect of every parliamentary candidate. At the beginning of March the statement was duly sent off. Given that it was in complete harmony with Labour's 'six pillars of peace'[114] (no doubt due to the fact that Philip Noel-Baker

---

[114] See below, 201.

was instrumental in drafting both documents), Ramsay MacDonald speedily endorsed LNU policy and Labour candidates had no difficulty in replying since their answers were provided by Noel-Baker.[115] Lloyd George did not reply to the statement although the Liberals (and Sir John Simon in particular) lent their voices to the cause of arbitration and the Optional Clause.

The Conservative Party election manifesto was vacuous on the League, but the party produced 'notes on [the] LNU statement on international policy' which emphasised the government's successes in foreign policy and Austen Chamberlain's devotion to the cause of peace. With regard to the Optional Clause, it said, firstly, that it was unclear whether the LNU was suggesting that Britain should make reservations; secondly, that it had been common ground for all parties that 'certain important reservations' should be made; and, thirdly, that as long as this was the case it was not clear that anything would really be gained by such conditional acceptance. Mention was made of the 1926 imperial conference and it was argued that the Kellogg pact made signature of the Optional Clause less important. This was because 'the Pact in itself tends to close the famous gap in the Covenant'.[116]

The LNU's branch level work was reminiscent of the disarmament campaign. The 2,767 branches[117] were asked to find leading members of the local community to present the general council's 'statement of policy' to candidates and to elicit their views in writing so that they could be published. Meanwhile, headquarters had constituency maps indicating local branches; indices were prepared of constituencies, branches and candidates; detailed files were built up containing correspondence and press reports; and backward branches were chased up and offered help in April.

In many ways the grass roots campaigning of the LNU was successful. It provided a large number of articles for provincial (and dominion) newspapers; it provided speakers for over a thousand meetings and conferences on the 'statement of policy'; and it collected the views of a large number of candidates. But weaknesses in the LNU's campaign were apparent and efforts were patchy. Many branches did not forward the 'statement of policy' to candidates early enough for the replies to get the maximum footage in the local press and district councils did not provide the hoped-for back-up support. Although some did render valuable service, others were indifferent and sometimes distinctly unhelpful. Branch secretaries were found to be 'lacking in political judgement and quite incompetent' for campaigning work;[118] leading local figures were averse to subscribing to political activities which they had not anticipated when agreeing to join the Union; and there were also cases not only of inefficiency but of gross partisanship. However, the Union as a whole did succeed in avoiding being drawn into controversy about partisanship – although this was probably because its role in the election campaign was only peripheral.

---

[115] Conversation with Noel-Baker, June 1980.

[116] CUL, Baldwin papers, 133.

[117] This is the Jan. 1929 figure.

[118] Report to Council, 27–9 June 1929, international arbitration, disarmament and security committee, minute 51, BLPES, LNU IV.37.

Conclusion

The LNU's attempt to persuade the government to accept the Optional Clause offers an excellent case study of the extent of the public's impact on foreign policy. It is also an extremely pertinent episode, inasmuch as a belief in the wholesomeness and efficacy of public opinion lay at the basis of the Union – and, arguably, of the League itself. The very clear conclusion, however, is that despite the apparently favourable circumstances, the campaign was a complete failure. The government was naturally concerned about what would later be called its image, and it was also worried about the Optional Clause becoming a party political issue. But there is no evidence that it was moved to think again about its Optional Clause policy by the efforts of the LNU – and if the Union could not succeed on this issue, it surely raised the question of whether it would be able to exert an independent influence on anything.

There were three factors which appeared to be working very strongly in the Union's favour in this matter. In the first place, its leaders could be seen as responsible people, in no way anti-establishment, and with entrée to the highest ranks of government. Indeed, one of these leaders, Cecil, was in the Conservative government until 1927. Secondly, they were campaigning on an issue which, at one level, had a great appeal for a law-abiding people who tended to look on international relations as if they were (or should be) like a game of cricket. At a more general level, advocacy of the Optional Clause could mobilise the tremendous will for peace which was manifest in the country after the trauma of the Great War. And, thirdly, this potential was actually tapped in that the LNU was a large and growing organisation which was roused to a considerable height of enthusiasm by the disarmament and arbitration campaign. Recalling an earlier jingle, one might say that the LNU had the people, had the issue and (just about) had the money too. And yet it failed.

On closer inspection this failure cannot be seen as very surprising. Firstly, despite all the links and courtesies between the LNU's leadership and the government, the latter viewed the former with considerable reserve, if not suspicion. Chamberlain later described the executive committee as 'comprising some of the worst cranks I have ever known, led by Cecil';[119] and a non-official source spoke of the LNU's leadership as 'a group of doctrinaire professors, disgruntled generals, and disappointed admirals, to which is added a miscellaneous collection of visionaries and elderly women'.[120] Nor could the government fail to note the growing alignment between the arguments of the LNU and the Labour Party. For example, Lord Parmoor could just as easily have been speaking for the LNU as he was for the Labour Party when he explained Labour's policy in the House of Lords.[121] Clearly, the mere fact that at the formal level relations between the LNU and the government were generally good was not going to cut much political ice with the latter.

Then, secondly, there is the inescapable fact that influential members of the government – particularly Hailsham (who was Attorney General until March

---

[119] Chamberlain to Tyrrell, 13 Feb. 1933, UBL, Chamberlain papers, AC 40/509, quoted in Christopher Thorne, *The limits of foreign policy: the west, the League and the far eastern crisis 1931-33*, London 1973 (first publ. 1972), 220.

[120] Major E. W. Polson-Newman, 'The League of Nations Union', *The English Review*, May 1929, 579.

[121] See House of Lords *debs.*, 8 Feb. 1928, 76-8.

1928 when he became the Lord Chancellor) and Bridgeman (the First Lord of the Admiralty) – were basically out of sympathy with the LNU's policy on the Optional Clause. This, quite apart from the understandable touchiness of a government at being told what to do in foreign policy by a domestic pressure group – and Austen Chamberlain provided a number of examples of that – meant that the LNU was, in a very real sense, pushing against the Conservative grain. In these circumstances, the reversal of a well-established and stoutly-defended policy was in any event most unlikely, particularly so in view of the fact that it had been attacked in a smoothly-orchestrated campaign. Backing down under public pressure is always hugely unattractive to governments. The government was only likely to move if it met a more or less irresistible force.

This draws attention to the third reason for thinking that the LNU never really had much chance of success in its Optional Clause campaign: its lack of political clout. The LNU's strength, in terms of its ability to recruit and propagandise, was its concentration on a single issue and its non-partisan character. But in terms of its capacity to bring effective pressure to bear on the government, these were also its weaknesses. The Union could be seen as a collection of do-gooders and cranks which did not hold together as an electoral force. Accordingly, there was no inducement for the government to pay heed to its strident calls. In the context of British politics the LNU was a flimsy edifice. It could argue and campaign but it was not in a position to make the government feel threatened.

It was this political weakness which was exposed by the Optional Clause campaign. Once the LNU had set out on this road a public clash with the government was inevitable. The only surprising thing is that Chamberlain initially responded in such a low-key way after his rebukes to the Union in 1925. But when he came out of his corner the fight was short and sharp. The LNU had to bow to the government or lose its standing in Britain as a non-partisan body. Quite understandably, it chose to bow. And then the reconciliation was swift. For although the government was not politically threatened by the LNU, it did not want to alienate the LNU's supporters. After all, an election was in the offing. So the weaker party having given way, the quarrel was made up. At least in respect of the Optional Clause at this time, the hope that British public opinion could play an important role in the making of foreign policy had proved to be ill-founded.

It is ironic that at the very moment when the government was firmly rejecting the LNU's call to sign the Optional Clause, it was, in fact, beginning to move in that direction. But there is no ground for thinking that it was being pushed there by the efforts of the LNU. Thus the reasons for the government's changing attitude must be sought elsewhere. The question arises whether, if domestic public opinion had so little influence, 'world public opinion' as allegedly represented by the League of Nations Assembly might have been the force which was propelling the British government down the path to the Optional Clause. It is therefore to Geneva that attention will now be turned.

5

The Assembly of the League of Nations and British Policy

The first part of this book has shown that in its early years the League Assembly played an important role in promoting compulsory adjudication. In 1920 the Optional Clause emerged at the first Assembly and in 1924 the fifth Assembly produced a draft treaty – the Geneva Protocol – which went far beyond the Optional Clause by providing for a comprehensive system for the pacific settlement of all disputes. The favourable attitude of the British Labour government in 1924 was an important factor in the emergence of the Protocol, but the Conservative government which succeeded it in November of that year took a different line and soon rejected the Protocol. However, the Protocol and its principles – arbitration, security and disarmament – were dear to the hearts of many at Geneva and attempts to resurrect it during the next few years placed Britain in a defensive position.

From the perspective of the British Conservative government, the fifth Assembly had run away with the bit between its teeth. But although the provisions of the Geneva Protocol – such as accepting the Optional Clause – were considered quite impossible, Austen Chamberlain recognised that the Protocol had also been the product of a deep-seated sense of insecurity in Europe. Just as MacDonald had realised that something was needed to replace the Draft Treaty of Mutual Assistance, so too did Chamberlain recognise that it would be disastrous to reject the Protocol without putting anything in its place: Europe would be left even more unsettled and unstable and the close relationship with France – upon which Chamberlain intended to base his foreign policy – would be impossible. Diplomatic soundings during the winter of 1924–5 suggested that, generally speaking, the Protocol was not regarded as a satisfactory substitute for a defence pact, and British thoughts were already turning in the direction of an Anglo-French security guarantee when Stresemann came forward with an offer to guarantee Germany's western frontiers. This was the alternative for which Chamberlain had been searching: it offered France security against Germany; it opened the door to Franco-German rapprochement; and it would not only draw Germany away from the Soviet Union but would restore Germany to its rightful place in the comity of nations by bringing it into the League as a permanent member of the Council. Negotiations took place at Locarno on this basis.

The Locarno treaties were concluded in October 1925 and entered into force when Germany joined the League in September 1926. The most important part of Locarno was the Treaty of Mutual Guarantee whereby, with Britain and Italy acting as guarantors, Germany, France and Belgium confirmed Germany's western frontiers and the demilitarisation of the Rhineland. Disputes between Germany and France and Germany and Belgium were to go to arbitration, conciliation or adjudication. The award of the Nobel peace prize to Chamberlain, Stresemann and Briand[1] lent weight to Chamberlain's claim that Locarno marked 'the real dividing line between the years of war and the years of peace'.[2] This appreciation of the value of Locarno was not shared by Germany's eastern neighbours. Poland and Czechoslovakia had at least as much reason as France and Belgium to fear a resurgent Germany, but they were far less reassured by Locarno than the two west European states. Germany had only promised that it would not use force to change its eastern frontiers; arbitration was not obligatory; and, in the event of an unprovoked attack, all they had was a French pledge to give them intermediate aid. Since Britain would not guarantee European security east of the Rhine,[3] Chamberlain recommended that other states should make regional arrangements on the lines of Locarno, but there was no likelihood of Germany entering into an eastern Locarno. The disquiet felt by Poland, in particular, meant that it was especially anxious to resurrect the Geneva Protocol. Many other League members were of a similar mind: those who on general grounds had shared the fifth Assembly's dream of peace; those who were particularly devoted to juridical principles; and those who had urgent anxieties about their security. There were, therefore, frequent expressions of support for the 'principles of the Protocol' at successive Assemblies and several attempts to recreate it in whole or in part. And because compulsory arbitration and the Optional Clause were part and parcel of the Protocol, Britain could not forget the question of the Optional Clause. Thus from 1924 to 1929 Britain was constantly on guard at Geneva, ready to counter Protocol-like initiatives and so prevent anything that might lead her in the direction of the Optional Clause.

The sixth (1925) Assembly

After the excitement of 1924 the sixth Assembly was bound to be anticlimactic, especially since attention centred on the secret, off-stage negotiations for a Rhineland pact. The British foreign secretary was determined that the pre-Locarno talks should not be complicated by any Genevan attempts to try to salvage the Protocol of 1924,[4] and he accordingly told the Assembly that he

---

[1] Strictly speaking, the prize for 1925 was held back and later awarded jointly to Chamberlain and Charles Dawes, the American banker whose report on German economic problems provided for the stabilisation of the German currency and annual reparations payments on a fixed scale. The 1926 prize was awarded jointly to Briand and Stresemann.

[2] Quoted in C. A. Macartney and others, *Survey of international affairs 1925*, ii, London 1928, 56.

[3] Chamberlain had great difficulty in persuading a reluctant cabinet to accept Britain's Locarno obligations and the dominions refused to accept any obligations at all. On Locarno see Sibyl Crowe, 'Sir Eyre Crowe and the Locarno pact', *English Historical Review* lxxxvii (1972); J. B. Duroselle, 'Reconsiderations – the spirit of Locarno: illusions of pactomania', *Foreign Affairs* l (1972); George Grün, 'Locarno, idea and reality', *International Affairs* xxxi (1955); Douglas Johnson, 'The Locarno treaties', in Neville Waites (ed.), *Troubled neighbours*, London 1971, 115; Anne Orde, *Great Britain and international security 1920–26*, London 1978, 89–98.

[4] See, for example, Chamberlain to Briand, confidential, 24 July 1925, and minute by Tyrrell (who became permanent under secretary on Crowe's death in Apr. 1925), 15 July 1925, PRO, W 6867/9/98 FO 371/11066. Germany had responded positively to the French note inviting her to enter into firm negotiations on 27 Aug. On 4 Sept., three days before the Assembly opened, it was announced there would probably be a meeting later that month to discuss a possible pact. On 15 Sept. the French, British and Belgian governments formally invited the German government (together with

could not accept the 'Latin . . .. logic' of the Protocol. Instead, as he had told the Council in March, he was adopting the wiser, practical, pragmatic approach taught by English history. British policy was directed towards supplementing the Covenant 'by making special arrangements . . . to meet special needs' in the region with which Britain was 'most intimately associated' and which had 'too often been the origin and the theatre of war'.[5]

Chamberlain impressed the delegates and was 'cheered to the echo',[6] but it was not popular to tell the Assembly that it was misguided in wistfully 'caressing the memory or the ideal of the Protocol'.[7] And when the French told delegates what they wanted to hear, they seized the leadership of the Assembly. In a brilliant performance that brought storms of applause and was deemed by the French-Canadian Assembly president, Dandurand, to be too eloquent to be translated, Paul-Boncour stole the show with his reply to Chamberlain. '[W]agging an accusing forefinger' in the direction of British delegates 'to give point to his hints at secret diplomacy, the old game of the silent Chancelleries',[8] he insisted that only an Assembly had the right to destroy the work of a previous Assembly. 'The time has not yet come', he cried,

> for us to fling over the Protocol that purple pall beneath which the dead gods sleep. The structure we once built on the shore of this lake is still there, firm and unshaken. The passing wave may distort and dim its image, but its essential features form once again in the passing river. The fragmentary structures in which diplomacies have felt obliged to put their faith can only be built upon the plan which we have drawn.[9]

French stock appreciated further and that of Britain correspondingly declined in the discussions in the third committee that led to the establishment of the Preparatory Commission for the Disarmament Conference.[10] The positions of

---

those of Poland and Czechoslovakia) to attend the conference at Locarno and this was accepted by Germany on 26 Sept., the day the Assembly closed. The conference began on 5 Oct. and the Locarno pact was initialled on 16 Oct.

[5] League of Nations, Records of the sixth Assembly, plenary meetings, text of the debates, *LNOJ*, special supplement no. 33, 1925, (*LNA6* debs.), fifth plenary, 10 Sept. 1925, 38–9.

[6] *Manchester Guardian*, 11 Sept. 1925. See also *The Times* of the same date.

[7] *The Times*, 16 Sept. 1925. Only Ishii of Japan gave the same message in a speech that went unremarked. However, not all delegates unreservedly supported the Protocol.

[8] *Manchester Guardian*, 12 Sept. 1925.

[9] *LNA6* debs., seventh plenary, 11 Sept. 1925, 55.

[10] The Preparatory Commission arose out of a Spanish resolution (approved by Britain and France) calling on the Council to make 'preparatory arrangements for a conference on the reduction of armaments'. Its consideration in the third committee led to lively discussions which revealed Britain and Italy as being in opposition to all the rest who were led by the Netherlands and Hungary (with French support). Whereas Britain argued that it would be premature to convene a general disarmament conference at an early date, the opposite view was that the League should forge ahead and hold a conference. At the same time, the League Council was criticised for inactivity and the Co-ordination Commission (which replaced the Temporary Mixed Commission in October 1924 and co-ordinated its work with that of the Permanent Advisory Commission) was criticised for being undemocratic. The Foreign Office thought the creation of the Preparatory Commission demonstrated that 'practical common-sense has once again suffocated in the Geneva atmosphere' and Chamberlain agreed with the Admiralty that 'This is folly': Minutes by Campbell and Chamberlain, 29, 22 September 1925, PRO, W 9183/9/98, W 8922/9/98 FO 371/11066. However, Chamberlain had heeded Cecil's urgings that to oppose the creation of the Commission would 'destroy both our reputation and our influence': telegrams from Cecil to Chamberlain and Chamberlain to Cecil, 18 Sept. 1925, W 8907/9/98 FO 371/11066. None the less, the UK line was

the two countries had seemingly reversed, with France appearing to want to move forward on disarmament while Britain was apparently obstructive. It was, said Cecil (who became leader of the British delegation when Chamberlain left Geneva), over disarmament that Britain's whole attitude became suspect. Whatever Britain did was attributed to hostility to the League and a determination to impair its efficiency. It was thought to be 'out to object to everything'[11] and 'public opinion both inside and outside the League' developed 'a marked anti-British bias'.[12] Arbitration (in the broadest sense) was not the mainspring of discontent with Britain, but it was an important issue, and one on which British policy had to be explained in order that there should be no misunderstanding of her position.

Unlike disarmament, arbitration seemed to be steadily advancing. A sizeable number of arbitration treaties had been concluded in 1925, many of them 'all-in' treaties that provided for the peaceful settlement of all disputes.[13] Many delegates, especially the Latin Americans, continued to declare their support for compulsory arbitration and the Optional Clause, and an ill-fated Swedish resolution calling for a general arbitral convention based on the relevant provisions of the Geneva Protocol gave them an extra opportunity to emphasise this aspect of the Protocol. The Swedish resolution, though irritating, did not present any problems for Britain.[14] Likewise, a Swiss resolution calling for the renewal of Optional Clause declarations did not put her in a defensive position.[15] For other delegates whose countries had not signed the Clause were

so unpopular that the British member of the third committee made a short statement at the end of the proceedings. This was to avoid any misunderstanding or misrepresentation of the British attitude to disarmament.

11 Undated note by Cecil on the sixth Assembly and disarmament (received in the Foreign Office on 5 Oct. 1925, PRO, W 9457/9/98 FO 371/11067.

12 Telegram from Cecil to Chamberlain, 21 Sept. 1925, PRO, W 9102/9/98 FO 371/11066.

13 Apart from Locarno and the renewal of existing treaties, twelve such treaties were concluded: five arbitration treaties and seven arbitration and conciliation treaties. In addition Siam made a series of treaties of friendship, commerce and navigation providing for disputes to be settled by arbitration or the PCIJ. By contrast no treaties of arbitration or arbitration and conciliation had been concluded in 1920; in 1921 there was one treaty of arbitration and conciliation; in 1922 there was one arbitration treaty; in 1923 there were three treaties; and in 1924 there were three arbitration treaties and two arbitration and conciliation treaties.

14 It was irritating inasmuch as Chamberlain had warned Sweden in March that not only would his country not accept universal compulsory arbitration, but he would also look unfavourably on any attempt to resurrect any part of the Protocol. Undén protested that he was not trying to do this, only to promote the widest extension of compulsory arbitration. The sub-committee that examined the Swedish resolution concluded that 'It was important to avoid anything which seemed necessarily to imply re-opening the discussion upon an isolated part of the Protocol, and on the other hand it appeared unwise to decide in advance that the best way of encouraging the development of arbitration was to draw up and submit for acceptance by various nations a general and uniform system of procedure': League of Nations, *Arbitration and security: exposé of the declarations and suggestions made at the sixth Assembly and at the Council, with a view to the pacific settlement of disputes*, prepared by the legal section of the secretariat, 5 Feb. 1926. Instead, the committee – and subsequently the Assembly – expressed itself in favour of arbitration and adopted a Japanese suggestion that a study should be made of the views that had been expressed in the Council and the Assembly on the general question of pacific settlement. The Scandinavians had been seeking to develop compulsory arbitration and the Optional Clause ever since the first Assembly.

15 See Annex 7 to League of Nations, Minutes of the first committee (constitutional and legal questions), *LNOJ*, special supplement no. 34, 1925 (*LNA6 first committee*), and Motta's remarks to the Assembly, *LNA6 debs.*, sixth plenary, 11 Sept. 1925, 42.

also apprehensive about the propriety and implications of supporting the resolution, with the result that its exhortatory element was removed and it was also made clear that in approving the resolution there would be 'no question of exerting pressure' or implicitly criticising non-signatories of the clause.[16]

But while Britain, as a member state, was not in an exposed position during the first committee discussion of the Swiss resolution, the British representative, Hurst, might have felt some personal embarrassment. A year earlier Hurst had supported the Optional Clause on behalf of a Labour government. In 1925 he had to take a different line on behalf of a Conservative administration, and it was therefore particularly necessary that there should be no misunderstanding of present British policy. Hence he 'bang[ed] the door on any prospect of British ratification of the Optional Clause'.[17]

Hurst's statement was 'followed with keen attention by many members of the public' and 'made a deep impression on the Committee'.[18] But it was not allowed to pass unchallenged. Buero of Uruguay pointed out that Hurst was wrong in saying that all Britain's arbitration treaties contained the vital interests formula as there were no reservations in the Anglo-Uruguayan treaty; O'Higgins disassociated the Irish Free State from the statement;[19] and Rolin of Belgium took issue over Hurst's general considerations lest they should 'stem the general and very strong current . . . within the Assembly in favour of the compulsory competence of the Court'.[20]

It was said that 'outside opinion' could not understand and was even 'somewhat revolted by' Britain's refusal to sign the Optional Clause.[21] This was hardly fair, as many other members were in the same position. But it reflected the general hostility towards Britain and the unpopularity of her attitude towards arbitration. As the Assembly drew to a close, Cecil explained his country's policy in order to try to allay the impression that his country had turned against the League. But the one part of his speech that was not 'fairly well received' was what he had to say on arbitration.[22] And this was rubbed home when delegates warmly applauded de Jouvenal of France for insisting that arbitration (backed up by sanctions) was the first of the three principles of peace (contrary to Cecil's insistence that it was not the foundation but the coping stone).

Having been both surprised and impressed by the tremendous desire at the Assembly to develop compulsory arbitration, Cecil had suggested during the

---

[16] As amended, the resolution simply asked that those states whose declarations would shortly expire should have their attention drawn to 'the measures to be taken, if they consider it proper, in order to renew in due course their undertakings'. It was, said Motta, 'simply a friendly act of encouragement': LNA6 debs., fourteenth plenary, 22 Sept. 1925, 103, 104.

[17] Wilson Harris (Geneva) to Murray, 19 Sept. 1925, Bodl. Lib., Murray Papers.

[18] *Manchester Guardian*, 19 Sept. 1925. It is unnecessary to summarise Hurst's statement to the first committee as its substance was the same as the reply that Chamberlain had given to the National Council for the Prevention of War in response to its petition calling for signature of the Optional Clause: see above, 61–2. For Hurst's statement see LNA6 first committee, fifth meeting, 21–3.

[19] See below, 165, n. 39.

[20] See LNA6 first committee, fifth meeting, 23.

[21] *Manchester Guardian*, 28 Sept. 1925.

[22] Cecil to Chamberlain, 25 Sept. 1925, UBL; PRO, Chamberlain papers, AC 52/141 and FO 800/ 258. It was also criticised by the *Manchester Guardian* which neatly juxtaposed Chamberlain's 'almost unintelligible' letter to the NCPW (see above, 61–2) with the report on Cecil's speech: editorial, 'Compulsory arbitration', 28 Sept. 1925.

Assembly that Britain might respond to continental opinion by indicating that it would not object to others entering into an agreement on the lines of the Protocol. And when he returned to England he came out firmly in favour of accepting the Optional Clause. After all, as both he and Chamberlain had told the Assembly, Britain had, in practice, always been ready to arbitrate,

> and I do not think it at all probable that we should wish to refuse arbitration in the future. It may well be that we should do wisely to accept . . . the 'Optional Protocol' . . . . we should nearly always gain by arbitrating . . . questions before The Hague Court. Moreover . . . we could sign . . . with the reservation . . . [of] questions involving our national honour or vital interest or any questions arising out of warlike operations. It may be said that that would not mean very much, but it would be unquestionably welcomed as a step towards arbitration by those States who have come to believe in arbitration with an almost unreasoning faith, and it certainly would not do us any harm.[23]

But nothing happened as a result of this suggestion. The foreign secretary had rejected Genevan criticism of his country (which he regarded as the League's most 'disinterested friend') and would 'not abate one jot of our principles to curry favour with the Assembly or its [sic] critics'.[24] No doubt he saw no reason to pander to Genevan whims by reconsidering something that had been rejected so recently. And there is no indication that Foreign Office officials saw any need to reconsider the Optional Clause. As will be shown in chapter 7, the Optional Clause was reconsidered in the summer of 1926 in a different context, that of the forthcoming imperial conference, but without any change in policy. Britain therefore went to the seventh Assembly still firmly set against the Optional Clause and compulsory arbitration.

The seventh (1926) Assembly

The outstanding event of the seventh Assembly was the historic moment when, amidst loud handclapping, Stresemann pushed his way through a disorderly crowd in an oppressively hot Assembly hall, mounted the tribune, and nervously took up Germany's membership of the League. Then came Briand's unforgettable welcoming speech which ushered in what was widely seen as the new era of peace in which arbitration was to hold a central position:

> We have done with the black veils of mourning for sufferings that can never be appeased, done with war, done with brutal and sanguinary methods of settling our disputes. True, differences between us still exist, but henceforth it will be for the judge to declare the law. Just as individual citizens take their difficulties to be settled by a magistrate, so shall we bring ours to be settled by pacific procedure. Away with rifles, machine-guns, cannon! Clear the way for conciliation, arbitration, peace!
>
> Arbitration! That word is now at the height of its prestige and its power. Arbitration treaties are increasing; nation after nation is promising to abjure war and

[23] Note on the sixth Assembly and disarmament by Cecil, PRO, W 9457/9/98 FO 371/11067. In March he had only suggested that Britain should hint at a willingness to sign.
[24] Telegram drafted by Chamberlain on 22 Sept. 1925, PRO, W 9012/9/98 FO 371/11066.

to accept intermediaries. All these undertakings are building the path of peace; all are permeated with the spirit of the League; and for that reason all nations should devote themselves heart and soul to the League's defence.[25]

Arbitration did, indeed, seem to be marching forward at an impressive pace. Almost twice as many treaties of arbitration or arbitration and conciliation were concluded in 1926 as in the previous year (although most of the twenty-two such treaties were between states that already enjoyed good relations and were already devoted to the juridical ideal). The Council's report on the secretariat's survey of such treaties had reaffirmed the desirability of the principle of arbitration, and delegates publicly yearned for a general arbitral scheme. There were initiatives in this direction and British delegates had to speak out on two occasions: to prevent compulsory arbitration being declared a 'fundamental rule which should govern the foreign policy of every nation';[26] and to say that Britain would have to abstain on a draft recommendation that states sign the Optional Clause.[27] But on neither occasion was Britain on its own and the proposers did not try to press their point.

The reason for this hesitancy was twofold. Firstly, a breathing-space seemed appropriate while Germany found its feet at Geneva: it was not, therefore, a time for action. Secondly, those who were most devoted to the juridical cause had more immediate matters on their minds. The entry of Germany into the League had sparked off an internal crisis and the first (legal and constitutional) committee was preoccupied with settling the remaining questions that had arisen.[28] In 1927 the resentment of the juridically-minded at what they saw as

[25] League of Nations, Records of the seventh ordinary session of the Assembly, plenary meetings, text of the debates, *LNOJ*, special supplement no. 44, 1926 (*LNA7* debs.), seventh plenary, 10 Sept. 1926, 53, 54.

[26] This was part of a Yugoslav resolution which had been introduced during the third committee's discussion of the Council's reports on the studies by the League secretariat of proposals for pacific settlement and the extent to which recent treaties and conventions had contributed to general security. The Council had laid special emphasis on the value of Locarno and the proposal amounted to a direct invitation to endorse the principles of the Protocol as applied regionally in the Locarno treaties. The sub-committee of the third committee that was charged with drafting an appropriate resolution was weighted in favour of the great powers and the draft Yugoslav resolution was rejected. Onslow, the British representative, explained that he could not accept compulsory arbitration and, at his suggestion, not only was the word 'arbitration' not qualified by the adjective 'compulsory' but conciliation was given equal weight with arbitration.

[27] This was during the first committee's consideration of the amended Yugoslav resolution which had been forwarded for an examination of its legal aspects. Henri Rolin of Belgium tried to introduce amendments calling on states to consider accepting the Optional Clause on the grounds that this would facilitate the 'intensive development of the practice of arbitration'. Hurst at once explained that it would be 'most embarrassing for his Government – which a few weeks hence would be considering the question as a whole [at the imperial conference] – to find that its representative . . . had voted for a resolution which prejudged the whole matter': League of Nations, Minutes of the first committee (constitutional and legal questions), *LNOJ*, special supplement no. 45, 1926, (*LNA7* first committee), ninth meeting, 30. Rolin withdrew his amendments after objections had been raised by the representatives of Japan, India, Australia, Canada and Venezuela.

[28] In essence, the League Council Crisis arose out of the simmering discontent of the lesser powers at the superior status enjoyed by the permanent members of the Council and these feelings were exacerbated by the manner of its solution. The special Assembly that met confidently in March to arrange Germany's entry into the League, collapsed within ten days after only three plenary meetings and in an 'atmosphere of suspicion, rumour and intrigue' and 'murmurs of revolt' over the unrecorded 'secret and mysterious conversations' between the Locarno powers: Arnold J. Toynbee, *Survey of international affairs, 1926*, London 1928, 48–9. The problem was that although it was

the violation of international egalitarianism was to be translated into action. But for the time being it was as if the 'League Council crisis' had knocked the stuffing out of the Assembly. Apart from the completion of the Slavery Convention, nothing of substance was achieved. Work was slacker for the British than in previous years (until a last-minute frenzied rush); there was little entertaining; and even Chamberlain and Cecil seemed to be 'at a loose end'.[29] Proceedings drew dismally to a close in a 'spirit of apathy' with the Assembly hall emptier than ever before for the President's closing speech, an occasion that was 'in nearly all respects beneath the dignity of the League'.[30]

Underlying the apathy of the 1926 Assembly, however, was the growing suspicion among those who were in favour of compulsory arbitration and the Optional Clause that Britain was engaged in 'malicious opposition'.[31] This had emerged in the previous year (as Locarno was being negotiated) and had been fuelled by the Council crisis of March 1926. But Britain paid little attention to these feelings. The Scandinavians and the Dutch, for example, were thought by Britain to be 'played out powers' who were 'up to mischief', and were treated to paternal advice about holding 'exaggerated opinions'.[32] Even the allegedly 'sniffy' attitude of The Times was of 'no importance',[33] but it was irritating that so many 'fictions' about British motives should have gained currency at Geneva.[34] And so, in his speech during one of the closing plenaries, Cecil reminded journalists that they had a 'great responsibility' and that they did not serve the cause of peace by reporting foundationless stories 'of combinations and intrigues and desires for domination and duplicity'.[35] And, since many of the

accepted that Germany should have a permanent seat on the Council, Spain, China, Poland, Brazil (and later Persia) also demanded that they be accorded this elevated status. A way out was found in May when a special committee on the composition of the Council proposed that Germany's inclusion as a permanent member of the Council should be accompanied by the addition of three so-called 'semi-permanent' seats to which non-permanent members could be re-elected. That is, when one-third of the non-permanent members retired at the end of their three-year term, some, like Spain, could count on getting the necessary two-thirds majority vote for re-election. Hence the term 'semi-permanent'. However, such members were not to exceed one-third of the non-permanent members and the Assembly could at any time decide by a two-thirds majority to hold a new election for all the non-permanent seats on the Council. Apart from Brazil and Spain, who walked out of the League in a huff (the former permanently, the latter temporarily), the other claimants to permanent seats acquiesced and the path was clear for Germany to enter the League at the seventh Assembly. However, the small states – particularly the Dutch and Scandinavians – were still angry in September, especially when they were forced to vote simultaneously on the entry of Germany and the reconstitution of the Council.

[29] See Cadogan's letters from Geneva to his wife, 7–23 Sept., CCAC, Cadogan papers, ACAD 3/2; Cecil to Chamberlain, 21 Oct. 1926 and Hurst to Cecil, 7 Oct. 1926, PRO, W 10048/10048/98 FO 371/11096; Manchester Guardian and The Times, 27 Sept. 1926.

[30] Manchester Guardian, 27 Sept. 1926.

[31] The Times, 25 Sept. 1926. The grounds for this were seen in Britain's insistence that the League should 'go slow' over disarmament and the proposed world economic conference; in Chamberlain's castigation of the Permanent Mandates Commission for exceeding its competence; and in Cecil's suggestion that a committee should examine what was and what was not the legitimate business of the League.

[32] See Tyrrell to Chamberlain, private, 8 Sept. 1926, UBL, Chamberlain papers, AC 53/561; Chamberlain to Tyrrell, 10 Sept. 1926, AC 53/562.

[33] Hurst to Cecil, 7 Oct. 1926, PRO, W 10048/10048/98 FO 371/11096: 'It may be that it is becoming traditional with the "Times",' he said.

[34] Cecil to Chamberlain, 21 Oct. 1926, ibid.

[35] LNA7 debs., fifteenth plenary, 24 Sept. 1925, 107.

criticisms of Britain were attributed to the French delegation's daily news conferences, the British made changes at the next Assembly (and, as a result, had 'very little difficulty' with the press).[36]

But this was the only way in which the seventh Assembly can be said to have affected British policy. Chamberlain and his advisers remained supremely confident of the wisdom of British policy. A little more decorum could be introduced into proceedings that often resembled a bear-garden, and Britain could improve the presentation of its policy, but there was no need to question the wisdom of that policy.

The small states, on the other hand, left Geneva feeling frustrated and angry. They had always resented the privileges of the permanent members of the Council, but in the early years, when Britain and France did not think the League very important, the Assembly had been their forum in which they could make their voices heard. However, once the great powers began treating the League as an important factor in international politics and sending their leaders to the Assembly as well as the Council, the organisation seemed to be turning into 'more or less an implement in the hands of the great powers, and . . . no more a real League of Nations'.[37] In this way the inherent rivalry between the Assembly and the Council was coming to the surface. Sooner or later the small states were likely to assert themselves, and in trying to take the League back in the direction they wanted to go they were likely to return to their beloved Protocol.

The eighth (1927) Assembly

The eighth Assembly met at a time when there was much dissatisfaction regarding the absence of progress on disarmament. In 1925 and 1926 it had been possible to overlook the lack of results on the ground that disarmament would come in consequence of an improved international atmosphere. But in 1927 the international climate looked less rather than more promising, as unresolved problems in great power relations began to show through the cracks in Locarno. The breakdown of the spring meeting of the Preparatory Commission was a blow to proponents of disarmament, and events that summer confirmed the small states' belief that the great powers were intent on maintaining their predominance and thrusting the principles of the Covenant into the background.[38] Disarmament was not going to come if they continued to allow it to be tackled in isolation from the principles of arbitration and security. They determined to act. And so it came about that 'one of the most striking features'

[36] Onslow to Tyrrell, private and confidential, 26 Sept. 1927, PRO, W 9382/9382/98 FO 371/12686.
[37] Nansen to Cecil, private and confidential, 15 July 1927, BM, Cecil papers, Add. MS 51099. See also F. P. Walters, A history of the League of Nations, London 1969 (first publ. in 2 vols, 1952), 290.
[38] The evidence lay in the by-passing of the League in the ill-fated Coolidge naval conference; in Cecil's resignation which evidenced British ill-faith in the whole disarmament exercise; in de Jouvenal's refusal to join the French delegation to the eighth Assembly on the grounds that France had not submitted disputes to the League which should have been submitted; and in the fact that instead of discussing important questions, the Council restricted its agenda to matters of 'third-rate importance' whilst serious matters were dealt with secretly, and to the benefit of the powerful, at Locarno tea-parties: ibid. 343.

of the eighth Assembly 'was the emphasis which was once more laid on the interdependence of arbitration, security and disarmament'.[39] The Protocol 'kept coming up about every half hour'[40] and, said Noel-Baker, '[o]pinion in the Assembly . . . is absolutely unanimous for an outlawry of wa[r], for a great extent of arbitration, and, indeed, for a virtual return to the Protocol. Only Chamberlain is against it'.[41]

In fact Chamberlain was not alone. But since he took it on himself to save the League from itself (as he saw it), it was unnecessary for anyone else to stand against the rhetorical tide. On 10 September Chamberlain's blunt rejection of the Protocol became 'the most discussed speech that there has ever been'.[42] Observers were said to be mystified at 'the mood of exasperation' that produced 'plain speaking almost to the point of brutality'[43] from a British foreign secretary. But from the beginning the eighth Assembly had been characterised by plain speaking rather than the usual 'exchange of complimentary banalities'.[44]

Having 'made up their minds to be brave'[45] the small states bitterly criticised the great powers for abusing the League. When Hambro, president of the Norwegian Chamber of Deputies, 'went for the Council and the "Big Four" with his gloves off' he was warmly applauded and hailed as 'a leader of the Opposition'.[46] Chamberlain's speech, on the other hand, was 'icily received'[47] by an 'awed' hall;[48] was denounced by the British opposition and League enthusiasts; and was 'very unpopular in the Secretariat' although delegates generally agreed that 'it was very honest and a good thing that the British view should be so clearly made known'. Yet, it was wondered, why had Chamberlain sounded defensive and struck a discordant note when his message was not a new one? Anthony Buxton, a British member of the secretariat, went some way towards guessing the truth when he said that Chamberlain sounded 'as if he felt he had been baited and was hitting back as hard as he could'.[49]

However, Chamberlain had not been goaded into action by Hambro, nor by the expression of similar complaints by de Brouckère of Belgium, Löfgren of Sweden and van Blokland of the Netherlands. Rather, it was the obstinacy of van Blokland in refusing to withdraw a resolution that produced Chamberlain's 'clear warning' that Britain would not be pushed into fresh engagements. But before discussing the Dutch resolution, it is first necessary to deal with another instance of small state insubordination: a Polish resolution renouncing aggressive war which took up a great deal of time and left Britain exposed in respect of the Optional Clause.

[39] Arnold J. Toynbee, *Survey of international affairs, 1928*, London 1929, 48.
[40] Anthony Buxton to Cecil, 30 Sept. 1927, BM, Cecil papers, Add. MS 51113.
[41] Noel-Baker to Murray, 9 Sept. 1927, Bodl. Lib., Murray papers.
[42] Noel-Baker to Cecil, 17 Sept. 1927, BM, Cecil papers, Add. MS 51106; Bodl. Lib., Murray papers.
[43] *Manchester Guardian*, 12 Sept. 1927.
[44] The *Journal de Genève* at the beginning of the eighth Assembly, cited in Margaret Burton, *The Assembly of the League of Nations*, New York 1974 (first publ. 1941), 209.
[45] Noel-Baker to Cecil, 17 Sept. 1927, BM, Cecil papers, Add. MS 51106.
[46] *Manchester Guardian*, 14 Sept. 1927.
[47] Buxton to Cecil, 30 Sept. 1927.
[48] *Manchester Guardian*, 12 Sept. 1927.
[49] Buxton to Cecil, 30 Sept. 1927.

The Polish resolution

As soon as the British arrived in Geneva, Sokal, the permanent Polish delegate to the League, told them that he intended to introduce a proposal whereby League members would agree not to embark on wars of aggression. His avowed intention was to refurbish 'some of the provisions of the Covenant which public opinion suspected had become a little rusty' in order to 'allay the uneasy feeling that the League was failing to achieve its purpose'.[50] But his real aim was to wring from Germany something which Poland had not obtained in 1925: a pledge to arbitrate disputes. When Cadogan and Hurst had failed to dissuade Sokal, Chamberlain warned the Pole against 'the danger of re-opening in any form the questions raised in the discussions of the famous Protocol' and against casting doubts on the value of Locarno.[51] Instead, Britain would support a resolution endorsing the 'principles of Locarno' – provided that Chamberlain was first shown a draft of the resolution and that it was acceptable to both the French and the Germans.

As far as the French were concerned, they were already aware of Sokal's intentions and would have found it difficult not to support their eastern ally. On 6 September, two days after their interview, Sokal handed Chamberlain the text of a resolution which had been approved by Briand and which now proclaimed *all* war illegal. '[A]lthough absurd and even in some respects comic', it was unacceptably dangerous:

> If we were to exclude the possibility of war as a final solution, we should have to accept the idea of some form of compulsory arbitration. Moreover, if any outbreak of war entailed the obligation on Members of the League to apply sanctions, which is the logical outcome of the principle that all war is illegal, that would be extending enormously our obligations under Article 16 . . .. Evidently . . . we could not accept the Polish resolution as it stood.[52]

The Germans were also alarmed and rushed to tell the British (who had offered to act as go-between with the Poles) that they would be in an invidious position if they had to denounce the resolution in the Assembly hall. Moreover, such a denunciation would leave Franco-German détente in tatters. The only thing to do was to bring the Poles to heel. Hurst produced an innocuous redraft of the Polish resolution and Chamberlain told Sokal that if he proceeded with his unaltered resolution, 'I would oppose it from the tribune, in order that by taking this burden upon myself I might prevent a fresh row between France and Germany'.[53]

The following day, 7 September, Briand and Stresemann accepted Hurst's redraft but Sokal said that his government was insisting on a modification that would have extended the original obligations. Chamberlain refused to accept it and the Germans were 'incensed', believing Poland's only object was to put them in the wrong. Instead, Hurst, Sokal, Fromageot (the French legal adviser)

---

[50] Memorandum by Cadogan, 2 Sept. 1927, enclosure in Chamberlain to Tyrrell, 3 Sept. 1927, PRO, W 8313/8313/98 FO 371/12686; *DBFP* iii, 327.
[51] Memorandum by Chamberlain, 4 Sept. 1927, enclosure in Chamberlain to Tyrrell of same date, PRO, W 8388/8313/98 FO 371/12686; *DBFP* iii, 328.
[52] Cadogan to Villiers, 7 Sept. 1927, PRO, W 8572/61/98, FO 371/12675.
[53] Chamberlain to Tyrrell, 19 Sept. 1927, UBL, Chamberlain papers, AC 54/482.

and Gaus (the German legal adviser) got together and produced a joint resolution. No sooner had this been done than Sokal turned round and demanded that the phrase 'All pacific means must be used for settling disputes' be amended to 'All disputes must only be settled by pacific means'.[54] Neither Hurst nor Gaus nor Fromageot saw any point in agreeing to something that was either meaningless or worthless, but Sokal said he had definite instructions and proceeded to leak his resolution to the press.

Chamberlain rejected Hurst's advice to let Sokal's resolution be killed in committee rather than lay himself open to criticism by opposing it in the Assembly. But, just at the moment that Chamberlain was hoping Briand would intervene 'and take a part of the load off my shoulders',[55] Warsaw responded to British pressure and Sokal's game was at an end. The British envoy in Warsaw was assured that Zaleski, the Polish foreign minister, had never contemplated opposing the wishes of Britain and France[56] and, on 9 September, Sokal duly moved the 'approved' resolution. It was unanimously adopted by acclamation in the third committee and, in a roll-call vote on 24 September, the Assembly declared that all wars of aggression were, and always would be, prohibited and that every peaceful means must be used to try to settle every kind of dispute.[57] This was 'nonsensical', said Kirkpatrick; 'quite stupendously silly', said Villiers; 'but, at least, harmless', reminded Campbell.[58]

There was, however, one by-product of the Polish resolution which put Britain on the defensive and increased pressure on her to accept the Optional Clause. This was Germany's acceptance of the Optional Clause as a device to win popularity and dish the Poles. The German legal adviser, Gaus, had advised that this step would not add to Germany's legal obligations since Germany had already renounced the use of force to change its eastern frontiers. But it would strengthen Germany's hand in refusing an eastern Locarno. Thus, immediately after declaring his support for the 'declaration concerning wars of aggression', Stresemann announced Germany's acceptance of the Optional Clause. He received tremendous applause and his act was regarded as having great symbolic importance. Germany had only belonged to the League for a year and to the

---

[54] Minute for Chamberlain by Hurst, 8 Sept. 1927, enclosure in Chamberlain to Tyrrell, 10 Sept. 1927, PRO, W 8603/8313/98 FO 371/12686.

[55] Minute by Chamberlain, 8 Sept. 1927, ibid.

[56] The first official explanation of Sokal's actions was that there had been a misunderstanding at Geneva, then that there had been confusion owing to the Zaleski's illness and crossed telegrams. Finally Zaleski said Sokal was a 'damned liar' who had been egged on by friends in the secretariat. Chamberlain was willing to accept Zaleski's explanation 'as far as that turns on his determination not to forfeit my good will or confidence & I readily accept his description of M. Sokal': Muller to Chamberlain, strictly confidential, 7 Oct. 1927; minute by Chamberlain, 21 Oct. 1927, PRO, W 9753/61/98 FO 371/12686. However, Chamberlain and his advisers suspected there had been a French hand in the matter. As Tyrrell put it: 'They were the cats paws of the French & were had': Minute, 21 Sept. 1927, PRO, W 8834/8313/98 FO 371/12686.

[57] League of Nations, Records of the eighth ordinary session of the Assembly, plenary meetings, text of the debates, LNOJ, special supplement no. 54, 1927 (LNA8 debs.), ninth plenary, 9 Sept. 1927, 84; League of Nations, Minutes of the third committee (reduction of armaments), LNOJ, special supplement no. 57, 1927 (LNA8 third committee), seventh meeting, 47; Eighth Assembly. Report of the British delegates to the Secretary of State for Foreign Affairs, London, 25 November 1927, Misc. No. 1, (Command paper 3008), 1928.

[58] Minutes by Kirkpatrick and Villiers, 29 Sept., 4 Oct. and undated minute by Campbell, PRO, W 9221/61/98 FO 371/12675 and W 9355/61/98 FO 371/12676.

PCIJ for six months. But here was Stresemann showing that Germany was an exemplary League member and that, as a great power, it was able to accept the Optional Clause with ease.

In this way Germany appeared to be strengthening the system of the Optional Clause. And since Britain's critics could also point to the 1924 French declaration accepting the Optional Clause (while conveniently ignoring the fact that it had not been ratified), it was becoming increasingly difficult to justify Britain's non-signature by reference to its position as a great power.

The Dutch resolution

Unlike the Poles, the Dutch did not consult the British before they 'suddenly' sprang the 'ridiculous proposal' that the Assembly should 'perform the remarkable feat of investigating the fundamental principles of the Protocol without re-opening a discussion of that document'. 'This, of course, at once threw everybody into commotion', reported Cadogan, and the British swiftly summoned a special meeting of BED. Chamberlain won the BED's agreement that if private persuasion failed, Chamberlain should 'in the last resort' make 'a public declaration, to prevent any such absurd and mischievous proposal being passed on for the delectation of an Assembly Committee'.[59] He was also given assurances of Baldwin's support for whatever he might consider necessary to avoid being 'plunge[d] . . . into the Protocol quagmire again',[60] and 'begged' Blokland, the Dutch foreign minister, to remove from his resolution everything except the reference to disarmament. At a second meeting, Blokland agreed not to come to a final decision until the end of the opening plenaries. Meanwhile Chamberlain arranged for Politis of Greece (one of the authors of the Protocol) to tell the Assembly, without renouncing the Protocol, that it was inopportune to discuss it.

Politis's eloquent, two-hour speech was described as a 'veritable manual of League politics' which 'entered into the heart of the world problem'.[61] It was also well-timed since Politis spoke immediately after Hambro, whose despondent view he rejected. But his appeal to wait patiently was seen by the small powers as an acceptance of impotence, an abandonment of the League's great work. It cost Greece a seat on the Council and it did not sway Blokland, who told

---

[59] Cadogan to Villiers, 7 Sept. 1927, PRO, W 8572/61/98 FO 371/12675. The relevant part of the resolution stated that 'without reopening the discussions on the Geneva Protocol of 1924, it is desirable to consider whether the time has not yet come to resume the study of the principles on which the Protocol was based'. These principles should be studied together with the report of the Preparatory Commission: LNA8 debs., third plenary, 6 Sept. 1927, 41. Although it could be given 'a fairly innocent meaning everybody would understand that as a matter of business anybody who voted for the Resolution in that form was prepared to accept the Protocol of 1924 in substance': 'The work of the eighth Assembly of the League of Nations' (Record of an address by Sir Hilton Young, a substitute delegate to the Assembly, at Chatham House on 13 Oct. 1927), *International Affairs* vi (1927), 373.
[60] See Baldwin to Chamberlain, 6 Sept. 1927, PRO, Chamberlain papers, FO 800/261.
[61] *Manchester Guardian*, 9 Sept. 1927.

Chamberlain that he would neither withdraw nor modify his resolution unless others endorsed what the Greek had said.[62] No-one else had the 'courage' to do so,[63] and it was therefore up to Chamberlain to try to quash the resolution.

The 'cold douche of common sense': Chamberlain's speech to the Assembly

Chamberlain well knew the unpopularity of his 'views on the great questions which may be summed up in the word "Protocol" ', but he did not flinch from administering 'the cold douche of common sense' that was 'repugnant to the races who habitually express themselves in a much more rhetorical form' and were 'less careful about the precise meaning of the words [which] they use and the undertakings they give than is compatible with our sense of what we owe to ourselves and others'.[64] And so, after rejecting Hambro's criticisms of the Locarno tea parties, Chamberlain dealt with each of the 'principles of the Protocol'. Starting with disarmament he suggested that the failure of the Coolidge conference was a disappointment from which they could draw the lesson to be patient and work slowly but steadily towards their goal. His country was second to none in its desire for a real and large reduction of armaments and its interest and its effort lay not only in words or speeches but also in deeds. Which country, he demanded, 'carrying our load of responsibility for the peace of so many and such scattered countries, in such varied conditions, would have done more? Is there any country, I would even ask, that would have done as much?'.

Next he turned to arbitration and begged his audience 'to bear in mind the special conditions of the British Empire':

> Ours is not a unitary system of government such as prevails in your countries. We are a great community of free and equal nations, each autonomous, united in the oldest league of peace in the world. It is not easy for an Empire so constituted always to

[62] The British legation at The Hague was 'almost astonished' that Blokland 'should take so public an opportunity of reverting to a subject on which His Majesty's Government are known to have such definite views'. However it was thought that the resolution was part of an effort by Blokland to educate a complacent public. He could not express in plain language his fear that in a future war Germany might well invade the Netherlands, but he wanted the Dutch 'to understand that it would pay Holland to play a leading role among the second class Powers in the League, sharing the part with Belgium. His ultimate aim is to create an impression that in the event of either of these two little countries . . . being threatened, they would take common action to safeguard their interests both in and out of Europe'. Accordingly, he was working for a new treaty to replace the 1839 treaty with Belgium and to do so he had to create a favourable impression on Belgium and 'flatter his countrymen by making them feel that Holland was taking a leading part in the deliberations of the League'. Another reason was his desire to cut a figure among the smaller states as he did not have the international reputation of his predecessor, Karnebeek. The speech had received governmental approval before Blokland went to Geneva and there could be little doubt that Blokland 'was fully aware . . . of the risk he ran of incurring a rebuke from you, Sir . . . .. I submit however that His Excellency probably felt that if he was successful, by acting as he did in furthering his larger policy . . . he would have rendered greater service to the cause of European peace than had he remained silent': W.E. Houstoun-Boswall (second secretary, The Hague) to Chamberlain, 14 Sept. 1927, PRO, W 8804/61/9 FO 371/12675.

[63] Cadogan to Villiers, 11 Sept. 1927, PRO, W 8693/61/98 FO 371/12675.

[64] Chamberlain to Baldwin, personal, 16 Sept. 1927, UBL, Chamberlain papers, AC 54/31.

accept the obligations that can be readily undertaken by a State homogeneous, compact, and speaking by the voice of but a single Government.

It is not easy, and it would not be right, to accept obligations unless we not only have the intention, but know that we have the power, to fulfil them. We are sometimes thought to be backward. There is an undercurrent of suggestion that, because we cannot participate in all the plans that are framed, we are stopping the progress of the League and are an obstacle in its way. I beg you to think of what we have done.

Britain had, he thought, 'arbitrated more grave problems than any other country in the world' and only a few days earlier had accepted the Council 'not as conciliator but as judge' over the frontier of Iraq, making concessions, moreover, that had not been required by the Council so as to make that judgement acceptable to Turkey.

Coming now to security, Chamberlain directed the full force of his words on those who, finding the security provisions of 'the famous Protocol exactly suitable to their conditions . . . cannot understand why anyone else should be unable to accept what is so advantageous to them'. Britain had accepted the Covenant. It had accepted Locarno open-eyed, knowing that when it guaranteed Belgium 'long years ago' it had cost her a million men. 'Yet, you ask us to do more!' he exclaimed. 'Could not some of you do as much before pressing us to go further?'[65] he demanded 'with out-stretched, accusing finger':[66]

I repeat, you say it is not enough. You invite us to take for every country and for every frontier the guarantee which we have taken for one by the Treaty of Locarno. If you ask us that, you ask us the impossible. Our strength, great as it may be, is not equal to the task with which you would charge us. [At this 'there was marked uneasiness on the French and Polish benches'.] . . .. You do not know what you ask us. You are asking nothing less than the disruption of the British Empire. I yield to no one in my devotion to this great League of Nations, but not even for this League will I destroy that smaller but older league of which my own country was the birthplace and of which it remains the centre.

Addressing the Dutch directly, Chamberlain said they were entitled to hang on to their hopes and work towards the day when the Protocol would prevail. But they should consider what was involved in their resolution. It was impossible to take up the principles of the Protocol without reopening discussions of the Protocol itself: 'what useful purpose could we serve, what evil consequences might we not incur, if we reopen those troubled debates before there has been, from any quarter, any indication of a change of mind'? Chamberlain was grateful to Politis for the 'ruthless logic with which he pursued the argument of the Protocol' and for pointing out the prematurity of trying to block up the gaps in the Covenant. They should recognise that gaps were necessary. It was the openings in buildings that 'give us power to breathe', the passages that 'give us power to move' and it was this that made 'the difference between a habitation and a tomb'.

Finally, he told the silent hall not to underestimate the authority that the League had already acquired. He had attended every Assembly and Council meeting because his government

---

[65] LNA8 debs., eleventh plenary, 10 Sept. 1927, 97.
[66] Manchester Guardian, 12 Sept. 1927.

bases its whole policy upon the League; because no country, however powerful, even to-day can disregard your moral judgement, or can be deaf to the advantage of being able to come here before you, or to your Council, to plead its cause, to receive your approval, and to justify itself before the world.

They had accomplished much, they would accomplish more. They shared the same faith in the League even if they did not all view its future in the same way. And Chamberlain's way was not a series of 'hasty', 'dramatic', 'sensational steps' but that of the slow, steady and sturdy growth of the acorn into the oak.[67] Chamberlain's speech was a 'welcome relief' to the British delegation, who agreed with the foreign secretary that it had 'done good'.[68] As Edith Lyttleton, put it, it was 'naturally a cold wind, but a bracing one':

Nothing was more palpable than the gradual change of atmosphere it brought about; the mists lifted, and it was recognised, although with irritation, that Great Britain had done a good deal already and was prepared to do more. It was in a large measure due to this speech that the subsequent efforts of the Committees, that the debate on their reports were as practical and weighty as they were. The will for Peace was never more strongly manifested, all the more real because feet were treading the ground. There was no doubt a great deal of criticism of the British, freely indulged in, but I am much mistaken if this was not mixed with admiration of the Foreign Secretary's plain speaking, and with welcome of the sense of reality which he has engendered.[69]

The first grudging recognition of what was practical came from Blokland who announced at the end of the same plenary meeting that he was modifying his resolution into a call for a study of the principles of arbitration, security and disarmament 'as provided for in the Covenant'. But he made it quite clear that he was only doing it because of British pressure, and he insisted that the British were wrong in thinking that he had ever wanted anything other than 'a calm and reasoned discussion of the problems raised by the Covenant'.[70]

'I suppose it must be acknowledged that the Dutchman has tried to meet our wishes and perhaps what he has done was done with the best intentions', said Cadogan. But personally he was 'rather aghast' at the new version, for Britain could no longer use the excuse that it 'would be useless and perhaps presumptuous' to join in discussions on the principles of the Protocol.[71] As it happened, these discussions gave rise to a proposal aimed at allowing those who

---

[67] LNA8 debs., eleventh plenary, 10 Sept. 1927, 98; Manchester Guardian, 12 Sept. 1927.
[68] See Cadogan to Villiers, 11 Sept. 1927, PRO, W 8693/61/98 FO 371/12675; Chamberlain to Tyrrell, private, 15 Sept. 1927, UBL, Chamberlain papers, AC 54/480.
[69] Lyttleton (substitute delegate to the Assembly) to Onslow, 25 Sept. 1927, PRO, W 11208/9382/98 FO 371/12686. However, it was not quite the end of the Protocol. Despite warnings from Chamberlain and Onslow, Paul-Boncour introduced a resolution that would have led to a discussion of it. But after Chamberlain spoke 'pretty frankly', Paul-Boncour agreed to 'try to find what Beneš once by misadventure called a "texte euneque" [castrated text]'. This was that governments that were willing and able should indicate the extent and circumstances in which they would be able to give effect to obligations under Article 16 of the Covenant: Cadogan to Villiers, 18 Sept. 1927, PRO, W 8979/61/98 FO 371/12675. It became one of the questions that fell within the remit of the new Arbitration and Security Committee.
[70] See LNA8 debs., eleventh plenary, 10 Sept. 1927, 104. See also Loudon's remarks to LNA8 third committee, third meeting. 21.
[71] Cadogan to Villiers, 11 Sept. 1927, PRO, W 8693/61/98 F 371/12675.

wanted to do so to travel down the arbitral path. Thus Britain had to take care that it was not carried along with them on a slippery slope to the Optional Clause.

Nansen's draft optional convention and the emergence of the Committee on Arbitration and Security

The amended Dutch resolution was submitted to the third committee. When it came up for discussion, Nansen, the Norwegian explorer and High Commissioner for Refugees, made a suggestion which, he said, was based on that of the Netherlands but could equally well be dealt with on its own merits. This was that the League should draft

> a simple treaty which should enable Members of the League which desired to do so to promote the more general acceptance of obligatory arbitration. There was already an optional clause attached to the Statute of the Court under which States which desired to do so could accept the jurisdiction of the court in legal disputes. The draft now put forward simply proposed that a similar arrangement should be drawn up under which States could accept also compulsory arbitration in non-legal disputes if the Council was unable, under Article 15 to secure settlement of them.[72]

> An optional arbitration treaty would be like the scaffolding of a system of universal arbitration, which can be built in brick by brick as each group of countries is in a political position to sign arbitration treaties *inter se*.[73]

In making this recommendation, Nansen went to great pains to reassure the British that he had no intention of trying to force them to participate in such a treaty. This was accepted by Hurst, who seems to have determined the British line. The minute in which Hurst advised Onslow (who had taken over from Chamberlain as head of the British delegation) why Britain should neither oppose the Nansen proposal nor adopt an attitude of disinterest, is quoted at length as it clearly explains his reasoning:

> Dr. Nansen seems to have . . . indicated that his proposal was founded on the idea expressed in the Secretary of State's speech, that any movement among States who were able and willing to make progress along the line of further obligations for the compulsory arbitration of disputes would be welcome. Also that he was willing to reshape his proposal into any form which would make it acceptable.

---

[72] *LNA8* third committee, fourth meeting, 27. The 'Draft Optional Convention' stated that: 'The Signatory States undertake to submit all questions of every kind arising between them, which it has not been possible to settle within a reasonable time by the normal methods of diplomacy, either to judicial decision or to decision through the procedure defined in the following articles.' In respect of legal disputes the signatories would 'recognise as compulsory, *ipso facto*, and without any special agreement the jurisdiction of the Court'. In other disputes, if a settlement could not be reached through the League Council under Article 15 of the Covenant, the dispute would be referred to arbitration. If the parties could not agree on the arbitrators, the Council would, by a majority, settle the points at issue. The parties would undertake to accept and carry out in good faith the award of the arbitrators: ibid. 27–8. Nansen later explained that states would be able to make reservations to the convention.

[73] *LNA8* debs., twentieth plenary, 26 Sept. 1927, 174. Cf. Lange's explanation to the first committee: League of Nations, Minutes of the first committee (constitutional and legal questions), *LNOJ*, special supplement no. 55, 1927 (*LNA8* first committee), fifth meeting, 22, 26.

I think it would be well to take him at his word. The present form of his proposal is really a resuscitation of the arbitration clause in the Protocol of 1924, and, as such, would presumably be unwelcome to His Majesty's Government.

This form would tend to leave any Government which failed to accept it in a position of isolation, or at any rate in an unfavourable position. Abstention would expose His Majesty's Government to continual pressure by other States in favour of acceptance, because acceptance was the path of progress. It would also lend itself to party politics at home. Any such result should be avoided.

On the other hand, the optional clause contained in the Statute of the Court has avoided these results. We made it abundantly clear at the time that we participated in the preparation of that clause that we should not sign it, but by taking part in the shaping of it we could and did secure that non-signature was not regarded as leaving us in an inferior position.

A clause on the lines of the optional clause in the Court Statute is really the best method of giving effect to the Secretary of State's idea that those States which can make progress along the lines of compulsory arbitration are welcome to do so. That clause is limited to what are known as justiciable disputes. Dr. Nansen's scheme would cover non-justiciable disputes and would provide for the compulsory reference of such disputes to some form of pacific settlement.

Some general instrument enabling those who wanted to do so to adopt obligations for the compulsory reference of these non-justiciable disputes to settlement by peaceful means would be an advantage even to His Majesty's Government, who would be non-signatories. At present the matter has to be regulated by bilateral treaties, and there has been a tendency among recent bilateral treaties covering the pacific settlement of non-justiciable disputes to refer them, in case of the failure of other means, to the Court at The Hague. It is undesirable, and in my opinion almost dangerous, that States should be making agreements which will impose upon the Court at The Hague the obligation to deal with political disputes. It will tend to blur the distinction between disputes that can be settled by the application of a rule of law and those which cannot, and judges are only in place in disputes of the former character.

If we could secure the adoption of a general instrument on the lines of the optional clause in the Court's Statute covering non-justiciable disputes, it would tend to discourage States from making bilateral treaties, and thereby eliminate the danger of such bilateral treaties containing undesirable clauses. I think, on the whole, we should gain if Dr. Nansen's proposal were allowed to . . . be put into good shape.[74]

After Pearce of Australia had been reassured that Nansen's proposal would only mean compulsory arbitration 'for those nations who wished to have it',[75] the third committee quickly agreed that Nansen's proposal was politically acceptable. However, there was no agreement in the first committee (which examined it from the legal point of view) because of differences about the best way of peacefully settling disputes and doubts about whether the proposal involved a model treaty or a general arbitral convention. Resort was had to a joint sub-committee of the first and third committees. With only one day in which to report, the joint sub-committee simply recommended that the proposal

[74] Quoted in Cadogan 'Memorandum on the proposal by Dr. Nansen at the eighth ordinary session of the League of Nations for a draft optional convention for obligatory arbitration of disputes', 9 Nov. 1927, PRO, PRA (27)11, W 10499/61/98, FO 371/12676.
[75] See LNA8 third committee, sixth meeting, 43. Brookes of South Africa, whose government was 'still opposed' to compulsory arbitration, also raised this point but was told by Lange that the proposed convention would be optional: LNA8 first committee, fifth meeting, 23.

be further examined by the proposed Security Committee[76] and set out the points to be considered.[77] This was approved by the Assembly on 26 September in a lengthy resolution calling on the Preparatory Commission to create a committee on arbitration and security (CAS) 'without delay'.[78]

Policy evaluation and preparation for the Committee on Arbitration and Security (October–December 1927)

There was no enthusiasm in Whitehall for the new League committee. As Cecil had been told in 1925 when the Preparatory Commission was established, 'These things which often have an innocuous appearance at the outset can have an unpleasant habit of developing into an early embarrassment and, once a League Committee is set up, we can quite soon be confronted with a request to agree to something most inconvenient.'[79] On learning that the Preparatory Commission was to have an offspring, Shone, a clerk in the western department, minuted that the 'creation of still another League Commission is exasperating. But fresh review of the principles of the Protocol is inevitable and to that we

---

[76] The Security Committee was created to disguise the 'complete deadlock which had arisen on nearly all the major questions before the Preparatory Commission': Major-General A. C. Temperley, *The whispering gallery of Europe*, London 1938, 73. The third committee had run into a quarrel between the French (who insisted that the deadlock in the Preparatory Commission arose from divorcing disarmament from security) and the Germans (who insisted that the Assembly had recognised that the time was ripe for a definite step to disarmament and that this was warranted by political conditions). The outcome was a compromise whereby the Preparatory Commission would establish an off-shoot committee to deal with security. As far as Britain was concerned, there was no reason to regret the introduction of security into disarmament discussions since this presented fewer difficulties than disarmament, the discussion of which Britain would be glad to see postponed.

[77] It was explained that this was because it was 'apparent that the importance of the first step towards disarmament depended upon the measure of security attained, and, consequently, the first effort made to ensure security, to develop arbitration, must be continued henceforward, so that, when the Preparatory Commission had finished its technical work, the States would be in a position to indicate to the Conference as complete a measure of disarmament as possible': *LNA8* third committee, eighth meeting, 53. The committee was accordingly asked to make 'An investigation . . . into the means of fostering and encouraging the acceptance of the Optional Clause . . . and the conclusion of special treaties for judicial settlement, arbitration and conciliation.' In making this investigation the committee was instructed to pay 'special attention' to conciliation 'the value of which cannot be exaggerated'; '[v]ery special attention' to 'the question of the relations between the Council's and the Assembly's mediatory action and the procedures of arbitration and conciliation'; and, in studying compulsory arbitration, consider how a convention 'could be given sufficient flexibility to enable the contracting States to regulate their engagements in accordance with their special conditions': memorandum by Cadogan, 9 Nov. 1927, PRO, PRA 27(11), W 10499/61/98, FO 371/12676; *LNA8* first committee, annex 4a.

[78] Resolution V adopted on 26 Sept. 1927: *LNA8* debs., twentieth plenary, 177–8. The security aspect of the committee's work falls outside the scope of this book but it is discussed in Cadogan's 26 Oct. memorandum (*DBFP* iv. 219) and was thus summarised by Kirkpatrick: '(1) The Preparatory Committee is in theory to continue to prepare a basis for a disarmament conference. This is the sop to Germany. (2) The Preparatory Committee is to study the question of security – a sop to France. (3) The members of the League are to consider the question of concluding agreements of the Locarno pattern and to state what they can do to support the Council in time of war. This is a sop to Great Britain': Minute, 27 Sept. 1927, PRO, W 9063/61/98 FO 371/12675. The committee was also asked to examine a Finnish proposal for assisting victims of aggression.

[79] Telegram to Cecil (approved by Baldwin in the absence of Chamberlain), 17 Sept. 1925, PRO, W 8824/9/98 FO 371/11066.

must devote ourselves now.' 'I agree', said Tyrrell, the permanent under secretary. 'Let us start at once.'[80]

This brought the Optional Clause once more to the attention of policy-makers, for Britain had to decide 'whether we shall say: "Your move" to the others or whether we are prepared to make any further advance and, if so, how far'.[81] Ronald Campbell, a senior member of the western department, accordingly included the Optional Clause in his survey of recent criticism that Britain was supposedly blocking 'further progress along the path of arbitration, security and disarmament'.[82] It was commended to Chamberlain as '[a]n excellent paper',[83] but Campbell's conclusion that Britain could do no better than 'stand fast on the defence of our policy and our actions, as made by the Secretary of State at Geneva last month',[84] was not based on a serious questioning of the basis of that policy. There was no need to do this in view of the general satisfaction felt by the British delegation to the eighth Assembly.[85] And, in respect of the Optional Clause, this was not only the conclusion indicated by the old memoranda that Campbell dug up; it was also the obvious one in view of the fact that Chamberlain felt 'bound by the strong opinions expressed by the Lord Chancellor, the Attorney General & Lord Haldane reaffirmed just a year ago by the Cabinet'.[86] Hurst's view that there would be no progress towards security and disarmament unless nations knew disputes would be settled peacefully and that Britain should accordingly re-examine whether it could show a greater willingness to enter into arbitration agreements was thus rejected by Chamberlain. For, as was manifest when policy came to be discussed by the relevant Cabinet committee,[87] compulsory arbitration and the Optional Clause were regarded as intimately linked.

Although there had been had been no suggestion in the Foreign Office that Britain should accept the Optional Clause, 'the Attorney General repeated with some emphasis his objections to the signature of the clause' and he was 'supported in a general way' by the rest of the Cabinet committee. However,

---

[80] Minutes by Shone and Villiers, 2 Sept. 1927, PRO, W 8979/61/98 FO 371/12675.

[81] Minute by Kirkpatrick, 27 Sept. 1927, PRO, W 9063/61/98 FO 371/12675.

[82] 'General survey', annex 3 to Campbell memorandum on 'Arbitration, security and disarmament', 8 Oct. 1927, W 11899/61/98, DBFP iv, 211.

[83] Minute by Tyrrell, 14 Oct. 1927, ibid.

[84] 'General survey', annex 3 to Campbell memorandum, 8 Oct. 1927.

[85] Although one delegate described the Assembly as 'listless', it was generally thought to have been a good, business-like affair – perhaps 'one of the best so far'. Chamberlain's speech had made the Assembly 'pull itself together' and mitigated 'the usual faint hostility' towards Britain (although unpopularity had to be lived with since, to be popular, one had to be 'either Latin, or Slav, which is the same thing in all relevant essentials, or small'). Criticisms by the representatives of small states were 'irritating and ignorant' attempts to magnify their importance. And the Protocol had been mischievously dug up because 'busybodies had idle hands and the proverbial agent was ready to find them the proverbial occupation': Hilton Young to Onslow, 4 Oct. 1927; Lyttleton to Onslow, 25 Dec. 1927, PRO, W 11208/9382/98 FO 371/12686.

[86] Minute, 7 Nov. 1927, PRO, W 10403/61/98 FO 371/12676. This was a reference to the discussions prior to the 1926 imperial conference.

[87] This was the cabinet committee on policy for reduction and limitation of armaments which had responsibility for the Preparatory Commission and hence also for the new League committee which was to be its offshoot. The committee members were: Salisbury (in the chair), Worthington-Evans (secretary of state for War), Hoare (secretary of state for Air), Bridgeman (First Lord of the Admiralty), Cushendun (Chancellor of the Duchy of Lancaster) and Hogg (attorney general). Cadogan was joint secretary to the committee.

Samuel Hoare, the secretary of state for Air, while acknowledging his complete ignorance of the subject, suggested that the Optional Clause should again be 'carefully considered with a view to seeing whether, without damage to our interests, we could now sign the clause, with reservations, in order to allay the criticism which is being levelled against HMG both at home and abroad'. But all that happened was the recirculation of a 'number of old papers'[88] with the inevitable decision that Britain could neither accept the Optional Clause nor 'a similar clause in bi-lateral agreements'.[89]

The explanation to be given for Britain's refusal to sign the Clause was that 'the peculiar position of the British Empire' meant that any such undertaking 'would have to be conditioned by so many reservations as to make the agreement worthless'[90] – the line that the government was taking that winter in response to the LNU's Optional Clause campaign. In respect of political disputes Britain's representatives were to urge the advantages of conciliation. But, in accordance with Hurst's advice (which had been endorsed by Chamberlain), it was agreed that Britain could lend a hand in drawing up a treaty as suggested by Nansen – providing that it was a model bilateral treaty and not an optional general convention. (The latter was objectionable because it was thought that by agreeing to such a convention 'we should subsequently have to resist the demand that we sign it in the same way as we have now to refuse to sign the "optional clause" ' and because Britain could not recommend to others what it would not do itself.)[91] Britain did not, however, have to block any attempts by others to conclude a general convention covering justiciable disputes – providing that care was taken not to 'use language which may hereafter hamper the Government in resisting political pressure at home to secure the adoption by this Country of the Optional Clause':

> Broadly speaking, wherever it is feasible our vote should always be cast on the side of arbitration, and where, as in our own case, it is not possible to go very far in that direction, every method of conciliation, as distinguished from arbitration – such, for example, as are contemplated in the Locarno Treaty – should be eagerly embraced.[92]

---

[88] Minute by Campbell, 14 Nov. 1927, PRO, W 10680/62/98 FO 371/12678. The papers that were circulated were those produced in 1926.

[89] Cabinet, reduction and limitation of armaments, committee on policy, minutes of a meeting held on 15 Nov. 1927, secret, PRO, PRA (27) 2nd cons. CAB 27/361.

[90] Reservations would have to be made of disputes arising out of naval belligerent action; any matter affecting inter-imperial relations; and 'until we have received their consent any matter which might react on the internal or external affairs of any of the self-governing Dominions' (on which Britain was bound by the 1926 imperial conference). 'Lastly, there must be a general reservation in regard to those disputes which touch the vital interests, independence and honour, of the State. The truth is that in vital matters we can bind the British Government but we cannot bind the British Parliament in whom, of course, ultimately the power rests. We could not deliver the goods. Such reservations would in our case rob of any real significance any general reference of justiciable disputes': Report of the cabinet committee on policy for reduction and limitation of armaments', signed by Salisbury, 23 Nov. 1927, PRO, CP 193(27) W 11069/61/98, DBFP iv, 229. See also PRA (27) 2nd cons.

[91] PRA (27) 2nd cons. See also minute by Hogg (attorney general), 22 Dec. 1927, PRO, W 549/28/98 FO 834/36; minute by Chamberlain, 27 Oct. 1927, annex 2 to memorandum of same date on 'The present situation in regard to disarmament', CP 256(27), W 10423/61/98; PRA(27)4 CAB 27/361; DBFP iv, 219; minutes by Hurst and Kirkpatrick, 3 Nov. and minute by Chamberlain, 7 Nov. 1927, PRO, W 10403/61/98 FO 371/12676; note by Salisbury, secret, 1 Nov. 1927, PRO, PRA (27)5 CAB 27/362.

[92] Report of Cabinet committee, 23 Nov. 1927.

If this did not represent a change in the substance of policy, it did reflect Chamberlain's and Cushendun's desire to adopt a positive attitude and minimise the opportunities at Geneva for criticising Britain. The Cabinet confirmed the recommendations of its committee on 24 November.

The British memorandum for the Committee on Arbitration and Security

The Committee on Arbitration and Security (CAS) was set up on 30 November 1927.[93] Its first session was a purely formal affair. Beneš of Czechoslovakia was elected chairman, Undén of Sweden and Urrutia of Colombia were elected vice-chairmen, and a programme of work was adopted. This was divided into three parts, only one of which is relevant to this book: the study of arbitration that was undertaken by Holsti of Finland.[94]

By Christmas, the members of the League had received a questionnaire asking for their views on the subjects before the committee and Hurst produced the British memorandum in reply. This was important for the committee since it was held that Britain's attitude 'was likely to prove the most important single factor determining the success or failure of the Committee'.[95] And it was important in respect of the Optional Clause because, although the arguments were not new, it was a carefully considered pronouncement that represented Britain's formal position up to the general election of 1929.

The British memorandum began by distinguishing between justiciable disputes (which arose from a conflict of rights) and non-justiciable disputes (where there was 'a divergence of view as to ... political interests and aspirations'). Arbitration treaties were those providing for the submission of justiciable disputes to a tribunal entitled to give a binding decision. The value of arbitration lay not in the rendering of a decision but in the willingness of disputants to accept that decision. Hence Britain did not believe that arbitration needed to be backed up by force (as did the French) but that, generally-speaking, the only sanction for arbitration treaties was public opinion. And so, whatever the League did to promote such treaties, it had to bear in mind the willingness of public opinion in any country to carry out an adverse decision. A treaty that went further than this was not merely 'useless' but might also embitter relations and set back the steady advance in arbitration if it failed to achieve a solution to a dispute in 'a moment of grave importance'. Governments recognised by their

[93] In accordance with the Assembly resolution, the Preparatory Commission charged the new committee with considering 'the measures capable of giving all states the guarantees of arbitration and security necessary to enable them to fix the level of their armaments at the lowest possible figures in an international disarmament agreement'. The members of the Committee on Arbitration and Security (CAS) were those who were represented on the Preparatory Commission (apart from the United States which refused the invitation to sit on a committee whose functions included an examination and elaboration of the Covenant). The Soviet Union sent an observer and Turkey was invited to serve on the committee in March 1928 (when it was first represented on the Preparatory Commission).

[94] In this respect Holsti's task was twofold: to make a study of Nansen's proposed optional convention and to examine the common features of arbitration treaties in order that they might draw up a model convention. The two other parts of the programme were the study of security undertaken by Politis, and the examination of Articles 10, 11 and 16 of the Covenant undertaken by Rutgers of the Netherlands.

[95] Arnold J. Toynbee (with V. M. Boulter), *Survey of international affairs, 1928*, London 1929, 83.

reservations to such treaties that there were certain justiciable questions that they could not submit to arbitration. For while reservations might vary in form, 'their existence indicates the consciousness on the part of Governments that there is a point beyond which they cannot count on their peoples giving effect to the obligations of the treaty'. Likewise the framers of the Covenant recognised that it was 'not feasible to embody in [Article 13 of] the Covenant a definite and comprehensive obligation to arbitrate all justiciable disputes'. 'Mere omission of the limitations on the obligation to arbitrate justiciable disputes which now figure in arbitration treaties would not promote the progress of arbitration', wrote Hurst:

> What is necessary is to overcome the difficulties which have caused the insertion of these limitations, and for this time is necessary. As nations get to understand each other better, as the respect for international law gets stronger, and as a sense of security increases, it will become more easy for States – even those whose interests are world-wide – to accept comprehensive engagements to arbitrate justiciable disputes. Some States are already in that fortunate position. Others less fortunate must approach thereto by degrees.

However, even states that could not yet accept the unrestricted obligation to submit to compulsory arbitration might be helped to move in that direction. Firstly, it would be useful to consider whether a provision that had been included in many of Britain's recent multilateral conventions – the undertaking to submit disputes over the application or interpretation of a treaty to the PCIJ – might be generally included in treaties. If this happened, 'the field within which all justiciable disputes will be arbitrated will steadily expand'. Secondly, and more importantly, the scope of agreements dealing with justiciable disputes could be expanded by pledging all parties to accept arbitration in advance. Britain was at present bound by eleven such treaties all of which, however, included the vital interests formula. Although, as had been pointed out there had to be reservations, it might be the moment to re-examine the vital interests formula.

Having dealt generally with compulsory arbitration, the British memorandum turned to the Optional Clause. The Optional Clause had not been widely accepted because

> the considerations which deter States from accepting binding obligations to arbitrate all justiciable disputes operate in varying degrees as regards other foreign States. In contracting an international obligation towards another State a country must take into account the nature of its relations with that State. Obligations which it may be willing to accept towards one State it may not be willing to accept towards another. Reservations and exceptions which it may think necessary as regards one State may not be considered necessary as regards another. The method of signing a general undertaking, even when coupled with the power to make exceptions as to the categories of disputes to be arbitrated, lacks the flexibility which enables the measure of the obligation to be varied in the case of the particular States towards which the obligation is being accepted. More progress is likely to be achieved through bilateral agreements than through general treaties open to signature by any State which so wishes.

Non-justiciable disputes should never be submitted to the PCIJ but could be best dealt with through the procedure of conciliation which was, at present, all that was possible. Nansen's proposal for a general convention for the peaceful settlement of all types of disputes might be useful if there were any states that were able and willing to sign it. But, even if only a few states found themselves in such a position, it would still be useful to have a model for any future agreements.[96]

The work of the Committee on Arbitration and Security

At the end of January 1928 Holsti, Politis and Rutgers met with Beneš in Prague to agree on the reports that had been drawn up on the basis of the replies from Britain and other countries. The reports did not reach Britain until Cushendun was about to depart for Geneva to represent Britain at the CAS meeting on 20 February. This did not matter since Sugimura (the League under secretary-general) had reassured Britain that he heartily agreed with the British government's views, and he had shown Cadogan the 'quite sound' draft which McKinnon Wood (the acting director of the legal section of the League secretariat) had written for Holsti. This had maintained that the aim of promoting and generalising arbitration agreements was 'to some extent achieved by constant discussion at Geneva'. And although it drew attention to the possibilities of drawing up a general arbitration convention – as suggested by Sweden and Norway with the strong support of Belgium – it also pointed out the 'difficulties and disadvantages' of such a course – as indicated by Britain and Germany – before inclining towards drawing up a 'model' treaty.[97]

When, however, Cadogan studied Holsti's report at Geneva, he found that the 'well-considered adjustment of the [various] points of view'[98] was a bit too well-adjusted in one direction for Britain's liking. The proposed Swedish treaty – with its objectionable provisions for compulsory arbitration and compulsory adjudication – had found its way into the report as one of the avenues open to the committee. And during the opening three days' 'flow of oratory',[99] Undén of Sweden received support when he pressed for a general 'all-in' treaty, notwithstanding several objections that it was futile to try to achieve such a treaty at that time.

When the committee began going through the memoranda which had been presented to it, Cushendun made it clear that Britain would only accept a recommendation drawing states' attention to suitable types of treaties, and he would certainly not agree to participate in drawing up a general treaty. For, he said, 'an attempt to reduce to one common type the varying practice of a great number of States, as embodied in existing bilateral treaties, so far from carrying

---

[96] 'Observations of His Majesty's Government in Great Britain on the programme of work of the Committee on Arbitration and Security of the Preparatory Commission for the Disarmament Conference' in CAS, docs.

[97] See memorandum by Cadogan, 20 Jan. 1928, W 1335/28/98, DBFP iv, 258; 'Memorandum on arbitration and conciliation' submitted by M. Holsti to the Committee on Arbitration and Security for consideration at its second session, CAS, docs., paras 27–49.

[98] Beneš to first Session of the CAS, cited in Cushendun to Chamberlain, 25 Feb. 1928, PRO, PRA (27)35 W 1773/28/98, CAB 27/362, CAB 21/309.

[99] Cadogan to Campbell, 22 Feb. 1928, W 1714/28/98, DBFP iv, 278.

us any further along the road to security, would have the opposite effect'.[100] The Italian and Japanese delegates strongly supported him, as did the representatives of Chile, Germany and Canada. But Undén struggled to keep alive the idea of a general treaty, backed by Politis (who had always been a 'Protocol man'), and with the tacit sympathy of Paul-Boncour (one of the principal proponents of the Protocol). Since the reports before the committee had 'examined, or at least mentioned, all the divergent opinions', each delegate found 'a text suitable to his case' and little progress was made. However, the delegates were agreed on one thing: the need to produce practical proposals. A drafting committee of twelve offered 'a very pleasant refuge to a distracted committee which cannot discover its own mind', and it was entrusted with the task of coming up with something to satisfy everyone: a model conciliation treaty (as favoured by Britain) and a model general treaty (to satisfy Undén and his supporters).[101] However, it was clearly understood that the CAS was not thereby expressing a preference for general treaties, and the British, Japanese and Italians stated that they had in no way modified their positions.

Instead of trying to reconcile the irreconcilable, the drafting committee adopted an approach which enabled speedy progress: by producing a set of treaties which, it was hoped, 'would provide sufficient variety to meet the desires and conditions of different Governments'.[102] The drafts were then scrutinised by a final drafting committee of three in which Hurst had no difficulty persuading his co-members, Politis and Baron Rolin-Jaequemyns of Belgium, to agree to provisions deemed important from the British point of view. Within a few days there were six 'model' treaties dealing with arbitration, conciliation and security. These had received their 'first reading' by the time the committee adjourned on 7 March and, in addition to agreeing the resolutions recommending the treaties to the Assembly, the committee had also approved a resolution on the Optional Clause.

Holsti's report had drawn attention to the eighth Assembly's view that it would be desirable to encourage acceptance of the Optional Clause. But he did not know what states could do 'beyond recognising, as they already do recognise, that the development of the court's jurisdiction under the optional clause . . . constitutes an important application of the principle of arbitration'.[103] Asked to translate this into a resolution, the drafting committee came up with a formula strongly urging states to accept the Clause and pointing out that they could do so with reservations. Cushendun assented to this but decided that he needed to make a statement 'to avoid the possibility of any embarrassing misunderstanding'.[104] 'By accepting this draft', he said,

> we are not making any practical proposal. What we are doing is to reiterate in strong terms the opinion that has been expressed before, that as many States as possible

[100] Cushendun to Chamberlain, 25 Feb. 1928.
[101] Ibid.
[102] See CAS, third session, 6; statement by Beneš in League of Nations, Minutes of the third committee (reduction of armaments), LNOJ, special supplement no. 67, 1928 (LNA9 third committee), second meeting, 10.
[103] Holsti memorandum in CAS, docs.
[104] Cushendun to Chamberlain, 7 Mar. 1928, W 2342/28/98, DBFP iv, 296.

should sign this clause if they find it in their power to do so, for they will, to that extent, be contributing towards the security of the world.

He sincerely wished that his country's circumstances allowed it to sign this valuable clause. But this was impossible because its interests were 'so complex, so scattered, and . . . so dependent upon not one Government, but a number of equal Governments'. None the less, his government did want to encourage those who did not have the same difficulties to sign the Clause and, in so doing, he wanted it 'quite clearly seen that we have not in any way abandoned the position that we took up, or modified it at all in any way when we have made ourselves responsible for this draft'.[105]

When Cushendun returned to London, it was unnecessary for the relevant Cabinet committee to consider the League committee's arbitration activities since Britain's position had been fully safeguarded and this aspect of its work was, in effect, complete. The drafts were given a swift 'second reading' in the summer of 1928 at the third session of the CAS. By the close of this third session, the CAS had drafted ten model treaties, of which only the six which dealt with arbitration and conciliation are relevant to this book. Earlier, in March 1928, the CAS had just drawn up three model multilateral treaties on the grounds that these 'presented more difficulties from the drafting point of view' and they could easily be adapted to serve as model bilateral treaties. Britain accepted this, as it was made quite clear that the committee had 'no intention of indicating thereby any preference for general conventions'.[106] However, in deference to Cushendun's insistence that bilateral treaties were of equal value, three model bilateral treaties were added at the third session. These treaties, together with appropriate resolutions, were then forwarded to the ninth Assembly in September 1928.

At this Assembly, the three multilateral treaties were combined into one treaty – the General Act.[107] This Act had four chapters, the first three of which corresponded to each of the multilateral treaties. Chapter I provided for disputes to be submitted to conciliation. Chapter II provided for the compulsory submission of all legal disputes to the PCIJ or an arbitral tribunal (with the option of a preliminary procedure of conciliation by mutual agreement). Non-justiciable disputes were to go to conciliation and, if that failed, to arbitration. Chapter III provided for the compulsory arbitration of non-justiciable disputes. Chapter IV contained general provisions of the kind found in the preceding chapters. This was intended for states willing to settle all disputes peacefully and was represented as a means of implementing the 1928 Kellogg peace pact. States could accede to all or any parts of the treaty and could also make reservations to their acceptance. However, although 'any class of dispute' could be reserved, states had to do so 'with greater definition' than the vital interests formula,[108] a

---

[105] Statement by Cushendun at 12th meeting of second session of the CAS, 5 Mar. 1928, PRO, W 2298/28/98 FO 411/7.

[106] See Cushendun to Chamberlain, 7 Mar. 1928.

[107] The General Act is printed in LNOJ, special supplement no. 63, Oct. 1928. It is simply and clearly explained in League of Nations, The League from year to year (1 Oct. 1927–1 Sept. 1928), Geneva 1929. See also John Fischer-Williams, 'Model treaties for the pacific settlement of disputes', International Affairs vii (1928); James Shotwell and Marina Salvin, Lessons on security and disarmament from the history of the League of Nations, New York 1949; CAS, third session, 6–8.

[108] Cushendun to Chamberlain, 7 Mar. 1928. See also Toynbee, Survey of international affairs, 1928,

step favoured by Hurst and suggested in the British memorandum (although it alarmed the Admiralty and was disliked by the Germans). The combination of the multilateral treaties in the Act did not amount to any significant alteration in the model conventions, but Britain had neither expected the treaties to be combined in this way nor that there would be an attempt at the forthcoming Assembly to endorse the approach of the General Act as preferable to the limited, bilateral approach favoured by Britain. Such an outcome was highly undesirable since it represented, in effect, an arbitral convention on the lines of the Geneva Protocol – the very thing that Britain had been opposing at previous Assemblies. Thus, as will now be shown, the ninth Assembly was not an easy one for Britain.

The ninth (1928) Assembly

The ninth Assembly met at a time of increasing difficulty in great power relations. Germany was becoming increasingly assertive and uncooperative, and Cushendun (who led the British delegation) was preoccupied with preliminary negotiations for the evacuation of the Rhineland, without which, Germany insisted, Franco-German relations would never be normal. But, despite discordant notes, the Locarno melody played on among the great powers. Moreover, the small states were happier than in 1927, their mood of anxiety and scepticism having given way to hope. The signing of the Kellogg-Briand pact a few days before the Assembly opened was regarded as auspicious and the work of the CAS was welcomed as a job well done. But although the small states spoke of the eventual rather than the immediate realisation of the principles of the Protocol, they were not content to leave the arbitral principle alone. Compulsory arbitration was still high on their agenda and the subsequent emergence of the General Act bore witness to their determination to press ahead whenever they could.

The draft model treaties that had been produced by the Committee on Arbitration and Security were referred to the third committee and those relating to arbitration and conciliation were, in turn, sent to the first committee. In this last committee two views emerged. The first, put forward by Undén of Sweden, was that the multilateral treaties should be merged into a single convention, on the lines of the eventual General Act. This was in order to avoid possible difficulties if a dispute arose between two states, each of which had accepted different model treaties (the argument being that there would then be no contractual agreement to submit the dispute to pacific settlement). The second view, expressed by Tumedei of Italy, was that this 'would only raise . . . further difficulties and it was on the whole better to leave things where they were'.[109]

87–8; CAS, third session, 6–7; Politis to League of Nations, Records of the ninth ordinary session of the Assembly, plenary meetings, text of the debates, LNOJ, special supplement no. 64 (LNA9 debs.), eighteenth plenary, 25 Sept. 1928, 168.

[109] Roberts (assistant to the British delegate) to Kirkpatrick, 22 Sept. 1928, W 9183/28/98, DBFP v, 467. For the views of Undén and Tumedei see League of Nations, Minutes of the first committee (constitutional and legal questions), LNOJ, special supplement no. 65, 1928 (LNA9 first committee), fifth meeting, 27–8, 30.

No agreement was reached and, on Hurst's suggestion, the first committee representatives on the liaison sub-committee of the first and third committees were given the job of trying to solve the problem. Hurst was invited to join the sub-committee but 'thought it better not to do so as our point of view . . . had already been put . . . and it seemed better that new minds should be brought to bear' on the matter.[110] This was a mistake.

Just under a week later, on 20 September, the British were 'rather surprised' to learn from the official journal that the sub-committee was proposing:

> not only to throw the three model conventions into one but to merge them into a final act or instrument of some kind to which everyone would be at once invited to accede. We were still more surprised when Monsieur Politis, who had apparently joined the sub-committee, presented the results of their work. He explained that in place of a preamble the new instrument was preceded by a long draft resolution, that the system of signatures followed by ratifications had been replaced by that of accessions and that the document now put forward was not a model offered as a basis for negotiations, but was an instrument which it was hoped the Assembly might approve at its present session. In order to bring this instrument into force it would be sufficient for any two states to adopt any part of it. He went on to say that the adoption of this proposal would have the effect of inaugurating what he might call 'a juridical union of civilised states' analogous to the Universal Postal and Telegraphic Union.
>
> This sudden development came as a considerable shock to our own and the Dominion delegations and . . . an attempt was made to agree upon some common policy [at a BED meeting]. Hurst explained that our objections to the proposal were two-fold. Firstly, the model bilateral treaties seem to have disappeared altogether from view and the 'bilateralers' relegated, morally speaking, to an inferior position. Secondly, he was afraid that if such a general act were now approved and a considerable number of states failed to accede afterwards, the effect upon the prestige of the League would be most unfortunate . . .. both Gaus and Fromageot had admitted . . . in strict confidence, that neither of their Governments were likely to become parties to such an instrument but on general political grounds their delegations were not prepared to oppose the proposal.[111]

The third British objection, which Hurst did not mention to the BED, was that 'the idea of any open general treaty of this nature was distasteful to HMG who foresaw that they might be subject to constant pressure to accede to it'.[112] The Australians duly protested at what had been done as soon as the first committee met and the Indians later dissociated themselves from the final discussions on the General Act. But the Irish felt 'bound to vote for it' as they

---

[110] Ibid.

[111] Ibid. For Politis's report on the work of the liaison committee see *LNA9* first committee, ninth meeting, 58–65. Cf. Politis to *LNA8* third committee, fourth meeting, 30. The first committee members of the liaison sub-committee were Undén, Rolin and Gaus – the legal advisers of Sweden, Belgium and Germany. Politis was one of the third committee representatives on the liaison sub-committee. It was explained that the reason for using the word 'act' was because the instrument would become a convention only when states had adhered to it and, therefore, the latter term was 'inaccurate and premature'. The term 'act' 'involved no idea of special solemnity', explained Rolin, the rapporteur. 'It had seemed that this was the only suitable technical word apart from the word "model", which had been discarded as it might give rise to ambiguity': *LNA9* first committee, eleventh meeting, 70.

[112] Report by Cadogan on the ninth Assembly, 26 Nov. 1928, PRO, W 11286/8860/98 FO 411/8.

could see 'no substantial difference between the three model conventions and the general act'.[113] Since Britain had agreed in the CAS to a resolution recommending that all states should adopt the model treaties, Hurst 'found it very difficult to produce any convincing argument on the other side'.[114] But while he could not stop the General Act going through, he could make sure that British policy was not compromised.

At the first opportunity in the first committee Hurst protested at what the sub-committee had done. Politis had agreed with Cushendun in February that it was 'at present . . . absolutely impossible in practice to conclude a general arbitration treaty between all States and covering all disputes'.[115] Everybody was interested in arbitration, said Hurst, but there were two doors they could open, the bilateral and the multilateral doors, both of which 'led to the same point, namely, obligations to accept arbitration for the settlement of disputes'.

> That, he thought, was a fair statement of the position, which remained unchanged. The position had been defined with precision over and over again in the meetings of the Committee on Arbitration and Security . . . .. States were not all in the same position, and therefore it was necessary to allow for a passage by what he had described as the two doors. Whichever door was chosen, the result would be the same. One door must not be labelled: 'For the good boys', and another 'For the bad boys' . . . .. M. Politis had compared the new system to be created by the General Act with something similar to the Universal Postal Union, and had thus left out of account the other door through which equally good boys could walk, namely, bilateral treaties and special negotiation, which would lead to the same results.[116]

Since Ito of Japan had also protested and Italy was obviously not going to accept the General Act (although France had cast its lot with the small states in keeping with its attitude towards the Geneva Protocol), quick backtracking was in order. Politis urged that those who wished to travel down the arbitral path should be allowed to do so. There had, he insisted, been a misunderstanding. They had never intended to upset the system on which the CAS had settled. They did not want to show either a theoretical or political preference that might put moral pressure on those who could only accept bilateral conventions. The General Act would be completely voluntary and if Hurst wanted to suggest any amendments these would doubtless be readily accepted.

And so they were. Hurst's amendments giving an 'equal blessing' to bilateral treaties met with no objections and Politis bent over backwards to ensure that the British viewpoint was fully taken into account. Hurst insisted on checking the Assembly resolution on the General Act but he found nothing to fear and Politis made a point of assuaging any British apprehensions when he introduced the Act to the Assembly. On 26 September when the Assembly approved the General Act, Nansen expressed gratification that his proposal had led to an Act that would result in 'the same progress in respect of non-legal disputes . . . [as had] been made in respect of legal disputes by means of the optional clause'.[117] But, as in 1920, words were cheaper than action. The Act entered into force on

---

[113] See Roberts to Kirkpatrick, 22 Sept. 1928; *LNA9* first committee, eleventh meeting, 77.
[114] Roberts to Kirkpatrick, 22 Sept. 1928.
[115] Politis to CAS, second session, quoted by Hurst to *LNA9* first committee, tenth meeting, 67.
[116] *LNA9* first committee, tenth meeting, 67–8.
[117] *LNA9* debs., nineteenth plenary, 26 Sept. 1928, 180.

16 August 1929 after being ratified by Sweden and Belgium. When Henderson announced in 1930 that the British government was 'favourably disposed' towards its acceptance, only four states (Denmark, Norway, Sweden and Belgium) had accepted the whole of the Act and just two states (Finland and the Netherlands) had acceded to all but its provisions regarding the 'arbitration' of political disputes.

The remainder of this part of the tale may be quickly disposed of. The resolution on the Optional Clause that had been drafted by the CAS is discussed in the Commonwealth context as it was amended on the initiative of the Canadians,[118] and the end of the ninth Assembly brought the end of Genevan pressure on the Conservative government in respect of the Optional Clause. Its minimal effect on that policy was once more evident in the annual stocktaking in the Foreign Office.

There had been, in 1928, a 'growing violence of . . . criticism of every action of the British Government'.[119] But although it was generally agreed that there had to be better organisation in the making and execution of policy, only Hurst suggested taking the criticism seriously. The general view was that League criticism was par for the course. Britain was almost alone in trying to follow a policy that was in the best interests of the League. Signing the Optional Clause – or even the Geneva Protocol – would only briefly put paid to criticism. 'For all practical purposes', it was thought, 'resort to these expedients may be dismissed as unlikely to prove of any real or permanent value in enhancing our reputation at Geneva.'[120]

Hurst, on the other hand, argued that even if critics were out to say their worst about the government, they were still 'intelligent enough to choose for the purpose any joints in the armour which they think they can pierce'. There was little doubt that Britain gave foreign delegations the opportunity to accuse it of being obstructive and he, himself, 'put this down wholly to the manner in which we oppose proposals which we dislike'. Maybe, as Cadogan suggested, Britain gained popularity by saving others 'from their own folly'. But the same result could be achieved with greater profit. 'Not infrequently we can be induced to take the labouring oar in opposing a scheme which other delegations are anxious to see rejected' when a more delicate handling would lead to others incurring the odium of defeating a resolution. And even if Britain did have to make the running, 'the work of strangling a proposal could often be done more gently and more effectively'.[121]

In fact, at the ninth Assembly Hurst had, to Britain's advantage, followed his own advice. For although British policy on the Optional Clause and compulsory arbitration was undoubtedly unpopular, it did not figure prominently in the catalogue of criticisms of Britain's role at that Assembly. For this Hurst should be given a good deal of the credit.

[118] See below, 183–4.
[119] Britain was accused of being 'reactionary. . . obstructi[ve] . . . delaying disarmament, pandering to the French, engaging in plots and conspiracies against the peace of the world, and even preparing for a new war': editorial, 'Great Britain and the League', *The Times*, 27 Sept. 1928
[120] Memorandum by Selby, 21 Sept. 1928, PRO, W 10894/10894/98 FO 371/13402.
[121] Undated memorandum, ibid. The file also contains a memorandum in which Cadogan argued that Britain was gratefully relied on to 'see to it that . . . plausible and specious proposals are not put to the severe, and possibly inconvenient, test of experiment'.

Conclusion

'World opinion', as represented at Geneva, had no significant impact on Britain's Optional Clause policy. But it could not be ignored to the same extent as public opinion at home. In consequence, members of the government and their officials had to give the Optional Clause much closer attention than they would have wished, and eventually made one small concession. In itself, this was of no great moment. But it may have helped to prepare the mental ground for much larger concessions in response to more compelling pressures which were at the same time emerging from another quarter.

There were two related ways in which the Optional Clause and associated issues forced themselves on the attention of the government as the result of the activities of the League Assembly. In the first place, the matter was under frequent discussion at Geneva. As a leading member of the organisation, Britain could not avoid contributing to those debates, and knew that her contributions would be closely studied by other members and appear in the official records of the League. Such formal, international, pronouncements had to be presented with greater care than, say, a speech at a political gathering or even a contribution to a parliamentary debate. They would have to offer either a considered response to the initiatives of others or a careful reply to criticisms of British policy, or both. And at all times British spokesmen had to be constantly on guard lest they compromise Britain's overall policy on the Optional Clause or provide any levers for further pressure on Britain to change that policy. The League, it must be remembered, existed at a time when concern for consistency and legal niceties was particularly high in international relations. In consequence, much care and effort went into the formulation of statements to the Assembly of Britain's position on the Optional Clause. It is interesting, for example, to compare Cushendun's inept performances in the House of Lords in November 1927 and February 1928[122] with the carefully-prepared memorandum submitted to the League's Committee on Arbitration and Security and the statement that Cushendun delivered to that committee. It is thus wrong to regard Cushendun's statement to the Arbitration and Security Committee as 'little more than what by now had become constant British practice when cornered: a groan about the hideous complications caused for poor Britain by the empire about her neck'.[123] Cushendun was carefully putting the British position on record.

Then, secondly, the frequent debates at Geneva about the Optional Clause and compulsory arbitration meant that Britain felt obliged to work out the best possible grounds for her negative policy in these regards. These exercises did not lead to a questioning of the general policy which was being defended: that was not their purpose (although such questioning could, in principle, have resulted, and the two Cecils – Robert Cecil and Cecil Hurst – did in fact suggest that a fundamental re-examination should take place). The point in this connection is that it was in consequence of Britain's membership of the League that she looked closely from time to time at her overall policy towards the Optional Clause and how it could be justified. Had Britain not been exposed to debate at

[122] See above, 79-80.
[123] W. J. Hudson, *Australia and the League of Nations*, Sydney 1980, 120-1.

Geneva, avoidance of the Optional Clause could easily have been regarded as simply a 'good thing' for Britain, and almost as a reflection of her traditional posture. In the event Britain had positively to think about her policy, albeit on the basis of a negative premise.

As it happened, one small shift did emerge. For by the beginning of 1928 Britain had decided that she would not oppose the wish of the vociferous proponents of compulsory arbitration (in the widest sense) to travel down that path – provided that it was clear that Britain had no obligation of any kind to travel with them. As has been pointed out, the resultant General Act was irrelevant so far as the strengthening of the international juridical system was concerned,[124] and only one part (Chapter II) specifically provided for compulsory adjudication and compulsory arbitration. However, it was widely seen as linked to the Optional Clause and, in fact, almost all those states that eventually signed the Optional Clause also acceded to the General Act.[125] One is left to wonder whether any pressure to sign the Clause via, as it were, the Act, might have been brought to bear on Britain – and whether it would have been successful – had she not come to sign it by another route. As Britain was very much aware in connection with the debates on the Optional Clause at Geneva in the period 1925–8, the impact of a thin end of a wedge can be no less in international relations than in other walks of life.

In the event, however, the General Act did not serve as a wedge which prised open the way to Britain's signature of the Optional Clause. The League Assembly's activities kept the issue very much before both the Foreign Office and the Cabinet. But the issue which led to a number of officials and ministers changing their opinions and confirmed the views of those who had already done so, arose far from Geneva. The New World came in to strengthen, indirectly, the arguments of the Old, this being by way of the American offer to Britain of a new arbitration treaty. The issue which had loomed the largest in Britain's fears about the Optional Clause was the perceived non-arbitrability of disputes involving belligerent maritime rights. As a result of the American offer Britain was forced to think again about this matter – and one of the main obstacles on the path to signature of the Optional Clause proved to be not nearly so insuperable as had hitherto been imagined.

[124] J. Brierly, 'The General Act of Geneva', The British Year Book of International Law 1930, xi, London 1930; H. Lauterpacht, The function of law in the international community, Hamden, Conn. 1966 (first publ. 1933), 374–8.
[125] At its height, when over half the members of the League were bound by the General Act, only one such state, Turkey, was not also bound by the Optional Clause.

6

The United States and British policy

At the end of 1927 the American secretary of state, Frank Kellogg, gave Britain two unwelcome surprises. These were his proposals, firstly, for a new bilateral arbitration treaty and, secondly, for the multilateral arrangement which became known as the Kellogg pact (or the Kellogg–Briand pact, or the Pact of Peace). Both played a part in developing Britain's Optional Clause policy in that they helped to clear the path towards signature.

The relevance of the proposed arbitration treaty is that it forced the Conservative government to consider exactly and specifically whether certain interests were so vital that Britain could not, under any circumstances, submit them to arbitration or adjudication. Most important among these was the hitherto sacrosanct doctrine of 'high' belligerent maritime rights (BMR) – i.e. taking a wide interpretation of the rights granted under international law to a belligerent navy in wartime. This doctrine had thus far constituted a major, if not the major, obstacle to accepting the Optional Clause, and was also a serious bone of contention between Britain and America. As a result of the examination of this thorny question an important section of the Cabinet concluded that it was no longer necessary or worthwhile trying to maintain high BMR *vis-à-vis* the USA, and that a BMR reservation should not be attached to the proposed arbitration treaty. Although no decision was taken on this matter before the general election of 1929, the change of opinion which its discussion induced cleared the path to the Optional Clause. For the acceptance by some important Cabinet members that Britain could submit BMR disputes with America to arbitration meant that they could hardly object to lesser issues being submitted to this procedure. Moreover, the process of considering the arbitration treaty also revealed a considerable advantage possessed by the Optional Clause over an arbitration treaty: accepting the Optional Clause was a unilateral step which did not require the approval of other signatories, whereas arbitration treaties could involve long and tedious negotiations. It was partly on this ground that the subsequent Labour government preferred the Optional Clause to arbitration treaties.

The Kellogg pact was less important in the development of Britain's Optional Clause policy, but it is appropriate that it should be briefly discussed since it was seen as having implications for another vital interest which had earlier been held to constitute a barrier to accepting the Optional Clause, namely, Britain's position in Egypt.[1] Until this point the Conservatives would undoubtedly have regarded this whole matter as highly unsuitable for compulsory arbitration, both because of the perceived interests at stake and because Britain's legal position was dubious. The negotiations over the Kellogg pact led Britain to make a formal statement which was regarded as a sufficient safeguard not only for

[1] See above, 48.

Britain's freedom of action in Egypt but also in other areas in which it had a special interest. And although this was not unchallenged, it was on the books and available for future use. Thus, when the matter of the Optional Clause was reopened in the spring of 1929, a formula was on hand for protecting Britain's interests in Egypt, the Persian Gulf area and Afghanistan. This provided the basis for a reservation to be included in a possible British declaration accepting the Optional Clause and obviated the need for further lengthy heart-searching over this very sensitive issue.

The Kellogg pact also bears on Britain's Optional Clause policy in two other ways. Firstly, once Britain had signed the pact, it was easier for proponents of the Optional Clause to argue for the acceptance of the Clause: one step towards the pacific settlement of disputes should be followed by another. And, secondly, the pact contributed to the building up of an atmosphere of peace and optimism which was a propitious context for the signature of the Optional Clause.

The Kellogg pact

The Kellogg pact stemmed from a proposal made by the French foreign minister, Briand, in April 1927 on the tenth anniversary of America's entry into the First World War. Hoping to curry favour with the Americans and in emulation of American diplomatic style, Briand sent a message to 'the American people' suggesting a Franco-American agreement to 'outlaw war' between the two countries.[2] The unexpected popular success of the proposal on the other side of the Atlantic was such that in June Briand sent Kellogg the draft of a formal agreement. It was brief, having only two substantive articles. Firstly, America and France were to agree to 'condemn recourse to war and renounce it respectively as an instrument of policy towards one another'; secondly, whatever dispute might arise between them, its settlement was 'never to be sought by either side except by pacific means'. For the time being, the draft treaty lay shrouded in secrecy (it was not published until January 1928) while Kellogg decided what step to take. But the idea of a treaty renouncing war continued to attract considerable support within the United States. Two Columbia academics (one of them Shotwell who had been credited with inspiring Briand's offer) had produced their own treaty in May; and in December two leading senators who could not be ignored, William E. Borah of Idaho, the Republican chairman of the Senate foreign relations committee (who was also credited with inspiring Briand) and Arthur Capper of Kansas (who was also on the foreign relations committee), introduced to the Senate resolutions calling for the outlawing of war.

It would have been imprudent to ignore these indications of American opinion, especially with a presidential election year coming up. And so it came about that at the end of December 1927, out of the diplomatic blue and amidst the widest publicity, Secretary of State Kellogg sent a note to the French declaring that the American government accepted Briand's June treaty – on condition that it be thrown open for every other state to sign. At the same time

[2] On the origins of the proposal, see Robert H. Ferrell, *Peace in their time: the origins of the Kellogg-Briand pact*, New Haven, Conn. 1952, and James Shotwell, *War as an instrument of national policy and its renunciation in the Pact of Paris*, London 1929, 39ff. See also David Hunter Miller, *The Peace Pact of Paris: a study of the Briand–Kellogg treaty*, New York 1928.

he offered France a new arbitration treaty making it clear that, whether or not it was accepted by France, he intended to offer identical treaties to every other state which had an arbitral agreement with the USA. His hope was that these would 'ultimately be universally accepted and prove a real step in advance in the education of public opinion of the world for the promotion of peaceful settlement of disputes'.[3] In so doing, Kellogg envisaged the multilateral pact as establishing the general principle of renouncing war in international relations, and the arbitration treaties as the means of implementing that principle.

Kellogg's peace pact offer was a rude shock for Britain, which had had no inkling that he would act in this way. Numerous enquiries the previous summer had revealed only that Kellogg did not intend to make an agreement with France which he would not also make with Britain and Japan. At the time Chamberlain had commented that Briand 'did not always work out his suggestions beforehand in practical form and therefore . . . sometimes found that they led into unexpected difficulties'.[4] But he had certainly not expected Briand's attempt to gain diplomatic advantage to rebound on Britain. In Britain's eyes Kellogg's proposed multilateral pact was an ill-considered and dangerously ambiguous document which had been put forward to reap electoral dividends. 'I do not think that there is any reality behind Kellogg's move', Chamberlain told Esmé Howard, the British ambassador in Washington. 'Kellogg's main thought is . . . of the Republican Party. It is one more instance of the common practice of the State Department to use foreign politics as a pawn in the domestic game.'[5]

Howard's reports from Washington confirmed the view that Kellogg's thinking on the proposed peace pact was distinctly fuzzy. Just as President Wilson had a few years earlier tried to represent a legal commitment (Article 10 of the League Covenant) as if it were a moral commitment, so too did Kellogg try to represent his pact as if it were of a moral nature. His suggestion was, he said, 'really in the nature of a declaration against war which, though abstract, would have great moral value on public opinion in the countries that signed it and on public opinion generally'.[6] Howard thought that 'a declaration renouncing *all war* in the future on the part of any Government is really nothing but sheer hypocrisy and humbug because no Government can obviously consent to renounce the right to defend itself if attacked'. But when he tried to point out to Kellogg that 'it was impossible to be too clear in the wording of international Treaties', the secretary of state 'indignantly' said that of course states would retain the right of self-defence; it was '[q]uite unnecessary' to say so in the pact.[7]

None the less Howard urged the need to respond positively to the American proposal, which Kellogg was 'most anxious to get . . . through by hook or

---

[3] Telegram from Howard (British ambassador to Washington) to Chamberlain, 30 Dec. 1927, A 1/1/45, DBFP iv, 242.

[4] Telegram from Houghton (American ambassador to London) to Kellogg, personal and confidential, 6 July 1927, USNA, 711.4112/125.

[5] Chamberlain to Howard, private, 13 Feb. 1928, Chamberlain papers, FO 800/262, DBFP iv, 275. Kellogg initially sought to satisfy American public opinion and embarrass Briand, whose offer had caused him discomfort. But in February 'the American Secretary of State began to undergo a momentous change of heart: *he began to believe that a multilateral treaty really would be a great gift to the world*': Ferrell, Peace in their time, 164.

[6] Telegram from Howard to Chamberlain, 12 Jan. 1928, A 290/1/45, DBFP iv, 251.

[7] Howard to Chamberlain, private, 2 Feb. 1928, Chamberlain papers, FO 800/262, DBFP iv, 268.

crook'.[8] On the one hand it might be useful if its successful conclusion led America to adopt a more positive and concrete policy against war. On the other hand its rejection would not only be a misfortune in the year of a presidential election but it might also 'set back the tide' which was 'beginning again to flow fairly strongly in this country in favour of cooperation with the rest of the world'.[9] But it was one thing for Britain to sign a bilateral pact with the USA and another to sign a multilateral pact 'with Powers who do not have our standard and whose past does not encourage us to place unlimited faith in their loyalty to "a scrap of paper" ', said Chamberlain. 'I confess that I don't think the world will gain anything by merely helping Mr. Kellogg over his electoral fence.'[10]

Meanwhile, the French had also been dismayed at the multilateralisation of the peace pact, fearing that it would conflict with and inhibit the use of force to uphold the treaty of Versailles, the League Covenant and the Locarno treaties.[11] But since Kellogg vehemently refused to contemplate either a bilateral pact or to limit the condemnation to wars of 'aggression', the reluctant French agreed to a joint submission of their correspondence on the pact to the governments of Britain, Germany, Italy and Japan.

In April 1928 a new phase in the negotiations began when Kellogg circulated to the great powers a note which incorporated Briand's draft pact recast in multilateral form. The French responded by circulating a new, expanded draft which safeguarded France's existing rights to use force. Britain, believing that some of the French fears were reasonable, and wanting to maintain Franco-German détente by reassuring France of British support when appropriate, attempted to have the two drafts submitted to a committee of jurists but quickly dropped the idea when Kellogg expressed his displeasure. '[L]egal experts', he said, 'existed mainly to discover difficulties and not to smooth them out.'[12] Similarly, a proposal to have a conference of foreign ministers to discuss the pact foundered on Kellogg's rejection of it as 'useless and even harmful'.[13]

The adoption of Kellogg's draft rather than that of the French was ensured by the end of April. This was firstly because of a speech by Kellogg to the American International Law Association in which he answered European fears by offering a series of interpretations to demonstrate that the French desiderata could be satisfied within the framework of his own draft.[14] The second important factor was Germany's unconditional acceptance of Kellogg's proposal on 27 April.

[8] Howard to Chamberlain, 27 Jan. 1928, A 903/1/45, DBFP iv, 263.
[9] Howard to Chamberlain, 2 Mar. 1928, A 1774/1/45, DBFP iv, 293. An additional reason was that the Foreign Office was impressed by Cecil's ability to influence opinion in favour of the pact: McKercher, Second Baldwin government, 107.
[10] Chamberlain to Howard, 13 Feb. 1928, Chamberlain papers, FO 800/262, DBFP iv, 275.
[11] See Tyrrell (permanent under secretary of the Foreign Office) to Drummond, 8 Feb. 1928, A 995/154/45, DBFP iv, 270; memorandum by Hurst, 30 Jan. 1928, A 691/1/45, DBFP iv, 265; Claudel (French ambassador to Washington) to Kellogg, 21 Jan. 1928, 711.5112France/119, FRUS, 1928, i, 6ff.
[12] Telegram from Howard to Chamberlain, 3 May 1928, A 2979/1/45, DBFP v. 337. Cf. Paraphrase telegram from Houghton to Kellogg, 3 May 1928, 711.4112Anti-War/29, FRUS, 1928, i, 50.
[13] Telegram from Chamberlain to Howard, 3 May 1928, A 2978/1/45, DBFP v, 338.
[14] For Kellogg's 'interpretations' see Documents on international affairs, 1928, ed. John W. Wheeler-Bennett, London 1929, 3–5. See also paraphrase telegram from Houghton to Kellogg, 27 Apr. 1928, 711.4112Anti-War/17, FRUS, 1928, i, 40–1; paraphrase telegram from Kellogg to Houghton, 30 Apr. 1928, 711.4112Anti-War/19, FRUS, 1928 i, 41.

Germany had nothing to lose by this and American favour to gain, but it wrecked Anglo-French attempts at a joint European response and cut the ground from under the argument that the pact clashed with obligations under the Locarno treaties and the League Covenant, Germany being a signatory to both agreements.

By mid-May these developments, together with the evidence of strong public support for the pact and American pressure on Britain to fall into line, led the Cabinet to conclude that Britain, too, would have to accept Kellogg's draft pact. For present purposes it is only necessary to look at one of the problems facing Britain in accepting the Kellogg pact. This was its implications for Britain's special position in the Middle East, which Crowe had regarded as a major obstacle in the way of accepting compulsory arbitration and the Optional Clause.[15]

When Britain granted independence to Egypt in 1922 it had reserved certain questions to Britain's 'absolute discretion'. Among these was the 'defence of Egypt against all foreign aggression or interference, direct or indirect'. Foreign governments were notified of the limitations which Britain placed on Egypt's legal and political freedom. The termination of the British protectorate in Egypt did not, they were told, involve any 'change in the status quo as regards the position of other powers in Egypt itself'. What this meant was spelled out in a paragraph stating that the 'special relations' which existed between Britain and Egypt under the terms of the British declaration granting independence to Egypt were a vital interest, as had been 'long recognised by other Governments'. The British government would not brook any interference in the affairs of Egypt by any other power and would use 'all the means at their command' to repel aggression against Egypt.[16] This statement became known as the 'British Monroe Doctrine' because of its similarity to the American Monroe Doctrine in Central and Latin America.[17] The problem facing Britain was that although the phrase in the Kellogg pact renouncing 'war as an instrument of national policy' did not prohibit wars of self-defence, it did prohibit 'war made in pursuance of a policy announced to all the world that a state will reply to certain acts by a resort to war'. And Britain's intimation to other countries that it would not tolerate interference in Egypt 'was meant to indicate that in the last resort Great Britain would go to war against a Power which interfered with Egypt'.[18] This objection was equally valid in respect of America's Monroe Doctrine, but Kellogg did not want any reservations: he wanted his pact to be as simple and straightforward as possible in order to maximise its moral effect. Moreover Kellogg saw no point in contemplating circumstances where it might be necessary to use force and the State Department thought there was no likelihood of any state threatening either Britain's position in the Middle East or that of the United States in Latin America.

---

[15] See above, 48.

[16] The note, dated 15 Mar. 1922, is printed in HMSO, *Command paper* 1617 (1922). See also *DBFP*, i, appendex, paras 96-7.

[17] The Monroe Doctrine had been enunciated by President James Monroe in 1823 when he warned outside powers against interfering in the affairs of Central and Latin America. The term 'British Monroe Doctrine' was coined by Lord Lloyd, High Commissioner for Egypt and the Sudan 1925-9. See Chamberlain to Stamfordham (secretary to the king), 13 Nov. 1927, UBL, Chamberlain papers, AC 54/206.

[18] Memorandum by Hurst, 20 Apr. 1928, A 2542/1/45, *DBFP* v, 314, annex.

While it was comforting for Britain to know that Kellogg accepted that Britain was as entitled as the United States to have a Monroe Doctrine, it was not enough to rely on the opinion of an American secretary of state and run the risk of being legally hamstrung in using force to defend Britain's interests in the Middle East. As Chamberlain explained to the American ambassador:

> as between us and the United States I thought there was a complete understanding and I feared nothing; but this was a Pact to which an unknown number of nations were to be asked to adhere. Our obligations would be undertaken therefore not only towards the Government of the United States but towards other signatories; it was therefore necessary in our view that they should understand the treaty in the same sense as we and the Americans did and that our common interpretation should be authoritative if at any time the Hague Court [the PCA] or the Permanent Court of International Justice or any other arbitral tribunal had to pronounce upon our obligations . . .. If any doubt arose on the question of law the Council [of the League] would take the advice of the Permanent Court of International Justice and unless either the text of the treaty itself clearly embodied Mr. Kellogg's intentions or some other authoritative document could be pleaded, we might find ourselves condemned for exercising our right to take action in conditions where Mr. Kellogg had clearly intended to reserve that right alike to the United States and to us.[19]

If the United States refused to insert a reservation to protect its Monroe Doctrine, it would be hard for Britain to justify an attempt to introduce an amendment to safeguard the British Monroe Doctrine. But Hurst did not see how America could refuse such a reservation unless 'the treaty is intended to be a dead letter and . . . merely a vote catching expedient'.[20] Thus it was that the lengthy, carefully-reasoned reply which Britain sent to the United States on 19 May set out the former's understanding of the pact when read in conjunction with Kellogg's April 'interpretations' and included a paragraph covering the British Monroe Doctrine.

This paragraph, which became known as the 'British reservation', drew on the wording of the note which had been produced in 1922 stating Britain's special interests in Egypt. But the 'British reservation' was not geographically limited to Egypt. It was also intended to cover the Persian Gulf states and Afghanistan. Britain had not formally declared its position in the Persian Gulf and Afghanistan as it had in the case of Egypt, and there were good arguments for not doing so. On the one hand it might imperil the achievement of friendly relations with Afghanistan and Saudi Arabia and, on the other, it might offend Afghan susceptibilities and encourage the Afghans to think that they could count on British support against Russia under any circumstances. However, the immense strategic importance of Afghanistan and the Gulf to the British empire meant that they had to be included in any declaration of a British Monroe Doctrine. A declaration mentioning only Egypt might be interpreted as a signal that Britain was no longer vitally interested in the Gulf and, even though it could not be publicly stated, the CID held that Britain could never be

---

[19] Chamberlain to Howard, private and confidential, 25 May 1928, A 3599/1/45, DBFP v, 358 (summarised in B. J. C. McKercher, *The second Baldwin government and the United States, 1924–1929: attitudes and diplomacy*, Cambridge 1984, 116–18). See also paraphrase telegram from Houghton to Kellogg, 25 Feb. 1928, 711.4112Anti-War/98, *FRUS, 1928*, i, 73–4.
[20] Memorandum by Hurst, 20 Apr. 1928.

indifferent to any foreign interference in Afghanistan. Thus, although the 'British reservation' was generally taken as referring only to Egypt, it was cast in a form which had a wider scope in justifying the retention of the right to use force as a measure of self-defence in

> certain regions of the world the welfare and integrity of which constitute a special and vital interest for our peace and safety. His Majesty's Government have been at pains to make it clear in the past that interference with these regions cannot be suffered. Their protection against attack is to the British Empire a measure of self-defence. It must be clearly understood that His Majesty's Government . . . accept the new treaty upon the distinct understanding that it does not prejudice their freedom of action in this respect. The Government of the United States have comparable interests any disregard of which by a foreign Power they have declared that they would regard as an unfriendly act. His Majesty's Government believe, therefore, in defining their position they are expressing the intention and meaning of the United States Government.[21]

When the British note was received, the State Department told the press it would oppose any reference to 'special regions' being included in the pact but assumed that Britain would make a unilateral declaration on this point at the time of signature. In private, however, and to the disquiet of the Foreign Office, the Americans said that the only thing they found difficult to accept in the British note (which also dealt with other matters such as its obligations under the League Covenant and Locarno treaties) was the 'British reservation'. Kellogg did not see why Britain needed it and could not afford to run this minimal 'risk'; it had 'opened a veritable Pandora's box of difficulties' since other states might thereby be encouraged to develop their own Monroe Doctrines.[22] A suggestion by Hurst that the way out of making a reservation might be to place a broad interpretation on the proposed pact, whereby it would be seen as a guarantee of the *status quo*, was scotched by the belief that it would be unacceptable to Kellogg and because Japan decided not to reserve its special interests in Manchuria. Accordingly, the Foreign Office concluded that it would have to press for the inclusion of the British Monroe Doctrine in the pact. However, when Kellogg opened the next round in the negotiations on 23 June by circulating another letter (this time to fourteen governments so as to include all the Locarno powers and – at Britain's request – the dominions and India) it was obvious that America was clearly and firmly opposed to any reference to Britain's Monroe Doctrine being included in the pact. Kellogg now quoted the 'interpretations' he had made in April and resubmitted his almost unaltered pact with what was, in effect, a demand that it be accepted without qualification or hesitation. However, the absence of any reference to the 'British reservation' was seen as according with private assurances that Britain need feel no anxiety on the point; Kellogg recognised Britain's right to maintain such a policy and was content to let the British doctrine stand unchallenged. Hurst accordingly advised Chamberlain that Britain should protect its doctrine by making

[21] See telegram from Chamberlain to Howard, 16 May 1928, A 3340/1/45, *DBFP* v, 349; *Correspondence with the United States ambassador respecting the United States proposal for the renunciation of war* (United States, No. 1), (*Command paper* 3109), 1928, item 2.
[22] Paraphrase telegram from Houghton to Kellogg, 25 May 1928, 711.4112Anti-War/98, *FRUS*, 1928, i, 74. France had special interests in Siam, Italy in Albania and Japan in Manchuria.

a definite pronouncement on some appropriate occasion, such as ... the moment of signature of the Peace Pact .. ... No-one would be asked to accept this statement; they would be left to object to it if they thought it necessary to do so. No State is likely to do so, least of all the United States as they have their own Monroe Doctrine to consider.[23]

However, as Craigie, the head of the American and African department, pointed out, Kellogg had signalled that he wanted unconditional acceptance and a British declaration along the lines of Monroe's famous doctrine would be ill-received. Kellogg would not reserve the American Monroe Doctrine and a British declaration would place the American government in an embarrassing position with its public, probably creating difficulties with the Senate at a time when Anglo-American relations were poor. A declaration would also offend Egypt, which was undesirable since Britain wanted to support the 'moderate' Egyptian government that was in power. If a declaration omitted the Gulf states and Afghanistan, it 'would create the impression that we no longer claim any special interests in those countries'. But if they were included in a declaration 'the offence given would be out of all proportion to the advantage gained'.[24]

Although the Cabinet would not accept any limitation on Britain's right to exercise its Monroe Doctrine, it agreed not to force the issue of including it in the pact and it was also decided that Britain should not make any declaration when the pact was signed in Paris on 27 August 1928. Instead, in July when Britain agreed to the pact, it contented itself with repeating the understanding that it did not 'prejudice' Britain's freedom of action in 'certain regions'.[25] At the same time, Britain formally notified other governments of its doctrine by despatching to Geneva, for circulation to League members, copies of the two notes to America in which the doctrine had been postulated.

On the day that the pact was signed, Kellogg (whose ill-temper had been a feature of the negotiations) was all sweetness and light at a private meeting with Cushendun (who signed the pact for Britain and India). Kellogg thanked Britain for helping to promote the pact and spoke frankly of unofficial American criticisms of the 'British reservation'. He had, he said, responded by pointing out that no reservations were being made; that every nation had the right to defend itself and would be the 'laughing-stock of the world' if it did not; and that, of course, Britain, like America, had special interests (in respect of which he specifically mentioned Egypt but on which Cushendun deemed it wisest to say nothing).[26] Immediately after the Kellogg pact had been signed by the fourteen original signatories, it was opened for acceptance by other countries by means of a circular letter which Kellogg sent to forty-eight governments and an invitation which France extended to the Soviet Union (since the latter did not

[23] Memorandum on the 'Peace Pact', 29 June 1928, A 4479/1/45, *DBFP* v, enclosure in 403.
[24] Memorandum by Craigie (head of the American and African department), 'Draft treaty for the renunciation of war, with particular reference to the question of the "special regions" mentioned in paragraph 10 of the British note of May 19, 1928', 29 June 1928, A 4519/1/45, *DBFP* v, 404. See also McKercher, *Second Baldwin government*, 121.
[25] See *Further correspondence with the government of the United States respecting the United States' proposal for the renunciation of war* (United States No. 2), (*Command paper* 3153), 1928; Atherton (US chargé d'affaires in London) to Kellogg, 18 July 1928, 711.4112Anti-War/159, *FRUS, 1928*, i, 112–14.
[26] Memorandum by Cushendun, 27 Aug. 1928, A 6092/1/45, *DBFP* v, 451.

have diplomatic relations with the USA). By the end of the year forty-six countries had intimated either their adherence or their intention to adhere.

Predictably, the Soviet Union, Egypt and Persia made it clear that in adhering to the pact they did not accept any reservations to it. This was specifically aimed at Britain although, as has been shown, Britain had not actually made a reservation. But it was a way for these countries to state their position formally just as Britain had found a way of publicly declaring a vital interest in respect of which it would not renounce the use of force. There was a certain amount of embarrassment involved in this procedure in that it drew attention to the limitations which Britain placed on Egypt's freedom of action and, as Persia and the Soviet Union recognised, the limitations did not stop at Egypt. But on the other hand, this aspect of the British national interest had been implicitly sanctioned by the United States, which was the only country that could have effectively called it into question. And it was because of the United States that Britain was led to a public proclamation of its Monroe Doctrine at Geneva. If, therefore, the question of accepting the Optional Clause were reopened, Britain had a basis on which to draft a reservation regarding the Near East. Thus, the danger which Sir Eyre Crowe had foreseen in the Optional Clause had, to all intents and purposes, been removed. In this sense, Britain's path to the signature of the Optional Clause had been largely cleared of a substantial obstacle, for hitherto it had been assumed by Conservative governments, almost without question, that one of the reasons which made signature impossible was Britain's need to protect her interests in the Middle East.

The Anglo-American arbitration treaty and the problem of belligerent maritime rights

When Kellogg proposed multilateralising Briand's peace pact in December 1927, the identical arbitration treaties which he offered to conclude with Britain, France and other countries were, in effect, part of a package deal. As Kellogg saw it, the peace pact was going to establish the general principle of renouncing war and the arbitration treaties would be the means of implementing that principle. And so, on 29 December, Kellogg handed Esmé Howard a draft treaty which was, apart from a reference to the dominions, the same as the one he had handed the French ambassador the day before. Howard commended the treaty to Chamberlain, pointing out that Kellogg was consulting senate leaders to ensure Congressional approval (a fence at which previous arbitration treaties had fallen) and saying that he thought it represented a real attempt by the American government to make a definite move in the direction of world peace. He, himself, regarded it as a 'distinct advance' over the shortly-to-expire 1908 Root treaties[27] inasmuch as Kellogg had omitted the vital interests formula (because, said Kellogg, 'as a lawyer [h]e had never been able to understand the real value of these words').[28]

[27] Howard to Chamberlain, 30 Dec. 1927, A 154/154/45, DBFP iv, 244. The Franco-American treaty expired on 27 Feb. 1928, the Anglo-American treaty on 4 June 1928 and the Japanese-American treaty on 24 Aug. 1928. Since being signed in 1908, they had been renewed at five-yearly intervals: in 1913, 1918 and 1923.

[28] Telegram from Howard to Chamberlain, 30 Dec. 1927, A 1/1/45, DBFP iv, 242. Article 1 of the

The new arbitration treaty was an even more unwelcome surprise to London than the proposed peace pact both because of the manner of its presentation and because of the omission of the vital interests formula. In a long letter to Howard, Chamberlain complained bitterly of Kellogg's cavalier approach to diplomacy:

> I think we have real reason to complain . . . . [O]nce again . . . Kellogg flings a new proposal at our head without one word of preliminary discussion. Nay, it is worse than that; for he instructed [Ambassador] Houghton to enquire last Summer whether we should be prepared to renew the existing [arbitration] Treaty in its present form and to tell me that there was no question of any alteration or extension. If he changed his mind, were we not entitled to some friendly private warning? And would not good manners and good policy alike have indicated that before framing his text he should make some enquiry as to whether the words which suited him were equally suitable to the conditions of the British Empire?
> He takes the contrary course. He excepts every question which the United States were ever likely to have covered by the old formula of 'vital interests, honour and integrity'. He does not stop to consider whether his new phrase gives equal protection to the other party. You know our difficulties about going to arbitration on the exercise of our belligerent rights at sea before a tribunal which must necessarily be constituted of Powers who have never accepted the doctrines laid down by our Admiralty Courts . . . . Obviously, Kellogg has here raised a question of the greatest difficulty for us and one which is particularly embarrassing in the present state of our relations with the United States. And it is no consolation to me to think that he has done so in good faith as complete as his ignorance![29]

The difficulty facing Britain was, indeed, considerable. It was clear that Britain could not insert the vital interests formula into the new treaty. Not only had Kellogg made it clear that he would not have it but also, although the formula was included in all but one of Britain's arbitration treaties,[30] it had increasingly fallen into desuetude and disfavour since the war. Any attempt by Britain to include it would lay the country 'open to the criticism that we had

---

treaty of 1908 stated: 'Differences which may arise of a legal nature or relating to the interpretation of treaties existing between the two contracting parties and which it may not have been possible to settle by diplomacy shall be referred to the Permanent Court of Arbitration established at The Hague by the convention of the 29th July, 1899, provided, nevertheless, that they do not affect the vital interests, the independence, or the honour of the two contracting States, and do not concern the interests of third parties.' Article 3 of the new treaty stated: 'The provisions of this treaty shall not be invoked in respect of any dispute the subject matter of which – (a) Is within the domestic jurisdiction of the high contracting parties. (b) Involves the interests of third parties. (c) Depends upon or involves the maintenance of the traditional attitude of the United States concerning American questions, commonly described as the Monroe Doctrine.' In March 1928 Kellogg suggested amendments in order to emphasise the link between the arbitration treaty and the Bryan (conciliation) treaty of 1914. The Bryan treaty provided that after diplomatic methods had failed, all disputes, whatever their nature, and whose settlement was not provided for or achieved under existing arrangements, should be referred to a permanent conciliation commission. Hostilities should not begin and war should not be declared during the investigation or before the commission had reported.

[29] Chamberlain to Howard, private, 13 Feb. 1928, UBL, Chamberlain papers, AC 55/266; FO 800/262, *DBFP* iv, 275.

[30] Britain's only unlimited arbitration treaty – unlimited both as regards duration and scope – was the 1918 treaty with Uruguay (ratified in 1919). This was because of Britain's desire for greater Uruguayan support in the prosecution of the First World War and in order to obtain, for allied use, the German ships lying in Uruguayan ports.

made no advance in the last twenty years'.[31] This meant that Britain had either to reserve BMR specifically, or find another reservation which would serve the same purpose, or accept an arbitration treaty which would allow the arbitration of disputes arising out of the exercise of BMR. This presented a serious dilemma since the last course seemed unthinkable, the second course would be exceedingly difficult, and the first course could cancel out any potential benefits from the treaty and possibly worsen already poor relations with America. This was because it was thought that current difficulties were largely attributable to naval differences.

The naval problem in Anglo-American relations

When the twentieth century opened Britain's naval strength had been based on the 'two-power standard regardless of flag' (i.e. Britain's navy was to be as strong as the combined strengths of the next two most powerful navies in the world). By the outbreak of the 1914 war the standard had fallen to 'sixty-per-cent above Germany', and by the end of the war Britain had lost its naval supremacy. In 1920, therefore, the best the Admiralty could hope for was the 'one-power standard', that is a navy that was equivalent in strength to that of the United States. Meanwhile, in 1915, the General Board of the United States navy had recommended that American sea-power should be 'second to none'. That is, the American navy was to be at least equivalent in strength to that of the other single most powerful navy in the world – in other words the British navy. This, combined with America's determination that Britain should never again be able to subject it to blockade in war-time, led to a naval building race between Britain and the United States before the war was hardly over. It was a race which Britain did not welcome and could not afford. The Washington treaty of 1922, which marked Britain's formal renunciation of naval supremacy, was welcomed as offering a check on naval rivalry in capital ships and aircraft-carriers. However, the respite was only temporary and limited since it led to greater rivalry in the unrestricted classes of cruisers, destroyers and submarines at a time when the British navy was operating under severe financial restrictions. The burden of debt and economic weakness resulting from the loss of Britain's export trade had prompted Lloyd George to initiate the 'ten year rule' at the end of the war. That is, he told the service chiefs that they need not anticipate a major war occurring within the next ten years. When Churchill became Chancellor of the Exchequer in 1924 and was confronted by a gloomy financial outlook, he used the intimate knowledge he had gained as Asquith's First Lord of the Admiralty (from 1911 to 1915) to set about cutting naval expenditure. This immediately led to a clash with Bridgeman, the First Lord of the Admiralty, over the 1925–6 naval estimates, an experience Bridgeman described as 'two days of desperate fighting in the Cabinet'.[32] Each successive

---

[31] Cabinet memorandum by Chamberlain, 'The Franco-American draft pact of perpetual friendship and the American draft of an arbitration treaty to replace the Anglo-American arbitration treaty of 1908', confidential, 24 Jan. 1928, CP 22(28), DBFP iv. 262.

[32] Quoted in Stephen Roskill, Naval policy between the wars, i, New York 1968, 447. The only support Bridgeman received was from Amery, his predecessor at the Admiralty.

year saw a repetition of the struggle over the naval estimates and each year the service chiefs were told that they should continue to work on the expectation that they would not be involved in a serious conflict for another ten years. Eventually, in June 1928, the CID accepted Churchill's suggestion that the 'ten year rule' should stand unless a decision were taken to alter it. For the navy, the self-perpetuation of the 'ten year rule' meant that it was almost impossible for it to maintain its strength by modernising existing ships, let alone keep up with the United States in the competitive building of new ones.

In the summer of 1927 Britain accepted President Coolidge's invitation to a naval limitation conference to be held in Geneva in the hope of finding some way out of the naval race and arriving at a workable *modus vivendi*. Unfortunately, not only were the conference preparations poor, but the fact that the British and American navies relied on cruisers that fell into different categories offered ample scope for disagreement. The conference quickly broke down over the issue of parity[33] and this caused Chamberlain more concern than anything he had so far had to deal with as foreign secretary.[34] Already-poor relations were worsened. Kellogg 'became petulant and niggling',[35] and the Foreign Office was seriously alarmed at the propaganda mileage that the American 'Big Navy League' (the epithet given to protagonists of a big US navy) was getting out of the breakdown of the conference. It was being cited as yet another example of Britain's untrustworthiness and of the way in which Britain had repeatedly let down the United States.[36] The fact that Robert Cecil resigned from the government as a direct result of the failure of the conference apparently gave added credence to the arguments of the Big Navy League.[37]

As the Foreign Office pondered the lessons of the Coolidge conference, it seemed more and more evident that the differences over cruisers were only the *apparent* reason for its collapse. Instead, the fundamental problem was identified as the question of belligerent maritime rights (BMR). The essence of this was

[33] Britain's navy was made up of 5,000-ton cruisers (which had 6-inch guns) because Britain could not afford 10,000-ton cruisers and because it needed a large fleet to protect its widespread and vulnerable lines of imperial communication. The United States navy was based on the longer-ranging 10,000-ton cruisers (which had 8-inch guns) because it had fewer fuelling bases and because it had its eyes on the Pacific Ocean. In terms of total tonnage, Britain had the larger navy. However, the United States had the advantage that their '8-inch' cruisers could sink '6-inch' cruisers before the latter were within firing distance of the larger ships. The American cruisers built after the Washington treaty of 1922 were also technically superior to, and markedly more successful than, the British *Kent* and *London* cruiser classes of 1924–6 which were poorly protected and had high silhouettes. For these reasons the British rejected the American proposal that discussions should be based on tonnage. Britain argued that arms limitation should centre upon finding some mutually acceptable ratio or equation. On the cruiser question and the Coolidge conference see McKercher, *Second Baldwin government*, 55–76; Dick Richardson, *The evolution of British disarmament policy in the 1920s*, London 1989, 119–39; and David Carlton, 'Great Britain and the Coolidge naval conference of 1927', *Political Science Quarterly* lxxxiii (1968).
[34] Chamberlain to Howard, private and personal, 10 Aug. 1927, Chamberlain papers, FO 800/261, *DBFP* iii, 503.
[35] McKercher, *Second Baldwin government*, 80.
[36] See, for example, Cabinet memorandum by Thompson (clerk in the American and African department), 'The future of Anglo-American relations', 17 Nov. 1927, A 6768/133/45, *DBFP* iv, 227. See also McKercher, *Second Baldwin government*, 84–5.
[37] See above, 66; 'Memorandum by Mr. Craigie respecting the effect on public opinion in the United States of Lord Cecil's resignation from the government', 11 Oct. 1927, A 6019/93/45, *DBFP* iv, 212; McKercher, *Second Baldwin government*, 79–80, 85–6.

that America had made it quite clear that the United States would never again tolerate the restrictions which had been imposed by the British blockade during the First World War, and it was therefore building a navy strong enough to break any blockade in any future war. The validity of this argument was seen in the serious debate about the possibility of Britain and America being drawn into war with one another as a result of the latter's determination to uphold its interpretation of its rights as a neutral during war.

Britain's naval policy in the First World War had been based on 'high' BMR. That is, Britain took a wide interpretation of the measures which a belligerent was allowed to take under the rules of international law. Practically every neutral state, including the USA, took a 'low' interpretation of BMR. That is they held that international law only allowed a much more restricted range of measures than those taken by Britain. The law in this respect was in fact uncertain. The principal agreements governing BMR up to the war – the Declaration of Paris of 1856 and the Declaration of London of 1909 – had not withstood the impact of technological advances in naval warfare, and each belligerent had acted in ways which were contrary to their provisions. After the First World War broke out, Britain and the United States had reached deadlock over the interpretation of BMR and the work of the blockade department of the British embassy in Washington was to 'keep the United States quiet and . . . secure her grumbling acquiescence to the blockade'.[38] Of course, things changed in April 1917 when Germany's resort to unrestricted submarine warfare brought the United States into the war against the central powers. But it was clear that America was determined never again to tolerate interference with its interpretation of its rights as a neutral. Hence the naval race with Britain.

In the autumn of 1927 the British embassy in Washington was urging the importance of settling Britain's outstanding differences with America over BMR, saying that otherwise there would be dire consequences. For example, a letter from the British military attaché in Washington (which was strongly endorsed by Howard and officials at the Foreign Office) held that:

> The American doctrine of 'freedom of the seas' and the British practice of blockade are irreconcilable. It is therefore misleading to speak of war between Great Britain and the United States as 'unthinkable'. If we adhere to our historic policy of blockade, when we are a belligerent and the United States is a neutral, we will be confronted by a choice of one of two evils, either a war with the United States in which, as we cannot develop our full strength we will be beaten, or the maintenance of peace with the United States at the price of national humiliation. This dilemma can be avoided only by discarding in advance, when we are still at peace, such portions of our blockade policy (and this may mean the whole of it) as may be necessary to conform to the American doctrine of 'freedom of the seas'. The fact that the British blockade of Germany was one of the main factors in obtaining victory for the Allies in the late war is irrelevant if in a future war (and it is the future, not the past, we now have to consider) it is going to lead to our defeat at the hands of America. Blockade is a weapon of war itself unsatisfactory in modern conditions, so we will not lose much if we abandon it. If we are not willing to do this to ensure peace with the United States, it is fatuous not to prepare seriously for the eventuality of war with that Power.[39]

[38] Lord Percy of Newcastle, *Some memories*, London 1958, 48–9.
[39] Colonel Pope-Hennessy to General Charles (War Office), 10 Oct. 1927, enclosure in Howard to Tyrrell, 12 Oct. 1927, A 6213/133/45, DBFP iv, 214.

The problem was rendered urgent by the distinct possibility that the United States would call an international conference for the recodification of maritime law during war. Howard argued that Britain should come to an arrangement with America before a conference were held. Otherwise they would run into the same difficulties as they had at the Coolidge naval conference – 'only the results will be infinitely worse as regards Anglo-American relations'.[40] If a conference actually did produce an agreement on BMR, it was thought inevitable that these would be set at a low level. As Vansittart (head of the American and African department until February 1928) put it: 'At an International Conference we should be squeezed and get little for it. Previous agreement with the United States will make it harder for the others to stand out; and the United States themselves will be easier to deal with à deux.'[41]

Hurst thought the American department was exaggerating the problem: not only had the Americans admitted in practice that Britain's exercise of BMR in the war had been perfectly legal, but it was both undesirable and unnecessary to come to an agreement on the matter.[42] Chamberlain, however, shared the view that an agreement was desirable and in December 1927 he obtained Cabinet approval for the setting up of a CID sub-committee (under Lord Salisbury's chairmanship) to consider fully the whole subject of BMR.[43]

At the outset, all the members of the sub-committee apart from Cushendun agreed that Britain could neither compromise on BMR nor allow any dispute arising out of the exercise of BMR to be taken to arbitration. However, over the fifteen months that the sub-committee sat, the majority of its members came to share the Foreign Office view that not only could Britain compromise on BMR, but it could also agree to arbitrate disputes arising out of the exercise of BMR. The reason for this change was due to its detailed consideration of the draft

---

[40] Ibid.

[41] Memorandum, 19 Oct. 1927, A 6057/133/45, DBFP iv, 216.

[42] It was undesirable because if Britain maintained its naval superiority, an agreement would hinder the exercise of blockade in a future war. On the other hand, if Britain lost its naval superiority an agreement would prevent Britain protecting its shipping during a conflict. It was unnecessary because of the existence of the League of Nations. The United States was the only important naval power outside the League and, if collective security were applied and all League members co-operated loyally, the only neutral American trade which could give rise to a dispute would be direct American seaborne trade with the Covenant-breaker. However, not only were the rules of international law adequate and well-established in this respect, but disputes arising out of the exercise of BMR during the Great War had concerned neutral trade with the enemy via the *territory* of neutral states – a problem which would not arise if the League continued to grow in strength: 'Memorandum by Sir C. Hurst on Sir Maurice Hankey's paper on "blockade and the laws of war" ', 10 Nov. 1927, annex II to Chamberlain memorandum, 14 November 1927, CP 286(27), A 6673/133/45, DBFP iv, 224.

[43] For the establishment of the sub-committee and its terms of reference see McKercher, *Second Baldwin government*, 92–102. The sub-committee was composed of Salisbury (Lord Privy Seal, in the chair), Chamberlain, Balfour (Lord President of the Council), Bridgeman (First Lord of the Admiralty), Sir Philip Cunliffe-Lister (President of the Board of Trade), Viscount Peel (First Commissioner of Works), Cushendun (Chancellor of the Duchy of Lancaster) and Sir Douglas Hogg (attorney general who became Lord Chancellor on 28 Mar. 1928 and took the name Hailsham). The expert assessors were Admiral of the Fleet, Sir Charles Madden (First Sea Lord and chief of the naval staff), Hurst and Hankey. The following changes were made while the sub-committee was sitting: Amery (colonial and dominions secretary) was added on 17 Oct. 1928; Tyrrell was added to the expert assessors and replaced on 26 July 1928 by Ronald Lindsay; and Sir Maurice Gwyer (procurator-general and Treasury solicitor) was added to the expert assessors on 19 Jan. 1928.

arbitration treaty which Kellogg had offered Britain at the end of 1927 and which was referred to the sub-committee in October 1928 after the Foreign Office had failed to find any satisfactory way of reserving BMR from the scope of the proposed treaty.

The British response to the proposed Anglo-American arbitration treaty

There were three aspects of Kellogg's draft arbitration treaty which commanded British attention. Two of these concerned points which could easily be reserved. The third aspect, the problem of safeguarding BMR was, as has been shown, of the greatest difficulty. It led to lengthy deliberations and the absence of a positive reply to the United States, for it was impossible to devise a formula which would safeguard BMR and be acceptable to the United States, and it was also impossible to get Cabinet agreement on dropping the BMR reservation. However, these discussions were important in preparing the path towards the Optional Clause because leading policy-makers changed their views on BMR and on how to ameliorate Anglo-American relations. Although the context in which arbitration was discussed at this time was limited, it was important in the development of Conservative opinion on arbitration in general, resulting in a less unfavourable attitude to the Optional Clause.

The first aspect of Kellogg's arbitration treaty was the one-sided advantage it gave America in providing that the senate should approve the *compromis* for every arbitration. This could easily be rectified by an amendment providing that the *compromis* should also meet with 'the approval of the Parliament or Parliaments of such parts of [H]is [Majesty's] dominions as may be concerned'.[44]

The second aspect which concerned Britain was the reference to the Monroe Doctrine, which safeguarded the United States *vis-à-vis* Central and Latin America but not Britain *vis-à-vis* the Middle East. The Kellogg pact negotiations showed that America would not challenge Britain's right to assert its own Monroe Doctrine. Accordingly, Britain could negotiate for the explicit American Monroe Doctrine reservation to be replaced by an alternative clause referring to 'the policy proclaimed in the past by either of the High Contracting Parties in relation to particular areas wherein such party possesses special interests which it is bound to uphold in the interests of its security'.[45]

The third aspect of the draft treaty, that of finding a way of excluding BMR from its scope in the absence of the vital interests formula, defied the ingenuity of the British legal advisers. What was needed was somehow to devise a reservation which would (a) safeguard BMR, (b) get through the American senate, and (c) be acceptable to the American government. Yet it was clear that

---

[44] The original draft article had been amended in accordance with the decision of the 1926 imperial conference that each dominion should separately sign and ratify treaties: Chamberlain to Balfour, private and confidential, 10 May 1929, UBL, Chamberlain papers, AC 55/24; 'Revised draft treaty of arbitration with the United States', 4 Apr. 1928, A 2358/154/45, DBFP iv, 341.

[45] Article 2(c) of the amended British draft treaty. First report of the sub-committee of the Committee of Imperial Defence, 'The renewal of arbitration treaties', 13 Feb. 1929, CP 40(29), DBFP vi, appendix II (CID:BR first report). See also Chamberlain memorandum for the Cabinet, 24 Jan. 1928, CP 22(28), DBFP iv, 262.

Kellogg would not accept any substantive amendments to the 'model' treaty which he was then negotiating with several countries and which was so intimately linked in his mind's eye with the Peace Pact.

After two-and-a-half months had gone by, Chamberlain told Kellogg in March 1928 that his government was 'very carefully considering' the draft arbitration treaty and was in touch with the dominions on the matter. A reply would be sent as soon as possible.[46] A month-and-a-half later, in April, Chamberlain told Houghton, the American ambassador, that the draft treaty did not altogether 'meet the necessities and obligations of the British Empire' in respect of Egypt. However, 'considerable progress' had been made before Easter. Chamberlain had circulated his 'first thoughts' to the Cabinet and the dominions but so far only one dominion had replied. In view of the 'convenience' of the dominions likewise expressing their 'first impressions' and because of the long distances involved, Chamberlain thought they might have to extend the existing treaty (which was due to expire on 4 June) for a short period 'in order to give us sufficient time to reach agreement'.[47] At the beginning of May Howard formally proposed an eight-month extension but also intimated that he expected to be able to make some suggestions on the new treaty within a few days. It was not, however, constitutionally possible for the United States to extend the treaty without submitting it as a formal agreement for the approval of senate, and Kellogg told the British that he did not think it 'would make much difference whether the Root Treaty was extended or not';[48] they could perfectly well get along without a treaty for a few months. May passed and the treaty expired in June without Britain making any proposals because it could not safeguard BMR in a way that would be acceptable to the Americans.

Chamberlain had not been disingenuous in April in telling the Americans that progress had been made. It was thought that Malkin had found a solution: a reservation limiting arbitration to disputes which were susceptible to a decision on the basis of a *recognised rule of international law* and that each *compromis* would prescribe the rule of law that the tribunal was to apply. Thus, if a dispute involving the exercise of BMR were to arise, Britain would argue that there was no general agreement on this body of law and that the dispute could not, therefore, be submitted to arbitration. Malkin, himself, did not think much of his suggestion, which he said he had written 'to ease my conscience'.[49] But it had the merits of being in line with a suggestion by the South African prime minister and of being consistent with Britain's past practice.

The suggestion had been taken up and a draft treaty was submitted for Cabinet approval, only to be withdrawn after Hurst pointed out that the proposed line of argument could be used to undermine the finality of decision which Britain had claimed for its prize courts during the war. It was, he pointed out, 'impossible to claim finality for the national prize court decisions on the ground that the decision of the court is based on international law, and at the same time to

[46] Telegram from Chamberlain to Howard, 13 Mar. 1928, *DBFP* iv, 308. On 8 Feb. the Cabinet decided to consult the dominions but it was a month before a despatch was sent. See also confidential note by Kellogg of a conversation with Howard, 3 Mar. 1928, USNA, 711.4112A/13.
[47] Chamberlain to Howard, 26 Apr. 1928, A 2845/1/45, *DBFP* v, 325. See also telegram from Houghton to Kellogg, 27 Apr. 1928, 711.4112Anti-War/17, *FRUS, 1928*, i, 39–40.
[48] Kellogg to Houghton, confidential, 22 May 1928, 711.4112A/24, *FRUS, 1928*, ii. 947.
[49] Malkin to Hurst (Geneva), 7 Mar. 1928, A 2100/154/45, *DBFP* iv, 299.

refuse international arbitration on the ground that there is no international law for an international tribunal to apply'.[50] Hurst and Malkin both thought an arbitration treaty with the USA would be little more than a 'gesture in favour of the principle of arbitration' because the senate would 'prevent the arbitration of any dispute which is inconvenient for the United States'.[51] But they recognised the political urgency of making a treaty. If none were made Britain would stick out like a sore thumb from other states. The American elections that autumn meant that it would be difficult to negotiate fruitfully with the United States between the summer of 1928 and the inauguration of the new president the following March, and it was also thought that Coolidge would be easier to deal with than his probable successor, Hoover.

The summer came and went without any progress. Anglo-American relations deteriorated in the wake of the Anglo-French naval agreement,[52] and the successful conclusion of the Kellogg pact in August did nothing to disperse the growing cloud of hostility and suspicion. Hurst was now suggesting that Britain should seriously consider whether there was any acceptable alternative to an arbitration treaty with the USA. In April Hurst had suggested that the Optional Clause might provide a way out of the dilemma. If Britain accepted the Optional Clause (and did not proceed with the proposed US treaty) there would be no problem about reserving BMR as this was exactly 'what Geneva is expecting if Great Britain signs the optional clause. Though the objections to such a course are many', he continued, 'it is difficult to escape the feeling that they may be less than those attendant upon the conclusion of a treaty with the United States in the wording now proposed.'[53]

In October America again pressed Britain for a reply on the proposed arbitration treaty and was again told that the delay was due to the tardiness of the dominions. Hurst now came up with another idea: to treat the Kellogg pact as a living reality which had opened 'a new chapter in international relations'. Britain could argue that this meant that in the future it would only be involved in war in self-defence or in pursuance of its obligations under the League Covenant and the Locarno treaties. In that event Britain could, he thought, justifiably argue that all disputes arising out of belligerent action were political rather than legal. He therefore recommended an arbitration treaty under which legal disputes would go to the PCA or PCIJ and political disputes would be sent to conciliation commissions (with the proviso that, in accordance with Article 15 of the Covenant, parties could appeal to the League Council against the recommendation of a conciliation commission). A further provision would make it clear that disputes arising out of collective security measures were political, not legal. (The British Monroe Doctrine would also be reserved.) Hurst's scheme

[50] Memorandum by Hurst, 5 Oct. 1928, annex to PRO, CP 303(28), CAB 24/198; *DBFP* v, 479. The CID sub-committee that examined the renewal of the arbitration treaties held that Hurst's argument was not conclusive: 'For our Prize Courts administer what we claim to be international law. If we decline an arbitration on the ground that some other countries do not recognise the same rule of law as ourselves it does not appear to us to forfeit our claim that the rules on which our Prize Courts work are correct': CID:BR first report.

[51] Memorandum by Hurst, 'The draft Anglo-American arbitration treaty', 25 Apr. 1928, A 2800/154/45, *DBFP* v, 324.

[52] See Roskill, *Naval policy*, i. 544–9; idem, *Hankey, man of secrets*, ii. London 1972, 476–9; McKercher, *Second Baldwin government*, 140–58; Richardson, *Disarmament policy*, 177–87.

[53] Hurst memorandum, 25 Apr. 1928, A 2800/154/45.

would, in his own words, 'not juridically add anything to ... [British] commitments', but it would safeguard BMR from arbitration. His French and German counterparts had intimated their governments' willingness to go along with this line, but in putting this proposal to the USA it would be necessary to be careful.[54]

This was the best that anyone had been able to come up with and, in October 1928, Cushendun (who was standing in for Chamberlain during the latter's illness) took Hurst's suggestion to the Cabinet which decided to refer the Anglo-American arbitration treaty (together with several other arbitration treaties that were under consideration)[55] to the CID sub-committee which had been set up at Chamberlain's behest in December 1927 to examine the general question of BMR.

As autumn turned into winter, there was no sign of any improvement in relations and Cushendun tried to impress on the Cabinet that something had to be done urgently. Believing that the majority of his Cabinet colleagues were so preoccupied with departmental business that they had 'little comprehension of the serious consequences which might follow a false step on our part at the present juncture',[56] he circulated a lengthy memorandum by Craigie. This pointed out the advantages of friendly relations with the United States, the need for collaboration on important problems and suggested that it was in Britain's 'ultimate interest to approach the settlement of outstanding Anglo-American differences in a spirit, not of jealous bargaining, but of broad conciliation'.[57] It was swiftly followed by a rejoinder from Churchill[58] and, when Chamberlain returned to work on 27 November, Cushendun advised him that 'there were pretty sharp divisions of opinion' on '[b]y far the most important matter you will have to deal with'.[59] It is unnecessary to outline in detail the debate that continued for the next two months.[60] The reports of the CID sub-committee clearly reveal both why there was a division of opinion and why the majority of the sub-committee's members decided that it was necessary to bow to the necessity of

54 Hurst memorandum, 5 Oct. 1928, annex to CP 303(28).

55 Namely, the Anglo-French treaty (due to expire in Oct. 1928), the Anglo-Italian and Anglo-Spanish treaties (due to expire in Feb. 1929), and a proposed arbitration treaty with Germany: Cabinet meeting, 17 Oct. 1928, PRO, CAB 47(28), W 10033/9560/98 FO 371/13402.

56 Cushendun to Chamberlain, 22 Nov. 1928, UBL, Chamberlain papers, AC 55/127.

57 If this were not recognised, Britain and America alone would have no arbitration treaty 'at a time when the air is full of the word "arbitration" ... .. Such impotence in negotiation could only be justified by the frank admission either that relations are already so strained that no further negotiations on these points are possible or that a progressive deterioration in those relations is inevitable and has been discounted in advance': 'Outstanding problems affecting Anglo-American relations', 12 Nov. 1928, annex to note by Lord Cushendun, confidential, 14 Nov. 1928, CP 344(28), DBFP v, 490.

58 Churchill opposed any attempt to abandon BMR or cut down the British navy down by agreement with 'a New England backwoodsman' (Coolidge). Such a move was unnecessary, impossible and it 'would divide the Conservative Party from end to end on the eve of the Election. There would be a stand-up fight in all the Constituencies' and this would 'destroy us as a political force': 'Anglo-American relations', 19 Nov. 1928, secret, CP 358(28), DBFP v, 497. See also Cushendun's counter-memorandum, 'Anglo-American relations', 24 Nov. 1928, CP 364(28), DBFP v, 500.

59 Cushendun to Chamberlain, 22 Nov. 1928, UBL, Chamberlain papers, AC 55/127.

60 This is fully discussed in McKercher, Second Baldwin government, 177ff.

conceding, in a limited context, the possibility of arbitrating disputes involving BMR.

The reports of the sub-committee of the Committee of Imperial Defence on belligerent maritime rights and Anglo-American relations

The sub-committee of the CID produced two reports: one on the Anglo-American arbitration treaty in February 1929 and one on BMR in March. Of these only the first report – on the Anglo-American arbitration treaty – need be dealt with at any length. But, to put this matter in context, the second report – on BMR (which as it happens was never discussed by the Cabinet) – must first be briefly discussed.[61]

The sub-committee report on BMR dealt with the discussions that had been held regarding the level of BMR which Britain should claim in a future war or in possible peace-time discussions regarding the matter. Apart from Cushendun, who had from the beginning recommended abandoning high BMR,[62] the sub-committee unanimously recommended that 'policy should be based on the assumption that belligerent rights must be maintained as high as possible'. This was because by abandoning high BMR 'we should throw away one of our most potent weapons' for achieving the object of war – namely bringing pressure to bear upon an enemy.[63] However, the phrase 'as high *as possible*' (emphasis added) reveals a crucial problem: how far was it going to be practical to claim high BMR, given American opposition to this stance? Here the members of the sub-committee differed. On the one hand there was what might be called the 'Foreign Office lobby', which thought that political wisdom dictated a

[61] See ibid. 132–9, 159ff. for a full discussion of the second report of the sub-committee of the CID on belligerent rights, 'Maritime belligerent rights', 6 Mar. 1929, BR 82 (General 91/5), *DBFP* vi, appendix III (CID:BR second report).

[62] Ibid. When he first went to Geneva, Cushendun maintained that 'what the Admiralty said was good enough for him' but, '[a]s time went and he heard the other side, he became a severe critic of the more extreme pretensions of some of the Service departments': Major-General A. C. Temperley, *The whispering gallery of Europe*, London 1938, 80. He began to catch what Bridgeman called 'the Geneva microbe' (Bridgeman to Baldwin, 23 Dec. 1928, Baldwin papers, vol. 63, quoted in Richardson, *Disarmament policy*, 187) as early as Nov. 1927 when he confided to Chamberlain that he thought Britain should abandon or modify its traditional policy on blockade. But he didn't know what, if anything, he should do: 'I don't want to signalise my entrance to the Cabinet by propounding an idea which all my colleagues might think preposterous, and earn for myself at once the reputation in the Cabinet of being a "crank", a "little-Englander" & God knows what rot more', he explained: Cushendun to Chamberlain, private and confidential, 4 Nov. 1927, UBL, Chamberlain papers, 54/387. 'Les grands esprits se rencontrent!' replied Chamberlain who also disagreed on specific points. 'My mind was working on the same lines while I was out at Geneva and there I spoke to the Prime Minister on the subject. When I came home I found that independently of me and of each other the Office here and Esmé Howard in Washington had raised the same question. So there are four of us at least who, quite independently, have drawn the same conclusions from recent events': Chamberlain to Cushendun, confidential, 7 Nov. 1927, PRO, Chamberlain papers, FO 800/288. Hankey had been 'horrified' when, at the first meeting of the CID sub-committee, Cushendun, who arrived first, had told him of his views. 'I took him up', he wrote in his diary, 'and we had a furious argument which lasted until the Ctee [sic] had assembled. Why are these supposed "Die-hards" with their big chins and obstinate faces such funks when it comes to the point? He reminded me of Carson in the war – always pessimistic': Diary entry, 11 Jan. 1928, CCAC, Hankey papers, 1/8.

[63] CID:BR second report. The definition was provided by Lord Stowell (1745–1836) a judge of the High Court of Admiralty from 1798 to 1828.

compromise with the United States. On the other hand there was what might be called the 'Admiralty lobby' which insisted on complete freedom of action for the British navy. The latter was a powerful group and had the Cabinet secretary machinating vigorously on its behalf behind the scenes.[64] So much importance did the Admiralty attach to this question that any other viewpoint was regarded as almost treasonable, and, since its negotiating style was heavy-handed and intransigent, there was scarcely scope for compromise within the sub-committee. Personal antipathy between Bridgeman and Chamberlain widened the breach between the two sides.

The sub-committee report on the proposed Anglo-American arbitration treaty also revealed sharp differences between the Admiralty and Foreign Office 'lobbies'. Here the issue was immediate: in the current discussions with the United States on the treaty should the issue of BMR (irrespective of the height of BMR which might be claimed in a conference or a conflict) be reserved? The 'Foreign Office lobby' came to the conclusion that BMR should not be reserved, to which the Admiralty took very strong exception. The inevitable outcome was a split report on the arbitration treaty. But, even so, it marked a step forward because, in the limited matter of the arbitrability of BMR, the majority (Salisbury, Hailsham and Cunliffe-Lister [the President of the Board of Trade] together with Chamberlain and Cushendun) supported the Foreign Office line.[65] While this was admittedly a very limited context in which to allow the arbitration of disputes involving BMR, it had important implications. For the consideration of the Anglo-American arbitration treaty had, like the Kellogg pact, focused attention on the determination of which specific interests were, from the Conservative point of view, absolutely vital. BMR had hitherto been sacrosanct and had loomed large in objections both to compulsory arbitration and to arguments for the necessity of including the vital interests formula in arbitration treaties. Yet leading Conservatives now concluded that there were circumstances in which Britain could forego a reservation of BMR. And having gone that far towards compulsory arbitration, they were unconsciously moving

---

[64] Baldwin rejected Hankey's threat to resign over BMR as an improper conception of the role of a civil servant, just as he had rejected Hankey's presumption in suggesting that he should be made a member of the BMR sub-committee rather than an expert assessor like the other civil servants. However, Hankey played an important role in the sub-committee and in December 1927, being 'very disturbed' by a conversation with Tyrrell, Hankey had determined to 'start my own propaganda': Hankey diary, 12 Dec. 1927, CCAC, Hankey papers, 1/8. This included lengthy correspondence with Balfour who was too unwell to attend the sub-committee meetings, attempting to nobble Tyrrell – despite Hankey's claim, repeated by Roskill, there is no evidence that this was successful – and protesting about Chamberlain's 'extraordinarily irregular procedure' in Cabinet: See Roskill, *Hankey*, ii. 452–4; PRO, CAB 63/40; BM, Balfour papers, Add. MSS 49704, 49705, 49709; McKercher, *Second Baldwin government*, 180–1.

[65] The minority (Bridgeman, Amery and Peel) supported Balfour's proposal that BMR should be reserved from the treaty 'until such time as agreement has been reached as to what those rights are': CID:BR first report. (Balfour had excused himself from signing the report because he had been absent from most of the meetings.) However, at the beginning of February, 'with the exception of Willie [Bridgeman] who looked very unhappy, we were all rather persuaded' by Hailsham that it would be better to sign the treaty without reservation and then try to codify BMR: Amery diary entry, 1 Feb. 1929, *The Leo Amery diaries*, I: *1869–1929*, ed. John Barnes and David Nicholson, London 1980, 585. But, with Hankey's assistance, conviction swiftly evaporated after the meeting and the minority view was accordingly included in the report: Amery diary entries 1, 4 Feb. ibid; and McKercher, *Second Baldwin government*, 190–1.

towards accepting the possibility of adhering to the Optional Clause. Although the legal adviser had pointed out as early as 1924 that Britain could reserve BMR from the scope of the Optional Clause, it was none the less the case that BMR had continued to loom large in Conservative objections to the Clause. Now, however, they were in a position to appreciate that the Optional Clause could be accepted in such a way as not to jeopardise interests which were considered vital – and, further, that those interests could be protected in a much less controversial way than would be involved in the negotiation of a bilateral arbitration treaty.

The starting-point of the sub-committee's report on the proposed arbitration treaty was the question whether there was any point in concluding such a treaty with the United States. Balfour and Bridgeman held that there was none because of the problem of reserving BMR, and suggested that the Kellogg pact should be used to justify this stance. The rest of the sub-committee rejected this both because Kellogg saw the arbitration treaties he was negotiating as complementary to his Peace pact and because, if the pact meant anything, it pointed to the necessity of developing the machinery for the peaceful settlement of disputes. An arbitration treaty might, they thought, improve Anglo-American relations, whereas the failure to make a treaty would probably worsen them, for it would play into the hands of the American Big Navy League which could then argue that Britain was stepping backwards whilst the rest of the world stepped forwards. At the same time, the failure to conclude a treaty could make for domestic problems because of the steady pressure from the government's critics who kept asking questions about its policy on 'all-in' arbitration treaties and the Optional Clause. The sub-committee as a whole accordingly came down in favour of an arbitration treaty with the United States. It was agreed on reserving the British 'Monroe Doctrine' and requiring parliamentary approval before every arbitration. But it split over the question whether there should be any reservation regarding BMR. Hurst's October 1928 suggestion of capitalising on the Kellogg pact to justify drawing a distinction between legal and political disputes (so that the exercise of BMR should fall into the latter category) was rejected because it was thought unwise to attempt to define vital interests. This was because no-one could foresee what vital interests might arise in the future as a result of technological advances and changing circumstances and because, ingenious as was the argument which Hurst suggested to justify drawing the distinction, it was thought that such an amendment would be unacceptable to the United States. Several sub-committee members thought it would make it more difficult for Britain to avert or refuse to attend an international conference on belligerent rights at sea. Britain was therefore left with '[a]t best . . . a choice of evils': a straightforward reservation of BMR or no such reservation at all.

The majority – Salisbury (the chairman), Chamberlain, Hailsham, Cunliffe-Lister and Cushendun – reluctantly concluded that the former course held greater risks. A BMR reservation would be unacceptable to the USA and, by preventing the successful conclusion of a treaty, would wreck 'the whole structure of a new departure in cordial relations' with that country. It would lead American public opinion to determine never again to allow Britain to exercise high BMR and would also probably lead to America convening a conference on the subject. Britain would have to attend such a conference where it was expected that pressure from other states would be bound to result in BMR being set at a lower level than Britain could expect from an arbitration based on America's naval instructions in the Great War.[66] 'We have', said the majority, 'not so much to fear from arbitration upon the uncertain law as it stands as from being faced with the amended law which American public opinion would demand at the Conference.'[67]

Moreover, given that Britain's prize courts had purported to administer international law, an unwillingness to settle differences involving BMR through an impartial tribunal would 'be represented as equivalent to an announcement to the world that we do not intend to be bound by International Law, but only by the standard of our own necessities'[68] – a charge which had often been levelled against Britain in the past. Yet, as Hurst pointed out, the legality of Britain's exercise of BMR would always be controlled by prize courts, which could invalidate any action that they determined to be inconsistent with international law:

> One has only to remember a case like the 'Zamora' in 1916 (where the Privy Council held to be invalid a measure which His Majesty's Government had taken for the purpose of requisitioning neutral property and thereby increasing the economic pressure on the enemy) to see that such restrictions as the naval authorities suffered from during the late war were not at all due to international engagements, whether ratified or unratified, by which His Majesty's Government had bound themselves in time of peace. People are apt to forget today the extent to which all through the late war the enemy played into our hands by the successive blunders which he committed at sea, thereby enabling His Majesty's Government to introduce all manner of novel measures under the guise of retaliation which no British prize court would have tolerated if the enemy had not made these mistakes.[69]

There was no inevitability about an arbitral award being adverse to Britain, and the 'mere presence' of the British member on a tribunal would be 'no inconsiderable guarantee of an equitable decision'. And in any case, even when Britain was not a party to an arbitration involving BMR, an arbitral decision would weigh with Britain since '[t]he point of view of the world opinion which would accept [the awards] . . . and the attitude of neutrals generally must react upon any inclination of ours to exercise Belligerent Rights in defiance of those decisions even though we may not have recognised their validity'.[70]

The majority also saw some positive arguments in favour of accepting the arbitrability of BMR. They held that the omission of a reservation of BMR would enable 'the signature of the Treaty [which] would produce great advantages not only in the sphere of general policy, but even in respect of Belligerent Rights themselves'. It would deprive the Big Navy League of its oft-used argument that a big navy was needed to prevent Britain from interfering with neutral trade during a war and this would help to ease the naval race. It would, in Chamberlain's view, enable the President to resist Senate pressure for

---

[66] A technical committee, chaired by Hurst, had revealed that British and American instructions during the war had only differed on one major point: See CID:BR second report.
[67] CID:BR first report.
[68] Ibid.
[69] 'Memorandum by Sir Cecil Hurst on Sir Maurice Hankey's paper on "blockade and the laws of war"', 10 Nov. 1927, DBFP iv, 224, annex.
[70] CID:BR first report.

a conference on BMR. Even if a conference on BMR were held, Britain could argue that it had already demonstrated its amenability and could refuse to attend it unless the subject matter were restricted to codifying or harmonising existing practice:

> In fact, our situation would be so strong that not only could we resist anything below the level of the American Instructions, but even in the solution at the Conference of the ambiguous points that lie between ourselves and the United States we ought to do very well.[71]

In the event of a war, the omission of the BMR reservation would help an American president to adopt the posture of a 'friendly neutral' since he could always point out to a restive public that arbitration lay in the background.[72] And since arbitration would be a leisurely process, there would be no risk of precipitate presidential action.

Finally, the majority of the sub-committee saw no practical benefit from trying to maintain high BMR against the United States, since this would only end in humiliation or war. It might, however, be possible to get a relatively good deal from America there and then. The Foreign Office did not believe that there were any differences of principle barring the way to an agreement, and while that might be difficult to achieve, it was thought that agreement was possible and that it might enable Britain to continue to maintain a relatively high level of BMR. In any case, as American sea power continued to grow it was probable that that country would become an advocate of high BMR. Meanwhile, as British naval power declined *vis-à-vis* the United States, it was probable that Britain would want the arbitration of disputes arising out of the exercise of BMR by the United States. To reserve BMR would therefore deprive Britain of a means of limiting America's claim to exercise a wide measure of freedom of the seas.

The minority of the sub-committee comprised the trio of Bridgeman (First Lord of the Admiralty), Amery (secretary of state for the dominions and First Lord of the Admiralty in the previous Baldwin administration) and Peel (First Commissioner of Works). They did not advocate an out and out reservation of BMR, only that disputes arising out of the exercise of BMR should be reserved 'pending agreement as to what those rights are'.[73] This should be accompanied by a proposal indicating Britain's willingness to begin discussion of the subject at an early date. In suggesting this they warned that the 'advantages to be gained' from the course proposed by the majority were 'so small and problematic and the risks so serious that no Government ought to accept them except in circumstances of great danger which certainly are not at present visible'. For while the risk of a big American navy was 'not very alarming', the loss of high BMR certainly was alarming.[74]

In the view of the minority it would, firstly, be a policy of weakness to allow the arbitration of questions involving BMR. They were 'profoundly sceptical' as

---

[71] CID:BR second report.

[72] On the other hand, the Admiralty held that in any case America would be, if not an ally, then a 'friendly neutral' or at least a 'long-suffering neutral'.

[73] CID:BR first report.

[74] Memorandum by Bridgeman, 'Arbitration treaty with the USA', 11 Feb. 1929, PRO, CP 35(29) CAB 24/201.

to the likelihood of its improving Anglo-American relations for they could see no evidence of a conciliatory attitude on the part of America. For example, within a few days of ratifying the Kellogg pact, the senate had passed a bill for building fifteen cruisers in three years. And whereas Britain, unlike France (which had no scruples about criticising distasteful suggestions), had constantly appeased America since the war, it was Britain not France which was constantly being attacked in congress. Secondly, the minority thought that omitting a BMR reservation would not avert a conference on the subject: 'The Americans will be just as aware as we are ourselves that the concession is made to *force majeure*, and it will not render them less anxious to compel further concessions' – it might even make them more anxious to call a conference and clear up the law. It was necessary to face the regrettable fact that a conference on BMR was likely, that Britain would have to attend it, and that it would not be possible to restrict the scope of discussions. If the results of the conference were acceptable to Britain and the USA, then Britain could drop the BMR reservation. But Britain should, in the meantime, maintain it on the reasonable ground of wanting to wait until the law on belligerent rights had been cleared away by the conference. In this way Britain would retain a larger measure of initiative in dealing with the question and, if the Senate would not accept the treaty 'because of the temporary reservation, the onus of having caused a breakdown would clearly rest with them'.

The third argument used by the minority was that if Britain 'gave way' to America, it might be unable to refuse other countries' requests for similar treaties based on the American model. Denmark and Holland, that had both offered to conclude 'all-in' arbitration treaties with Britain, were states which had been neutral during the war and had objected to British naval operations. Had such 'all-in' arbitration treaties then been in existence they would have 'proved an immeasurable handicap' and arbitrations under such treaties 'will handicap us in future wars, since they will be binding for all time and in all wars'.

The fourth objection saw the non-reservation of BMR as the beginning of the downhill trip for Britain,

> the beginning of concessions, which will afterwards make it difficult for any Government to stand firm. In time these rights will be whittled away, not only in arbitrations to which we are a party, but in arbitrations arising out of wars in which we are not engaged, the decisions of which will become established precedents.[75]

And the 'whittling away' process would not stop there for it would apparently also lead downhill towards the Optional Clause. While admitting that the United States would not be a party to any proceedings before the PCIJ, they pointed out that nearly every other power would turn to the PCIJ for a judgment. Having listed the nationalities of the judges, they immediately asked whether 'a Court so constituted would endorse a high level of maritime rights?' – a question which went unanswered as if it were self-evident that it would not. Moreover, they drew upon Malkin's 1924 memorandum on the Optional Clause to point out that 'a Court composed of international lawyers' would tend 'to

[75] CID:BR first report.

apply the rules which they will find in text-books'.[76] And then, as if the Optional Clause did not allow reservations, they held that it was 'too great a risk' to entrust the future employment of BMR 'to the decisions of some such tribunal' to which 'any nation, however small, will be able to bring us to arbitration'.[77]

Their final objection was the weightiest at that time and was the reason why no decision was taken on the arbitration treaty before the 1929 general election. A failure to safeguard BMR would 'split the Conservative Party from top to bottom'[78] and the timing was inopportune: 'the last few months of a Government's term of office is an extraordinarily bad time for announcing a great concession to a foreign State'.[79]

The avoidance of a decision on the arbitration treaty

Anglo-American relations were still in a worryingly poor state when the sub-committee of the CID completed its work and presented its two reports – on the Anglo-American arbitration treaty in February and BMR in March. Relations were better than they had been in the second half of 1928 but the Big Navy League was still strong and was on the lookout for any opportunity to justify expanding the American navy by representing British behaviour as hostile. The 'fifteen-cruiser bill', which had encountered stiff opposition in February 1928, was due to come up again at the beginning of 1929. And towards the end of December 1928 Howard had reported that Senator Borah, the chairman of the Senate foreign relations committee, was going to reintroduce his resolution calling for a conference on BMR as an amendment to the bill.[80] This was almost certainly assured of passage since it now had the approval of Senator Hale from Maine, the chairman of the naval affairs committee. Howard himself continued to favour a settlement over BMR or freedom of the seas as a means of depriving the campaign for a larger American navy of its *raison d'être*. And he did not see the cruiser bill as something to be deplored since he thought its failure would lead to 'a campaign of still greater violence and calumny against Great Britain'.[81] All the conversations he had had with American leaders indicated that they wished to eliminate naval competition and establish a sound relationship with Britain on the basis of 'enlightened self-interest'. Just as the CID sub-committee was compiling its report on the Anglo-American treaty,

[76] See above, 26.
[77] CID:BR first report.
[78] Memorandum by Bridgeman, 'Arbitration treaty with the USA'.
[79] CID:BR first report.
[80] In Feb. 1928 Borah had introduced a resolution into the Senate as an amendment to the naval construction bill. This called on the president to summon a conference for the codification of wartime maritime law. Although the committee on naval affairs did not accept Borah's amendment, it had been allowed to stand over to the next session.
[81] Howard to Chamberlain, private and confidential, 25 Jan. 1929, PRO, Chamberlain papers, FO 800/263; *DBFP* vi, 354. The Congressional debate on the 'fifteen-cruiser bill' showed very hostile attitudes to Britain and there was a frequent refrain that the United States needed a fleet large enough to protect its commerce. (The only navy strong enough to be a threat was the British navy.) Howard feared that unless the situation as regards naval construction improved before 1931 (when the Washington treaty came up for revision), the 'Big Navy Party' might obtain an invincible hold on Congress through its insinuations and propaganda.

news arrived that the cruiser bill had been passed. The Borah amendment had been replaced, however, by one (proposed by Senator Reed of Missouri) which did not make it mandatory on the president to summon a BMR conference. But the likelihood of it being held remained on the cards since Howard reported that Hoover was personally anxious to settle the question and would take it up at an early date.

Chamberlain was perplexed about American policy and did not seem to be getting far in limiting naval competition or persuading America to stay its hand in calling a conference on BMR. But he and his Foreign Office advisers had come to the conclusion that the key to improving Anglo-American relations did not lie in settling differences over BMR but in concluding an arbitration treaty which did not reserve BMR. This was explained by Chamberlain to Howard at the beginning of February:

> Ever since my return to work [on 27 November] I have been busily engaged . . . on the consideration of the differences which have arisen between us and America and in search of a solution for them. These difficulties are three in number: naval strengths, the new Arbitration Treaty and belligerent rights; and we have moved for long in a vicious circle which we have not hitherto been able to break. Belligerent rights are the factor which is common to all three questions; and at one time, in agreement with the Office I had come to the conclusion that it was at this point that we must attack our problem. But, no sooner had we reached this conclusion, first formed in the Office and later somewhat reluctantly adopted by me, than both the Office and I began to doubt the wisdom of it; and I have now come definitely to the conclusion that we should approach the problem of American relations through the Arbitration Treaty . . . . What worries me in the conduct of foreign affairs . . . is when I myself do not know what I want . . . when I have not got a policy. This has been my position ever since the breakdown of the Geneva [Coolidge] Conference [of 1927] and it has caused me more anxiety than anything else in our foreign relations. Now at last I see light. Whether I can carry the Cabinet or not I do not know, for the decision at which I have arrived is one which I should have regarded as quite out of the picture when, with my colleagues, I set out on this enquiry . . . .. The conclusion . . . I have . . . reached . . . is that amongst the risks which in any case we run there is less risk in accepting arbitration on any dispute arising out of our exercise of belligerent rights than in maintaining the attitude which all governments in this country have previously adopted that this was a subject upon which we could not accept any reference to arbitration.
>
> You will realise that this conclusion came as a shock to me, as it did to those other colleagues who, having taken part in our prolonged discussions, finally came to the same view. It will be an even greater shock to members of the Cabinet who have not trodden the same weary road and, though I think that the Lord Chancellor's agreement [i.e. Lord Hailsham who had independently reached the same conclusion] will carry great weight with them, I cannot at present foretell what the decision of the Cabinet may be.[82]

---

[82] Chamberlain to Howard, strictly personal and confidential, 5 Feb. 1929, UBL, Chamberlain papers, AC 55/282; A 2116/12/45, *DBFP* vi, 359. On 25 Jan. Malkin had written a memorandum in which he, too, had at last cleared his own ideas 'on the subject of the "vicious circle" '. The term 'vicious circle' was, he thought, misleading since it suggested that all three of the matters Chamberlain mentioned in his letter had to be settled. Malkin thought it was only essential to settle one of them immediately. Naval limitation could be postponed until 1931 when the Washington treaty was due for discussion. With regard to BMR he thought that even if a treaty could be agreed 'the result in our relations with America would not be good'. It would not eliminate the risk of

Having thus made up his own mind, Chamberlain was anxious to get his policy through the Cabinet. The sub-committee's report on the proposed arbitration treaty was submitted as an urgent matter directly to the Cabinet rather than to the CID and discussed on 15 February, two days after it had been completed. Chamberlain was forced to recognise that it would not be easy to get a decision from the British and dominion governments. But he pleaded that delay would be dangerous. It would, perhaps, only be possible to postpone the matter without injury if the government had a definite policy and could indicate to the Americans that it meant business. However, the cabinet supporters of the 'Admiralty line' (Balfour, Bridgeman, Amery and Churchill) had submitted memoranda as ballast for the minority's case, and insisted that 'contentious questions ought not to be taken up at the very end of the life of a Parliament and . . . ought to be deferred for a few months'.[83] '[I]f it were known that we had cast our belligerent rights upon the waters', said Bridgeman, 'there would be a split in the Conservative Party from top to bottom'.[84] The discussion was inconclusive and was 'eventually adjourned in order to allow the other members to take part at a later meeting'.[85]

In March Chamberlain was forced to accept a ten-day delay because of Churchill's absence and he had no choice other than to accept Baldwin's decision that the matter could not be considered before Easter because of the absence of the prime minister, himself, and Bridgeman. However, Baldwin did not keep it a secret from Hankey that he wanted to delay discussion for as long as possible and the most likely reason is that he did not want the differences over the treaty to split the Cabinet on the eve of the general election.

In April Chamberlain was still trying to impress on the Cabinet his 'greatest anxiety' over Anglo-American relations and warning them of 'impatience' in Britain, 'nervousness' in the dominions, 'the constant liability of new and disturbing rumours in the US', and that the Foreign Office was 'left in a position of difficulty and even of some peril'.[86] But he knew he could get no large policy decisions and not only was there no decision on the arbitration treaty before the election but the CID sub-committee's report on BMR was not even discussed.

In the event Britain never did have to thrash out the problem of BMR and the arbitration treaty. The general election of 1929 led to the downfall of the

---

serious difficulties arising if Britain were a belligerent and its negotiation would raise severe difficulties on both sides of the Atlantic. Accordingly, it was arbitration that had to be settled and in order to get an arbitration treaty Britain would have to run the risk of not reserving BMR. The clinching factor was that 'what we have to fear is not the possibility of having to arbitrate the question, but either a declaration of war or the stoppage of supplies by the United States. The existence of an arbitration treaty covering such disputes could not increase this risk, and might diminish it': A 708/302/45, DBFP vi, 353. This no doubt explains why Hankey records in his diary on 7 Dec. 1928 that 'Austen Chamberlain suddenly came out [in Cabinet] in favour of Freedom of the Seas.' On 26 Jan. 1929 he found Chamberlain 'sounder than before on Belligerent Rights': CCAC, Hankey papers, 1/8.

83 Cabinet meeting, 15 Feb. 1929, PRO, Cabinet 7(29) CAB 23/60. See also Amery diary entry for 15 Feb. 1929, Leo Amery diaries, 586–7.

84 Memorandum by Bridgeman, 'Arbitration treaty with the USA'.

85 PRO, Cabinet 7(29) CAB 23/60.

86 Cabinet meeting, 11 Apr. 1929, PRO, Cabinet 16(29) CAB 23/60. Chamberlain did, however, get agreement that during their discussions on naval limitation Cushendun and Craigie could show America that Britain meant business.

Conservative government and its replacement in June by a Labour government under Ramsay MacDonald. Both MacDonald and President Hoover were personally interested in naval disarmament and when MacDonald visited Hoover in the autumn of 1929 it was thought best not to risk overcongesting the agenda or hindering discussions by raising the contentious issue of BMR, although it did crop up. However, by the autumn of 1930 the American government no longer wanted to discuss BMR, let alone have a conference on the question: its navy department had realised that it was not in America's interests to whittle down BMR. Meanwhile, although the American embassy intimated from time to time that it would like a reply on the proposed arbitration treaty, the new secretary of state, Stimson, did not share his predecessor's preoccupation with constructing a network of arbitration treaties.

The Labour government followed its predecessor in using the problem of dominion consultation as an excuse for doing nothing about the proposed Anglo-American treaty. However, in 1930 it was necessary to think about it because of the imperial conference that year. The foreign secretary, Arthur Henderson, thought it best to ignore the proposed treaty unless the Americans made a definite move – in which case one suggestion was that Britain should recommend that the US accept the Optional Clause! Since this was hardly practical politics, Henderson advised that if Britain had to conclude a treaty it should not reserve either the British Monroe Doctrine or BMR.[87] The Admiralty and Hankey were up in arms at the thought of 'voluntarily surrendering one of our greatest weapons in time of war and one of the great safeguards against another Power declaring war against us'.[88] But, interestingly, none of the members of the Cabinet committee that considered the question – not even the First Lord of the Admiralty – supported the Admiralty's contentions. However no firm decision was taken as it was decided that Britain should, if necessary, press for a wider agreement on the pacific settlement of disputes. And at the subsequent imperial conference, the proposed arbitration treaty was discussed at a private meeting in Downing Street, a meeting for which no papers were circulated and of which no records were kept.

[87] This was because an attempt to reserve BMR would lead to a discussion of the question and thence to a 'revival of . . . agitation in the US' which would destroy considerably improved relations. If the omission of a BMR reservation provoked debate in Britain it would be less harmful than one on the other side of the Atlantic. Moreover, events such as the London naval treaty of 1930 and the changing American attitude to BMR had 'somewhat diminished the weight to be attached to the arguments of the minority' of the CID sub-committee on BMR: 'Memorandum by the Foreign Office on the views set out by the First Lord of the Admiralty regarding the problem of the reservation of belligerent rights in connection with the conclusion of an arbitration treaty with the United States', 14 Oct. 1930, PRO, CP 342(30) CAB 24/215; memorandum by Arthur Henderson (foreign secretary), Aug. 1930, 'US proposals for an arbitration treaty to replace the Root-Bryce treaty of 1908', E(b)(30)9, CP 335(30) CAB 24/215. See also Henderson to Hankey, secret, 28 Oct. 1930, Henderson papers, FO 800/282.

[88] Britain should use every means to dissuade the United States from pressing the proposed arbitration treaty but, if 'relentlessly pressed', Britain should reserve BMR even at the risk of a BMR conference being called: memorandum by the naval staff, 8 Oct. 1930, attached to note by Alexander (First Lord of the Admiralty): 'United States arbitration treaty. Admiralty views as to reservation of belligerent rights', PRO, CP 331(30) CAB 24/215; Hankey to Henderson, secret, 21 Oct. 1930, Henderson papers, FO 800/282; Minute by Hankey for MacDonald, secret, 10 Oct. 1930, PREM 1/99. The justification for omitting a BMR reservation to the Optional Clause did not apply in this case since, in practice, the Optional Clause had only been accepted *vis-à-vis* members of the League.

As it happened, the United States did not press and the whole question vanished from sight without an arbitration treaty ever being concluded. A few years later, in 1938, the problem of BMR again came to the fore with the approach of the Second World War. Difficulties were perceived because there was no BMR reservation in Britain's acceptance of the Optional Clause. This was due to expire in February 1940. Urgent discussions both in Cabinet and in a special Cabinet committee resulted in a note being sent to the secretary-general of the League of Nations when war broke out. It denounced Britain's obligations under both the Optional Clause and the General Act (which had been accepted in May 1931) on the grounds that 'the Covenant has, in the present instance, completely broken down in practice, that the whole machinery for the preservation of peace has collapsed, and that the conditions under which His Majesty's Government accepted the Optional Clause no longer exists'.[89] In the event the renunciation of these obligations caused no problems. BMR was just not the issue in the Second World War that it had been in the First World War, and President Roosevelt was a more than friendly neutral prior to America's entry into the war in 1941.

Postscript: the impact of Britain's acceptance of the Optional Clause on its policy towards arbitration treaties

The inter-relationship between Britain's policies towards the Optional Clause and arbitration treaties is underlined by the way in which the acceptance of the former led to the downgrading of the latter. In September 1929 Britain signed the Optional Clause with reservations. In November, after examining Britain's arbitration policy, Malkin (who was now senior legal adviser) advised the foreign secretary that there was no point in negotiating arbitration treaties with co-signatories of the Optional Clause since any such treaty would be subject to the same reservations as Britain had attached to its declaration accepting the Clause. With regard to non-signatories of the Optional Clause it was preferable that they should be persuaded to accept the wider obligation of the Optional Clause, for 'one of our principal motives in signing the Optional Clause was to induce other states to follow our lead, and thus extend as far as possible the operation of arbitral machinery for the settlement of justiciable disputes'. If any state would not accept the Clause, it was better to have an arbitration treaty than nothing at all. But Malkin did not expect Britain to renew its existing arbitration treaties 'since they all, with one exception, contain the old exclusion of vital interests, etc'.[90] which was frowned on by the Labour administration. Additional reasons for extending the system of the Optional Clause at the expense of arbitration treaties was the desirability of increasing the jurisdiction and prestige of the PCIJ; the fact that states could make reservations to the Clause without the bother of the negotiations involved in reaching an arbitration agreement; and that it would be easier in this way to maintain

---

[89] Letter sent to the secretary-general of the League, 7 Sept. 1939, PRO, W 12888/107/98 FO 371/24014.
[90] Note by Malkin on 'Bilateral arbitration treaties', 1 Nov. 1929, PRO, W 11454/6685/98 FO 371/14134.

identical Commonwealth commitments.[91] Cecil, who had been brought back to the Foreign Office to advise on League policy, agreed with Malkin:

> The weight of argument seems to me on the side of relying on the Optional Clause alone & not concluding any more bilateral treaties for justiciable disputes only – apart from exceptional cases like the U. S. A. What we want is not so much arbitration with this or that country but a system of arbitration as the alternative to the international expedients which have hitherto existed.[92]

And Dalton, Henderson's second-in-command at the Foreign Office, agreed with Cecil. The five countries which had approached Britain for 'all-in' arbitration treaties – Denmark, Norway, Sweden, Switzerland and Spain – and which also had accepted the Optional Clause, were accordingly informed that, for the above reasons, Britain felt that nothing further was necessary. This was symptomatic of the more general fact that in the thirties the popularity which 'all-in' arbitration treaties had enjoyed in the twenties waned very considerably, with the result that they soon lost their prominence on the international stage.

Conclusion

It is not surprising that the Conservative government did not in the end come to any decision on the Anglo-American arbitration treaty or settle the perceived differences with the United States over BMR. The Foreign Office was, it is true, arguing that the settlement of these issues was imperative, for it was naturally alarmed at the poor state of Britain's relations with the strongest power in the world. And, given the extent to which this state of affairs was attributed to the policy of maintaining high BMR (especially when it was doubtful whether Britain could maintain such a policy against American wishes in the event of a war), it was to be expected that the Foreign Office would wish to lower BMR and not exclude them from the scope of an Anglo-American arbitration treaty. On the other hand the Admiralty continued to maintain that the navy must retain its freedom of action to act in war-time, notwithstanding its awareness of just how weak the empire's maritime defences were. The weight of naval tradition, together with the experience of the Great War, pointed the admirals and their officials firmly in this direction. Given such divergent approaches on a matter of considerable sensitivity and the split in the Cabinet to which they had led, prevarication was the order of the day. With an election in the offing, it made good sense for Baldwin to postpone a decision.

From the perspective of this book, however, the discussion of the arbitrability of BMR assumes considerable importance. For it resulted in the Conservative government being forced to re-examine what had hitherto been automatically taken for granted: whether it was vitally necessary that BMR should never be the subject of international arbitration. The Admiralty continued to regard this policy as written on tablets of stone, a view which was reflected in the suggestion

[91] Ibid. That is, apart from the Irish Free State which had independently accepted the Optional Clause. It would 'probably be impossible' to continue the system of concluding treaties applicable to the whole Commonwealth. It was also thought that it would be easier to propose acceptance of the General Act to the House of Commons and the dominions.
[92] Minute, 13 Nov. 1929, ibid.

made in the minority report on the Anglo-American arbitration treaty: that the compulsory arbitration of disputes involving BMR would lead to the compulsory adjudication of such disputes by the PCIJ – which was quite unacceptable. But, worried about the possibility of conflict with the United States, the Foreign Office decided that the time had come to alter Britain's traditional position. And those members of the government who were not imbued with jingoism or the Admiralty way of looking at things also concluded that Britain's interest was changing. Thus they thought it was necessary to contemplate the submission of disputes arising out of the exercise of BMR to an arbitral tribunal, although (with the exception of Cushendun) they also advocated maintaining BMR at the highest possible level. This meant, at least in principle, that the way to the acceptance of the Optional Clause was largely cleared. For as Hurst, the Foreign Office legal adviser, 'keeps on saying whenever we discuss it', 'belligerent rights constitute the only reason why we object to compulsory arbitration'.[93] Most members of the sub-committee on BMR did not, Salisbury told Chamberlain, go so far as to regard this as the only reason. But it was certainly the case that the importance of safeguarding Britain's conception of BMR had been the chief argument against accepting compulsory arbitration and compulsory adjudication. Now that a very weighty segment of opinion had decided that, compatibly with Britain's best overall interests, BMR could be taken to an international tribunal, the main argument against the Optional Clause was very considerably weakened.

However, although Hurst had argued that in comparison with the Anglo-American arbitration treaty, the Optional Clause was much simpler and less hazardous, government ministers did not go on in the early months of 1929 to a direct consideration of whether Britain should go the whole hog and accept the Optional Clause. But, as will be shown in the next chapter, when the Optional Clause became an urgent issue in a different context (that of the dominions), policy makers at both the political and official levels did not react with the sort of automatic hostility which would have been routine only a few years earlier. Instead they were able to consider the matter in an atmosphere in which a positive decision was by no means excluded. And this was so because they were now in a position to provide immediate drafts of the specific reservations which were deemed necessary to protect Britain's vital interests. It is true that it was decided that the Optional Clause should only be accepted after the Anglo-American treaty had been concluded. (It was also held that 'as a general principle the reserves to be made in the treaty with the United States and those made when signing the Optional Clause should be identical'.)[94] But the chief barrier to the idea that the Optional Clause was in principle unacceptable had fallen, and this resulted from the urgent consideration in 1927-9 of Britain's relations with America.

There is, of course, little profit in speculating on 'what might have been', but it is possible that if the Conservatives had been returned to Office in 1929, they might soon have accepted the Optional Clause. In the first place, some dominions were anxious to do so. Secondly, Baldwin had promised that Chamberlain could remain at the Foreign Office, and Chamberlain clearly

---

[93] Salisbury to Chamberlain, confidential, 21 Dec. 1928, UBL, Chamberlain papers, AC 55/461.
[94] See record of a meeting in the Foreign Office on 5 Apr. 1929, W 3236/21/98, *DBFP* vi, 391.

regarded the Anglo-American treaty as an urgent necessity. And if the Cabinet had approved the arbitration treaty, there is good reason to suppose that it would have accepted the Optional Clause with the reservations suggested in the spring of 1929. In short, acceptance of the Optional Clause was on the cards before the 1929 general election. As has been argued, the chief obstacle had been removed by developments in Anglo-American relations since 1927. But the impetus which was taking Britain forward along the now more or less open path to signature came from Canada's announcement in January 1929 that it was about to accept the Optional Clause. This threatened the unity of the empire and caused Britain to do some quick thinking about how this danger could be averted. Accordingly, it is now necessary to turn to the influence of the dominions on this aspect of British foreign policy.

7

The Dominions and British Policy

During the early part of the twentieth century, over a period of no more than two decades, the British empire underwent a profound constitutional change. Prior to the First World War its foreign policy was determined in London by the British government. By the 1930s the dominions[1] had received what was to all intents and purposes sovereign statehood, and the Commonwealth[2] grouping had been formally declared a free association of equals. During the transitional period the doctrine of *inter-se* was developed in an effort both to conceptualise the changes which had manifestly taken place and to underline the links with the past. The doctrine had only a short life, but it was during its ascendancy that the attitude of Britain to the Optional Clause was being intensively discussed. And *inter-se* was seen to have a most important bearing on the matter.

Inter-se

The doctrine of *inter-se* was developed by the British government in an attempt to cope with practical and constitutional problems which arose out of the development of the Commonwealth. Before 1914 the dominions had no voice in the foreign policy of the British empire (although they did have some freedom in commercial matters). At the imperial conferences of 1907 and 1911, for example, there was some clear and severe criticism of Britain's failure to consult the dominions, even on issues that directly concerned them, but it was sharply dismissed. The dominions were told by Britain's prime minister, Asquith, that the control of foreign policy could not be shared. The First World War changed all that. In 1914 the British declaration of war automatically included the dominions but as the war dragged on and its costs mounted, the dominions' contribution and their increasing assertiveness regarding their own, individual,

---

[1] That is Canada, South Africa, Australia, New Zealand and, after 1921, the Irish Free State. Newfoundland was a dominion only in name and, after going bankrupt in 1933, came under the control of Britain. In 1949 Newfoundland became a Canadian province with the same standing as other Canadian provinces.

[2] Although Lord Rosebery used the term 'commonwealth' in 1884, this was forgotten and it was Lionel Curtis who coined the expression 'Commonwealth of nations'. 'During the War when we were busy contrasting our ideals with those of the empires of Central Europe . . . statesmen began to use the phrase in their speeches', he said. In 1917 the imperial conference used the term and thereafter it was used with increasing frequency until, in 1921, it was established as a new official designation of the empire. But, as Hancock pointed out, 'the name empire . . . proved itself tough'. In the years following the Irish 'treaty' 'a conservative interpretation of the name commonwealth began to gain currency', one which was restricted to Britain, the dominions and, usually, India. In this book the term 'Commonwealth' will be used in the latter sense, the term 'empire' referring to Britain and its dependent territories: W. K. Hancock, *Survey of British Commonwealth affairs*, i: *Problems of nationality 1918–1936*, London 1937, 52–62.

interests required Britain to take account of their views. This led in 1917 to the creation of the Imperial War Cabinet to discuss the conduct of the war and the Imperial War Conference to consider inter-imperial affairs. That United Kingdom ascendancy was giving way to dominion equality was, moreover, acknowledged that year when the imperial conference resolved that the constitutional relationship should, in future, be based on 'a full recognition of the dominions as autonomous nations of an Imperial Commonwealth and of India as an important portion of same'. Accordingly, the dominions and India were recognised as having 'the right' to 'an adequate voice in foreign policy and in foreign relations'. It was also agreed that there should be developed 'effective arrangements for continuous consultation in all important matters of common Imperial concern, and for such necessary concerted action, founded on consultation, as the several Governments may determine'. At the war's end the dominions other than Newfoundland came onto the international stage by attending the peace conference, by signing the peace treaties (albeit subsumed under 'British empire'), and by becoming founder-members of the League of Nations. These privileges were also extended to India (which had lost more men in the war than any of the dominions) although it did not have dominion status and its international voice was that of the India Office in London.

Membership of the League of Nations meant that at Geneva the dominions could, if they wished, conduct themselves independently of Britain and of one another. In 1920 the foreign policies of the dominions were embryonic but over the next few years, and in varying degrees, the dominions asserted their independence by developing foreign policies which were not identical with those of Britain. This automatically raised fundamental constitutional questions about the relationship of the Commonwealth countries to each other and the rest of the world. Britain's response was the doctrine of *inter-se*, which was premised on the centrality in the empire/Commonwealth of the British Crown. As the king was a single person, it was asserted that the Crown was also juridically indivisible, and that, accordingly, Britain and the dominions could not, among themselves, engage in the full range of relationships which were usually open to sovereign states. By virtue of their shared loyalty to the king,[3] they enjoyed a special kind of relationship which was not international and was not governed by international law. The doctrine did not long survive, for its internal contradictions soon became evident. On the one hand was an empire with a single constitutional head, and, on the other, members pursuing independent external policies. Indeed, one dominion, the Irish Free State, pointedly rejected *inter-se* at the outset by registering the 'Irish treaty'[4] with the

[3] Although the Irish Free State rejected dominion status, it recognised the 'British Crown or . . . the person of the King' as 'the only bond linking together the various nations of the British Commonwealth': Timothy A. Smiddy, 'The position of the Irish Free State in the British Commonwealth of nations' in *Great Britain and the dominions* (The Harris Foundation lectures, 1927), Chicago 1928, 117. It was because of this that in 1932 the other dominion premiers pleaded (unsuccessfully) with De Valera not to remove the oath of loyalty to the king from the Irish constitution.

[4] That is 'The articles of agreement for a treaty between Great Britain and Ireland, 1921'. Britain contended that the agreement was not an international treaty because it had been concluded between two members of the Commonwealth. On the registration of the Irish 'treaty' see D. W. Harkness, *The restless dominion: the Irish Free State and the British Commonwealth of nations, 1921–1931*, London 1969, 57–63, and appendix B. Harkness, however, exaggerates the Irish role in the

League secretariat in 1924. And by 1931, with the Statute of Westminster effectively recognising the full sovereign statehood of the dominions,[5] the doctrine had lost much of its significance. As one writer has said, it was '[b]orn a dying duckling'.[6] None the less, for a brief while the doctrine was important, being a transitional device which formed 'a perhaps essential stage in the process, *ex uno plura*, of the Commonwealth' whose constituent parts were constantly moving towards independence.[7]

It was at this stage in the evolution of the Commonwealth that Britain found itself receiving hints and nudges, of varying strengths, that it should sign the Optional Clause. The British government of 1924-9 deemed it essential that if Britain accepted the Clause at all, it had to be done conjointly with the dominions and in identical terms. Furthermore, one of those terms must be that inter-imperial disputes – the phrase 'intra-imperial' was never used – should be withheld from the jurisdiction of the Permanent Court. All this was seen as a corollary of *inter-se*, which made the relations between Britain and the dominions of a special, non-international nature. Given that the Commonwealth members had a common allegiance to a single head, it was necessary that they all march in step in so important an international matter. And it was also necessary that any disputes which arose among themselves should be settled within the family, according to its own procedures, and not adjudicated by an international court. If the doctrine of *inter-se* were not maintained with regard to the PCIJ, it would be that much more difficult to assert it in respect of other matters. This was, for several reasons, seen as a very slippery slope.

The first danger was the belief that 'impossible situations might be created'[8] in the event of war if it were not maintained that the British empire/ Commonwealth was one unit. This was because it seemed logically impossible for the king, as the head of every Commonwealth country, at one and the same time to be both at war and at peace with a foreign power. Thus it was that Leo Amery, the secretary of state for the colonies and dominions in the second Baldwin administration, wrote that the king had been perturbed by the implication in a newspaper article that the 1926 imperial conference had materially altered the position of the king. 'The British Crown is one in space and time', wrote Amery.

> Above all, as no loyal subject of the King can be at peace with the King's enemies though there is no definite obligation as to the extent of the aid which he should render, so too no Government of the Empire can be neutral in the proper sense when the King is at war anywhere, though of course, it may not decide to do anything active. That unity of the Crown is the basis of all co-operation and development, and

disintegration of imperial unity in the 1920s and he overemphasises intra-imperial conflict at the expense of important aspects of co-operation.

[5] On the impact of the dominions' emergence as sovereign states, see Lorna Lloyd and Alan James, 'The external representation of the dominions, 1919–1948: its role in the unravelling of the British empire', *The British Year Book of International Law, 1996*, xlv, Oxford 1997. On sovereignty see Alan James, *Sovereign statehood: the basis of international society*, London 1986, passim.

[6] S. A. de Smith, *The new Commonwealth and its constitutions*, London 1964, 11, quoted in J. D. B. Miller, 'The decline of *inter-se*', *International Journal* xxiv (1969), 766.

[7] J. E. S. Fawcett, *The inter-se doctrine of Commonwealth relations*, London 1958, 45–6.

[8] Imperial conference, 1926, interim report no. 2 of the Cabinet committee on questions affecting inter-imperial relations, June 1926, PRO, E(B)12 CAB 32/49.

the one fatal heresy to guard against is the idea that there are many different Crowns or that the King is King in different parts of the Empire in different senses.[9]

Dropping inter-se would, secondly, endanger preferential trading tariffs within the Commonwealth. These tariffs effectively constituted a system whereby dominion foodstuffs were imported duty-free into Britain while foreign foodstuffs were taxed. Conversely, British manufactures were allowed into the dominions at lower tariffs than those imposed upon foreign goods. There were signs that states entitled to most-favoured-nation treatment were becoming inclined to challenge the Commonwealth's preferential trading tariffs in view of the new status of the dominions. Previously, Britain had argued that the dominions were not covered by arbitration clauses in commercial treaties because they were not 'foreign'. If the doctrine of inter-se were dropped, the Commonwealth trading system might be taken to arbitration with the result that Britain would either have to drop concessions to the dominions or extend the benefits of concessions to any country entitled to most-favoured-nation treatment. Since it was the dominion leaders who had invented preferential tariffs and pressed them on Britain, it was thought that they, rather than Britain, stood to lose, and it was therefore believed in the Foreign Office that there might be 'alarm in certain quarters'[10] at the prospect of the preferential tariff system being submitted to arbitration.

The third effect of dropping inter-se would be to end the common nationality of all members of the British imperium (subsequently enshrined in the British Nationality and Status of Aliens Act of 1941–3). This would mean that British subjects connected by birth or residence with one part of the empire/Commonwealth would be foreigners in other parts. As such they would be liable to treatment as aliens. The fourth effect of dropping inter-se would be on the diplomatic unity of the empire. Because it could be regarded as one entity for diplomatic purposes, Britain could, on occasion, claim to speak on behalf of the dominions.[11] But the advantages were not all one-sided. For in an inter-se context it was possible to maintain that a British diplomat accredited to a foreign country represented the dominions as well as Britain. And, conversely, it made it possible for a foreign diplomat in London to represent his country vis-à-vis the whole Commonwealth. To drop the diplomatic unity of the empire/Commonwealth would have left the dominions almost entirely bereft of diplomatic representation. Canada, it is true, obtained the right to separate diplomatic representation in Washington as early as 1920, but the Canadian minister would have been closely tied to the British embassy – to the extent that

[9] Amery to Sir Sydney Low, 29 Nov. 1926 (the day after Low's article appeared in the *Sunday Times*), PRO, PREM 1/91. Low (1879–1932) was lecturer in constitutional history, University of London, and author of a textbook, *The governance of England*.

[10] 'Memorandum by the legal advisers of the Foreign Office respecting compulsory arbitration', 4 Mar. 1926, PRO, CP 257(26), W 6559/30/98 FO 371/11868; *DBFP* ii, 68, annex (legal advisers' memorandum, Mar. 1926).

[11] For example, in 1924 Chamberlain asked the League Council to postpone discussion of the Geneva Protocol on the grounds that he spoke the minds of not one, but 5 or 6 governments. A year earlier Cecil had spoken on behalf of Australia, and in Aug. 1928 Cushendun expressed 'the satisfaction, the gratitude and the good intentions' of the New Zealand government when Sir James Parr's train was delayed – and did so 'without any prior authority and yet without exciting any comment': C. A. W. Manning, *The policies of the British dominions in the League of Nations*, London 1932, 34, 129.

when the British ambassador was absent the Canadian minister would take charge of the embassy. The then opposition leader, Mackenzie King, vehemently denounced this arrangement as compromising the distinctness of Canadian representation and it not until the beginning of 1927 that Vincent Massey took up his appointment as Canada's first minister to the United States. (The proposal that the Canadian minister be able to take charge of the British embassy had been withdrawn). Meanwhile, the Irish Free State was the first into the diplomatic field by establishing a permanent delegation to the League of Nations in 1923 (Canada and South Africa following suit in 1924 and 1929) and by the appointment of Professor Smiddy as its minister in Washington in 1924 – more than two years before Canada made a comparable move.[12] However, it was only in 1929 that the Free State opened further legations (in Paris, Berlin and the Vatican City) – the year in which South Africa opened legations in Rome, Washington and The Hague. By then Canada had opened legations in Paris (1928) and Tokyo (1929) and the Canadian Department of External Relations had grown from minuscule to tiny.[13] But this was scarcely adequate apparatus for more than minimal diplomatic relations, and the other dominions still relied almost entirely on Britain for their diplomatic representation. Thus, the abandonment of *inter-se* could be seen as having a possibly very serious effect on the international position of the dominions.

Finally, and most importantly from the present perspective, there was the danger that dropping *inter-se* would enable any organ of the League, such as the PCIJ, to assert its right to consider any dispute between two members of the Commonwealth, and Britain certainly did not want outsiders discussing Commonwealth matters. One bone of contention already existed between India and South Africa over the latter's treatment of people of Indian origin. India had also made itself a critical observer of the administration of mandates in general and the South West African mandate in particular. Accordingly, whenever the Optional Clause was considered, this was one reason why it was held that the doctrine of *inter-se* should be carefully protected.

[12] Smiddy was sent to Washington in 1922 as the Irish Free State commissioner. In 1923 his government told him 'he could regard himself as a Permanent Official of the Free State'. It was not, however, until Esmé Howard (the British ambassador to Washington) had formally notified the American government of the desirability of appointing an Irish representative and Secretary of State Hughes had formally approved the proposal, that Smiddy presented his letters of credence: Harkness, *Restless dominion*, 63–6. Characteristically, Smiddy went alone to present his letters to the president, unlike Massey of Canada who had been 'very anxious' to be accompanied by Howard in order to make it 'clear to the public that Great Britain approved of the establishment of a Canadian legation and that the two missions were on friendly terms': Vincent Massey, *What's past is prologue*, London 1963, 122. Washington did not appoint a representative to the Irish Free State until 1927. When the Australian prime minister, Hughes, announced his plan to send an ambassador to Washington it 'met with such ridicule in Australia that for the time the plan was dropped': W. J. Harte, *The control of foreign policy in the British Commonwealth of Nations*, London 1932, 8. An Australian representative was sent to Washington in 1930.

[13] In 1925 Canada's Department of External Affairs contained only two administrative officers and an under secretary. By 1930 the number of administrative officers had risen to seven. In New Zealand a department of external affairs had been set up in 1919 solely for the purpose of administering the Samoan Mandate, but in 1926 Prime Minister Coates announced the establishment of a prime minister's department which would contain one officer charged with looking after the incoming material on imperial and foreign affairs.

In 1921 the dominions and India had followed Britain's lead in not accepting the Optional Clause when adhering to the Statute of the PCIJ. At the fifth (1924) Assembly, Britain's Labour government was in favour of the Optional Clause and Canada, too, on its independent judgement, favoured the acceptance of compulsory jurisdiction.[14] This was also the position of the Irish Free State – although it did not seem to have given the matter much thought. Australia and New Zealand, by contrast, only agreed to move forward on the Clause for the sake of imperial unity. However, the return to power of the Conservatives in November 1924 resulted in Britain reverting to its previous position. Now Canada was held back on the Optional Clause by Britain's appeal to the principle of imperial unity and, more generally, Britain made use of the doctrine of *inter-se* to justify her own failure to make a positive move on the subject.

In these ways Britain could be seen as using the using the device of *inter-se* to maintain control of the foreign policies of the dominions. This was not without internal departmental strains in the British civil service. A former Dominions Office[15] official recalled that it was necessary 'to press sometimes vigorously for the full recognition of the equal status of the Dominions, against the hesitations of the F.O. who were still wedded to the conception of a common policy for the Empire', and that at one interdepartmental meeting, 'the argumentation was so fierce that it ended with Harding [assistant under secretary] and Hurst sitting glaring at each other and neither saying a word'.[16]

More specifically, a recent study of the Commonwealth has used the example of the Optional Clause to show how Britain was able to 'bull-doze' a dominion into toeing the British line. However, the same author also cites '[t]he Optional Clause controversy' as 'perhaps the best illustration of the growing 'ungovernability' of the Commonwealth relationship'.[17] For by the end of 1928 Canada was threatening to go ahead and sign the Optional Clause, possibly on its own. There were indications that the Irish Free State would do likewise and that, unlike Canada, the Irish would have little compunction about acting independently. And so, paradoxically, *inter-se* became a ground not for holding back on the Optional Clause, but for moving forward. For if two dominions were determined to sign, this became an argument for all the others doing likewise, as this would now be the only way of everyone keeping in step, and thus preserving the doctrine of *inter-se*. Hence the British government's advisers started to make preparations for a possible signature. As it turned out, unity could not be maintained on this point (and the Labour government of 1929 did not regard such unity as vitally important).

[14] See above, 45 and below, 163.

[15] The Dominions Office was established in 1925 at the insistence of Amery who saw it as a means of promoting his own vision of the empire and of weakening the authority of his rival, Chamberlain. However, the Dominions Office was never strong and it was treated by the Foreign Office as its inferior.

[16] Unpublished memoirs of C. W. Dixon (a member of the Colonial Office who transferred to the Dominions Office in 1930), quoted in Joe Garner, *The Commonwealth Office 1925–1968*, London 1978, 50. The meeting was in preparation for the 1926 imperial conference. 'Only the ingenuity of Batterbee [senior assistant secretary in the Dominions Office] in evolving an acceptable compromise succeeded in thawing the scene': ibid.

[17] See Robert F. Holland, 'The Commonwealth in the British official mind: a study in Anglo-dominion relations 1925–1937', unpubl. DPhil diss. Oxford 1977, 257, 131–2.

The doctrine of *inter-se* was soon to fall into desuetude. But throughout the second half of the 1920s, it was *inter-se* which both assisted in holding the dominions back so far as the Optional Clause was concerned – and then contributed significantly to pushing Britain towards the Optional Clause at the start of 1929.

The dominions in international relations

In addition to fostering a sense of individual rather than imperial identity in the dominions, the First World War also fostered dominion nationalism. This was accompanied by a mood of isolationism arising partly from a preoccupation with internal developments. It was also partly due to a general feeling that Europe and its troubles were far away – a feeling most famously expressed in Dandurand's remark to the fifth (1924) Assembly that Canada lived in a 'fire-proof house'. The sheer distance from Europe of Australia and New Zealand made it difficult for them to be actively involved in League affairs. It was, for example, much easier for the Antipodean dominions to choose their delegates to the League Assemblies from politicians who happened to be in Europe when the Assembly met – on one occasion the Automobile Association was, at the last moment, used to track down Bruce, who was holidaying in France – a problem which South Africa solved in the early years by appointing Robert Cecil and Gilbert Murray (both of them resident in Britain) to its delegation of three.[18] And policy formation was hindered by the slowness of communication: in 1924 the secretary-general's annual report did not reach Australia until after the Australian delegation had set sail for Europe; it was only in December 1924 that New Zealand received a copy of the Geneva Protocol which had been approved by the Assembly at the beginning of October; and the Australian government did not receive a full report of the proceedings at the fifth (1924) Assembly until the head of Australia's delegation got back to Australia in January 1925.

But dominion isolationism was not just due to geographical distance. There was a also a sense in which the dominions felt themselves remote from European affairs and were not really interested in international relations. Geographically-speaking, the Irish Free State was comparatively close to Geneva but its position in Britain's shadow led to its being described as 'un île derrière un île';[19] a country that was

> cut off to an extraordinary degree from the mainstream of Western European life, at least until the late 1950's . . . [with] a tendency to ignore . . . international issues . . ..
> Foreign policy, except in relation to Great Britain, usually evoked little or no interest and played no part in parliamentary or electoral politics.[20]

[18] Cecil was a South African delegate in 1920, 1921 and 1923. Murray served on the South African delegation in 1921 and 1922.

[19] That is Ireland was 'an island behind an island': Jean Blanchard, *Le droit ecclesiastique contemporain d'Irelande*, Paris, 1958, 11, quoted in Basil Chubb, *The government and politics of Ireland*, London 1970 (repr. 1980), 46.

[20] Ibid. 46–8. Cf. Patrick Keatinge, 'Ireland and the League of Nations', *Studies* lix (1970), 140; Stephen Barcroft, 'Irish foreign policy at the League of Nations 1929–1936', *Irish Studies in International Affairs* i (1979), 19–21.

And so it was with the other dominions. In the 1925 Australian general election, Charlton (the leader of the opposition Labour Party) suggested that his country should not participate in foreign affairs; Massey (the New Zealand prime minister from 1912 to 1925) did not think that the dominions should have been admitted to the League; in 1930 it was said that for the majority of New Zealanders '[f]oreign affairs . . . do not exist';[21] and South Africa was turned inwards on itself. Meanwhile Canada shared the isolationism of the United States. By 1925 the only real interest the Canadian parliament and public had shown in the League was the size of Canada's contribution to the budget. According to Dandurand, he, Lapointe and Prime Minister Mackenzie King were the only politicians with a serious interest in foreign affairs. And even in 1929, when Canada had a seat on the League Council, King privately thought it 'an absurdity, this running to & fro to mix in European affairs'.[22] It was, therefore, hardly surprising that the League did not count for much to the peoples of the dominions and most of their politicians.

However, as Manning pointed out, there was one thing which did interest several dominions in the League – the opportunity to emphasise 'their . . . status within the British Commonwealth. They were concerned to get their equality with Great Britain affirmed and recognised on paper. The best way to do it was to become independent in the League'.[23] This was true of three out of the five dominions – the Irish Free State, Canada and South Africa – so that, according to one observer, not only were the meetings of the British empire delegations (BED) at Geneva marked by plain speaking, but there was also less unanimity in the Commonwealth than between France and the Little Entente or in the Spanish-American bloc.[24] It should be noted, however, that the dominions were not all equally determined to assert their independent status, Australia and New Zealand generally being rather backward in this regard. Indeed, so loyal and so conservative was New Zealand that a British official who had been posted there reported that New Zealand regarded itself 'almost as divinely inspired to be the saviour of the Empire against itself – in other and cruder words, that she almost alone amongst the dominions has any sense of decency'.[25]

[21] 'New Zealand impressions', memorandum by Philip Nichols (UK liaison officer to the New Zealand government, 1928–30), 16 Apr. 1930, PRO, U 280/32/750 FO 426/2.
[22] Diary entry, 20 Feb. 1929, *The MacKenzie King diaries*, Toronto 1973.
[23] C. A. W. Manning, draft manuscript 'The policies of the British dominions in the League of Nations', vi. 10. Cf. idem, *Policies of the British dominions*, 138–9.
[24] Major-General A. C. Temmperley, *The whispering gallery of Europe*, London 1938, 110–11. In 1928 Dame Edith Lyttleton (a British delegate to the Assembly) pointed out that '[t]he British are not in such a strong position as the French who can always bring their Latin Allies to heel with a word, almost a gesture. But', she concluded comfortingly, 'the combined weight of the British Empire can be all the more powerful for being intelligent and individual, and this is easily secured. The dominion delegates for the most part are ill informed about European and Eastern affairs, and are ready to take a lead': undated memorandum, ?Oct./Nov. 1928, PRO, W 10894/10894/98 FO 371/13402.
[25] Nichols memorandum, 'New Zealand impressions'. Thus Sir Francis Dillon Bell, close adviser on constitutional questions to Coates (after the latter became prime minister in 1925), described the 1931 Statute of Westminster as 'the damned Statute of Westminster': W. D. Stewart, *Sir Francis H.D. Bell*, Wellington 1937, 262, quoted in Angus Ross, 'Reluctant dominion or dutiful daughter? New Zealand in the inter-war years', *Journal of Commonwealth Political Studies* x (1972), 35. New Zealand did not adopt the Statute of Westminster until 1947.

The most significant assertion of dominion independence from Britain in the 1920s was their non-participation in the Locarno treaties of 1925. By refusing to join Britain in guaranteeing Germany's western borders, the dominions made clear their aloofness from the security concerns of Europe and their unwillingness automatically to go to war alongside Britain.[26] Locarno struck at the doctrine of inter-se by suggesting that Britain and its colonies could be at war while the overseas dominions were at peace. It was the 'first official recognition of the limited liability of the dominions' and was, for this reason, described by Smuts as 'cutting the heart out of the Empire'.[27] It also had important practical implications for the defence of the empire. In addition to its obligations under Locarno, Britain, as the leading member of the League, had to be able to act with a firm hand in Europe. At the same time it was burdened with the responsibility for imperial defence in the Pacific despite the run-down of its military might and the emergence of Australia and New Zealand onto the international stage. Although Australia had begun constructing its own navy in a limited way before the war, it made cuts in the twenties so that an Australian delegate to the tenth (1930) Assembly roundly declared that: 'Australia tells the world, as a gesture of peace . . . that she is not prepared for war'. The Australian government had 'run its pen through the schedule of military expenditure with unprecedented firmness' and had 'reversed the policy . . . of compelling the young to learn the arts of war'.[28] New Zealand did contribute money for imperial defence but the amount was too small to make much difference to Britain's load. It did, however, mean that New Zealand had a greater interest in the state of the British navy than did any other dominion apart from Australia. Accordingly, because both were dependent on the British navy for their defence, New Zealand and Australia shared the British Admiralty's concern over BMR and looked at the Optional Clause from the same perspective as the Admiralty. This, together with their fears about Japan challenging their 'white' immigration policies and their inclination to follow the lead of the British Conservative government at Geneva, made them a restraining influence on Canada's desire to accept the Optional Clause. It also meant that they were critical of the Labour Party's favourable attitude towards the Optional Clause – hence their awkwardness in 1924 at the fifth Assembly and in 1929 when the Labour government decided to accept the Clause.

The fifth (1924) Assembly set the pattern for the way in which the Commonwealth's policy on the Optional Clause was to develop over the next few years, reflecting and in one case modifying the attitudes which had emerged in the various dominions earlier in the 1920s.

[26] Both Massey and his successor, Coates (New Zealand prime minister 1925–38), would willingly have ratified Locarno. New Zealand did not sign because of its 'desire to avoid any outward appearance of disunity within the Empire': J. B. Condliffe, 'The attitude of New Zealand in imperial and foreign affairs', Great Britain and the dominions (The Harris Foundation lectures, 1927), 378.

[27] Harte, Control of foreign policy, 14–15. In this respect, however, it is worth noting that the abortive Anglo-French treaty of guarantee of June 1919 expressly provided that it should impose no obligation on the dominions. Article 49 of the Irish 'treaty' of 1922 stated that 'save in case of actual invasion the Irish Free State shall not be committed to active participation in any war without the consent of the Oireachtas': ibid. 6, 8.

[28] Quoted by Professor Sir William Harrison Moore in 'The dominions of the British Commonwealth in the League of Nations', International Affairs x (1931), 379. The word 'military' included naval expenditure.

The dominions and the Optional Clause 1920–5

In 1920 Canada, like the rest of the Commonwealth, followed Britain's lead in not accepting the Optional Clause. But while Britain's voice can be detected in the Canadian government's explanation of its policy, there could also be heard the voice of a smaller power which supported compulsory adjudication but recognised the necessity, for the time being, of accepting that the great powers would not grant this authority to the Court. And, while there were some isolationist senators who opposed having anything to do with the new Court, there were others, such as Senator Dandurand, who expressed 'surprise' that Canada had not signed the Optional Clause.[29] The suddenness with which they learned of Britain's favourable attitude towards the Clause at the memorable fifth (1924) Assembly, meant that at first the Canadian delegate, Skelton, could only murmur about Canada's general sympathy with compulsory arbitration. By the end of the Assembly, however, Ottawa had given its authorisation for Canadian delegates to go full steam ahead, and Dandurand accordingly told the plenary session that, 'it is my firm conviction that Canada, faithful to her past, will be prepared to accept compulsory arbitration and the compulsory jurisdiction of the Permanent Court of International Justice'.[30]

However, when the Canadian delegation returned home with a Protocol that included sanctions as well as compulsory arbitration, the government was displeased. Against the advice of Dandurand, an inter-departmental committee supported Mackenzie King in recommending the rejection of the Geneva Protocol. At the same time the committee recommended (with a view to the Canadian reply on the Protocol not sounding completely negative) that Canada should declare its willingness to consider accepting the Optional Clause.[31] The recommendation was accepted and, two days after the committee had reported to King, Canada told the British government that:

> as Canada believes firmly in submission of international disputes to joint enquiry or arbitration and has shared in a certain number of undertakings in this field, we should be prepared to recommend acceptance of compulsory jurisdiction of Permanent Court in justiciable disputes, with certain reservations, and co-operation in further consideration of method of supplementing the provisions of the covenant for settlement of non-justiciable issues.[32]

[29] Canadian Senate *debs.*, 19 May 1921, col. 509, PRO, W 6399/22/98 FO 371/7035. On the other hand, another senator had 'no hesitation whatsoever' in asserting that Canada was not 'in any way interested in this matter [of the PCIJ]. Canada will never be interested in any matter submitted to this tribunal . . . we do not have the means to join all these fancy schemes': ibid. cols. 2819–21. See also Doherty (minister of justice 1911–21 and delegate to the League of Nations 1920–21) to the Canadian Senate on 28 Apr. 1921, in *Documents on Canadian foreign policy, 1917–1939*, ed. Walter A. Riddell, Toronto 1962, 404–5.
[30] League of Nations, Records of the fifth Assembly, plenary meetings, text of the debates, *LNOJ*, special supplement no. 23, 1924 (*LNA5 debs.*), twenty-eighth plenary, 2 Oct. 1924, 221.
[31] See Richard Veatch, *Canada and the League of Nations*, Toronto–Buffalo 1975, 56–7 and Gwendolen Carter, *The British commonwealth and international security: the role of the dominions 1919–1939*, Westport Conn. 1971 (first publ. 1947), 120.
[32] Governor-general of Canada (General Lord Byng) to Amery, 4 Mar. 1925, PRO, W 1860/9/98, No. 7, FO 411/2. Canada's statement to the League was, however, more guarded, saying only that Canada would be prepared to consider accepting the Optional Clause. See also *Documents on Canadian foreign policy*, 417; C. P. Stacey, *Canada and the age of conflict*, II: *The Mackenzie King era*, Toronto–Buffalo–London 1981, 63–4; and *Protocol for the Pacific Settlement of Disputes: correspondence relating to the attitudes of the dominions*, London (*Command paper* 2458) 1925, no 8.

The Irish Free State was the only other dominion to declare itself in favour of the Optional Clause in 1924. This was in November when the foreign minister, Desmond Fitzgerald, told the *Dáil* that his country had recommended the immediate acceptance of the Optional Clause at the fifth Assembly[33] (although this does not appear in the Assembly records). The Free State's statement on the Geneva Protocol, however, strongly endorsed the idea of compulsory arbitration.[34]

Canada and Ireland were both drawn to supporting the Optional Clause and compulsory arbitration partly because they were both opposed to the military aspects of collective security. But they opposed this for different reasons. Canada not only feared that the application of League sanctions might draw it into conflict with its southern neighbour but also shared something of the United States' isolationist outlook – just as it shared the American sense of moral superiority over Europe. As Dandurand was wont to remind the League Assembly, Canada had developed – with the United States – the habit of resolving disputes through arbitration. Its three-thousand-mile frontier with the USA was unfortified and, he said, '[n]ot only have we had a hundred years of peace on our borders, but we think in terms of peace, while Europe, an armed camp, thinks in terms of war'.[35]

The Irish Free State's support for the Optional Clause and its opposition to military sanctions stemmed from its small-state mentality. Like other small states, it favoured the legal equality which the PCIJ offered in a dispute with a great power as well, no doubt, as finding attractive the thought of being able to take Britain before the Court. And, like other small states, it also emphasised that, '[t]he League should not rely on material sanctions but on the moral pressure of the world's opinion and, within this context arbitration would define and enhance international judgement'.[36]

Having said this, however, Irish policy towards the Optional Clause appears to have been based on an instinctive support for an ideal about which the government had only a vague notion, rather than forming part of a coherent foreign policy. Indeed, at the 1923 imperial conference, an Irish representative, MacNeill, said that 'the Irish Free State has arrived at nothing nearer to a definition of Foreign Policy than is expressed in its adhesion to the League of Nations'.[37] And although Fitzgerald told the *Dáil* that 'so far as I have gone into

---

[33] *Dáil Éireann debs.*, XI, cols. 1474–6, cited in Harkness, *Restless dominion*, 142; *Dáil Éireann debs.*, 6 Nov. 1924, PRO, W 10049/338/98 FO 371/10573.

[34] Carter, *Commonwealth and international security*, 121. The Free State did not join in the Commonwealth exchange of opinions but 'publicized its rejection [of the Protocol] through a statement in the *Dáil* which was subsequently transmitted to the Colonial Secretary and thence to the other dominions': ibid.

[35] Dandurand speaking to the League Assembly on 2 Oct. 1924, LNA5 debs, twenty-eighth plenary, 221. Cf. Dandurand's speech to the Assembly on 12 Sept. 1927: Records of the eighth ordinary session of the Assembly, plenary meetings, text of the debates, *LNOJ*, special supplement no. 54, 1927, (*LNA8* debs.), twelfth plenary, 113; Manning, *Policies of the British dominions*, 47–9. An additional reason for Canada's favourable attitude towards arbitration was that this accorded with the nature of Mackenzie King who, possibly as a legacy from his time in labour negotiations (his area of study), loved casting himself in the role of mediator.

[36] Copy of telegram from Amery to governor-general of New Zealand (General Sir Charles Fergusson), 13 July 1925, CUL, Baldwin papers, 132.

[37] London, *Command paper* 1987 (1923), 62, quoted in Harkness, *Restless dominion*, 54.

the matter, I would be entirely in favour of adopting the Optional Clause',[38] a few days earlier, in Geneva, O'Higgins had said that his government had not yet decided its attitude and wanted to go more fully into the practical aspects of the Optional Clause before signing it.[39] In fact, one of the 'practical aspects' which prevented the Irish government from signing the Optional Clause was that the Irish government was not clear whether it was bound by the Statute of the Court, which had been ratified by Britain before the Irish Free State came into being. But it was only after angry questions in the *Dáil* about why Ireland had not yet ratified the Statute that, in September 1926, a note was sent to the secretary-general asking that the Irish Free State be listed among the members of the PCIJ.[40]

South Africa does not appear to have had any interest in the Optional Clause, while Australia and New Zealand showed a distinct lack of enthusiasm for the Clause at the fifth (1924) Assembly. New Zealand was the only dominion to reply to MacDonald's tardily-despatched telegram inviting views on the Optional Clause. Its reply emphasised its distrust of the PCIJ on much the same grounds as English critics of the Clause and its belief that an adverse judgement was a 'foregone conclusion' in the vital matter of BMR was repeated in its reply on the Protocol.[41] On the other hand, Australia did not mention BMR in its reply on the Protocol. No doubt this was thought unnecessary in view of its outright refusal to countenance compulsory arbitration and because the return to power of the Conservatives on 4 November 1924 sufficed to allay any fears that BMR would not be safeguarded.

Both antipodean dominions were, however, particularly critical of Article 10.1 of the Geneva Protocol. This was the final agreed form taken by the 'Japanese amendment' (which had brought the negotiations over the Geneva Protocol to a temporary standstill because of Australian and New Zealand anxiety that it would enable the Japanese to challenge their 'white' immigration policies). The article stated that a country which was involved in hostilities over a matter which an international tribunal had ruled to be within the domestic jurisdiction of a state, would not be condemned as an aggressor if the dispute

---

[38] Dominions Office to Foreign Office, 11 Sept. 1925, PRO, W 8679/27/98 FO 371/11069. See also Dominions Office memorandum, 2 Mar. 1926, CP 257(26), paper D, FO 371/11868 (printed as annex 16 to *Command paper* 2458, 1925).

[39] See League of Nations, Minutes of the first committee (constitutional and legal questions), *LNOJ*, special supplement no. 34, 1925 (*LNA6* first committee), sixth meeting, 24–5. This statement was prompted by Hurst's explanation that one of the problems in Britain accepting the Optional Clause was that it 'required solidarity of action' by six nations. This had been 'construed as representing the considered views of not one Government but six'. O'Higgins accordingly wanted to make it clear that his country was sympathetically inclined towards arbitration and that Hurst did not speak for the Free State: see above, 94, but cf. riposte from Cooke of Australia.

[40] Hurst was sure the Irish Free State was bound by Britain's signature of the Court Statute but he thought the Free State had been prompted to take this step 'by extremist elements', that in so doing it had tried to minimise offence and that the letter to the secretary-general was of no great importance: minute, 7 Oct. 1926, PRO, W 9122/30/98, FO 371/11868.

[41] Fergusson to Amery, 6 Jan. 1925, enclosing memorandum signed by W.F. Massey (prime minister of New Zealand), PRO, W 993/9/98 FO 411/2. In Nov. Massey 'emphatically' endorsed the views of Crowe and 'wholly dissent[ed]' from those of Hurst. For, he said, the 'continental jurists' on the Court held views on BMR that were 'opposed to the principles long established in England and essential to the interests of Great Britain': Massey to Viscount Jellicoe (governor-general of New Zealand until 13 Dec. 1924), 3 Nov. 1924, PRO, W 10049/338/98 FO 371/10573.

were submitted to the League under Article 11 of the Covenant. The Australian government dismissed this provision as impractical and argued that there was no justification for placing disputes arising out of domestic jurisdiction on a different footing from any other arbitral award or dispute on which the Council had expressed a unanimous opinion. The New Zealand government's objections betrayed – as did its telegram on the Optional Clause – a general doubt as to the likelihood of the League Council or the Assembly supporting New Zealand's views, and a particular distrust of the PCIJ. 'Whatever the jurists at Geneva may think', the legal advisers of the New Zealand government believed there was a 'grave danger' that the PCIJ (consisting as it did 'mainly of foreigners') might hold that New Zealand's immigration laws were 'contrary to the comity of Nations' and were not solely a matter of domestic jurisdiction. The New Zealand government would 'never' consent to the Optional Clause.[42]

The British government's decision to reject the Geneva Protocol and its outright dismissal of the possibility of accepting the Optional Clause rendered further consultations on both subjects unnecessary for the time being. However, the fifth (1924) Assembly and the Geneva Protocol had provided the first occasion on which the dominions had expressed their opinions on the Optional Clause in either an international or Commonwealth context. And their attitudes had been revealed as divergent: Canada was clearly in favour of the Clause; the Irish Free State was in principle in favour of the Clause but had not thought through its policy; South Africa was not interested; Australia and New Zealand were hostile. Over the next five years the British government's task was to try to keep the dominions in line in order to protect the doctrine of *inter-se*. The subject of the Optional Clause was brought up again at the 1926 imperial conference and the British government reconsidered it in preparation for this conference.

Preparations for the 1926 imperial conference: the British government's reconsideration of the Optional Clause

There were two reasons for Britain placing the Optional Clause on the agenda of the 1926 imperial conference. The first was that Chamberlain, the foreign secretary, was using the dominions as a justification for British policy on arbitration and the Optional Clause. For example, in reply to several requests for 'all-in' arbitration treaties, he had said that the British government could not take any steps in this direction without having fully considered the question with the dominions. It was, therefore, at least necessary to go through the motions of consulting the dominions when the conference met in October 1926.

The second reason for placing the Optional Clause on the agenda of the conference was the apparent interest which some dominions were showing in the subject of arbitration and the belief that several of them wanted to move forward on the Optional Clause. It was widely known that Canada favoured its acceptance, the Irish Free State government supported it in statements to the *Dáil* and, although Australia had opposed any possible hint of a commitment to

---

[42] Ibid.

compulsory arbitration at the sixth (1925) Assembly, Chamberlain had learnt that South Africa's former indifference had apparently been replaced by support for the Optional Clause.

Preparations for the imperial conference began early in 1926. At the beginning of March, and at the behest of Chamberlain, the four Foreign Office legal advisers,[43] produced a memorandum on the Optional Clause (although it was regarded as being the work of Hurst). Whereas Hurst and Malkin had differed over the Optional Clause two years earlier – the former supporting it, the latter opposing it – the legal advisers were now unanimously agreed that, from the legal point of view, it would be advantageous for Britain to accept the Optional Clause with such reservations as were necessary.

The legal advisers' memorandum began by examining Britain's existing arbitral commitments. These were three-fold. Firstly, under Article 13 of the Covenant, Britain had accepted in principle that legal disputes should be submitted to arbitration. Secondly, Britain was bound by its arbitration treaties to submit legal disputes to arbitration unless they fell within the scope of the vital interests formula which was included in all but one such treaty. Thirdly, Britain had agreed that disputes relating to the interpretation or application of particular instruments should be submitted to arbitration or, more usually, to the PCIJ. These commitments left 'considerable gaps' so that '[i]n practice . . . international arbitrations only take place in cases where both parties willingly consent to the submission'.

The memorandum then turned to considering what would happen if a party refused to submit a serious dispute to arbitration or adjudication. The League Covenant obliged League members to submit a serious dispute to enquiry by the Council if they could not agree on submitting it to arbitration. While this was a satisfactory way of dealing with wholly political (or non-justiciable) disputes it was unsatisfactory for justiciable (or legal) disputes in which there was a conflict as to rights. This was because '[t]he Council is a political body, and it is as ill-qualified to decide a case which should be brought before a bench of judges as a tribunal of judges is ill-qualified deal with a political question'. The legal advisers thought it probable that in such disputes the Council would turn to the PCIJ for an advisory opinion. Accordingly, a state which wanted arbitration would be encouraged to take a justiciable dispute to the League Council under Article 15.1 of the Covenant. Although Britain had found it useful to adopt this procedure in 1922 to induce France to come to a settlement over the *Tunis Nationality Decrees*,[44] it was 'not a satisfactory application of the provisions of the Covenant' and it would 'tend, if it increases, to embarrass the Council and to complicate the working of the Covenant'. It was, however, appropriate to submit to the Council disputes which involved mixed considerations of politics and law and for the Council to turn to the Court for an advisory opinion on any legal point which was involved. And, in respect of purely political disputes, the existing machinery of the League was sufficient. For wholly justiciable disputes,

---

[43] That is Hurst, Malkin, Montagu Shearman and Eric Beckett. Shearman had worked on blockade in the First World War and was appointed a temporary assistant legal adviser in February 1919, an appointment which was made permanent in July 1919. In March 1925 Beckett was appointed assistant legal adviser and Malkin became second legal adviser.

[44] See above, 19–20 nn. 70–1.

however, the advisers held that 'the case for an advance is sufficiently strong to merit exploration'.

There were three main arguments that had been raised against compulsory arbitration and the Optional Clause but it was held that they did not withstand examination. The first was the 'great argument which is always relied on by those who oppose any acceptance of the principles of compulsory arbitration': the dangers resulting from submitting disputes involving BMR to this procedure. Although there were grounds for believing that the dangers would be less in the future than they had been in the past, because Britain would only be involved in naval action in pursuance of its obligations under Article 16 of the League Covenant, Britain could not submit such disputes to adjudication. To do so would 'provoke great alarm in the country and would lead to an agitation which it is desirable to avoid'. It would also imperil imperial unity since the Australian and New Zealand governments would oppose such an obligation. However, it would be possible to reserve BMR in a declaration accepting the Optional Clause and this right had been confirmed by Hurst's soundings at the fifth (1924) Assembly.

The other two objections to the Optional Clause were less weighty. These were 'that no sufficient confidence can be felt in an international tribunal unless His Majesty's Government have been parties to the selection of at least a majority of the members' and that 'in a really important case it might be impossible for His Majesty's Government to give effect to an adverse award'. It was not, however, believed that these objections outweighed the advantages of being able 'to obtain as of right' the compulsory adjudication of disputes. If it were decided by the government that it was desirable to make an advance in the direction of arbitration, the legal advisers recommended the limited acceptance of the Optional Clause as the best course since it could be taken unilaterally and without the bargaining involved in negotiating an arbitration treaty. In addition to reserving disputes involving BMR, the legal advisers suggested that acceptance of the Optional Clause should be based on reciprocity; that it should be limited to disputes arising out of events taking place after the date of the declaration; and that it should be of limited duration to allow the government to reconsider the obligation at regular intervals.

The legal advisers also thought that it would be necessary to discuss with the dominions whether it would be 'possible and desirable' to limit the acceptance of the Optional Clause in a way that would prevent other states from challenging the imperial preference trading system. Although, they said, 'it can hardly be denied that a country which has got an arbitration clause in its commercial treaty with us would be entitled to have the point submitted to arbitration as things stand', the risk might be diminished by the acceptance of the Optional Clause being effected by one instrument on behalf of the whole empire/Commonwealth. It was, in any case, recommended that this procedure should be adopted in accepting the Clause.

Finally, the legal advisers recommended that, before accepting the Optional Clause, a system should be developed for arbitrating petty claims put forward on behalf of the nationals of one state against another. Such claims required 'simpler and more expeditious treatment than is afforded by the cumbrous machinery of reference to the Permanent Court'. There was, at present, no system for securing the arbitration of such claims and 'wearisome and irritating negotiations' were usually necessary to obtain arbitration. This was because no state wished to admit its officials had blundered and 'considerable ingenuity' was displayed in arguing why a claim was bad and unsuitable for arbitration.[45]

Austen Chamberlain was struck by the lawyers' argument and kept for further consideration the memorandum and the accompanying papers which had been written by Crowe and Haldane in July 1924. He also formally asked, at the end of March, that the Optional Clause be put on the agenda of the imperial conference. Chamberlain's advisers were not all convinced of the merits of the lawyers' case. When the memorandum was circulated in the Foreign Office in May, Victor Wellesley (the deputy under secretary) recommended that the proposal should not be adopted. Recalling Sir Eyre Crowe's admonitions less than one-and-a-half years' earlier, Wellesley minuted that Britain should 'guard against lightly surrendering the reservation of vital interests which compulsory arbitration would involve'. 'I . . . cannot get away from the feeling', he wrote, 'that it is unwise to tie our hands more than is absolutely necessary'.[46] On the other hand, Forbes, a senior member of the treaty department, commented that: 'To resist this proposal for compulsory arbitration in the present day is very much like an attempt to swim against the tide'.[47] By June Chamberlain had decided that Britain's whole policy should be reconsidered at Cabinet level and he obtained the setting up of a Cabinet sub-committee which was by name concerned with examining the question of compulsory arbitration, but was in fact concerned with the Optional Clause.[48]

By the time that the sub-committee met on 27 July, Austen Chamberlain had made up his own mind in favour of accepting the Optional Clause. Having told the sub-committee why it was necessary to reconsider the question in preparation for the imperial conference and drawn its attention to the legal advisers' memorandum of the previous March, Chamberlain said he was concerned about being 'forced to adopt a dilatory attitude' at a time when other countries were increasingly tending to favour compulsory arbitration. Britain had, he said, supported compulsory arbitration for disputes arising between Germany and its neighbours and could be charged with 'recommending others to adopt a procedure which she refused to follow herself'.[49] When Lord Cave, Lord Chancellor and chairman of the sub-committee, asked 'what a first-rate power like Great Britain had to gain by acceptance of the principle of compulsory arbitration', Chamberlain replied that:

> acceptance of the principle by Great Britain would undoubtedly have a very great influence with other countries. On the other hand refusal to accept the principle

[45] 'Memorandum by the legal advisers of the Foreign Office respecting compulsory arbitration', 4 Mar. 1926, CP 257(26), *DBFP* ii, 68, annex (Legal advisers' memorandum).
[46] Minute, 18 May 1926, PRO, T 2845/1458/383 FO 372/2175.
[47] Undated minute, ibid.
[48] See 'Memorandum by Sir Austen Chamberlain on compulsory arbitration', 24 June 1926, CP 257(26), *DBFP* ii, 68; minutes of Cabinet meeting, 30 June 1926, PRO, CAB 43(26). The members of the sub-committee were Cave (Lord Chancellor, in the chair), Amery (colonial and dominions secretary), Hogg (attorney general), Cecil and Chamberlain. Salisbury (Lord Privy Seal), Balfour (Lord President of the Council) and Birkenhead (secretary of state for India) were appointed to the sub-committee but did not attend the meetings. Birkenhead did, however, submit a memorandum. Two Foreign Office officials attended the sub-committee's meetings as advisers: Malkin, who favoured accepting the Optional Clause, and Wellesley, who did not.
[49] Secret: Cabinet committee on compulsory arbitration in international disputes, proceedings, conclusions of meeting held on 27 July 1926, PRO, CA(26) 1st cons., CAB 27/330.

would give rise to misrepresentation of our motives in refusing. France and Germany would probably accept the principle on a reciprocal basis. The United States would not, however, accept it. There was a large influential body of public opinion in this country which supported the principle on general religious and humanitarian grounds.[50]

Robert Cecil, who had the previous year become a proponent of accepting the Optional Clause, supported Chamberlain but the rest of the sub-committee was impervious to their arguments. The counter-argument was set out in circulated copies of Crowe's and Haldane's 1924 memoranda and a paper in which Birkenhead reiterated the objections which India had had to compulsory arbitration under the terms of the Geneva Protocol. Indeed, the other members of the sub-committee not only found the arguments in favour of the Optional Clause unconvincing, but they also exaggerated the perceived dangers of accepting the Clause in a way which revealed deep-seated suspicion of the PCIJ. For example, Douglas Hogg, the Attorney General, said that he was completely opposed to the Optional Clause and that 'The British Government by accepting the Covenant had in effect pledged themselves to submit any suitable subject to arbitration. Under the proposals now in question the British Government must pledge themselves to submit unsuitable subjects to arbitration.' The Irish might take 'purely domestic questions before the Hague Court – for instance Irish appeals to the Privy Council' and, '[w]hile the Hague Court was suitable for minor questions, he [Hogg] doubted its suitability for the more important disputes, as at present constituted it [the PCIJ] facilitated political logrolling'.[51] When Cecil questioned Hogg's remark that the majority of judges knew neither French nor English, the latter replied that 'he had only stated that some of the members were not conversant with either French or English when originally appointed; and that several only understood one of the languages even now'.[52]

In addition to suspicion of the 'foreign judges' there was suspicion of the 'foreign procedures' of the PCIJ which were 'very dangerous' because the Court was not bound by rules of evidence as were British courts,[53] and there was distrust of foreign countries: 'in practice Great Britain would always implement her undertaking while other countries would try to find reasons for not submitting inconvenient cases to the Court'.[54]

Amery, the secretary of state for the colonies and dominions, introduced a new objection of his own. Having said that his experience in the *Mosul Case* made him reluctant to agree to submit important questions to the League Council (i.e. 'beyond the strict interpretation of our obligations under the Covenant'), he explained that '[t]he weakness of the Council . . . afforded no good reason for extending the jurisdiction of the Permanent Court'. Moreover, arbitration was not, said Amery, 'the only alternative to force: postponement often resulted in the peaceable solution of issues, the bitter effects of which disappeared with lapse of time'.[55]

[50] Ibid.
[51] Ibid.
[52] Secret: Cabinet committee on compulsory arbitration in international disputes, proceedings, conclusions of meeting held on 3 Aug. 1926, PRO, CA(26) 2nd cons., CAB 27/330.
[53] Hogg to CA(26) 1st cons. and repeated by Amery to CA(26) 2nd cons.
[54] Cave to CA(26) 2nd cons.
[55] Ibid.

Finally, there was the oft-used argument that Britain could not afford to tie its hands in advance. Of the four categories of disputes enumerated in Article 13 of the Covenant, only the first – the interpretation of treaties – was, said Cave, suitable for submission to the Court: 'the other categories were of such very wide character as to make it dangerous . . . to accept arbitration in all cases which might fall within them'.[56]

Cecil, Chamberlain and Malkin vainly endeavoured to overcome the prejudice of the majority of the sub-committee. At the first meeting Cecil followed Chamberlain in putting the case for the Optional Clause in a moderate way. He pointed out that in the past Britain had, on the whole, been willing to go to arbitration; he argued that it would be advantageous to Europe 'to persuade the smaller turbulent European Powers to accept the principle' of compulsory jurisdiction; and he asked whether the legal advisers could suggest further reservations to those which they had proposed in their March 1926 memorandum. But his arguments cut no ice and it was equally of no avail for Malkin to point out that there already was a danger that a dominion might take a dispute with Britain to The Hague; that this would not be increased by accepting the Optional Clause; and that it would be necessary definitely to agree on the doctrine of *inter-se* in drawing up the terms in which the Optional Clause would be accepted. Indeed, such was the hostility of almost all those present that, as Cecil pointed out at the end of the first meeting, 'if the objections to arbitration by the Hague Tribunal were as serious as the Attorney-General had represented, it was questionable whether Britain ought to agree to refer any question to the Court'.

When the sub-committee met a second time, Cecil moved into the attack, starting with the objections Hogg had made at the last meeting. There were, he said, no specific instances of logrolling and it had never been hinted that the PCIJ was anything but impartial. The French judge had, he reminded them, voted against the French government's contention that the *Tunis Nationality Decrees* were a matter of domestic jurisdiction. Britain had little to fear from the impartial decisions of the PCIJ, but there were good grounds for being apprehensive of the decisions of the Council because these were 'based on purely political considerations'. Finally, he appealed to his colleagues to recognise the value of adhering to the Optional Clause: 'it was not desirable to examine the proposal from the point of view of discovering what possible evil result should follow from its adoption and then to reject it. The proposal should be regarded from the point of view of what was best for Great Britain and the world'.

At the end of the second meeting the sub-committee came firmly down against accepting the Optional Clause. Chamberlain bowed to the will of the majority but Cecil refused to accept defeat. Cecil formally requested that his dissent be minuted in the sub-committee report and he reserved the right to explain his views to the Cabinet. Accordingly, in due course, two papers were circulated to the Cabinet: Cave's report setting out in careful detail the arguments that had been put to the sub-committee for and against accepting the Optional Clause before recommending that the Clause should not be accepted; and a memorandum by Cecil explaining why the Optional Clause should be accepted. The Cabinet accepted Cave's report and Cecil's memorandum only

---

[56] CA(26) 2nd cons. Amery shared Cave's objection on this point.

served to set his views before the Cabinet and to mark his growing alienation from his colleagues.[57]

The task of producing a paper on the Optional Clause for circulation to the dominions at the imperial conference fell to Sir Douglas Hogg, the Attorney General, with the assistance of Malkin and Harding of the Dominions Office. Hogg's memorandum contrasted sharply with Cave's considered report in the sweeping simplicity of the arguments presented against adhering to the Optional Clause (and which gave no indication that he had either read the legal advisers' memorandum or made use of Malkin's services). Hogg began by saying that the reason for raising the subject at the imperial conference was that it was essential for the Commonwealth to have a uniform policy on the Optional Clause. As he put it, this meant that they had to decide whether it was desirable for the Commonwealth to go further than Article 13 of the Covenant and 'agree in advance to submit to arbitration every dispute of this nature which may arise, *even though questions of vital interest, independence, or honour may be concerned*'.[58] There was no mention of the possibility of making reservations. Hogg then pointed out that the Optional Clause had been considered by the British government in 1920 and 1924 and that it had been rejected on both occasion. Dominion views as expressed in respect of the Geneva Protocol were summarised.

There were, said Hogg, two advantages in accepting the Optional Clause. Firstly, any steps which helped to convert public opinion away from the use of force would be valuable because it was vitally important to preserve peace and the Optional Clause would serve this cause. British acceptance of the Clause would have a general beneficial influence, particularly on 'the smaller turbulent foreign powers'. Secondly, acceptance of the Optional Clause would enable any part of the empire to take a dispute with another foreign state to the PCIJ if that other state had likewise accepted the Optional Clause without reservations.

On the other hand, there were five weighty disadvantages to accepting the Optional Clause. Firstly, both of the above-mentioned advantages were illusory. There was no prospect of either the Soviet Union or the United States accepting the Optional Clause. And although Britain would always execute the judgements of the PCIJ 'to the fullest practicable extent', other states could not be relied upon to do likewise.

Secondly, despite Britain's honourable attitude to legal decisions, it was impossible for a democratic state to bind itself in advance because a future

---

[57] See report of Cabinet committee on compulsory arbitration in international disputes, secret, 25 Oct. 1926, PRO, CP 359(26) CAB 27/330; memorandum by Cecil, secret, 23 Oct. 1926, CP 360(26) CAB 27/330.

[58] Imperial conference 1926, compulsory arbitration in international disputes, memorandum prepared for the imperial conference, secret, E.114, PRO, CP 359(26) appendix, CAB 27/330. Printed for the imperial conference as E(IR/26)2, Nov. 1926, CAB 32/57 (emphasis added). Cecil, however, thought the crucial questions were: 1. Was it desirable that judicial decision should take the place of war as a means of settlement of justiciable international disputes? (to which his answer was yes); 2. Would British acceptance of compulsory judicial decision in justiciable disputes have an important influence in promoting the general substitution of judicial decision for war as a means of settling such disputes? (to which his answer was yes); 3. Notwithstanding the advantages claimed as a result of an affirmative answer to the first two questions, would compulsory judicial decision of justiciable disputes involve such risks for the British empire that it should not be accepted? (to which his answer was no.)

parliament might refuse to pass legislation which was required in pursuance of an adverse judicial decision. However, it would always be possible in any given instance for a member of the Commonwealth to obtain from parliament an advance assurance that such legislation would be approved.

Thirdly, acceptance of the Optional Clause 'would involve the complete waiver of the right to reserve ... disputes touching the vital interests, independence or honour of the State'. The serious implications of such a 'waiver' on matters as important as the position of Britain in Egypt or immigration into the dominions would be unacceptable to public opinion throughout the empire.

Fourthly, the PCIJ was not 'English'. As such it was unsuitable for disputes of primary importance 'since it has decided not to be bound by any rules of evidence'. This made it 'very dangerous' to agree to be bound by the Court in advance of the emergence of any particular dispute.

Fifthly, the procedure for electing judges gave 'ample scope for political influence'. The scope for exerting such influence would be 'considerably accentuated' if it were known that a dispute pending between two states was going to be referred to the Court. In conclusion, therefore, Hogg suggested that it was premature to accept the Optional Clause and the Commonwealth should adopt India's suggestion that the question should rest for a few years until there had been more experience of the working of the Court.[59]

The Optional Clause and the imperial conference of 1926

The imperial conference met in London on 19 October 1926. On 4 November Hogg's memorandum on the Optional Clause was circulated to the dominion representatives on the committee on inter-imperial relations and the subject was discussed by the committee on 9 November.[60] The inter-imperial relations committee was preoccupied with the discussions leading to the Balfour Declaration – a landmark in the evolving constitutional structure of the Commonwealth and for which the conference is chiefly remembered. This stated that the dominions were 'autonomous Communities within the British Empire, equal in status, in no way subordinate one to another in any aspect of their domestic or external affairs, though united by a common allegiance to the Crown, and freely associated as members of the British Commonwealth of Nations'.[61]

As Balfour (the Lord President of the Council) said himself, the declaration only contained views which he had held and publicly expressed for many years, and he had 'merely fashioned into a new, elegant and acceptable form phrases

---

[59] Ibid.

[60] Those present at the meeting which discussed the Optional Clause were: Balfour (Lord President of the Council, in the chair), Chamberlain, Amery, Hogg, Mackenzie King (Canadian prime minister), Lapointe (Canadian minister of justice), Bruce (Australian prime minister) Coates (New Zealand prime minister), Hertzog (South African prime minister), Havenga (South African minister of finance), O'Higgins (Irish minister of justice and vice-president of the Executive Council), Fitzgerald (Irish minister of external affairs), Costello (Irish attorney general), Monroe (Newfoundland prime minister), Morine (Newfoundland minister without portfolio) and the Maharajah of Burdwan.

[61] *Imperial conference 1926: Summary of proceedings*, London (*Command paper* 2768), 1926, 9.

that had been tossed around, sometimes for years'.[62] But the declaration was important because it satisfied the *amour propre* of the dominions by clarifying dominion status and the nature of the Commonwealth without sacrificing the doctrine of *inter-se*. It was not surprising that the Optional Clause was disposed of in one meeting.

The only dominion that appeared to take an interest in the Optional Clause, let alone give any indication of having examined Hogg's memorandum on the subject, was Canada. Lapointe, a keen supporter of the League of Nations, the most influential French Canadian politician, and a man whose views on foreign policy were virtually identical with those of Mackenzie King (the dominant figure in Canadian politics), spoke for Canada on the Optional Clause. Having drawn attention to the expressed willingness of Canada to accept the Optional Clause in 1925, he read out a statement which took issue with four points in Hogg's memorandum. Firstly, said Lapointe, other states could be trusted to honour their commitments under the Optional Clause. Secondly, he held that parliamentary consent was required whether an international agreement was general or special. Thirdly, he pointed out that acceptance of the Optional Clause could be subject to reciprocity and a time limit could be placed on the duration of acceptance of the Clause. Fourthly, it was possible to make explicit reservations on matters of vital interest. Finally, Lapointe told the meeting that Canadian public opinion favoured compulsory arbitration and that, in his view, 'the gain to world peace involved in the acceptance and application of the principle of arbitral settlement may more than offset specific disadvantages'. However, Canada recognised that 'in a matter of such moment it may be desirable to await the test of time' and it was 'therefore prepared to postpone further consideration . . . for the present'.[63]

The other dominion leaders had little to say on the subject. Coates, the New Zealander, explained that 'it was difficult to say that [the] people [of New Zealand] understood all about the Court . . . they wanted to know what other countries were going to do before they committed themselves'. Hertzog, the South African prime minister, said that 'in South Africa the feeling was that if they could have arbitration, they should have it'. Bruce of Australia conceded that the Optional Clause was supported by a large number of Australians (the Australian League of Nations Union and some Australian MPs having begun pressing the Clause on the government). But Bruce thought 'there would be a complete revulsion of feeling if this proportion of the public realised that certain matters, however vital to the Empire, would have to be arbitrated'. Finally, Fitzgerald of the Irish Free State simply said that 'as far as public opinion had expressed itself' the Irish were in favour of it.[64]

At the end of the short, 'skilfully' handled discussion,[65] the committee had no difficulty in reaching an agreement which neither advocated adopting nor rejecting adhesion to the Optional Clause. It stated that 'no resolution should be proposed to the Conference on the question, it being understood that no

[62] Garner, *Commonwealth office*, 51.

[63] Committee on inter-imperial relations, ninth meeting, 9 Nov. 1926, PRO, E(IR-26), CAB 32/56.

[64] Ibid. Monroe of Newfoundland and the Maharajah of Burdwan also agreed to postponing discussion of the Optional Clause.

[65] See Amery diary entry, 9 Nov. 1926, *The Leo Amery diaries*, i, 1896–1929, ed. John Barnes and David Nicholson, London 1980, 478.

Government would take any action in the direction of the compulsory jurisdiction of the Court without bringing the matter up again for discussion'.[66] The committee's report, however, was completely in line with Hogg's proposal in stating that the committee was unanimous 'in favouring the widest possible extension . . . of arbitration . . . [but] it was at present premature to accept the obligations' of the Optional Clause.[67] This was most satisfactory for Britain, which thought that the question of the Optional Clause had been at least shelved until the next imperial conference, since it was assumed that 'consultation could hardly take place satisfactorily except around a table'.[68]

The imperial conference did give Britain a breathing space, but not the four years that were expected. The ease with which agreement had been reached was due to the relevant committee's preoccupation with drafting the Balfour Declaration and the good-natured, convivial atmosphere of the conference. But it did not weaken Canada's support which grew over the next few years. Australian support also grew and the Irish Free State continued to favour the Optional Clause whenever someone else brought it up. A turning point in the development of Commonwealth policy on the Optional Clause was reached in the summer of 1928, when both Canada and Australia came to believe that it was time to move down the path to the Optional Clause. And before long Canada had reached the stage of threatening that, if necessary, it would travel alone. It is, therefore appropriate to divide subsequent Commonwealth policy on the Optional Clause into two sections: the period up to the summer of 1928, and the period leading up to the 1929 general election in Britain.

The dominions and the Optional Clause 1927–8

On the surface, from the perspective of the British government, it would seem that the dominions were 'sound' during this period.[69] After the clamorous Assembly of 1927, and just as the LNU campaign for the Optional Clause was about to take off, Ivone Kirkpatrick, a second secretary in the western department, complacently minuted that: 'Canada is rather toying with the

[66] Committee on inter-imperial relations, ninth meeting.

[67] Report of the committee on inter-imperial relations, signed by Balfour, 18 Nov. 1926, secret, PRO, E 129 CAB 32/47.

[68] Minute by Campbell (senior clerk in the western department), 14 Nov. 1927, PRO, W 10860/61/98 FO 371/12678. See also Chamberlain's answer to a Commons question on 24 Nov. 1926, House of Commons *debs.*, 382.

[69] Holland has written that 'whilst the Locarno lull continued the Optional Clause was quietly ignored. But once signs of instability returned . . . pressure built up for a "forward move" at the League to stop the rot in Europe. The dominions were carried along by this current since, regarding League membership as the most solid evidence for their "international status" they were reluctant to do anything which detracted from the League's significance': 'Commonwealth in British official mind', 133. Donald Page ascribes the development of Canadian policy to campaigning by the Canadian League of Nations Society. As a result of what he describes as 'the greatest demonstration of public interest in Canadian external policy in the 'twenties', Skelton and King were led to review Canadian policy and 'allow Senator Dandurand to begin discussions at the diplomatic level on the acceptance of the Optional Clause': 'The Institute's popular arm: the League of Nations Society in Canada', *International Journal* xxxiii (1977–8), 53–4. See also idem, 'Canadians and the League of Nations before the Manchurian crisis', unpubl. PhD diss. Toronto 1972, 310. It may be suggested that both Page and Holland have succumbed to the *post hoc* fallacy. See Lorna Lloyd, ' "Equality means freedom to differ": Canada, Britain and the world court in the 1920s', *Diplomacy and Statecraft*, vii (1996).

proposal to sign. South Africa and the IFS are more or less indifferent and could probably be pushed into signing. Australia and NZ are hostile.'[70] Canada was, however, doing rather more than simply 'toying' with the idea.

It has been suggested that even though Mackenzie King was in a strong political position – he had just secured his first majority government and faced an opposition that was neither effective nor coherent – he might have found himself in an embarrassing position on his return to Canada after the 1926 imperial conference. This was because, despite King's support for an 'independent' Canadian foreign policy, he had 'abandoned' Canada's arbitration policy in deference to British objections. But Canada had been willing to give way on this point because it was not yet a high priority and she had had her way on other conference matters. And, while it is reasonable that King's critics should have shared the assumption that the promised Commonwealth consultation on the Optional Clause could only take place in the context of an imperial conference, it is important to note that, like Hertzog of South Africa (who also wanted to emphasise his country's 'independence') King found it politically expedient to do so in a moderate way. Moreover, in 1926 Canada was the only dominion that appeared to have given any serious consideration to the Optional Clause.

In the spring of 1927, Sir George Foster, an enthusiastic octogenarian supporter of the League of Nations, criticised the Canadian government in the Senate for failing to accept the Optional Clause because of the opposition of the British government and some of the other dominions. From the Canadian perspective, he explained, this step had the advantage of combining idealism with particular national interests. The Optional Clause provided 'a sheltered zone in which Canada should immediately place herself'. 'Here we are', he continued, 'on this American continent, with no-one to the north of us except the cold silence of the northern zone; no present enemy; and, I think, no possible enemy; and there is no other to the southern boundary than the people of the United States.'[71] And Canada would certainly never go to war with the United States.

Dandurand replied on behalf of the government that Canada had already indicated its support for the Optional Clause in its reply on the Geneva Protocol and that he had repeated this at the sixth (1925) Assembly. 'We can well afford to wait until the next [imperial] conference and see what will happen in the meantime', he said. Nine-tenths of Canada's disputes were with the USA which did not belong to the PCIJ. In the unlikely event of the USA adhering to both the Statute of the PCIJ and the Optional Clause, Canada would hasten to follow suit.[72]

Britain regarded the rebellious eighth Assembly as 'a very strong dominions Assembly' with harmonious and intimate relations between Commonwealth delegates.[73] This was partly due to the British delegates on League committees being specifically charged with keeping in touch with their dominion

---

[70] Minute, 1 Dec. 1927, PRO, W 11351/62/98 FO 371/12678.

[71] Canadian Senate debs., 30 Mar. 1927, V.LXII, no. 23, 261, PRO, W 4659/62/98 FO 371/12678.

[72] Documents on Canadian foreign policy, 417–19.

[73] Onslow to Tyrrell, private and confidential, 25 Sept. 1927, PRO, W 9382/9382/98 FO 371/ 12686. See also Onslow to Chamberlain, 26 Sept. 1927, and Lyttleton to Onslow, 28 Oct. 1927, W 11208/9382/98 FO 371/12786.

counterparts and partly because the proposed Dutch and Polish resolutions, which would have revived the arbitral provisions of the Geneva Protocol, necessitated frequent consultations. As soon as the Dutch resolution was tabled, Chamberlain convened a BED meeting. Explaining that the terms of the resolution and the history of the Protocol made this a matter on which 'any but a united front on the part of the British Empire delegations could not be lightly contemplated', he reminded the dominion leaders of the decision of the 1926 imperial conference on 'compulsory arbitration' and invited their views. The dominion delegates indicated that none of them had the authority to reverse their governments' attitudes on the Protocol; that they had no reason to think that their governments had changed their attitudes; and that they considered the Dutch resolution was 'inexpedient and inopportune'.[74] Dandurand, however, (who 'was most diffuse in his observations besides keeping us till 12.30 a.m.'):

> evidently still cherishe[d] a great sentimental enthusiasm for the principles of compulsory arbitration, in spite of the fact that Canada rejected the Protocol when faced with the practical commitments which it involved. It became necessary for Sir A.C. to express some astonishment that Senator Dandurand should contemplate with comparative equanimity the unlimited obligations of a revised Protocol – e.g., the obligation in certain circumstances to apply economic sanctions against the U.S. . . . or go to war in defence of Liberia, when Canada had not found herself able to become a party to Locarno which confined itself to matters of the most vital interest to Great Britain and was strictly limited in the obligations it involved. This was said and taken in very good part but the palpable hit gradually brought the Senator down to realities and, as recorded, he agreed with the other dominion delegates.[75]

Dandurand's speech on the final day of the opening plenary sessions did explain why his country was unable to accept the Geneva Protocol. He also emphasised the importance of the United States factor in Canadian foreign policy; reminded his hearers of the demilitarised Canadian-American frontier and the history of peaceful relations between these two countries; and repeated that his country supported the Optional Clause. He was not, however, taken seriously by the British who regarded him as 'a conceited, talkative, cocky little man, full of self importance'.[76]

---

[74] Memorandum for Chamberlain by Liesching (Dominions Office) and Cadogan, 7 Sept. 1927, PRO, W 8518/61/98 FO 371/12675. See also Liesching to Dixon (assistant under secretary, Dominions Office), 8 Sept. 1927, W 8693/61/98 FO 371/12675. On 19 Sept. Liesching reported to Dixon that a BED meeting that day had confirmed that dominion opposition to the Geneva Protocol remained unaltered and was 'if possible stronger than ever'. The Irish Free State delegate had not attended the meeting because the results of the Irish elections were coming through: W 9015/61/98 FO 371/12675.

[75] Liesching to Dixon, 7 Sept. 1927. 'You can never understand how long it took to overcome or rather outlast Senator Dandurand's volubility', Cadogan told Villiers: 7 Sept. 1927, W 8572/61/98 FO 371/16275.

[76] Onslow to Tyrrell, private and confidential, 25 Sept. 1927. See also Onslow to Tyrrell, private and confidential, 26 Sept. 1927, PRO, W 9382/9382/98 FO 371/12686; Cadogan to Villiers, 11 Sept. 1927, W 8693/61/98 FO 371/12675; minute by Chamberlain, 9 Nov. 1925, W 9478/9478/98 FO 371/11071. Dandurand was not, however, such a lightweight. He had been president of the 1925 Assembly and successfully championed Canada's bid for a Council seat in 1927: Lorna Lloyd, 'Le Sénateur Dandurand, pionnier du règlement pacifique des différends', Études Internationales xxiii (1992).

Kirkpatrick complacently dismissed Dandurand's speech as consisting 'chiefly of an offer to sign the optional clause',[77] but Skelton (King's influential adviser and the under secretary in the Canadian Department of External Affairs) was underlining Dandurand's words by privately informing the British delegation that acceptance of the Optional Clause was becoming an immediate Canadian foreign policy goal. Canada had 'given way' in 1926, but it was 'still very strongly in favour of compulsory arbitration and . . . signing the optional clause'. His government, he said, intended to raise the question soon but he took note of the objections of Australia and New Zealand and promised that they would receive serious consideration. Skelton did not, however, leave an Australian delegate under any illusion that he had been 'much shaken' by Australia's objections and the latter thought that he had only 'induced the Canadian Government to go more slowly'.[78]

Meanwhile the British LNU leadership saw Canada as a means of putting pressure on the British government. Their views were so much in harmony that Mackenzie King's formidable under secretary for external affairs, Skelton, relied heavily on the Union's Optional Clause pamphlet in a government memorandum advocating a forward move.[79] Personal relations were also good. Colonel David Carnegie, a member of the LNU executive with close Canadian links, spent six months helping the Canadian League of Nations Society with its Optional Clause campaign. When Cecil urged Dandurand that 'Canada could give a very effective lead to Great Britain by acting on its expressed intention of accepting the optional clause', Dandurand replied that 'Canada was moving in that direction'.[80] Canada's first steps were verbal. Skelton's suggestion of encouraging public discussion of the Optional Clause was followed by statements in the Commons that Canada was in favour of discussing with Britain its wish to sign the Clause. However, it took the signature of the Kellogg pact to spur Mackenzie King into doing anything more.

During this period the Irish Free State's policy on the Optional Clause remained little more than an instinctive support for the ideal of compulsory adjudication. While Canada was steadily moving forwards in 1927, the Free State did not march in step. The Assembly records contain no indication that Free State delegates ever mentioned the Optional Clause. When directly asked for the Irish view, the Irish delegate refused to give one since the delegation 'did not know what the policy of the new government would be'[81] – the results of the second general election that year were coming through during the Assembly.

In October 1927, Geoffrey Mander (a leading Liberal on the LNU executive who was elected MP for Wolverhampton in 1929) suggested to Gilbert Murray that the LNU should try to persuade the Irish Free State to sign the Optional Clause in much the same way as Cecil was recommending the Optional Clause to Dandurand. 'Prime facie one would think that they would be only too

[77] Minute, 5 Oct. 1927, PRO, W 9382/9382/98 FO 371/12686. For Dandurand's speech to the plenary meeting see *Documents on Canadian foreign policy*, 304–7.
[78] Note from Maxse (dominions information department), 23 Sept. 1927, PRO, W 9050/61/98 FO 371/12678.
[79] See Skelton memorandum, 12 Dec. 1928, NAC, MG J4, vol. 127, file 965, PCIJ reel C-2720.
[80] Veatch, *Canada and the League of Nations*, 59.
[81] Note from Maxse, 23 Sept. 1927.

delighted to do something sensible that England declined to do', Mander wrote to Murray.

> It would give them an opportunity of showing their independence . . .. I gather that Canada is well-disposed towards the idea, but Ireland, for obvious reasons, should be very much easier to move, and the advantages in thus breaking the Empire opposition to the clause would be great.[82]

A month later, however, Mander reported back to Murray that 'a very confidential source at Geneva' had confided to him that, although the Irish 'want to sign', they 'do not want to annoy the British at the moment because they are on good terms with them'. The Irish were mindful that the imperial conference of 1926 had bound them not to do anything without consulting the rest of the Commonwealth but:

> They . . . realise the importance of the question and in time can probably get Canada also. It is almost certain that before March 31st of next year [i.e. 1928] a letter will go to London raising the question, i.e. the 'further discussion'. It is exceedingly probable that before the Assembly of 1929 they will have signed the clause. I think one of their motives for postponement is to sign some time nearer to the moment when they may again become candidates for the [League] council.[83]

Such a letter was not sent before 1929 and the British Foreign Office was unaware of Ireland's interest in the Optional Clause. '[T]he Free State know and care nothing about the question', Kirkpatrick had minuted in September 1927.[84] Anglo-Irish relations were, indeed, quite good and 'British opinion as a whole basked in the happy delusion of Anglo-Irish reconciliation',[85] failing to realise the depth of bitterness in a country which had won independence only after a long and difficult struggle. During these years the Free State was overwhelmingly preoccupied with domestic problems relating to the 1922 'treaty' – at the expense of foreign policy. In 1926 the formation of the *Fianna Fáil* by De Valera provided an umbrella for the anti-'treaty' elements which opposed the oath of allegiance to the king and regarded the separation from the Free State of the six counties of Ulster as a betrayal of Irish nationalism. The two elections of 1927 demonstrated the increasing polarisation of Irish politics around the 'treaty' issue and the decline of the parties upon which Patrick Cosgrave's moderate, pro-'treaty' *Cumann na nGaedheal*, had depended. In 1927 the *Cumann na nGaedheal* Party lost the dominant position it had held since 1923 and, in July of that year, the development of Irish foreign policy was a casualty of the assassination of Kevin O'Higgins. O'Higgins, the vice-president and minister of External Affairs, had been one of the most formidable and impressive members of Cosgrave's administration. Now, however, the foreign affairs portfolio was tacked on to Patrick McGilligan's responsibilities as minister for Industry and Commerce. Relegated to a back seat in governmental business, foreign policy remained primarily focused on status, which had earlier been represented by the despatch of an envoy to Washington, the sending of a permanent official to the

---

82 Mander to Murray, 11 Oct. 1927, Bodl. Lib., Murray papers.
83 Mander to Murray, confidential, 7 Nov. 1927, ibid.
84 Minute, 26 Sept. 1927, PRO, W 9050/61/98 FO 371/12678.
85 Holland, 'Commonwealth in British official mind', 192.

League and the registration of the Irish 'treaty' with the League. In other words, 'Irish activity in the League was concerned principally with the definition of Ireland's relationship to Britain'.[86]

Australia was moving cautiously towards favouring the Optional Clause in 1927–8. At the eighth (1927) Assembly, during discussion of Nansen's proposed 'Optional Convention',[87] Sir George Pearce, the leader of the Australian delegation and a former minister of defence in Hughes's government, made quite clear Australia's opposition to any form of compulsory arbitration. It was, he reminded the Assembly, one of Australia's main reasons for rejecting the Geneva Protocol, and 'the reference to the first Committee . . . would be a waste of time when it was known that it could not be accepted by certain States represented at the Assembly'. However, when it was pointed out that the proposal was aimed at 'an optional clause concerning arbitration' similar to the Optional Clause of the PCIJ and that there was no question of compelling all states to make use of compulsory arbitration, he withdrew his objections to it being further examined.[88] A few days later Harrison Moore told the first committee that

> although representing a country which did not, at the present time, consider it essential to accept compulsory arbitration, [he] was sympathetically inclined to the Norwegian [Nansen's] proposal. The preparation of a model treaty was a task which the League might very profitably undertake.[89]

Seven months later, when the Australian House of Representatives debated the report of the Australian delegation to the eighth (1927) Assembly, Latham (the Attorney General) reminded the House of the decision of the 1926 imperial conference that the Optional Clause 'was of such fundamental importance' that it required further examination, and that:

> It had been agreed that no part of the Empire should take independent action in connection with it, but that there should be full consideration before anything was done. The Commonwealth Government was now agreed in [sic] a consideration of the subject of arbitration, and particularly of the Optional Clause. They hoped to be in a position at an early date to communicate with the other parts of the Empire with the object of arriving at a common agreement on the matter.[90]

What concerned his government was that the vagueness of international law introduced a 'considerable element of uncertainty' about the likely decisions of the Court. When such problems had been resolved his government hoped to be able to join with other Commonwealth countries in signing the Optional Clause. In so doing, there was one point on which Australia was clear: that it

[86] Norman MacQueen, 'Eamonn de Valera, the Irish Free State and the League of Nations, 1919–46', *Eire-Ireland* xii (1982), 113.

[87] See above, 106.

[88] League of Nations, Minutes of the third committee (reduction of armaments), *LNOJ*, special supplement no. 57, 1927 (*LNA8 third committee*), sixth meeting, 17 Sept. 1927, 43. See also Liesching to Dixon, 7, 19 Sept. 1927.

[89] League of Nations, Minutes of the first committee (constitutional and legal questions), *LNOJ*, special supplement no. 55, 1927 (*LNA8 first committee*), sixth meeting, 21 Sept. 1927, 25. Harrison Moore and Costello of the Irish Free State were subsequently appointed to the sub-committee which was set up to examine Nansen's proposal.

[90] House of Representatives *debs.*, 26 Apr. 1928, *Journal of the Parliaments of the Empire* ix, 701–2.

would be very unlikely that any member of the Commonwealth would desire to take inter-imperial disputes to the world court. A few months later, in August, Bruce, the prime minister, refused to commit himself to any course of action and there, for the time being, Australian policy rested.

It is surprising that the Australian government should have gone this far, given its position in 1924 and 1929. That it had done so was not known to Philip Noel-Baker, who was very closely involved in trying to push Britain down the path to the Optional Clause.[91] One explanation of Australia's forward progress might have been pressure on the government from the Australian League of Nations Union – in February 1929 the Australian government conceded that signing the Optional Clause 'would give satisfaction to public opinion which has recently been growing up on this question'.[92] But there is no reason to suppose that Australian public opinion was any more influential than public opinion in Canada and Britain. Another reason could have been the advocacy of the Optional Clause by the Australian Labour Party. Like its British counterpart, the Australian Labour Party supported internationalism and disarmament, and Charlton, the Labour leader who had been a delegate to the fifth (1924) Assembly, had responded to Latham's statement in April 1928 by advocating arbitration, the Optional Clause and the Geneva Protocol. But here, too, there is no reason to believe that this factor was significant. A more likely explanation is that the Australian government was being led to a serious examination of its whole policy on arbitration and the Optional Clause chiefly by recent developments at Geneva and by the information which it was receiving about the proposed Anglo-American arbitration treaty (which, because of its implications for BMR, aroused Australia's close concern). But there was no urgency about the process, and no sign that the government was thinking of raising the subject within the Commonwealth.

South Africa's policy up to the summer of 1928 can best be described as one of vacillating disinterest. Speaking in private at the eighth (1927) Assembly, South Africa seemed sympathetically inclined but in public it toed the Commonwealth line. The following year, when countries were changing paeans to the Kellogg pact, the South African delegate made the statutory genuflection. But his speech to the plenary meeting concentrated on his country's 'grave concern . . . [for] the well-being of . . . uncivilised races', and the necessity of preventing 'the savage hordes of Africa' from being 'trained and armed in accordance with modern military ideas'.[93]

New Zealand, whose general 'attitude may be summed up briefly as a fervent loyalty to the British crown, a distrust of constitutional changes within the Empire, lukewarmness toward the League of Nations, and readiness to co-operate in imperial, and especially in naval, defense',[94] remained utterly reliable on the Optional Clause. The New Zealand delegation joined the Australians in

91 Conversation with Noel-Baker, June 1980.

92 Copy of despatch from Mackenzie King to Amery enclosing telegram from the government of the Commonwealth of Australia, 23 Feb. 1929, PRO, W 2335/21/98 FO 371/14102.

93 League of Nations, Records of the ninth ordinary session of the Assembly, plenary meetings, text of the debates, LNOJ, special supplement no. 64, 1928 (LNA9 debs.), twelfth plenary, 11 September 1928, 93. Cf. Manning, Policies of the British dominions, 61–2.

94 J. B. Condliffe, 'The attitude of New Zealand on imperial and foreign affairs' in Great Britain and the dominions, 1927, 369.

being particularly critical of attempts to revive the Geneva Protocol at the eighth (1927) Assembly, and a resolution sent to the New Zealand government criticising the British government's 'lukewarm attitude towards arbitration and disarmament' drew the reply from the High Commissioner in London that 'I must say quite bluntly that I do not agree with the terms of the resolution; and, further, that I have reason to believe that the policy of the British Government receives the unqualified support of the Government of the Dominion of New Zealand.'[95]

The turning point in the development of Commonwealth policy on the Optional Clause: the Kellogg-Briand pact and the ninth (1928) Assembly

The summer of 1928 took some Commonwealth countries further along the path towards the Optional Clause and brought them close to accepting compulsory adjudication. Arbitration was on the dominions' minds before summer since Kellogg's proposed Anglo-American arbitration treaty (about which London kept them informed) directed their attention towards examining their attitudes towards arbitrating particular types of disputes. It was, however, the Kellogg pact – which was warmly welcomed by public opinion throughout the Commonwealth – that influenced policies on the Optional Clause. This was because it was seen as dictating a forward move on arbitration and adjudication in the immediate future, and it was Canada that moved first.

In August 1928, the Canadian leader, Mackenzie King, travelled to Europe to sign the Kellogg pact and he proceeded from Paris to Geneva to address the ninth Assembly. King found the latter experience an 'agonizing ordeal' and, '[a]fter a few days of misgivings about having 'really no message' and being 'fearful of pitfalls and commonplaces', he fell back on the well-worn theme of the lessons to be learned by Europe from Canada's example'.[96] He also fell back on another well-worn Canadian theme – but one which was much to the Assembly's taste – his country's support for compulsory arbitration and the need to develop the machinery for the pacific settlement of disputes in the wake of the Kellogg pact. 'I speak', he said,

> for the whole of Canada when I say that our experience leads us to favour, in so far as Canadian questions are concerned, the reference to arbitration of all international disputes of a judicial or legal nature and the settlement, by methods of conciliation or arbitration, of all other differences that may arise between Canada and any other nation.[97]

Canada was not the only dominion to speak in this vein. At the next plenary meeting, Blythe (the Irish Minister of Finance and Vice-President of the Council) declared that the Kellogg pact made resort to war 'an outrage' in 'the law of civilised society' and that a state had 'no more right than a private

---

[95] Sir James Parr to Mr. Manus (London Liberal Federation), 29 March 1928, PRO, W 3330/28/98 FO 411/7.
[96] H. Blair Neatby, *William Lyon Mackenzie King, 1924–32. The lonely heights*, London 1963, 264–5.
[97] LNA9 debs., seventh plenary, 7 September 1928, 61. At this Assembly, Mackenzie King was elected one of the six vice-presidents.

individual to attack and kill its neighbours'. Referring to what King had said a few days earlier, he did 'not hesitate to say that the Irish Free State is no less strongly in favour of arbitration than Canada. It is the duty of all the Governments which have signed the Kellogg pact to endeavour to bring about the conditions under which it can most surely achieve its object.'[98]

Neither New Zealand nor South Africa made any specific comment on arbitration in their Assembly speeches, but McLaughlin (the leader of the Australian delegation and a senator in the Australian parliament) indicated that the Kellogg pact had influenced his government's arbitration policy. Like King, McLaughlin had been in Paris to sign the pact and he told the Assembly of his belief that '[i]f ... nations renounce war ... some other means must be provided. Arbitration is a suitable method for disputes of a juridical nature, and some form of conciliation is necessary for disputes which do not lend themselves to settlement by arbitration or by the decision of the Permanent Court.'

However, McLaughlin made it clear that his country did not unreservedly support general compulsory arbitration. Like Britain, Australia preferred the bilateral rather than the multilateral approach to such matters, and McLaughlin reminded the Assembly that, although League members were bound to submit to the authority of the League when disputes arose, this did not include matters of domestic jurisdiction: 'Every country desires to be master of its own internal policy, and this fact should be kept constantly and clearly in view.'[99]

When the Assembly got down to committee work, Canada acted on its words. Early on in the proceedings of the first committee, Dandurand proposed that states be invited to explain exactly what uncertainties in international law prevented them from signing the Optional Clause. Persuaded to defer his proposal until the committee was actually discussing the Optional Clause, he reintroduced it at the end of the lengthy meeting when the first and third committees approved the text of the General Act. The meeting agreed, without debate, that the exhortatory resolution on the Optional Clause should have an additional paragraph in which states would be asked to 'indicate the questions of international law the elucidation of which would facilitate their acceptance of Article 36 of the Statute'.[100]

Dandurand probably made this move partly because he was impatient of British dilatoriness and was trying to use the Assembly to clear the path to the Optional Clause not just for Canada's sake, but for that of the world. Britain's leadership was essential for the success of the League, the Kellogg pact required states to settle all their disputes peacefully and Britain was the chief obstacle to the general acceptance of the Optional Clause. In private he told the British that Canada was about to sign the Clause. When Hurst 'expressed surprise' and reminded Dandurand that the 1926 Commonwealth agreement bound Canada to do nothing before the 1930 imperial conference, Dandurand replied 'in a bantering tone that he had drafted the 1926 resolution badly'. Canada was very soon to begin 'conferring through the circularizing of the sister-nations, without

[98] LNA9 debs., tenth plenary, 10 September 1928, 78–9.
[99] LNA9 debs., fifth plenary, 6 September 1928, 41.
[100] See League of Nations, Minutes of the first committee (constitutional and legal questions), LNOJ, special supplement no. 65, 1928 (LNA9 first committee), third meeting, 12 Sept. 1928, 15; joint meeting of first and third committees, 24 Sept. 1928, LNA9 first committee, 93 and LNA9 debs., nineteenth plenary, 26 Sept. 1928, 183.

waiting for an Imperial Conference'.[101] Perhaps because such information from Canada was similar to what Britain had heard the previous year, or perhaps because the British regarded Dandurand as a lightweight, there is no indication in the Foreign Office records of much attention being paid to this news. And in the Foreign Office post mortem on the Assembly, there was no mention of any difficulties with the Commonwealth.

Britain heard nothing of Canada's proposal to move ahead on the Optional Clause for several months. In December, however, Dandurand's initiative at the Assembly resulted in Britain receiving from Geneva a questionnaire on the Optional Clause. In September the British delegation had neither opposed nor commented on the additional paragraph. But now that the secretariat had acted on the resolution, the Foreign Office did not know how Britain could reply. Firstly, it was felt that Britain could not respond until the conclusion of the Anglo-American negotiations on the proposed arbitration treaty; and, secondly, a reply could not be sent without consulting the dominions. Hurst thought 'the simplest and wisest course' would be to ignore the questionnaire which is what he thought most states would do.[102] Chamberlain, none the less, directed that the dominions should be consulted and that copies of the questionnaire be sent to the Cabinet and the dominions. In the meantime the League was to be told that Britain's reply would be delayed. When the Dominions Office asked the Foreign Office about the reply, it was told that the Anglo-American negotiations, about which the dominions had been kept fully informed, was the reason for the delay. But then, in January, Canada took a further step forward by declaring that it was going to sign the Optional Clause.

The Canadian initiative and Commonwealth consultation on the Optional Clause, January–March 1929

On 23 January 1929 MacKenzie King telegraphed London to say that Canada had decided to accept the Optional Clause. The arguments to the contrary did not outweigh those in favour of taking this 'essential step towards establishing peace and removing fear and suspicion'. Recent developments – especially the Kellogg pact – had confirmed 'the necessity of working out means' for 'peaceful settlement of legal disputes by reference to [the] appropriate tribunal'.[103] In February the Canadian initiative became public when, in answer to a parliamentary question, King said that Canada was corresponding with other Commonwealth countries in accordance with its 1926 'undertaking not to sign formally until there had been an opportunity for discussion'.[104]

---

[101] Canadian Senate debs., 17 Apr. 1934, 249, quoted in Veatch, Canada and the League of Nations, 59.

[102] Minutes by Hurst and Campbell (head of the western department), 21 Dec. 1928, PRO, W 11436/309/98 FO 371/13391. Campbell accordingly suggested shelving the subject until 1 Mar. but Lindsay (who had become permanent under secretary in July 1928) said it was 'hard to think any answer will be easier on March 1 than today': minute, 24 Dec. 1928, ibid.

[103] Telegram from Mackenzie King to Amery, 23 Jan. 1929, (received 24 Jan. 1929), PRO, W 763/21/98 FO 371/14102.

[104] Documents on Canadian foreign policy, 421; Canadian House of Commons debs., 19 Feb. 1929, PRO, D 5429/29, W 6779/21/98 FO 371/14104; quoted by Cecil in the House of Lords on 1 May 1929, House of Lords debs., 289-90.

Britain did not react to the Canadian telegram with any alarm. Indeed, it does not seem to have been distributed with any sense of urgency. Three days after King's telegram had been received, Ronald Campbell (who had taken over from Villiers as head of the western department) minuted that he was not aware that the question of signing the Optional Clause was under consideration, although he did know that some of the dominions were 'definitely coming round to the policy of signing the Clause'[105] and this meant that the question would soon have to be reconsidered. Since Canada had raised the subject, the job of consulting the other dominions and disseminating their views was conducted by Ottawa. There was, it seems, no concern about that either, probably because it was anticipated that dominions other than the Irish Free State would apply the brake to Canada. In other words, they would tell Canada that they did not want to move forward speedily, and Canada would refrain from immediate action out of respect for the principle of imperial unity. In any case, the Dominions Office was sanguine that explaining the need for the Clause to be considered in connection with the draft Anglo-American arbitration treaty 'would doubtless suffice to check any precipitate action'.[106]

When New Zealand and South Africa received their copies of the Canadian telegram on the Optional Clause, they immediately telegraphed to ask Britain for its views – communications which crossed with a British telegram telling them that, as in the case of the League questionnaire, British policy could not be settled because of the Anglo-American arbitration treaty which turned largely on the question of BMR. South Africa duly sent Canada a 'very sensible telegram' which would hopefully 'damp[en] the ardour of the Canadian government'.[107] While sympathising with Canada's viewpoint, South Africa thought that the proposed Anglo-American treaty should be given priority and that 'the matter [of the Optional Clause] could very well stand over'.[108] New Zealand also agreed that the Optional Clause should be considered *after* the Anglo-American negotiations had been completed, as did Australia. But the Australian telegram added the rider that 'they consider it is undesirable to maintain *non possumus* attitude . . . for very much longer . . . . it would be advantageous to endeavour to reach some definite policy even before the next Imperial Conference'. As Bruce told King, Australia had been considering the question for some time. And, like Canada, Australia held that since the Kellogg pact had thrown on its signatories an obligation to submit all disputes to pacific settlement, it was necessary to review their attitude to the Optional Clause:

> with a view to drawing the clearest lines of demarcation possible between those differences which can be submitted to the Permanent Court of International Justice for judicial settlement and those for which some other form of peaceful settlement is desirable. In this connection they consider that it would be an advantage to agree in advance that all purely justiciable disputes susceptible of being settled by legal principles accepted by parties be submitted to the Court. Such a course would not only give satisfaction to public opinion . . . but . . . would tend to strengthen the Court.[109]

105 Minute, 27 Jan. 1929, PRO, W 836/21/98 FO 371/14102.
106 Minute by Clutterbuck, 31 Jan. 1929, PRO, DO 35/77.
107 Minute by Campbell, Feb. 1929, PRO, W 1409/21/98 FO 371/14104.
108 Telegram from Athlone (South Africa) to Willingdon (Canada), 15 Feb. 1929, ibid.
109 Telegram from Bruce to Mackenzie King, 23 Feb. 1929, PRO, W 1621/21/98 FO 371/14104.

At the beginning of March the Canadian government deferred to the views of the other dominions and informed Britain that it, too, was willing to wait until there had been sufficient opportunity to consider American policy on arbitration before moving ahead on the Optional Clause. King had bowed to the doctrine of *inter-se* in recognition of the importance of the Commonwealth relationship. At the beginning of May he affirmed in a newspaper interview that Canada had never considered signing the Optional Clause without the rest of the Commonwealth, but he was torn between, on the one hand, *inter-se* and, on the other, his support for the Optional Clause and his need to be seen to take an independent line within the empire. Reporting a parliamentary debate on 7 May, the British High Commissioner drew attention to the way in which King 'carefully . . . trims his sails to every gust from the Opposition that blows on this question' of the Optional Clause: '[A]ll I said', said King,

> was that Canada was prepared to sign the Optional Clause, but did not intend doing so without conference with other parts of the British Empire, as had been promised at the time of the last Imperial Conference: I made no statement to the effect that we would not sign the Optional Clause unless all parts of the Empire agreed. Our view is that there should be a conference in the first place.

Later, in answer to a supplementary question, King said that he assumed that the opportunity to confer (as agreed in 1926) would come at the next imperial conference. 'It may come before', he continued, 'but until it does come I should not like to say that Canada will take action on its own.'[110] *Inter-se* had triumphed for the time being.

Unfortunately, just as King had demonstrated his amenability to the Commonwealth factor, a statement in the House of Lords by Lord Hailsham (formerly Douglas Hogg, who had adopted this title on becoming Lord Chancellor in March 1928), was reported in the Canadian press in a way which was open to being misinterpreted as a pronouncement that the Optional Clause could not be signed without the agreement of all the dominions. This so infuriated King that he threatened to publish all the correspondence between Ottawa and London. Fearing that he might do just that, London quickly placated him. Such was the sensitivity of the dominions that, as Campbell remarked, the Dominions Office 'get into communication with us almost before any [parliamentary] Question appears on the Order Paper' lest 'we may say something which upsets them'.[111] Moreover, the British opposition was asking so many questions about the Optional Clause that in April the Dominions Office had warned the Foreign Office to avoid any statements which might give the 'misleading impression' that the dominions actually opposed signature of the Optional Clause. To do so would run the danger of a public denial by Mackenzie King or Hertzog and reveal that it was the UK which was the source of restraint.

Thus it was that Canada was in the vanguard of the Commonwealth at the beginning of 1929 but King's brave statement in January had become hesitant by

---

[110] See despatch from Sir William Clark (who had become the first British high commissioner to a dominion in Apr. 1928), received 21 May 1929, PRO, W 6779/21/98 FO 371/14104.

[111] Minute by Campbell, 19 Dec. 1928, PRO, W 12131/309/98 FO 371/13391. The opposition's parliamentary questions on the Optional Clause extended to Canadian policy as well as that of Britain.

May. It has been pointed out that Canada's willingness to take an initiative on the Optional Clause was quite striking in comparison with the 'negativism or inactivity which characterized so much of Canadian participation in League of Nations affairs'.[112] But as Canadian delegates had so often reminded the Assembly, Canada was geographically fortunate. This rendered acceptance of the Optional Clause 'virtually risk free':[113] there was little likelihood of it being brought before the Court since, even if the United States joined the PCIJ, there was no question of the US adhering to the Optional Clause; and there was equally no question of a Canadian-British dispute being taken to the Court. As Canadian delegates also pointed out, the country was historically inclined to favour compulsory arbitration and hence also the Optional Clause. And this inclination gave Canada kudos in a forum where compulsory arbitration and the Optional Clause had assumed a disproportionate importance in the search for peace. And so, what appears at first sight to be a striking initiative was not really bold. It was, however, an important initiative because Canada put the Optional Clause high on the Commonwealth agenda and Britain was made aware that not only Canada wanted to move forward on this matter. For the time being, the acceptance of the Optional Clause had, by common consent (except that of the Irish Free State, which must be dealt with separately), been postponed until after the conclusion of the Anglo-American negotiations for an arbitration treaty – which, in effect, meant until after the British general election of 1929. But in Britain the question of the Optional Clause was already being very urgently considered by the government's advisers.

The Irish Free State and the Canadian initiative on the Optional Clause

The Irish Free State chose to opt out of the Commonwealth discussions on the Optional Clause at the beginning of 1929, although it received full information on them. At the end of January, however, the Free State told Britain that it was prepared to conclude new, general arbitration treaties at the same time as the commercial treaties which it was in the process of negotiating with France, Spain and Italy. This news was received with alarm in Whitehall. The Dominions Office was worried; the Lord Chancellor, Hailsham, took 'a very grave view of the matter, and consider[ed] that it str[uck] at the root of the whole constitution of the British Empire'; and Austen Chamberlain thought it sufficiently important to bring it to the immediate attention of the prime minister and Cabinet.[114] This was because, as the Irish government was informed, Britain held it essential to maintain imperial unity in arrangements for settling by arbitration disputes 'which would otherwise lead to a rupture'. Britain did not, however, think it mattered if dominion commitments differed on 'questions of less importance, such as arise out of the interpretation of a treaty' providing they were in

---

[112] Veatch, *Canada and the League of Nations*, 60.
[113] Ibid., 61.
[114] Lindsay to Vansittart (private secretary to the prime minister), 2 Mar. 1929, CUL, Baldwin papers, 101. See also minutes by Batterbee and Harding, 27, 28 Feb. 1929, PRO, DO 35/77.

'general accord' with the Covenant and with any general treaties covering all parts of the empire.[115]

At the end of February Amery, the Dominions secretary, urgently telegraphed Canada asking the Canadian government to send the Free State the views of South Africa and Australia because, he said, there were indications that the Irish government was inclined towards joining in multilateral treaties for compulsory arbitration and negotiating separate, bilateral arbitration agreements. Canada swiftly did so but with no effect. On 8 March the Irish sent Ottawa a telegram pointing out the advantages of concluding individual treaties with the US. A few days later an Irish telegram to London elaborated on its position. This telegram reminded Britain that at the end of 1927 the Free State had expressed its belief that each member of the Commonwealth should conclude its own, separate, arbitration convention with the USA. Accordingly, the Free State was examining the desirability of concluding an Irish-American agreement at an early date 'so as to avoid any break in the continuity with the US of the . . . existing agreement'. Ireland's consideration of Kellogg's proposed arbitration treaty had confirmed its view of the desirability of separate conventions, and the Free State regarded the substitution of the Kellogg treaty for the Root-Bryce treaty of 1908 as an appropriate and convenient occasion for members of the Commonwealth to make individual treaties with the United States. 'The various arbitration treaties would adhere in essentials to the same form', it was suggested,

> and while such an arrangement would emphasise the Commonwealth polity it would, at the same time, remove that prospect of confusion and doubt as to the incidence of rights and obligations which a general treaty would inevitably reveal. H.M.G. in the Irish Free State do not anticipate any dispute between the U.S. and any member state of the Commonwealth which could not best be settled direct between the U.S. and the particular member state concerned. Direct communication and discussion would, in specific instances facilitate the settlement of the reference to the arbitral tribunal and of the question falling to be ruled, and in general the separate treaty arrangement would simplify and expedite the processes of the entire arbitration proceeding.

The despatch concluded by expressing the Irish government's 'hope' that the British government would assure them that Britain agreed with their views.[116] This was certainly not the case.

At the end of March Amery sent a very carefully-worded reply to the Irish government. Trying hard to avoid offending Irish susceptibilities, Amery agreed that it was in accordance with the principles of the 1926 imperial conference for dominions to negotiate and sign arbitral treaties of the sort that the Free State said it was contemplating with France, Spain and Italy. All the other dominions had, however, agreed that the renewal of such treaties should await the outcome of the current British-American negotiations and it was important for the Commonwealth to act jointly. There was, he said, no desire to commit any dominion to the policy of any one government. On the contrary, 'the only

---

[115] Batterbee (assistant secretary, Dominions Office) to Sir Claud Schuster (clerk of the crown in chancery and permanent secretary to the Lord Chancellor), 9 Mar. 1929, ibid.

[116] Despatch from McGilligan (minister for external affairs) to Amery, 18 Mar. 1929, PRO, W 6779/21/98 FO 371/14104.

desire of His Majesty's Government in the United Kingdom is that there should be complete co-operation in the formation of a common policy'. The 'complexity and difficulty' of arbitration required that there should be 'the fullest possible exchange of view[s]'. Britain had 'derived valuable assistance' from the other dominions and they would greatly appreciate any views which His Majesty's Government in the Irish Free State may be able to contribute'. He drew attention to the 1926 agreement on uniformity of action – from which no dominion representative had dissented – and to the Irish Free State's November 1926 memorandum stating that 'The King is the real bond [of the Commonwealth], and forms used in international treaties will be devoid of all meaning as long as they do not give complete expression to that reality.' Amery went on to say that 'the cohesive force, resulting from the bond of the Crown, and its effectiveness as a means of preserving peace and prosperity, would surely be seriously impaired if His Majesty's general arbitral obligations designed to be an alternative to war were different in respect of different parts of his Dominions'. Finally, Amery argued that if the arbitral agreements of one part of the empire were different from another it would not be possible to have co-operation and consultation for a common policy: a most difficult situation would arise if a serious dispute took place with a foreign country affecting two or more members of the British Commonwealth, one alone of which had a general arbitration treaty with the country in question covering the subject of dispute.[117]

The Free State did not reply before the general election but it is unlikely that Amery's arguments cut much ice. The Free State had, in effect, confirmed its rejection of *inter-se* and served notice that it would follow its own, independent line on arbitration. Its general dilatoriness in communicating with Britain and its practice of doing no more than voicing its support for compulsory arbitration and the Optional Clause perhaps suggested that the Free State would not now act swiftly. But, given the British government's concern to maintain *inter-se*, Amery had correctly perceived the portent of the Free State's message.

The British government's advisers prepare for acceptance of the Optional Clause

By March the Canadian government had come round to a 'satisfactory' position on the Optional Clause. But Britain had only gained a temporary breathing-space and was having to tread warily. It was clear that Canada wanted to move ahead and had only agreed to delay its hand. Australia had now come out in favour of the Clause, South Africa was making sympathetic noises, and there was no knowing what the Irish Free State might do. It was therefore sensible for the government's advisers to take preparatory steps towards signature. An additional reason for so doing was that the opposition parties were publicly committing themselves to the Optional Clause. Accordingly, members of the Foreign and Dominions Offices held two meetings in April in order 'that the advisers of H.M. Ministers should be clear in their minds on the various points that arose' 'on the question whether it would be possible for the Optional Clause

---

[117] Despatch from Amery to McGilligan, 22 Mar. 1929, PRO, OC(29)3 appendix A, CAB 27/392.

... to be signed by the units of the British Empire, and, if so, what reserves ought to be made in so doing'.[118] The Dominions Office was not, however, hopeful about the prospects of reaching an agreement without a Commonwealth conference: 'I very much doubt that it is possible to reach agreement with the Dominions on arbitration', said Batterbee, an assistant secretary in the Dominions Office. '[P]olitical issues are so tangled up with the legal issues that I doubt whether anyone short of the Dominion Prime Ministers is really capable to deal with them.'[119]

The discussions were conducted in the light of the views of the British government and such views as had been expressed by the dominions on the proposed Anglo-American arbitration treaty and in response to the Canadian initiative on the Optional Clause. The available material was somewhat patchy. Two Commonwealth members, New Zealand and India, had abdicated decision-making on the proposed arbitration treaty to Britain (India commenting that the matter 'was hardly of direct interest').[120] They had expressed no recent opinions on the Optional Clause and were hardly likely to present any sudden difficulties. South Africa's only position on the Optional Clause was that it was 'not prepared to accept jurisdiction of th[e] Court in all legal disputes',[121] but it had expressed views on the Anglo-American treaty which were taken into account. The Irish Free State had indicated that it wanted to go it alone in arbitration and had opted out of consultations on the Optional Clause, so that its attitude on specific points could only be guessed at. However, Canada and Australia had made known their considered views on both the Optional Clause and the Kellogg arbitration treaty. This information was sufficient to draw up a tentative list of possible reservations and for the British officials to begin thinking about which issues might give rise to difficulties.

At the first meeting in Hurst's room, on 5 April, the majority agreed that it was desirable to wait until the proposed Anglo-American arbitration treaty had been negotiated before considering the Optional Clause in detail. Three principles linked to this treaty were agreed on. Firstly, the Optional Clause should be 'regarded as embodying only the arbitration commitments which H.M. Government are prepared to accept vis-à-vis states other than the United States'. Secondly, the signature of the Optional Clause should not preclude the negotiation of arbitration treaties with states which had not accepted the Optional Clause. Thirdly, 'as a general principle the reserves to be made in the treaty with the United States and those made when signing the Optional Clause should be identical'.[122]

---

[118] Record of a meeting in the Foreign Office on 5 Apr. 1929, PRO, W 3236/21/98 FO 371/14103; *DBFP* vi, 391. Those present were: Hurst (in the chair), Batterbee (assistant secretary, Dominions Office), Dixon (acting assistant secretary, Dominions Office), Malkin, Beckett (assistant legal adviser, Foreign Office), Cadogan (assistant to the British delegate to the League of Nations), Craigie (head of the African and American department), Leeper (a senior member of the western department), Kirkpatrick (a senior member of the western department) and Prince George (the Duke of Kent, who was temporarily attached to the Foreign Office).

[119] Minute, 1 Feb. 1929, PRO, DO 35/77, quoted in Holland, 'Commonwealth in British official mind', 134.

[120] CID sub-committee on belligerent rights, confidential, B.R. 70, annex 1, appendix 3, 29 Jan. 1929, PRO, CAB 24/215.

[121] Telegram from Athlone to Willingdon, 15 Feb. 1929.

[122] Record of a meeting in the Foreign Office on 5 Apr. 1929.

It was also agreed that the discussion of the precise reservations might have to be postponed until the next imperial conference. None the less, the meeting proceeded to discuss, in a general way, the possible reservations which might be made to the Optional Clause. BMR was not discussed on the grounds that the subject was before the Cabinet. It is, however, appropriate that the dominions' views on this thorny subject should be reviewed before proceeding to the reservations that were discussed.

South Africa, Canada, Australia and New Zealand recognised the difficulty and delicacy of the subject of BMR. Both South Africa and Australia had suggested, with regard to the Anglo-American treaty, that arbitrations should take place 'according to the rule of law recognised by both parties or by principles agreed to between them' – a suggestion which Malkin had made the previous year but which had been dropped by Britain after Hurst had criticised it.[123] In its telegram on the Optional Clause, Australia had explained that the main difficulty in accepting it lay in the second and third sub-paragraphs of Article 36.2 of the Statute of the Court. These, it said, posed a danger not only to BMR but also to domestic jurisdiction (i.e. the possibility of Australia's 'white' immigration policy being challenged before the Court). Australia held that it would be 'unwise', to accept the phrase 'any question of international law . . . .. without some qualification as to what International Law is and what the Court is to apply'. Article 38 of the Statute was insufficient and it might be possible for the PCIJ to 'impose a rule of its own creation, although such a rule may never have been agreed to by a party to a dispute'. Likewise, Australia could not allow the Court jurisdiction 'in respect of a dispute covering 'breaches of an international obligation' unless they knew 'from what source such an obligation could flow'. The solution was thought to lie in limiting acceptance of the Optional Clause to disputes 'concerning the existence of any fact which if established would constitute the breach of an international obligation arising out of a treaty or of any of the rules of international law' formally accepted by parties to a dispute.[124] This suggestion was dismissed by Hurst who 'thought such a reservation would not help in the least in regard to belligerent rights, but might be used to exclude practically every dispute from arbitration'.[125]

The dominions had not been told about the British government's examination of BMR for fear of the information leaking out to the United States.

---

[123] This was the wording suggested by Australia. South Africa suggested excluding disputes the subject matter of which was 'not regulated either by any Convention, Treaty or agreement in force between the High Contracting Parties or by any rule of international law recognised by both High Contracting parties': CID sub-committee on belligerent rights, B.R. 70, annex 1, appendix 3. On Malkin's 1928 suggestion see above, 137–8.

[124] Copy of despatch from Mackenzie King (enclosing telegram from Bruce), 14 Mar. 1929, PRO, W 2335/21/98 FO 371/14102. If the suggestion were accepted, Australia suggested that 'a convenient procedure would be to communicate with the States members of the League of Nations asking them whether they would be prepared to accept a similar obligation. Our acceptance of the Optional Clause in its modified form vis-a-vis those states willing to be bound in the same way, might be recorded in an exchange of notes subsequently communicated to the League of Nations and to the Registrar of the Court'.

[125] 'Note of a meeting held in Sir C. Hurst's room at the Foreign Office on Thursday, April 25th 1929, to consider possible reservations to be attached to any signature of the Optional Clause of the Statute of the Permanent Court of International Justice': PRO, W 4155/21/98 FO 371/14103; *DBFP* vi, 421.

However, Canada was sensitive to the attitude of its southern neighbour and, on its own judgement, shared the views which had been held in the Foreign Office about the need to appease America on BMR. In respect of the proposed Anglo-American treaty Canada expressed optimism about the effects of the Kellogg pact in mellowing American attitudes so that it might not demand full neutral rights in respect of a belligerent that was defending itself against an aggressor. But it was conceded that 'this tendency has not yet definitely crystallised, and the difficulty in any case of obtaining objective tests of aggression must be recognised'. The Canadian government warned of the deleterious effects of 'any unqualified reservation' asserting Britain's right to enforce its own interpretation of BMR and of a failure by Britain to provide for the peaceful settlement of disputes which might ensue. Accordingly, Canada suggested it would be desirable to make an international agreement on BMR and that acceptance of the Optional Clause should reserve BMR 'pending codification' of the law.[126]

At the second interdepartmental meeting on 25 April,[127] Hurst produced a list he had drawn up on the basis of the previous meeting and the views which the dominions had expressed. The list did not include the condition of reciprocity or imposing a time limit on acceptance of the Optional Clause (which had been suggested by both Canada and South Africa) since these were taken for granted. But it did set out nine other possible reservations which were considerably more than any state had yet made. (If reciprocity and a time limit are counted as two reservations, no state had yet made more than four reservations to a declaration.) This led Leeper, a senior member of the western department, to ask whether other states might refuse to accept so conditional an acceptance of the Optional Clause. Hurst, however, assured him that not only was a state entitled to make any reservations it liked but also that 'it only meant that other states would only be bound towards this country in similar terms. The reservations were reciprocal'.

The first suggested reservation was that which had been proposed by Australia: inter-imperial relations. The meeting as a whole shared Batterbee's view that, while there would be 'some advantages' in drawing attention to *inter-se*, it would be better simply to find a form of wording which would exclude inter-imperial disputes from the purview of the Court but which would not draw attention to the doctrine. An explicit reservation of inter-imperial disputes would, it was held, 'lead to the inference that, in its absence, the Statute would be of inter-imperial applicability',[128] a point with which Hurst agreed. Such a reservation was, he thought, unnecessary since the Court only had jurisdiction in international disputes. However, as Malkin pointed out, 'whether more than one Dominion would agree with this view is, of course, another matter'.[129] It was

[126] CID sub-committee on belligerent rights, B.R. 70, annex 1, appendix 3; telegram from Mackenzie King to Amery, 23 Jan. 1929, PRO, W 763/21/98 FO 371/14102.

[127] Those present were Hurst (in the chair), Batterbee, Dixon, Malkin, Beckett, Leeper, Koppel (head of the dominions information department, Foreign Office) and Thompson (a member of the African and American department). Unless otherwise indicated quotations in this section are taken from the Foreign Office note of this meeting.

[128] Memorandum by Batterbee, 11 Apr. 1929, PRO, W 3336/21/98 FO 371/14103. See also Foreign Office note of meeting on 25 Apr. 1929.

[129] Minute, 17 Apr. 1929 ibid. Malkin agreed with Hurst that such a reservation 'would in principle be most undesirable'. Leeper, however, favoured such a reservation: see minute, 16 Apr. ibid.

hardly likely that the Irish Free State would publicly accept this, and Batterbee (who would have been 'content to leave it as an underlying assumption that the Court could not adjudicate between different parts of the Empire if Mr. Bruce had not specifically raised the question') thought that it would be easiest for the Irish Free State to agree to the assumption that such a reservation was unnecessary.[130] It was agreed that it would be best to try to reach an informal understanding on this question rather than making it the subject of a reservation.

The second possible reservation – of domestic jurisdiction – had been favoured by Canada, Australia and South Africa in respect of the proposed Anglo-American arbitration treaty and it had been suggested by Canada in respect of the Optional Clause. This reservation was rejected by Hurst as unnecessary and was strongly opposed by Beckett on the grounds that its inclusion would imply that the absence of such a reservation gave the PCIJ jurisdiction in matters of domestic jurisdiction. Batterbee, however, argued that Britain should not try to resist the well-known desire of several dominions to include such a reservation. Britain had accepted this reservation in the American draft treaty because there seemed no way of satisfactorily modifying it. Australia, which was strongly in favour of the reservation (because of its desire to reserve questions of immigration), would argue that if it was necessary to include the reservation in an arbitration treaty with the United States, it was necessary to include it as a reservation to the Optional Clause. Accordingly, the reservation was left to stand for the time being.

The third possible reservation was of disputes involving the interests of third parties. This was also a reservation which had been included in Kellogg's treaty simply because, it was thought, such a reservation had always figured in arbitration treaties. Likewise, it was thought that the dominions had not commented on it because they took this reservation for granted. However, the League's Security Committee, when drafting the General Act in 1928, had decided to omit this reservation. Instead, the General Act granted a third party the right to intervene in a dispute and being thereby bound by any decision; if a third party did not intervene, it would not be bound by the decision. Beckett agreed with the 'Geneva attitude' and Hurst, too, thought it 'logically . . . reasonable'. However, Hurst recognised that a 'practical politician' might not think so and Canada might find it difficult to persuade its public to accept broader arbitral obligations than did the USA. The reservation was put to one side for the time being and the meeting adopted Hurst's suggestion that a discussion paper be drafted both for general purposes and also so that the point could be further examined and discussed with the dominions if the government decided to move forward in the direction of bilateral arbitration treaties rather than the Optional Clause.[131]

The fourth possible reservation was the British Monroe Doctrine in the Middle East. This was adopted without discussion since 'the present Government

---

[130] Batterbee thought 'even the Irish Free State' would not wish to take the position that the PCIJ was the proper tribunal for inter-imperial disputes and that, although the Free State had registered the 1921 'treaty' with the League, 'they knew, even if they would not admit it, that they were wrong'. Dixon thought the Free State 'might accept a formula which left the legal position open but which would in practice result in such disputes not going to the Court'.

[131] It had been agreed on 5 Apr. that disputes arising with third parties should be excluded because such a reservation was included in the American treaty.

would never look at any proposal to accept the Optional Clause without such a reservation'. It is worth noting, however, that Australia, which was trying to carve out its own Monroe Doctrine in the Pacific, suggested amending the Anglo-American arbitration treaty in a way that would protect the regional interests of Commonwealth countries as well as excluding inter-imperial disputes. This was by reserving 'any questions affecting relations of the various parts of the British Empire *inter-se* or of any parts of the British Empire with regions in which the British Empire, according to its traditional attitude, has special interests'.[132]

The fifth possible reservation was Canada's suggestion for avoiding any difficulties arising out of the implementation of collective security measures by reserving 'operations against violators of the Covenant'. This had been included in the 1928 Franco-American arbitration treaty. Although Malkin wondered whether it was necessary, it 'was generally agreed that there was no objection to including this reservation and that it might prove to be a safeguard, though no-one regarded it as of first-class importance'.

The sixth possible reservation was of disputes arising out of past events. This had been included in five Optional Clause declarations, had been recommended by Australia, and had always been considered necessary by the legal advisers. This was because of the 'serious' risk that First World War neutrals (particularly Sweden) might seek adjudication on Britain's exercise of BMR during the war. It was accepted without discussion.

The seventh possible reservation, of territorial questions, had been suggested by the Colonial Office in order to protect Britain's position in the Falkland Islands and South Orkneys. Hurst thought the phrase 'territorial questions' too sweeping since it would exclude disputes such as those concerning the correct interpretation of a treaty delimiting boundaries. Batterbee had 'hoped' that this would be covered by the 'past events' reservation but it was agreed that it would be best to expand the 'past events' reservation with 'a phrase about "attempts to modify the territorial status quo existing at the present date" '.

The eighth possible reservation, of matters provided for in other treaties, was immediately accepted. The ninth possible reservation was Bruce's proposal to exclude matters where no recognised rule of international law existed and which was, as has been already indicated, dismissed by Hurst and the other officials.

By the end of the two meetings, therefore, the government's advisers had agreed on six possible reservations to a Commonwealth adhesion to the Optional Clause,[133] two were to receive further consideration,[134] and one had apparently been dismissed immediately.[135] This was the last time that the Optional Clause was discussed in Whitehall before the general election.

---

[132] CID sub-committee on belligerent rights, B.R. 70, annex 1, appendix 3.

[133] Namely, reciprocity, domestic jurisdiction, the British Monroe Doctrine in the Middle East, obligations arising out of the League Covenant, disputes arising out of past events (together with a phraseology which would cover attempts to modify the *status quo* existing at the time of signature), and matters provided for in other treaties.

[134] Namely, inter-imperial disputes (the officials believing that it might be best to try to reach an informal understanding on this question) and interests involving third parties (the officials proposing that this be examined further and discussed with the dominions).

[135] Namely, disputes where no agreed rule of international law existed.

Conclusion

Commonwealth policy up to and including the acceptance of the Optional Clause has been described as follows:

> The consultative 'system' . . . never matured into a process in which Commonwealth governments defined a common policy by hard negotiation, swapping quid pro quos and gradually opening up areas of consensus . . . .. from the British angle 'consultation' was a mechanism to provide an illusion of participatory policy-making whilst dominion leaders were, in fact, subtly drawn to underwrite U.K. decisions. From the dominion angle, it was a means by which U.K. policy could possibly be checked if it infringed dominion interests without carrying with it such a degree of commitment as to enmesh them in imperial interests. Both sides to the consultation, then, saw its interest in keeping its content vague and its political character indeterminate.[136]

Certainly, Commonwealth policy on the Optional Clause was not determined by 'hard negotiation' and it is difficult to see how it could have been so determined without dominion leaders coming together. For most of the 1920s only Canada had an independent policy on the Optional Clause and all (except the Irish Free State) were quite happy to follow Britain's lead on the basis of the doctrine of *inter-se*. The 1926 imperial conference discussion of the Optional Clause (by a committee preoccupied with other business) did indeed 'provide an illusion of participatory policy-making' which drew the dominions to 'underwrite' British policy. And the dominions certainly provided Britain with an excuse for its own inaction on arbitration in general and the Optional Clause in particular.

By the end of 1928, however, Canada was ready to push its policy on the Optional Clause. The 1926 imperial conference was sufficiently distant in time (as was the next imperial conference) for her to take a lead. At the ninth (1928) Assembly Canada had used the Assembly's support for compulsory arbitration to prompt the sending of a questionnaire on the Optional Clause to League members. Meanwhile, the proposed Anglo-American arbitration treaty had focused the attention of Commonwealth countries on considering the specific issues which could not be submitted to legal settlement. The Kellogg pact provided the justification for moving along the path to the Optional Clause at an early date and also brought the Australian government out in favour of the Optional Clause. In the event, Canada did not back down: it held back on the Optional Clause at the start of 1929, but only because the other dominions (apart from the Free State, which did not join in the Canadian-initiated consultations) held that the final steps down the path to the Clause might appropriately be postponed. A general commitment to compulsory adjudication could well wait until the terms of a particular arbitral commitment, which would have included all the dominions (except, perhaps, the Irish Free State), had been agreed. And it was reasonable to assume that it would not take long to conclude the treaty.

In 1929 Canada showed that a dominion could act as initiator and co-ordinator of Commonwealth consultations on a particular policy. That Britain could no longer take for granted the acquiescence of most of the dominions was illustrated in a minute by Kirkpatrick. 'Of course', he wrote, 'New Zealand are

---

[136] Holland, 'Commonwealth in British official mind', 143–4.

willing to defer to our views but it is satisfactory that Australia and now South Africa are with us.'[137] As it happened, Britain did not have to make up its mind on the Optional Clause in the early months of 1929 because there was no need to do so. The British foreign secretary was preoccupied with Anglo-American relations and was trying to get the Cabinet to move forward with him on this policy. His advisers were, however, beginning to prepare for acceptance of the Optional Clause. Although one reason for the officials' discussions was the opposition parties' support for the Optional Clause, the support given to it by the dominions was equally important. The advent in Britain of a Labour government in June 1929 led to a swift move to the end of the path to the Optional Clause, but the re-election of a Conservative government would probably have also had the same consequence. Perhaps progress might have been slower, but perhaps not. For, paradoxically, while the Labour government was willing to sacrifice *inter-se* in accepting the Optional Clause, a Conservative government might have moved speedily in the same direction out of a concern to preserve the doctrine. In retrospect, *inter-se* was on its last legs. But in 1929 the Conservatives were still wedded to the doctrine on account of their desire for imperial unity, and so might well have accepted the Optional Clause at an earlier rather than a later date. As it turned out, however, responsibility for the matter was now passed to an administration of a different political complexion.

[137] Minute, Feb. 1929, PRO, W 1641/21/98 FO 371/14104.

PART THREE

ARRIVAL, 1929

8

The Second Labour Government and Britain's Acceptance of the Optional Clause

The Labour Party and the Optional Clause, 1925–9

In 1925, after the second Baldwin government had rejected the Geneva Protocol, the Labour Party gave its approval to the Locarno treaties on the grounds that they made a contribution towards pacification in Europe. But the party did not regard the Locarno policy as a substitute for the Protocol. It was only a first step towards it, and was not much of one at that. Indeed, some Labour MPs had considerable reservations about whether Locarno had any value at all, and underwent a good deal of heart-searching before they felt able to vote for its ratification. This was because, from the Labour point of view, there were two serious defects in the Locarno treaties.

Firstly, given that the Labour Party as a whole regarded disarmament as an urgent matter, and its left-wing was pressing for 'disarmament by example', Locarno was sadly deficient when compared with the Geneva Protocol's provision for a disarmament conference. Secondly, Locarno was a regional security pact and, as such, was regarded as reeking of the balance of power and thus as a hangover of pre-war mentality. While German entry into the League was welcomed, the Locarno route to membership was seen as a divisive measure which drew Germany into the 'capitalist' camp against the Soviet Union. It was also objectionable because it bought the security of a handful of west European states at the price of increased insecurity in eastern Europe, where there were thought to be greater dangers to peace.

Accordingly, until 1928 when the General Act laid the ghost of the Protocol to rest, the Labour Party continued to maintain that the Geneva Protocol represented the correct approach to the problem of peace. This is not to say that the party was committed to every word in that document, for it was generally recognised as unsatisfactory from the British point of view. MacDonald and Parmoor both recognised that amendments might be necessary;[1] Snowden, Chelmsford and Haldane disliked it;[2] the rank and file objected to its coercive

---

[1] 'As you know, we never stood by every sentence and expression in the 1924 draft, which nevertheless was a very remarkable document as a first draft; we do stand, however, on the idea and outlook of the Protocol . . . .. So far as I am concerned . . . the 1924 draft shall be taken as a basis of consideration and not as a verbally inspired gospel': MacDonald to Murray, 12 Sept. 1927, Bodl. Lib., Murray papers. See also David Marquand, *Ramsay MacDonald*, London 1977, 356; MacDonald to Murray, 16 June 1925, Bodl. Lib., Murray papers; Chamberlain to Cecil, 19 June 1925, London, PRO, Chamberlain papers, FO 800/258; Parmoor to Murray, 2 Nov. 1935, Bodl., Lib., Murray papers.
[2] See Snowden's letter airing his 'doubts about the wisdom of the policy of the Protocol' in the *Manchester Guardian* two days after the publication of a letter by MacDonald supporting that document: *Manchester Guardian*, 14, 16 Sept. 1927. See also MacDonald to Scott, 13 Sept. 1927,

features;[3] and, early in 1925, the party's advisory committee on international questions was confidentially considering amendments which, among other things, would make the sanctions provisions less compelling.[4] However, the Protocol had propaganda value and was important in maintaining party unity. Just as a judicious emphasis on the pacific elements of the Covenant had earlier helped to swing the party behind a pro-League policy, so too did a judicious emphasis on the Protocol's provisions for disarmament and arbitration provide a means of overcoming the left-wing's suspicion of the League. Moreover, the party leadership found it useful to insist that recurring calls for unilateral disarmament were 'absolutely impossible'[5] in the light of the approach laid out in the Geneva Protocol.

For example, the party faithful were told that '[d]isarmament would not come until they had laid the first foundation of [d]isarmament – security against attack'.[6] Security, in turn, could not rest upon the physical foundations of weaponry but was to be found in people's attitudes. '[I]f we are to give peace to Europe', MacDonald proclaimed, 'we have to attack the psychology of the people. In the beginning, and as a start, peace is a purely psychological problem.'[7] And the Protocol's emphasis on universal arbitration provided the vital link between security and disarmament, the way in which a 'peace system' could be substituted for a 'war system'.[8]

Thus, whatever the deficiencies of the Geneva Protocol as a document, and whatever reservations there may have been about it within the party, it was none the less supported both publicly and privately by the party's leading spokesmen, and had an honoured place in the party's official pronouncements. The focus, however, was on conciliation, pacification, arbitration and disarmament – collective security being ignored, played down or rationalised out of existence. This meant that the General Act of 1928, with its emphasis on arbitration, could be wholeheartedly supported as a substitute for the Protocol. It also meant that because acceptance of compulsory adjudication was an

quoted in Marquand, *Ramsay MacDonald*, 468; Snowden to MacDonald, 14 Oct. 1927 and MacDonald to Snowden, 15 Oct. 1927, MacDonald papers, PRO 30/69/8/1. For the views of Chelmsford and Haldane see Marquand, *Ramsay MacDonald*, 356.

[3] H. R. Winkler, 'The emergence of a Labour foreign policy in Great Britain, 1918–1929', *Journal of Modern History* xxviii (1956), 257. Michael Gordon emphasises that since the rank and file were only committed to military sanctions as a matter of form, their support for this aspect of the Protocol was only verbal: *Conflict and consensus in Labour's foreign policy*, Stanford, Ca. 1969, 51–3.

[4] Winkler, 'Emergence of Labour foreign policy', 257.

[5] *Report of the twenty-eighth annual conference of the Labour Party, Birmingham, 1–5 October 1928*, 265. This was in response to a last-minute attempt to get 'a definite pledge . . . that the Labour Government within a year of coming into power will call a Conference . . . to prepare plans for Complete Universal Disarmament to be accomplished, let us say, in a term of four years . . . so that it can be accomplished in the life of one Labour Government': 263. That same year the ILP passed a resolution calling for 'the acceptance by this country of a policy of disarmament by example and to urge the settlement of . . . disputes by arbitration before an impartial tribunal': *Report of the annual conference of the ILP, Norwich, April 1928*, 75. See also Arthur Ponsonby, 'Disarmament by example', *International Affairs* vii, July 1928.

[6] Oswald Mosley seconding the 'Peace and disarmament' resolution at the 1928 Labour Party conference: *Report of the twenty-eighth annual conference*, 187.

[7] MacDonald to the House of Commons on 24 Nov. 1927, House of Commons *debs.*, 2096.

[8] 'Protocol or pact', reply by MacDonald to Chamberlain in the House of Commons on 10 Apr. 1925, quoted in *International Conciliation*, No. 212, Sept. 1925, 256. Cf. MacDonald to Murray, 16 June 1925, Bodl. Lib., Murray papers.

immediately practical step, the Optional Clause rose to the top of Labour's foreign policy agenda.

The importance of, and priority attached to, the Optional Clause was made explicit in the new party programme, *Labour and the nation*, which was adopted by the 1928 Labour Party conference. A future Labour government was pledged to erect 'six pillars of peace'. The first three pillars – which included '[i]mmediately accepting the Optional Clause' – were intended to provide a general sense of security and end appeals to force; the last three pillars were to shore up the foundations of peace.[9] This programme was 'accepted by the National Executive without the change of a comma'[10] and passed by the party conference almost on the nod, being no more than a reformulation of ideas which had for a long time had the party's support.

During the 1928–9 session of parliament Labour MPs continued to raise the Optional Clause and the government's general arbitration policy during question time (thereby posing difficulties for Foreign Office officials who were endeavouring to provide draft answers that were 'rather more non-committal than a blunt "No" ').[11] But as a question for major parliamentary debate, the Optional Clause had, by this time, clearly run its course. Thus, when Parmoor brought it up for debate in the Lords in November, the only other speakers in a sparsely-attended, hour-long debate were Cecil and Cushendun. Apart from bringing up the Kellogg pact as an additional reason for signing the Clause, neither Cecil nor Parmoor had anything new to say. As Cushendun pointed out he, too, had nothing to add to what he had already said in the Lords on six or seven earlier occasions. And there were only five speakers when Cecil brought it up for debate at the beginning of May 1929, although the debate was interesting because of the brevity and clarity with which government policy was criticised and defended.

The general election of 1929 was likewise marked by an absence of emphasis on the Optional Clause. Although the Labour manifesto told the country that 'Labour stands for [a]rbitration and [d]isarmament',[12] and the Liberals included among their 'watchwords' 'the substitution of arbitration for force, and an all-round reduction of armaments',[13] none of Labour's sixty-six election pamphlets

---

[9] The 'six pillars' were: (1) Renouncing war as an instrument of national policy and negotiating international agreements through the League of Nations; (2) Reducing armaments to 'the minimum required for police purposes', and in so doing, to make adequate provision for workers who would be displaced by disarmament; (3) *Immediately signing the Optional Clause* and accepting the General Act; (4) Promoting international economic co-operation and co-operating with the ILO; (5) Practising open diplomacy and making all agreements subject to ratification by parliament; (6) Systematically using the League to promote international co-operation. This meant accepting the implications of collective security and included following an anti-imperialist policy (emphasis added): Carl F. Brand, *The British Labour Party: a short history*, London 1965, 128; *Report of the twenty-eighth annual [Labour Party] conference*, Appendix X, 349–50. The 'six pillars' were drafted by Philip Noel-Baker and Leonard Woolf. Noel-Baker was, of course, a leading light in the LNU and Woolf, who was secretary of the party's advisory committee on international questions, was pro-League.

[10] Philip Noel-Baker, *The first world disarmament conference 1932–33 and why it failed*, Oxford 1979, 36, and conversation with Noel-Baker, June 1980.

[11] Minute by Broadmead (clerk in the western department), 17 Nov. 1928, PRO, W 11011/309/98 FO 371/13391. See also minutes by Campbell (head of the western department), Hurst and Locker-Lampson (parliamentary under secretary), 20 Nov. 1928, W 11111/309/98 FO 371/13391.

[12] 'Labour manifesto', in *British election manifestos 1918–1966*, ed. F. W. S. Craig, Chichester 1970, 57.

[13] 'Liberal manifesto', ibid. 62. The Liberals, however, put greater emphasis on disarmament: see

focused on foreign policy.[14] Apart from universal protestations of devotion to the cause of peace and disarmament, foreign policy was not an election issue. On polling day, 30 May, the Conservatives won the largest number of votes. The Labour Party, however, won the most seats.[15] On 5 June, when it was clear that Labour had enough seats to form a government (albeit one which would be dependent on the support of Liberal and independent MPs), Baldwin immediately resigned and MacDonald became prime minister of the second Labour government.

Drafting the Optional Clause declaration: Foreign Office difficulties

The foreign secretary in the second Labour government was Arthur Henderson, an easily-underestimated man if one judged him by his political nickname – Uncle Arthur – and the appearance he gave of being 'a rather stuffy, slow-going and slow-thinking professional politician'.[16] However, not only did Henderson become well thought-of in the Foreign Office, he was also one of the great successes of the ill-fated government. He was a simple, straightforward, deeply-religious man possessing good judgement, determination and utter integrity. He was also good at delegating work to his juniors and had a loyal, strong and harmonious political team.[17] His under secretary, to whom he gave the job of producing a draft declaration on the Optional Clause, was Hugh Dalton, a rising star who had written 'the most carefully worked-out argument for . . . [Labour's emerging] policy'.[18] Together with

ibid. 60-1. The Conservatives said that 'support of the League . . . and the pursuit of peace are the cardinal principles of Conservative policy'. But it was 'security on which peace depends' and Locarno was the 'key' to Britain's 'policy in Europe': 'Notes on the LNU statement on international policy', CUL, Baldwin papers, 133; 'Conservative manifesto' in British election manifestos, 53.

[14] However, 2 of the 20 standard pamphlets (as opposed to those prepared specifically for the election) dealt with issues directly relevant to the Optional Clause. These were on arbitration and the freedom of the seas.

[15] Labour had 288 seats, the Conservatives 260, the Liberals 59 and 8 MPs were independent. The Conservative vote rose by 616,875, Liberal votes by 2,379,763 and Labour votes by 2,900,435. As a percentage of the total votes cast, the Conservatives had 38.2% compared with 48.3% in 1924; the Liberals 23.4% compared with 17.6% in 1924; and Labour 37.1% compared with 33% in 1924.

[16] Leonard Woolf, An autobiography, ii, London 1980 (first publ. in 6 vols, 1960-9), 247.

[17] Carlton suggests that Henderson's political advisers in the Foreign Office formed an avant-garde which exerted 'considerable' influence over the foreign secretary because, unlike the officials, 'they were much more sympathetic to the Labour Party's distinctive foreign policies': David Carlton, MacDonald versus Henderson: the foreign policy of the second Labour government, London 1970, 20. However, this does not give enough weight to Henderson's firm commitment to party conference decisions. Carlton suggests that the extent to which Henderson devoted himself to other matters – India, Palestine, the economic crisis, and his one day a week as general secretary of the Labour Party – led to an unfortunate 'neglect of detail in foreign affairs': 22. But this underestimates Henderson's ability to depend upon and delegate work to junior ministers and the merits of refusing to be submerged by Foreign Office papers, unlike his predecessor, Chamberlain, and his successor, Simon. The more convincing assessment is that of Winkler and of Henderson's Foreign Office advisers: see Hugh Dalton diary entry, 17 July quoted in ibid.; Hugh Dalton, Call back yesterday: memoirs 1887-1931, London 1953, 223; H. R. Winkler, 'Arthur Henderson', in G. Craig and F. Gilbert (eds.), The diplomats 1919-1939, ii, New York 1972 (first publ. 1951), 319-22; The memoirs of Lord Gladwyn, London 1972, 39-40; Walford Selby, Diplomatic twilight 1930-40, London 1953, 3. Selby was Henderson's private secretary at the Foreign Office.

[18] Winkler, 'Emergence of Labour foreign policy', 257 n. 38. The book in question was Towards the

Philip Noel-Baker, Henderson's parliamentary private secretary, Dalton complemented Henderson's sound common sense with intellectual sophistication. Parmoor (the President of the Council and the Labour leader in the House of Lords) was the obvious spokesman on foreign policy in the upper chamber and Rennie Smith (who had joined Dalton in pressing the Conservatives on the Optional Clause in the last session of parliament) was the latter's personal private secretary. Finally, at the beginning of July, Cecil became Henderson's adviser on League of Nations questions and Will Arnold-Forster (who had worked with Cecil on blockade during the war, had been secretary of the LNU's Optional Clause Campaign and was a friend of Cecil, Noel-Baker and Dalton) was brought in as Cecil's secretary. If ever the Foreign Office was run by a pro-League team, it was in 1929. It was also a team which regarded the Optional Clause as an urgent matter. Not only was it the one, immediate step that could bring the swiftest results for a Labour government, it would also give the most effective 'proof of the pacific temper of Labour's policy'.[19]

As soon as he entered the Foreign Office, Henderson called together the heads of departments. He recalled working on the Geneva Protocol with 'real pleasure' and said he counted on them to help him make a fresh start on arbitration and disarmament. 'There could be too much "continuity" in foreign policy; on many matters his point of view was diametrically opposed to that of the late Government – on Russia, for example, and on the Optional Clause. The Government . . . was in favour of signing the Clause with the least possible delay.'[20] The king's speech confirmed this commitment and, just over two weeks after getting down to 'real work',[21] Dalton had produced a draft declaration and a memorandum for Henderson to put to the Cabinet.

However, the declaration was produced in an atmosphere of suspicion and distrust: distrust between ministers and officials and distrust arising out of Henderson's position in the government. Henderson only became foreign secretary on 10 June after a 'stand-up fight' with MacDonald, Jimmy Thomas and Philip Snowden.[22] The result was that:

---

peace of nations (London 1928) and Dalton acknowledged that Noel-Baker's 'ideas more than any man's, have helped me write this book': inscription on the fly-leaf of the copy he gave the latter. Noel-Baker said MacDonald had asked him why Dalton wrote the book as there was 'nothing in it'. Dalton had, said Noel-Baker, written the book to make himself an expert on foreign affairs and to get a job in the Foreign Office. Dalton was a 'blundering idiot' who had no understanding of the Optional Clause, the League or international affairs: interview with Noel-Baker, 12 Mar. 1973, conversation on 27 Mar. 1974, undated note of conversation in the late 1970s. Ben Pimlott also reports MacDonald's remark to Noel-Baker: *Hugh Dalton*, London 1985, 186.

[19] Labour party, international department, advisory committee on international questions, 'Suggested first measures which might be taken by a Labour government', private and confidential, Feb. 1929, no. 394B, CCAC, Noel-Baker papers, 2/3.

[20] Hamilton, *Arthur Henderson*, 284. Cf. Dalton, *Call back yesterday*, 218.

[21] Dalton diary entry, 17 June 1929. Unless otherwise indicated, references to Dalton's diary are taken from his private papers: BLPES, vol. 10.

[22] The phrase is Beatrice Webb's. See her diary entry for 6 June 1929 in *Beatrice Webb's diaries*, ed. M. Cole, ii, London 1956, 197. See also Harold Nicolson, *King George the fifth*, London 1952, 435; Dalton diary entry, 6 June 1929, and Dalton, *Call back yesterday*, 215; MacDonald diary entries, 7 Nov. 1928, 14 Apr. 1929, 1, 4 June 1929, MacDonald papers, PRO 30/69/8/1; Marquand, *Ramsay MacDonald*, 489–91; Snowden, *An autobiography*, ii, London 1934, 760–4; Carlton, 'Great Britain and the Coolidge conference', 15–6. Cf. Hamilton, *Arthur Henderson*, 281–2.

relations between MacDonald and Henderson became even worse than they had been before. Each had a new grievance against the other – Henderson, because MacDonald had tried to keep him out of the office on which he had set his heart; MacDonald, because Henderson had forced his hand. Each allowed the grievance to rankle, and each watched suspiciously for further acts of aggression in the future. Each found what he was looking for. MacDonald took charge of the central problem of Anglo-American relations himself, and he could not resist interfering in other areas of foreign policy as well. Henderson resented the interference, grumbled loudly to his friends . . . .. MacDonald, who was in any case prone to suspect others of conspiring against him, became more and more convinced that Henderson was not to be trusted, and less and less willing to listen to what he had said.[23]

Under these circumstances all contacts between Downing Street and the Foreign Office were delicate. Before June was over Henderson had a 'row' followed by 'an estrangement' of two days from his permanent under secretary, Lindsay, after discovering by chance that Lindsay had suggested an appointment to MacDonald and 'hinted [to MacDonald] at the difficulties over the signing of the Optional Clause'.[24] More frequently it was the prime minister, not the officials, who took the initiative in by-passing the foreign secretary.[25] For example, instead of passing over to the Foreign Office a suggestion that Brierly, Chichele Professor of International Law at Oxford University, should write a formal memorandum explaining why he was against signing the Optional Clause, MacDonald called in Noel-Baker to comment on Brierly's views. Of course Noel-Baker vigorously defended the Optional Clause,[26] but Henderson was 'a little vexed' to discover that his parliamentary private secretary had spent an hour-and-a-half discussing the Optional Clause with the prime minister. Noel-Baker in turn thought there were signs that Hankey, the Cabinet secretary, was 'at work' on MacDonald, warning him to be cautious and making him fearful that 'the Liberals will turn us out if we make no reservation on Egypt'.[27]

Meanwhile Dalton, who shared the widespread Labour distrust of Foreign Office officials as obstructionist and unsympathetic to Labour, and personally believed that the Office was riddled with Roman Catholics and/or homosexuals,

[23] Marquand, *Ramsay MacDonald*, 491. The king shared MacDonald's low opinion of Henderson. 'Henderson is a damned ass and very conceited', he said: quoted in Kenneth Rose, *King George V*, London 1983, 369. The result was that at times Henderson had to struggle against the awkward combination of 'the Palace and the P.M. [which] seem[ed] to be echoing one another': Dalton diary entry, 29 July 1929, quoted in Dalton, *Call back yesterday*, 227. The fact that Dalton did not get on with MacDonald did not help.

[24] Dalton diary entry, 29 June 1929.

[25] See diary entry for 2 Dec. 1929 in *Beatrice Webb's diaries*, 23; Dalton diary entry, 29 July 1929, quoted in Dalton, *Call back yesterday*, 226. Cf. Marquand, *Ramsay MacDonald*, 499–501; Lord Vansittart, *The mist procession*, London 1958, 375, 392–3.

[26] Noel-Baker defended the Clause using the arguments set out in the LNU's 1928 'Optional Clause' pamphlet and those which he put forward in the House of Commons in January 1930: see above, 70–4; House of Commons *debs.*, 27 Jan. 1930, 732–42. For Noel-Baker's memorandum of 11 July 1929 see PRO, PREM 1/72. For Brierly's views see 'Memorandum on the proposed acceptance of the "Optional Clause" in Article 36 of the Statute of the Permanent Court of International Justice', ('written in haste'), 9 July 1929, ibid. See also Brierly to Rosenberg (MacDonald's secretary), 9 July 1929, ibid.; J. Brierly, 'The judicial settlement of international disputes', *International Affairs* iv (1925); letter from 'a student of international law' (John Fischer Williams), *Manchester Guardian*, 22 July 1929.

[27] Dalton diary entries, 8, 9 July 1929. See also memorandum by Cecil of an interview with Lord Grey, 13 July 1929, BM, Cecil papers, Add. MS 51073.

approached the drafting of the declaration with unmasked hostility to the civil servants. Since Dalton was arrogant, abrasive and determined to 'get these buggers on the run',[28] life was not easy for those who had to advise him on the Optional Clause.

The Labour Party's advisory committee on international questions had suggested that only four conditions be attached to the Optional Clause – reciprocity, a reservation of disputes arising out of naval action taken on behalf of the League, a reservation of inter-imperial disputes and a fifteen-year time limit on acceptance. (It thought the last two could safely be omitted.)[29] Dalton was therefore astonished to discover that in April the government's advisers 'had manufactured 9 [reservations] for Austen!' Characteristically he blamed the officials for devising 'the maximum which ingenious caution could invent' and called on Henderson to put them in their place:

> Uncle summoned Lindsay, Hurst, Malkin, Selby & me to his room. He sat stubbornly in his chair & said that the Govt was in favour of signing the clause with the least possible delay. He did not wish to hear 'a lot of legal arguments' about reservations. He in his speeches had not spoken about reservations but about *signing the clause*. If, however, there were any real difficulties which they could put up he was willing to consider them, but he expected that, when they put up difficulties, they would also suggest means of overcoming them. All this produced rather a shattering effect! Hurst & Lindsay argued a bit, though uneasily. Malkin sat silent. ('Did you notice how Malkin behaved?' Uncle asked me afterwards. 'He never said a word but he looked as though he was going to burst!') I remarked, at one point in the discussion, that the dominions had been in advance of us on all this & that 'the block had been in London'. The late Govt, I said, had refused to do anything, either to sign the clause or to make bilateral treaties. Hurst, slightly nettled, said that the late Govt was not 'really malignant'. 'No', I said, 'they were not malignant, but they suffered from mental laziness & lack of grip.' After the meeting Uncle said to me, 'don't these chaps know what our policy is?'[30]

A few days later, when Dalton, Noel-Baker and senior officials from the Foreign, Dominions and India Offices met to begin considering the reservations to be made to the Optional Clause, the preliminary list that Hurst had drawn up in April was brought out. At first '[t]he atmosphere was bad . . . but [it] gradually improved'. Some reservations were dismissed 'by general consent', others were discussed 'at length', and others were dismissed by Dalton as 'flatly contrary to the policy of the Gov[ernmen]t'.[31] By the time they had reached the end, they

---

[28] Diary entry, 1 July 1929. See also Pimlott, *Hugh Dalton*, 192–3; *Memoirs of Lord Gladwyn*, 38–9.

[29] '[O]n a broad view', said the committee, 'there seems to be no sound objection whatever to . . . [the dominions] having recourse, if they so choose, to the Permanent Court' instead of the Judicial Committee of the Privy Council. The 15-year time limit was based on the unratified French declaration of 1924 but it was 'worth considering whether the time limit should not be omitted altogether' as there 'appears to be no substantial danger in omitting the time limit': Labour Party, advisory committee on international questions, 'Suggested first measures', CCAC, Noel-Baker papers, 2/3.

[30] Diary entry, 17 June 1929.

[31] Dalton diary entry, 20 June 1929. Hurst had suggested that Noel-Baker should attend and Arthur Ponsonby (who was under secretary at the Dominions Office) represented the Dominions Office. The officials who attended were Lindsay, Hurst, Malkin, Cadogan, Campbell and Kirkpatrick from the Foreign Office; Harding and Dixon from the Dominions Office; and Walton and Turner from the India Office. Lindsay had suggested that Hurst should chair the meeting and that it should be in

had, in fact, come to almost the same conclusions about the list as had the government's advisers in April, but Hurst was concerned about two reservations. The first was the proposal to reserve disputes involving BMR only to the extent that they arose out of action on behalf of the League. This was no more than Hurst had, himself, suggested in 1924 but he thought it wise to show the reservation to the Admiralty and, after obtaining Henderson's explicit consent, he was able so to do. The other reservation, the 'British Monroe Doctrine' which had been adopted without discussion in April because of the known views of the Conservative government, divided the committee and subsequently divided the Cabinet. When the Foreign Office pointed out Bruce of Australia's interest in this reservation, the 'distinctly helpful' representatives of the Dominions Office pointed out that neither Canada, South Africa nor the Irish Free State could be expected to agree to the reservation. Hurst subsequently tried to explain to Dalton that its omission presented difficulties, but Dalton thought he was engaging in 'legal subtleties'.[32] Henderson 'simply *won't have* the British Monroe Doctrine Reservation' he told a 'very worried' Hurst.[33]

When Dalton went through the Cabinet paper with Hurst, Malkin and Lindsay, it was the permanent under secretary's turn to bear the sharp edge of the doctor's tongue. At one of their meetings, he believed that Lindsay wanted

> to load the Cabinet paper with doubts as to whether the League Covenant, or the Kellogg Pact, would stand the strain of a crisis, to point out the tremendously important departure in policy involved in the Optional Clause, and generally speaking to smother [the] whole proposal in a featherbed of cautionary considerations. I said to him bluntly 'this is becoming more and more your paper, and less and less a co-operative venture'. I had already given notice that I should put in a paper of my own on political considerations, and I was prepared in this to defend Hurst's draft of acceptance, but all this elaboration of L[indsay]'s, I said, would simply make the document too long for most of the Cabinet to read, and would make some of them who were keen on our accepting go off in the deep end. I said also to L[indsay] 'should you not add, at the end of H[urst]'s exposition, "these considerations, pressed to their logical conclusion, make it undesirable that the OC should be signed at all?" ' He said, 'No, that would be a caricature'. The poor man has never, I think, been to Geneva.[34]

Eventually, Dalton was more or less satisfied. Although he thought Hurst's 'cautionary tome' was 'very long and that something shorter is needed for the Cabinet',[35] it is difficult to see how it could have been shorter. It was clearly written and explained the various considerations that had been taken into account. It was circulated to the Cabinet on 3 July, together with a draft declaration.

Hurst's room. 'I agreed', said Dalton, 'since H[urst] had taken the chair at an earlier meeting of a similar cttee': ibid. On the April meeting see above, 189–94.

[32] Although he thought Hurst had gone 'a good way to meet us' after the first Optional Clause meeting, Henderson suspected Hurst of 'complaining to the P.M. that we are unreasonably rushing him, & impatiently brushing aside his legal subtleties': Dalton diary entry, 26 June 1929. On 24 July Dalton noted that 'Hurst will be glad to be a judge [of the PCIJ] soon, & we will be rid of him.'

[33] Dalton diary entry, 1 July 1929.

[34] Dalton diary entry, 29 June 1929.

[35] Dalton diary entry, 1 July 1929.

The 3 July draft declaration

The proposed declaration accepting the Optional Clause ran as follows:

(1) On behalf of His Britannic Majesty's Government in the United Kingdom I accept,

(2) for a period of fifteen years and thereafter until such time as notice may be given to terminate the acceptance,

(3) in relation to any other State accepting the same obligation,

(4) the jurisdiction of the Court as compulsory,

(5) in all international disputes comprised in the categories mentioned in article 36 of the Statute,

(6) with regard to facts occurring or situations arising after the signature of the present declaration,

(7) other than disputes in regard to which the parties have agreed or shall agree to have recourse to some other method of peaceful settlement,

(8) or which arise out of action taken at the instance of the Council of the League of Nations, in pursuance of the obligations imposed upon Members of the League by the terms of the Covenant,

(9) and subject to the proviso that pending the conclusion of treaties regulating the situation in areas in which the Government of His Britannic Majesty claim to possess certain special interests, the exercise of the jurisdiction of the Court shall in the case of disputes arising out of action taken to uphold these special interests be dependent on the conclusion of a special agreement defining the point at issue and settling the terms of reference.[36]

After a brief introduction, the accompanying memorandum began by explaining why a fifteen-year time limit (paragraph 2) was suggested. Although, 'an irrevocable commitment' was 'undesirable', there were 'inconveniences' in having to renew a signature at the end of a stated time period and this was why it was proposed that the declaration should remain in force for fifteen years and thereafter until revoked. This was equal to the longest time limit that had been set by any of the fifteen declarations which had included such a condition (the usual limit being five or ten years). In any case, '[a]n arrangement on these lines is practically equivalent to a permanent commitment, as, unless there has been some change in the circumstances, withdrawal from . . . compulsory jurisdiction . . . would be regarded as a retrograde measure, and a Government would hesitate to take it'.

Reciprocity (paragraph 3) was a condition that was generally taken for granted in Optional Clause declarations. Because Article 36 of Court Statute was ambiguous on this point, it had to be stated explicitly and had therefore been included in the declarations of twenty-two out of the twenty-three states that had accepted the Optional Clause. Its absence would make it advantageous to other states not to accept the Clause, since a non-signatory could take a

---

[36] Henderson memorandum, 'The Optional Clause and possible reserves', circulated on 3 July 1929, PRO, CP 192(29), W 6556/21/98 FO 371/14104. The paragraphs have been numbered for ease of comparison with later drafts. Most of the memorandum is printed in *DBFP* vi, 759ff.

signatory of the Clause to the Court without having any corresponding liability to be taken to the Court.

The first of the specific reservations that had been suggested for the British Commonwealth was Australia's February 1929 proposal to exclude inter-imperial disputes. In the paper presented on 3 July this was dismissed as unnecessary and undesirable. It was unnecessary because '[a]ccording to the view held by this Government, the Court only has jurisdiction in *international* disputes, and a dispute between two units of the British Empire is not, and cannot be, in the strict sense of the term, international'. It was undesirable because such a reservation would imply that its omission gave the Court jurisdiction in inter-imperial disputes. Britain's position was well-known; it had been 'publicly stated at Geneva'; and in 1926 the special, non-international nature of inter-imperial relations had been 'fully understood' and formed the basis of much of the work of the imperial conference. It would be best to omit any such reservation and simply to tell the dominions that Britain held that the Court did not have jurisdiction in inter-imperial disputes. For, whereas

> [n]o Dominion is likely to contest it, or to make any attempt to refer [a dispute with Britain] to the Court . . .. to invite formal concurrence in any explicit statement that the International Court has no jurisdiction in inter-Imperial disputes would create difficulties for some of the Dominion Governments and it would be better to refrain from doing so.

The second specific reservation which had been suggested several months earlier, domestic jurisdiction, had emanated from Australia, Canada and South Africa. It had been criticised by the Foreign Office lawyers in April and was now held to be '[i]n theory . . . superfluous'. However, as shown by the recent American treaties, it had become common practice to include such a reservation in arbitration treaties. Although no such reservation had yet been made to the Optional Clause, 'the explanation . . . may be that most of the States which have accepted the clause are continental States to which this question is not one of great importance'. Despite the objections to such a reservation, '[p]ractical considerations' dictated its inclusion if the dominions wanted it. On the advice of the Foreign Office legal advisers, a reservation of disputes involving the interests of third parties was rejected as unnecessary. As had been pointed out in April, the League's Security Committee had regarded the interests of third parties as already being sufficiently protected by the Statute of the PCIJ,[37] and its view had been endorsed by the Assembly when the General Act was approved.

The sixth paragraph of the proposed declaration, reserving disputes or situations prior to signature, had been adopted without discussion in April,[38] and was said to be both reasonable and 'a matter of importance to Great Britain . . . by reason of the risk . . . of stale claims arising out of action taken during the late war being put forward by countries which were then neutral'. Similarly, the

---

[37] See above, 193. This was by reference to Articles 62 and 63 of the Statute which gave third parties the right to intervene in proceedings in which they had an interest.

[38] It had been extended to include situations arising before acceptance of the Optional Clause in response to a Colonial Office request that it be widened to protect Britain's position in the Falklands and South Orkneys.

seventh paragraph – reserving disputes where an alternative method of pacific settlement had been agreed on by the parties – had also been taken for granted in April. This was 'not a reserve in any proper sense of the term and need not be worded as such'. It was included so that disputes which were best suited to conciliation could be submitted to a conciliation commission and because some disputes were too small to warrant submission to the PCIJ, 'whose activities should be reserved for important cases'.

The eighth paragraph of the proposed declaration, reserving disputes arising out of military or naval action on behalf of the League, was justified in the following way. Until that time, successive governments had refused any arbitral commitments which might 'imperil' the exercise of BMR. However, it was no longer diplomatically wise to take refuge in the wide-ranging vital interests formula, and the problems of making an explicit BMR reservation had been revealed in connection with the proposed Anglo-American arbitration treaty. But if Britain were willing to base its policy on the assumption that all states would live up to their obligations under the Kellogg pact and the League Covenant, the difficulty might be 'overcome'. It followed from these treaties that Britain would, in future, only be at war either in self-defence or in pursuance of its obligations under the League Covenant. It would be reasonable to assume that if Britain were involved in a war of self-defence, the League Council would give effect to Article 16 of the Covenant and Britain could count on the co-operation of other League members. As Hurst had been arguing since 1924, it was hardly likely that action taken to uphold the Covenant and at the instance of the League Council would be questioned before an international tribunal. And this meant that in future Britain need not worry about the arbitration of disputes involving BMR.

If the above argument were accepted, there were two formulae that could be inserted into the Optional Clause declaration. The first – which was adopted – was a modification of the reservation that had been included in all Kellogg's arbitration treaties with European states. It excluded disputes arising out of British naval action when, without being the victim of an attack, Britain became a belligerent in order to uphold the Covenant. The second formula, which had been suggested by South Africa and had been 'frequently considered during the last two years',[39] was to exclude all disputes on matters as to which there was no recognised rule of international law. This had 'certain [unspecified] advantages and may be put forward in some quarters as the proper expedient which His Majesty's Government should adopt if they desire to accept an extended obligation to submit to compulsory international arbitration'. However, it was rejected because, as Hurst had pointed out, it weakened Britain's contention that its prize courts applied international law, and because so general a reserve 'might be used to exclude practically every dispute from arbitration'.

The final, ninth paragraph of the proposed declaration, protected the 'British Monroe Doctrine'. All America's arbitration treaties reserved the American Doctrine and Britain's interests in Egypt and the Persian Gulf were not only comparable to those covered by the United States' Doctrine but were 'even

---

[39] Australia had suggested a similar reservation but it had been dismissed by the government's advisers earlier that year.

more essential to Great Britain than is the integrity of the Monroe Doctrine to the United States'. But a reservation of disputes arising out of action to maintain these interests would have a much wider scope in respect of the Optional Clause than it would in a bilateral arbitration treaty with the United States. For it would exclude 'arbitration' with a third power that attempted to interfere in the Middle East as well as with regional powers – such as Egypt or Persia – regarding the legality of British actions affecting them. Because Britain had 'no secure legal basis for our claim to occupy in certain countries a special position, through which alone we can ensure the protection of our lines of communication to India and the East', it would be dangerous not to make such a reservation. And, because it was 'generally known in well-informed circles' that Britain's legal position was weak, 'the acceptance of an obligation to submit to arbitration any aspect of it which might come into dispute would be likely to give rise to a vehement political campaign in this country'.

There were three alternatives before the Cabinet. The first was to make no reservation of the 'British Monroe Doctrine' but this would 'reduce to vanishing point the chances of a treaty settlement . . . with Egypt', which was the only means of establishing Anglo-Egyptian relations 'on a basis of goodwill'. The second was to make an unqualified reservation but this was contrary to Labour's proclaimed pre-election policy. The third alternative was to limit the obligation to 'arbitrate' by stating that, until the conclusion of treaties to regulate the situation in any areas in which Britain 'claim[ed] to possess certain special interests', disputes arising out of British action 'to uphold these interests' could not be taken to the PCIJ unless a *compromis* had been concluded. This was 'avowedly a compromise, but [it] goes some way to meet the objections on either side' and was for this reason included in the draft declaration.

The 'Monroe Doctrine' reservation was the only part of the declaration that Henderson was unwilling to accept. Although, he said in an accompanying note to the Cabinet, he 'would have preferred that Great Britain should sign the Optional Clause unconditionally', the Cabinet could 'safely accept all the earlier parts of the formula'. But he was 'doubtful' about the ninth paragraph because it 'contains an important reservation of substance, and would introduce a new and undesirable form of procedure in connection with the submission of international disputes to the Permanent Court. On both grounds I am not sure whether it can be approved'.[40]

The declaration on the Optional Clause: inter-departmental disagreement

When Henderson's memorandum came before the Cabinet on 10 July, it was decided that a Cabinet sub-committee under MacDonald should consider the terms of the Optional Clause declaration.[41] This was because the Admiralty had

---

[40] Note by Henderson, 3 July 1929, attached to PRO, CP 192(29).
[41] The members of the sub-committee were MacDonald, Henderson, Alexander (First Lord of the Admiralty), Sankey (Lord Chancellor), Passfield (secretary of state for dominion affairs), and Wedgwood Benn (secretary of state for India): Cabinet meeting, 10 July 1929, PRO, CAB 28(29), CAB 23/61. The Cabinet had ruled that only decisions should be recorded in the minutes. This was because a 'very bad habit had grown up of recording observations from members of the Cabinet which, when looked at when the circumstances under which they were made and their context had

also circulated a memorandum saying that it viewed 'with much perturbation' the implications of the draft declaration for 'the chief weapon of this country'.[42] The other armed services were also alarmed.

In the first place, neither the Admiralty nor the Chief of the Imperial General Staff, General Milne, agreed with the assumption that Britain would, in future, only go to war either in self-defence or to uphold the Covenant. The 'gap in the Covenant' gave states the right to go to war when the Council failed to reach a unanimous report and the Admiralty said this would be most likely to happen when great powers were involved in a dispute – and when, accordingly, BMR would be important. Even if the Kellogg pact and the Covenant had ruled out war in Europe, neither instrument was applicable in Asia where, said Milne, British vital interests were 'confronted . . . by forces whose main object is to compass our destruction by every means in their power'.[43] The services could not, therefore, allow any possibility that the PCIJ might interfere in matters that were essential for imperial defence: the application of BMR and Britain's position in Egypt. The Admiralty's objections to the PCIJ having jurisdiction in disputes involving BMR (objections shared by the Air Staff)[44] were those that had been heard so many times in the past.[45] However, this was the first time the army and air force had had to justify to themselves and the Cabinet the need to avoid the possibility of the 'British Monroe Doctrine' being taken to the PCIJ. The importance of Britain's position in Egypt, said Milne, stemmed from its 'immense strategic importance . . . safeguarding, as it does, the vital artery of our Imperial communications in India, to the Far East and to our Dominions in the Pacific'.[46] Whereas there was genuine uncertainty surrounding the laws of naval warfare, there was no uncertainty about the weakness of Britain's legal position in Egypt. If, therefore, there were no reservation on this point, Egypt would quickly see that it did not need to negotiate a final agreement on outstanding differences over the 1922 treaty but could take these for settlement by the PCIJ. At some time Egypt would go on to challenge successfully the whole question of

faded from memory, gave most misleading impressions of the reasons why conclusions had been reached': MacDonald to Esher, 25 July 1929, MacDonald papers, PRO 30/69/6/32.

[42] Admiralty memorandum, circulated by Alexander, July 1929, PRO, CP 200(29), W 6730/21/98 FO 371/14104.

[43] Memorandum by General Milne, Chief of the Imperial General Staff, 15 July 1929, secret, PRO, OC(29)2 CAB 27/392.

[44] This was because aircraft were 'certain' to play an increasingly important role in future wars. For example, 'flying boats, operating in pairs or in larger formations, could effectively undertake the visit and search of suspected vessels, one or more machines remaining in the air as a safeguard against any attempt to escape or to offer obstruction to the boarding party': memorandum by Lord Thomson, secretary of state for air, July 1929, PRO, CP 237(29) CAB 24/205.

[45] Firstly, the 'biassed neutrals' who predominated among the judges would be bound to deliver adverse decisions on disputes involving Britain's exercise of BMR and might do so in the early stages of a war. Secondly, the Court could ask Britain to stop its practice of BMR even before a judgment had been given. Since the navy would almost certainly be instructed to execute the ruling, '[o]ur sea power will be stultified'. Thirdly, it was prudent to make it clear that Britain was not going to accept as binding rules to which it had never agreed and which it might be disinclined to obey in wartime. Finally, it would be 'very anomalous' if a court intended to handle justiciable matters should deal with questions that had 'such a political bearing on the security of a nation': Admiralty memorandum, CP 200(29).

[46] Memorandum by General Milne, OC(29)2. Thomson's memorandum pointed out that the Suez Canal and Persian Gulf were 'key areas from the point of view of our imperial air communications, no less civil than military'.

Britain's position in Egypt. Britain would then be forced to withdraw from Egypt and abandon its control of the Suez Canal and, if as a result it had to rely on the alternative Cape route, it would have to increase the number of troops stationed in India[47] and review the whole basis of the duties and strength of the British army. Although it was true that a 'Monroe Doctrine' reservation would be a completely new departure in Optional Clause reservations, it was essential in view of the peculiar political, economic and strategic conditions of the British Commonwealth. And, after all, if the United States could reserve its Monroe Doctrine in arbitration treaties, it was hardly unreasonable for Britain to follow the American example.[48]

Even though the Admiralty appeared to have changed its attitude by conceding that the League Council could 'endeavour to effect a settlement' of disputes involving BMR,[49] it had still given nothing essential away. Henderson's team was unimpressed by the proposal and the defence departments' arguments cut no ice. As they saw it, the services were getting 'quite out of hand' and dominating their political masters, as had happened in 1924.[50] For although Cecil and Parmoor were not altogether happy with other parts of the draft declaration,[51] the reservation of the 'British Monroe Doctrine' and the one the

[47] The only justification for the small size of the British army in India was that it could be rapidly reinforced via the Suez Canal.

[48] This, of course, ignored Henderson's point that such a reservation would be wider in respect of the Optional Clause than it would in a bilateral arbitration treaty. The Air Staff supported Milne. '[W]hilst appreciating that there may be overriding political considerations, [they] . . . hope[d] that it may be practicable to retain some such reservation as that proposed . . . in the final sentence of [Henderson's draft declaration] if, indeed, this cannot be strengthened': Air Staff note, attached to Thomson's memorandum, PRO, CP 237(29).

[49] Instead of the reservation of disputes arising out of action on behalf of the League, the Admiralty wanted the following reservation: 'other than disputes which arise out of war measures, HMG claiming that the pacific settlement of any such disputes shall be sought by submission to the Council of the League of Nations as laid down in paragraph 3 of Article 15 of the Covenant'. The Air Staff suggested, as an alternative wording, 'or which arise out of war measures other than those undertaken by a state which has contravened its obligations under the Covenant'. This would exclude from the PCIJ not only disputes arising out of war measures taken at the instance of the League Council, but also defence measures '(strictly in accordance with the Covenant) before the Council has issued any report': Note by the Air Staff, CP 237(29).

[50] See Cecil to Noel-Baker, confidential, 1 Aug. 1929, BM, Cecil papers, Add. MS 51107.

[51] The day after the Cabinet discussed the draft declaration, Parmoor told MacDonald that there should be no reservations but later he was willing to accept the conditions of reciprocity and a time limit. Reciprocity was 'obviously required' and, although there was 'a good deal to be said for omission of any time limit (as in treaty of Locarno) . . . if any time limit is to be specified the terms of the draft are right'. However, a reservation of 'alternative methods of settlement' was 'redundant' since it was already plain that Britain was free 'if the other disputant agrees' to try conciliation or go to a special arbitral tribunal. Both Parmoor and Cecil objected to the 'past disputes' reservation. Cecil thought it was not very happily worded, Parmoor believed it was so wide as to 'seriously damage our own signature and encourage future signatories likewise'. Both thought it was unnecessary. Cecil held that most questions arising out of the war had already been settled. Parmoor thought it unlikely that any neutral claims relating to the war would be raised now, but if they were, 'it is most unlikely that the Permanent Court would find "stale claims" valid'; if claims were not stale, they should be settled by the appropriate means. As far as the Falklands were concerned, it would be an 'excess of caution' to cover Britain's position when accepting the Optional Clause. 'It is most unlikely that so long-standing a title would now be challenged; it is most unlikely that, if challenged, our title would now be denied by the Court: but even at the worst, if our title were challenged, and were denied, that would be preferable (if the matter is viewed in proper perspective) to so sweeping a qualification of our acceptance of the rule of law in legal issues': Parmoor memorandum for the prime minister, 11 July 1929, PRO, W 6946/21/98 FO 371/14104; Parmoor memorandum, 'The Optional Clause. The

Admiralty demanded for BMR were not only contrary to Labour policy and the spirit of the Optional Clause, but were also thought to be unnecessary.

The reservation proposed in paragraph 8 of the 3 July draft declaration – excluding disputes arising out of naval or military action on behalf of the League – already provided for 'a hypothetical difficulty so improbable that it need not be taken into account', said Parmoor. The Admiralty's preferred reservation, limiting the reference of all war measures to the League Council, was 'unsound' in assuming that Britain needed to prepare 'for private war used as an instrument of national policy'.[52] Since Britain had pledged itself under the Kellogg pact to settle all disputes by peaceful means, it was no longer free to exploit the 'gap in the Covenant'. Cecil's objection to the Admiralty's reservation was weightier. It would be difficult, he pointed out, to justify referring an obviously legal question to a non-legal tribunal and Britain would come off worse. For whereas the Court had 'shewn itself remarkably free from undue national bias' the decisions of the Council were taken on the basis of political considerations and were determined 'by neutral members of the Council only' since disputants were debarred from voting. In any case, a majority decision against Britain would be as bad as a unanimous report, and a considerable minority in favour of Britain's opponent would be little better.[53]

To Cecil and Parmoor, the 'Monroe Doctrine' reservation was unnecessary, discreditable and contrary both to the spirit of the Optional Clause and to Labour Party policy. It was unnecessary for two reasons. Firstly, '[i]n these days of submarines and aircraft' the Suez Canal had lost its strategic value and it was 'surprising to hear that such a waterway . . . could be safely used for important military purposes'. Secondly, the reservation would not make Britain's position in Egypt any more secure. For while Britain's position there was legally tenable, a reservation would be seen as an admission that it was legally untenable. The result would be the opposite of what the army envisaged: Britain's negotiating hand would be weakened and, in effect, Egypt would have been invited to demand 'arbitration', a demand which Cecil thought Britain would be unable to refuse. Then, if Britain did appear before the Court, it would have prejudiced its position by as good as admitting that it did not believe its own case. It was for this last reason that Cecil thought the proposed 'Monroe Doctrine' reservation would 'not sound very creditable':

> After all, if we put into plain language what the reservation means . . . .. [i]t amounts to this: – that we are usurping a position in Egypt which we have no right to hold, – no doubt with the best of motives and results, – and that for that reason we decline to allow any dispute about it to go before the Court.[54]

Furthermore, a 'Monroe Doctrine' reservation would be contrary to the spirit of the Optional Clause in asserting that Britain wanted 'to be free to act illegally'

proposed reservations', 22 July 1929, OC(29)6 CAB 27/392 and Henderson papers, FO 800/280; Cecil memorandum for Henderson, 23 July 1929, Henderson papers, FO 800/280 and BM, Cecil papers, Add. MS 51081. Cf. 'Draft of declaration on signature of the Optional Clause' in Labour Party, advisory committee on international questions, 'Suggested first measures', CCAC, Noel-Baker papers, 2/3.
[52] Parmoor memorandum, 22 July 1929. For the Admiralty's reservation see above n. 49.
[53] Cecil memorandum for Henderson, 23 July 1929.
[54] Ibid.

and because it was 'dangerously vague and sweeping . . .. a standing incitement to others to stake out similar claims'.[55] Finally, it would be contrary to Labour Party policy inasmuch as the party had vigorously denounced the 'British reservation' to the Kellogg pact.

While the peacebuilders and defenders of the empire were disagreeing, the Dominions Office was also pondering the difficulties of a 'Monroe Doctrine' reservation. A circular telegram had been sent on 22 June, informing the Commonwealth that the British government had concluded that it was time to sign the Optional Clause and asking for views on the appropriate reservations which, it was hoped, would be few in number.

Only India replied expressing definite views on reservations before the Optional Clause sub-committee met on 25 July. But in the light of earlier correspondence and known views, it did not appear that there would be any difficulty over including a BMR reservation: Canada, Australia and South Africa had all recognised that it was a question 'both of great importance and great difficulty'.[56] However, it was 'very doubtful whether it would be possible to secure the agreement of all the Dominions' to take similar action on a 'Monroe Doctrine' reservation.[57] Some were in favour of it. The India Office regarded the reservation as 'of the highest importance'[58] because India was unable to rely on the Covenant for protection[59] and had its own area of special security interests.[60]

---

[55] Parmoor memorandum, 22 July 1929. It was also, he said, 'an impossible position to maintain vis-a-vis a member of the League, – a member who is also a member of the present Council'. (Persia had been elected to the Council in Sept. 1928.)

[56] The quotation, which came from a Canadian telegram, was used in Passfield's Cabinet memorandum of 16 July 1929: PRO, OC(29)3 CAB 27/392; W 6897/21/98 FO 371/14104.

[57] Passfield memorandum, 16 July 1929.

[58] Undated memorandum prepared in the India Office, circulated on 22 July 1929, PRO, OC(29)4 CAB 27/392. Both Hurst and the India Office held that the government of India was wrong in believing that India's special security needs were safeguarded because of the reservation of past disputes and its belief that either the Optional Clause or an arbitral agreement ceased to operate when the interests of third parties were involved: telegram from the government of India, 1 July 1929; minute by Hurst, 4 July 1929; Hurst to Walton (India Office), 15 July 1929, PRO, W 6452/21/98 FO 371/14104.

[59] This was, firstly, because two of its most important neighbours – the USSR and Afghanistan – were not members of the League. Although this did not bar them from 'assuming the obligation and obtaining the benefit' of the Optional Clause, it justified 'an attitude of caution in our dealings with them'. Secondly, two other neighbours – China and Persia – had not yet demonstrated that they had the capacity to carry out their League obligations: India Office memorandum, PRO, OC(29)4.)

[60] The USSR, as a potentially hostile power, had to be excluded from Tibet (sic.) and the importance Britain attached to the Persian Gulf for air and sea communications meant that no hostile power could be tolerated on its shores. This was why Mesopotamia had been occupied during the war and it was one reason why Britain wanted a strong, independent and friendly Iraq: PRO, India Office memorandum, 22 July 1929, OC(29)4. It was not thought that acceptance of the Optional Clause would be a hindrance to any measures Britain might need to take in the event of the Soviet Union invading Afghanistan and threatening India since 'the Afghan Government would certainly request and implore our assistance'. Equally, there was no justification for a reservation to prevent Britain's treaty with Afghanistan being taken to the PCIJ: 'The Government of India may sometimes have cut short petty disputes by unilateral action but their primary interest is that Afghanistan should be strong and that relations should be neighbourly and this must always be the mainspring of their policy. It is not likely that there would be a dispute in which issues of great importance to India were involved and in which there would be much risk of the Court deciding against us': Record by J. C. Walton (India Office) of interview with Sir F. Humphrys (British envoy extraordinary and minister plenipotentiary to Kabul, 1922–9), 2 July 1929, PRO, W 6452/21/98 FO 371/14104. 'It is satisfactory to see that the India Office have come to the conclusion that no reserve as to Afghanistan is necessary', said Hurst: Minute, 4 July 1929, ibid.

Australia and New Zealand could also be expected to favour a reservation safeguarding their lines of communication with Britain. And while South Africa was thought to be indifferent, it would probably go along with the reservation. However, Canada and the Irish Free State would be 'most unlikely' to agree because of their 'general attitude of disassociation from questions affecting the Near and Middle East'.[61] In the event, the problem of a 'Monroe Doctrine' reservation vanished. On 24 July, the day before the Optional Clause sub-committee meeting, Henderson circulated an amended declaration which, he said, had been produced 'in the light of recent discussions and communications from the Dominions'.[62]

The 24 July draft declaration

The new draft form of acceptance was as follows:

(1) On behalf of His Britannic Majesty's Government in the United Kingdom *and subject to ratification*, I accept

(2) for a period of fifteen years and thereafter until such time as notice may be given to terminate the acceptance,

(3) in relation to any other state accepting the same obligation,

(4) the jurisdiction of the Court as compulsory,

(5) in all international disputes comprised in the categories mentioned in Article 36 of the Statute,

(6) arising after *the ratification* of the present declaration, with regard to *situations or facts subsequent to* the said ratification,

(7) other than disputes in regard to which the parties have agreed or shall agree to have recourse to some other method of peaceful settlement,

(8) *(and subject to the proviso that His Britannic Majesty's Government reserve the right to require that proceedings in the Court shall be suspended in respect of any dispute which has been submitted to, and is under consideration by, the Council of the League)*.[63]

There were three ways in which this second draft differed from the first, two of them being uncontroversial. Henderson regarded it as 'essential' to sign the Clause at the League Assembly in September, but he had given an undertaking that Britain would not ratify the declaration until it had been discussed in the House of Commons: the first amendment made good this promise. The second change was to redraft the 'past events' reservation 'in a form which is clearer and accords with the formula . . . adopted by France, Germany, Belgium and other foreign countries'. The third change (paragraph 8) was substantive. The 'BMR' and 'Monroe Doctrine' reservations were replaced by a completely new one: a 'proviso' or 'so-called "French joker" '[64] which suspended proceedings in the Court while a dispute was before the League Council. As Dalton put it,

[61] Passfield memorandum, 16 July 1929.
[62] Henderson memorandum, 24 July 1929, W 7665/21/98, *DBFP* vi, 436.
[63] Ibid. Emphasis added to amendments to the 3 July draft.
[64] Dalton diary entry, 24 July 1929. This term arose from the fact that the 'proviso' was practically identical to a condition attached to the unratified French declaration of 1924.

This blots out belligerent rights, British Monroe doctrine (whether for unknown regions, or for Egypt etc. specifically named), & all arbitration 'compromis'. Cecil, Phil [Noel-Baker] & I hammer Hurst & bring him reluctantly into line. This final form [i.e. a declaration including the suspensory proviso] is to be our 2nd line of defence [in the Cabinet sub-committee]. The 1st is 'no reservations at all'. But this will be untenable & for demonstration purposes. I tell Hurst that the Secretary of State desires a minimum of this 'reservatory rigmarole'.[65]

It worked. The sub-committee approved the amended draft and recommended that it be stressed to the dominions that 'the most careful consideration ha[d] been given to the[ir] views . . . [and] express a strong hope that, in view of the importance of unanimity in this matter, they should concur in the proposed Declaration'.[66] On 26 July the Cabinet approved the declaration and decided it should be made at the forthcoming League Assembly. But approval was conditional on two requirements being met. The Foreign Office and services were to reach agreement on the 'French joker' or 'proviso' about which the services were unhappy, and the dominions were to give their approval to the draft declaration. In the event of a failure to agree, the question was to be referred to the prime minister.

After the Cabinet meeting on 26 July, Dalton noted dismally: 'The O[ptional] C[lause] isn't safe yet. We never seem to reach an end.'[67] The following day he felt more cheerful: 'Hurst has dealt with the reluctant Service departments over the OC. The Air Ministry was tearful & thought we should lose the next war. But the despatch to the Dominions, defending our proposed formula, has gone this morning. At last! Only just over a month before the Assembly meets.'[68]

Dalton had counted his chickens too soon for the services were not quite so easily put to flight. At the end of a lengthy meeting, Hurst and Malkin had failed to persuade the Admiralty and the Air Ministry (the War Office having entrusted the safeguarding of its interests to the former department) to abandon their demand that BMR should be reserved. The representative of the Air Ministry 'reluctantly acquiesced' when Hurst pointed out 'that this policy had been considered by the late Government last autumn and had been rejected because of the difficulties which it might create with the United States'. But the

---

[65] Ibid. Henderson's memorandum (which Dalton had drafted) explained, firstly, that Henderson would prefer to omit the paragraph 'and thus to sign the Clause without any reservation contrary to its intention and spirit'. If, however, such a reservation had to be made, Henderson thought the 'French joker' was 'the least objectionable form of words'. Hurst believed it would make a BMR or 'Monroe Doctrine' reservation unnecessary; it covered a number of dominion suggestions; it was practically identical with the 1924 French reservation; and Cecil, who 'fully shares my dislike of reservations of substance', did not object to it. The memorandum concluded by emphasising 'the extreme undesirability' of a specific 'Monroe Doctrine' reservation. 'To assert it as our predecessors did in connection with the Kellogg Pact, by reference to certain unnamed regions, is plainly inconsistent with the repeated declarations, and the whole international outlook, of the Labour Party. To assert it, on the other hand, with Egypt specifically named, would be to advertise the fact that our legal status in Egypt was untenable. We should thereby encourage the Egyptians to refuse to conclude a treaty by friendly negotiation and to insist on a reference of our legal rights to arbitration, which it would be very damaging for a Labour Government to refuse': Henderson memorandum, 24 July 1929.
[66] Report of Cabinet sub-committee on the Optional Clause, 25 July 1929 (initialled by MacDonald), PRO, CP 235(29) CAB 24/205.
[67] Diary entry, 29 July 1929.
[68] Diary entry, 30 July 1929.

Air Office official remained 'firmly convinced' that the 'proviso' was 'dangerous and inadequate' in the absence of a definite guarantee that the Council would not refer a dispute to 'arbitration'. And the Admiralty not only refused to believe Britain could only be involved in wars of self-defence or on behalf of the League but 'cannot persuade themselves that war may not emerge as the result of the inability of the Council to come to a unanimous agreement'. Hurst thought that the services would not press their point of view but he was wrong.[69] Alexander appealed to the prime minister, and MacDonald postponed the despatch of the telegram to the dominions, telling the Foreign Office to 'try to get an agreement on what seems to me to be a small point'.[70]

The Foreign Office responded by treating the difference as unimportant. Hurst said Alexander had probably only written to the prime minister in order to make it plain that his department had doubts about the effectiveness of the Foreign Office reservation. All that his letter indicated was that the Admiralty was concerned about the likely actions of the Council, but that department no doubt felt 'some hesitation in being too dogmatic' since it had less experience of Geneva than the Foreign Office. And it was the Foreign Office, not the Admiralty, that bore the major responsibility for ensuring that reservations were adequate.[71] This did the trick and, with MacDonald's personal approval, the telegram to the dominions was despatched posthaste.

This was, in effect, the end of the Admiralty's attempt to get a BMR reservation before the Optional Clause was signed. In view of Britain's previous attitude towards BMR and the Optional Clause, this is remarkable, and it is the change in the Admiralty's attitude that marks the real difference between the responses of Whitehall to the policy of the second Labour government and that of its predecessors. The reason for this probably lies in the Labour Party's general peace policy and in the personalities involved. The offer of a reservation that would allow disputes involving BMR to be brought before the League Council was, no doubt, the best hope the Admiralty had of 'protecting' BMR, for the Admiralty's arguments no longer carried their former weight. For all his characteristic vacillation, the prime minister had frequently denounced the premises on which Admiralty arguments were based and was disinclined to heed them. No doubt MacDonald was ignorant of the precise legal points involved in accepting the Optional Clause, but he was advised by politicians who were knowledgeable and he had called for advice from Noel-Baker – one of the most ardent advocates of the Clause. Moreover, despite the antipathy between MacDonald and Henderson, the foreign secretary and his team were far more formidable than either Alexander or Shaw. In any case, it is reasonable to think that neither Alexander nor Shaw did any more than put forward their departments' views. Both men were regarded as being under the thumbs of their departments,[72] but it was also the case that neither was one to champion his department. Shaw, the Minister for War, was a pacifist, who did not want 'to

[69] Minute by Hurst for MacDonald, 30 July 1929, PRO, PREM 1/72.
[70] Minute by MacDonald, 30 July 1929, on Alexander to MacDonald, 30 July 1929, ibid. While recognising that the 'French joker' went a good way towards meeting Admiralty views, the Admiralty feared that the PCIJ might be able to prevent the conduct of important operations if the Council referred a dispute involving BMR to the Court.
[71] Minute by Hurst, 31 July 1929, ibid.
[72] See Basil Liddell Hart, *The memoirs of Captain Liddell Hart*, i, London 1965, 148, 152.

have anything to do with war or military operations' and was 'content to play a somewhat passive role'.[73] Alexander, who had begun life as a stoker in the navy and risen to prominence in the Co-operative movement, was an able man but he did not have a strong personality. For MacDonald, as for Churchill in the Second World War, he was a good choice as one who 'served faithfully according to the policies and purposes of those who had put him in office'.[74] Finally, the secretary of state for Air, Lord Thomson, was MacDonald's closest friend in politics, and he, too, seems only to have passed on his department's views. In short, the service ministers do not appear to have sympathised with or pressed their departments' views strongly, whereas Henderson not only fought hard but had the backing of a formidable team and a prime minister who, on this issue, supported him.

Imperial disunity: the Australian 'blockade'

Having overcome the objections of the services, the next step was to obtain the agreement of the dominions. Three main problems arose. The first concerned Australia's alarm about the non-reservation of BMR. The second related to the method of settling inter-imperial disputes. And the third – which was closely connected with the second – had to do with the implications for the international status of the dominions of the manner in which inter-imperial disputes were to be excluded from the jurisdiction of the PCIJ.

The circular telegram of 1 August assured the dominions that Britain had taken their views into account and individual telegrams commented in detail on any specific points that had been raised. They were asked to reply quickly since it was 'earnestly' hoped to reach agreement before the League Assembly. 'You will . . . appreciate the immense impetus that would be afforded to the cause of world peace', they were told, 'if it were possible for action on this important matter to be taken simultaneously by all members of the British Commonwealth and for declarations in agreed terms to be signed during the Assembly.'[75]

Although all were agreed on the principle of signing the Clause, only the pliable government of India assented to the proposed British terms. The dominions were no longer willing to defer to British opinions: they had their own views and, as their replies revealed, these were strongly held. Thus the British Labour government precipitated a situation which tested the ability of the Commonwealth to consult effectively and reach consensus in a short space of time. Unless agreement were reached, the doctrine of *inter-se* would be imperilled. But although only the Irish Free wanted to throw *inter-se* overboard, the Commonwealth had developed to a stage where it was no longer possible to avoid facing the contradictions that were inherent in the doctrine.

Lord Passfield (formerly Sidney Webb) who headed the Dominions Office, was as undynamic as Alexander and, in respect of the Optional Clause, was probably

---

[73] Temperley, *Whispering gallery*, 119, 118.
[74] Roskill, *Naval policy*, i, 36. An additional reason might have been MacDonald's desire to keep control of Anglo-American naval negotiations.
[75] Circular telegram, 1 Aug. 1929, No. 108, PRO, W 7577/21/98 FO 371/14104; *DBFP* vi, 438, annex F.

no more than a tool of his officials.[76] Within the Dominions Office, policy seems to have been in the hands of Batterbee and Dixon. They had for some time been pessimistic about the prospects of agreement and endeavoured, therefore, to reach whatever outcome would be least damaging for imperial unity. They warned the Foreign Office again about the political sensitivity of the issue and the need to avoid offending dominion susceptibilities.[77] And well before the precise points of disagreement emerged, Batterbee was suggesting that the only solution to irreconcilable differences over reservations would be to follow the logic of Locarno. 'It is, of course, an axiom that the general scheme of the arbitration arrangements of all parts of the British Empire should be the same', he wrote,

> but the field of arbitration may well be different, as the practical problems of the various parts of the Empire are necessarily by no means identical. In other words, any one part of the Empire may well be at liberty to exclude particular subjects or interests from compulsory arbitration, provided that it is satisfied that this can be done without imperilling general Imperial interests, or, alternatively, if it is satisfied that general Imperial interests would be imperilled if these particular subjects or interests were not excluded.[78]

Batterbee was here thinking of the 'British Monroe Doctrine'. If his view was accepted, it would be possible for some, but not other, dominions to make a 'Monroe Doctrine' reservation: those – Australia, New Zealand and perhaps South Africa – that might be called upon to assist in preserving Britain's special interests. This would obviate the need to try to twist the arms of Canada and the Irish Free State to accept the reservation. As it happened, this was another problem that came to nothing. The British did not tell the dominions that the suspensory 'proviso' or 'French joker' was intended to safeguard the 'Monroe Doctrine' as well as BMR and none of the dominions raised the matter. However, the 'proviso' did divide the Commonwealth sharply and along the same lines as had been expected from an explicit 'Monroe Doctrine' reservation.

On the one hand, the Canadians and Irish Free State thought the 'proviso' was 'contrary to the spirit' of the Optional Clause,[79] and 'so wide that if adopted

[76] The reasons were threefold. Firstly, as his wife, Beatrice Webb, saw it, it was 'inevitable'. 'By temperament and training Sidney belongs to the Civil Service', she said: diary entry, 5 Feb. 1930, BLPES, Passfield papers, vol. 44. Secondly, the seventy-year-old minister was 'showing signs of age' and found the problem of Palestine alone 'a considerable burden'. Thirdly, because he was less interested in the dominions than in promoting welfare in the colonies, Passfield left 'little mark on the dominions side of the work': Joe Garner, *The Commonwealth Office 1925-1968*, London 1978, 17.

[77] Minute by Hurst, 9 July 1929, PRO, W 6898/21/98 FO 371/14104. Both Canada and the Irish Free State emphasised that they had been in the vanguard: as Britain was aware, Canada had 'concluded some time ago' that it should sign the Clause and the Irish Free State asserted that it had 'always been prepared to sign the Optional Clause with as few reservations as possible': telegram from Mackenzie King to Passfield, 19 July 1929, OC(29)7 CAB 27/392; telegram from the Irish Free State, 28 June 1929, W 6320/21/98 FO 371/14104.) Dalton was only too happy to tell the Commons it had been the previous administration that had been dilatory, not the dominions: House of Commons *debs.*, 5 July 1929, 454. An Irish request that the king's speech should make it quite clear that other Commonwealth governments had already raised the question of the Optional Clause was ignored.

[78] Passfield memorandum, PRO, OC(29)3, which combined parts of minutes by Batterbee and Harding, 9 July 1929, DO 35/79. See also Holland, 'Commonwealth in British official mind', 141.

[79] McGilligan (minister of external affairs, Irish Free State) to Passfield, 22 Aug. 1929, PRO, W 8260/21/98 FO 371/14105.

in unqualified form by various countries . . . it might prevent rather than facilitate a definite solution of legal disputes'.[80] 'The questions concerned are matters of law and fact and not matters of policy', insisted the Canadian government. 'Generally speaking a Court appears more suitable for their solution than a political body such as the Council.' In some cases the Council might usefully undertake conciliation, but there was a danger that if unanimity were not reached the dispute might remain indefinitely before it. It was therefore necessary to impose a definite time limit on the period during which proceedings before the Court should be suspended.[81]

On the other hand, the antipodean dominions reacted fiercely to the absence of a BMR reservation and, as in 1924, echoed the Admiralty. The present reservation was seen to be inadequate and BMR were so vital that they must not be jeopardised by a hasty decision. Australia repeated its call for a reservation of matters about which there was no agreed rule of law and, together with New Zealand, insisted that it would not be possible, before September, to give the matter the careful and thorough consideration that was necessary. Acceptance of the Optional Clause should therefore be postponed, possibly until after it had been discussed by the 1930 imperial conference.[82]

Governmental reaction to the antipodean problem

So far as New Zealand was concerned, the Foreign Office took the view that although its reply was 'not very satisfactory', there was no need for alarm. 'The New Zealand Government will . . . in accordance with their usual practice', said Malkin, 'ultimately accept the view of H.M.'s Government in the United Kingdom'.[83] The Australian reply, however, succeeded where the pleas of the Admiralty had failed. Henderson, Hurst and Noel-Baker were at The Hague, attending the conference on reparations and evacuation of the Rhineland and Lindsay, the permanent under secretary, advised the prime minister to acquiesce to Bruce's 'weighty proposal'. Although this conflicted with the British government's wish to sign the Clause at the Assembly, a delay would allow for lesser questions as well as important ones to be thrashed out. After all, he said, Australia was only taking the line that Britain had previously held:

> to refuse his appeal for further consideration (which would possibly involve the United Kingdom and some of the Dominions, but not all, signing the optional clause in September without any agreement having been reached on various outstanding

[80] Telegram from Mackenzie King to Passfield, no. 138, confidential, 9 Aug. 1929, PRO, W 8064/21/98, FO 371/14104; *DBFP* vi, 438, annex D.

[81] Ibid.

[82] See Bruce (prime minister, Commonwealth of Australia) to Passfield, no. 176, confidential, 15 Aug. 1929, PRO, W 8136/21/98 FO 371/14105; *DBFP* vi, 438, annex A; telegram from Bruce to Passfield, no. 177, secret, 15 Aug. 1929, PRO, W 7989/21/98 FO 371/14104; *DBFP* vi, 438, annex B; enclosure in Nichols (UK liaison officer to New Zealand government, 1928–30) to Koppel (head of the dominions information department, Foreign Office), 26 Aug. 1929, PRO, W 9505/21/98 FO 371/14106; paraphrase telegram from governor-general of New Zealand (General Sir Charles Fergusson) to Passfield, no. 90, secret, 10 Aug. 1929, W 7680/21/98 FO 371/14104, annex C; telegram from Fergusson to Passfield, confidential, 15 July 1929, PRO, OC(29)5 CAB 27/392.

[83] Minutes by A. W. A. Leeper (first secretary, western department) and Malkin, 13, 14 Aug. 1929, PRO, W 7680/21/98.

points) would mean the end of joint action in future in matters of common interest as to which any difference of opinion existed . . . [This was because] the action of the United Kingdom in this case would render it impossible in the future for us to object to similar independent action by the Free State or any other left wing Dominion.

The whole question of the signature of the optional clause has now got to a point where mere departments, with their Secretaries of State scattered over the country, are unable to deal with it efficiently, and I think that, in order to arrive at the urgent and important decisions which are now necessary, it would be advisable for you to summon immediately the Cabinet Sub-Committee on the Optional Clause.[84]

MacDonald acquiesced. 'Australia has undoubtedly called "check" and I see no way of moving further unless we are prepared to have a partial Dominion signature', he said.

This would be a mistake. The Australian P.M.'s telegram reads as a final decision. The silence of the Irish Free State [which had not yet given its views] is also unfortunate. I think we can make a satisfactory appearance at Geneva with the Australian formula though it is not what I should like. Owing to constitutional developments, we shall have to accept these impediments to the swift realisation of our will here. We must pay the price. The Cabinet Sub-Committee should be summoned and the position explained. I shall not be in London . . . but the position is so clear that my presence may not be necessary.[85]

Henderson's team was furious, and Parmoor considered resigning. Not only had Lindsay offered MacDonald 'tendentious advice which he knows is contrary to [the] [S]ecretary o[f] S[tate]'s point of view', not only had neither the foreign secretary nor his political aides been consulted, but Henderson could not leave The Hague for the sub-committee meeting. '[O]f course, we know his [Henderson's] point of view', Lindsay told Dalton. 'He wants to sign anyhow. But one can't simply take that line in a situation like this. It's much too important a question for any one department.'[86] 'Damn Lindsay!' fumed Dalton:

If Austen had been at the Hague & Baldwin in Worcestershire would he have acted similarly? Nothing but obstruction have we encountered except on the question of Egypt – obstructed by our officials, & our legal advisers, & the Service Depts, & the Dominions! Red tape wound tight round our legs. No movement anywhere along the front. And we may soon be bombed out of our offices, & thrown back into impotent opposition . . .. Suggestions that every home dept & every Dominion should be consulted before anything is finally agreed to be *said* even at Geneva . . ... No finality anywhere.[87]

[84] Minute by Lindsay for MacDonald, 17 Aug. 1929, W 8136/21/98, *DBFP* vi, 438.
[85] Minute by MacDonald, 18 Aug. 1929, quoted in W 8328/21/98, OC(29)13, *DBFP* vi, 440. The permanent under secretary of the Dominions Office also thought that 'discussion with the Dominions will almost inevitably take a considerable time': minute by Harding, 9 July 1929, PRO, DO 35/79.
[86] Dalton diary entry, 20 Aug. 1929. Pimlott believes that Dalton's letter to Henderson protesting at Lindsay's advice to MacDonald and asking Henderson to come to London was in retaliation for a tart reprimand by the permanent under secretary. This was after Dalton made embarrassing remarks about Egypt which had led the Egyptian prime minister to threaten to resign: *Hugh Dalton*, 192–3. This might have been a contributory factor but it seems clear that Dalton wrote because he was, quite simply, 'very angry' over the Optional Clause: Dalton diary entry, 20 Aug.
[87] Diary entry, 21–2 Aug. 1929.

By 'caving in' MacDonald was going back on the line that had been recommended by the party's advisory committee, taken by Henderson and his team in parliament and the Foreign Office,[88] and endorsed by MacDonald himself less than three weeks earlier. At the end of July Henderson had sent MacDonald a memorandum in which Cecil recommended the policy Britain should follow at the tenth Assembly in respect of arbitration, security and disarmament. MacDonald had approved signing the Optional Clause at the Assembly; approved a fifteen-year period of acceptance; apparently accepted that reservations should be limited to those compatible with Labour's declaration that they should not 'weaken the obligation to settle all disputes by pacific means'; and, most importantly from the present perspective, he had commented on the recommendation that (as the foreign secretary had 'made plain in Parliament') Commonwealth unanimity while desirable was not essential and its absence did not oblige Britain to postpone signature: 'Every effort shd. be made to get unanimity & only when we have failed shd. govt. tell them we shall sign. On an important matter like this a division amongst Dominions might be a serious departure, but it may have to be faced.'[89]

Yet now MacDonald regarded it as a mistake 'to have a partial Dominion signature'. To Henderson's peacebuilders, this amounted to allowing a conservative dominion a veto on Labour's foreign policy, and Noel-Baker was firmly convinced that the Australian telegram was the work of Hankey. He had suspected Hankey of putting the wind up MacDonald even before the Optional Clause had come before the Cabinet at the beginning of July, and he believed the Cabinet secretary had contacted his Australian cronies and arranged for Bruce to send his telegram.[90]

Henderson was 'splendid'.[91] Noel-Baker and Hurst, who were with Henderson at The Hague, jointly drafted a reply to Bruce. This was telephoned to London, together with a stiff note pointing out that Australia had not answered Britain's June request for observations. 'After mature reflection', which included taking account of the reservations Australia had suggested at the beginning of 1929, Britain had drawn up a formula which 'went to the limit of the substantive reservations which we thought it possible to accept'.

> The Australian Government now proposes again a reservation which, if it were adopted, would in the opinion of our legal advisers, render futile the signature of the Clause. Such a reservation we cannot accept, either now or in the future, however much 'consultation' we may have, unless we are to violate the pledges which we made

---

88 See Labour Party, advisory committee on international questions, 'Suggested first measures', CCAC, Noel-Baker papers, 2/3; Henderson to House of Commons, 5 July 1929, House of Commons *debs.*, 416; Parmoor to House of Lords, 1 May 1929, House of Lords *debs.*, 317–19; Minute by Kirkpatrick, 22 July 1929, PRO, W 7307/21/98 FO 371/14104.
89 See Cecil minute for Henderson, 29 July 1929, and undated minute thereon by MacDonald, W 7112/4373/98, *DBFP* vi, 437 nn. 4, 5.
90 There is no documentary evidence but Noel-Baker often expressed this view in conversation. The similarity of the arguments used by Australia and the Admiralty lends some weight to this view as does the fact that Hankey felt very strongly about maintaining high BMR.
91 Noel-Baker to Cecil, 23 Aug. 1929, Cecil papers, BM, Add. MS 51107.

before we took office and unless we are to flout the desires of the other Dominions to sign without substantive reservations.[92]

Britain should try to reassure Australia and try to negotiate. But, said Henderson, 'If the Australian Government does not agree, I think we should go ahead without them'.[93]

Cecil and Parmoor urged MacDonald and the Cabinet to stand by Labour policy and refuse to budge beyond a willingness to consult at Geneva. The government was committed to signing the Clause at the Assembly and failure to do so would 'not only disappoint the expectations of the world but also . . . do very grave injury to our political position at home'.[94] Bruce's telegram consisted of nothing new: the Australian government had put forward these arguments ever since coming to office, they were the same as those of the previous British government, and they were wrong. The previous government had so often used the dominions as an excuse for not acting that any such statement was 'subject to a very heavy discount at Geneva' and there was a 'grave danger in admitting the principle of a Dominion *liberum veto* in foreign affairs'. In any case, to accede to Bruce's request would not remove the threat to imperial unity, since Canada and the Irish Free State might insist on signing.[95]

When the Optional Clause sub-committee met at MacDonald's behest on 23 August, it did not share the prime minister's view that Britain 'must pay the price' for imperial unity by bowing to Australia's demands. Imperial unity was important but there was a limit to the extent to which this meant that Commonwealth members had the right to force one another's hands on a carefully-considered and important issue. It was decided that Britain should 'stand firm' for the time being. The lengthy response which Noel-Baker and Hurst had drafted to Bruce (and to which MacDonald made only minor verbal alterations) would be sent in the hope that its arguments might persuade Australia, and Henderson and MacDonald should make every endeavour to bring Australia into line through negotiations. If need be, Britain could assent to reducing the time-limit of the declaration from fifteen to ten years, but that was all.[96]

---

[92] Undated 'Note on the Optional Clause by Mr. A. Henderson', The Hague, received in Foreign Office on 22 Aug. 1929, PRO, W 8180/21/98 FO 371/14105; DBFP vi, 439.

[93] Undated note from Henderson to MacDonald, ?21 Aug. 1929, 'Present state of the correspondence with the dominions about the Optional Clause', Foreign Office memorandum, secret, 22 Aug. 1929, OC(29)13 W 8328/21/98, DBFP vi, 440.

[94] Parmoor memorandum submitted to the Cabinet on 22 Aug. 1929, PRO, OC(29)15 CAB 27/392.

[95] Cecil to MacDonald, 21 Aug.1929, PRO, PREM 1/72 and W 8259/21/98 FO 371/14105; Parmoor memorandum, OC(29)15; minute by Cecil, 20 August 1929, W 8568/21/98 FO 371/14105.

[96] The meeting was attended by Sankey (Lord Chancellor, in the chair), Passfield, Parmoor, Wedgwood Benn, and Alexander. Dalton was 'also present' as were Lindsay, Leeper and Malkin: Cabinet committee on the Optional Clause, conclusions of second meeting, 23 Aug. 1929, secret, PRO, OC(29) 2nd cons., CAB 27/392.

Twisting Australia's arm, I: A telegram

Britain's first means of persuasion, the telegram to Australia, was despatched on 23 August. It is worth summarising for two reasons. Firstly, it is a powerfully-argued restatement of Labour Party policy and, as such, stands in striking contrast to the views of previous governments. Secondly, the arguments that were later put forward in the white paper on the Optional Clause and during the ratification debate in the House of Commons are cogently expressed. They may be most conveniently set out at this point.

The telegram began by explaining that the British government attached great importance to accepting the Optional Clause because there was a danger of the Kellogg pact becoming 'no more than a scrap of paper' unless it were followed by definite acts to 'build up barriers against war'. The most effective of these would be the 'general acceptance for a system of law as a substitute for the system of armed force' which had been renounced in 1928; governments should not be 'deterred or detained by considerations less grave than those relating to the risks of war which have still to be removed'.

There were three reasons for wanting to sign the Clause at the tenth Assembly. Firstly, if MacDonald could do this himself, it would have 'a more powerful moral and political effect on the opinion of Europe and the world than signature later on when the Assembly is not in session'. Secondly, the British delegation would then be in a position personally to persuade other statesmen to follow the example of the British empire. In this way they could 'hasten the process of general acceptance'. Thirdly, it would do much to lift the negotiations of the Preparatory Commission on Disarmament 'out of the rut into which unfortunately they have fallen'. This was important as the next twelve months would be a critical period during which such an impetus would be particularly needed.

The telegram then proceeded to explain why Britain had to reject each of Bruce's reservations, starting with the wish to limit adjudication to cases involving branches of international law which, having been codified, had been accepted by the parties. There were three reasons why Britain could not, after careful consideration, agree to this. Firstly, it would mean restricting compulsory jurisdiction until the whole of international law had been codified. Given the speed at which this was taking place, this was 'equivalent to postponing till the Greek Kalends the effective acceptance of the Optional Clause'. Secondly, Britain could not at one and the same time argue that there was no established rule of law concerning BMR and that the war-time decisions of its prize courts were firmly based on existing international law, and therefore final. Thirdly, it would not be desirable to encourage states to look to the continental method of codification for the development of international law. The English common law approach, which would be entailed in accepting the Optional Clause, was preferable.

To restrict jurisdiction to disputes where the parties agreed on the rule to be applied by the Court 'would amount in practice to a reservation so wide as to rob our signature of the Optional Clause of all real value'. It in effect meant requiring a *compromis* and, if adopted by a 'disloyal' government, could be used like the discredited 'vital interests' formula to prevent adjudication. Australia's contention that there was no question of excluding the categories of disputes enumerated in Article 13 of the Covenant and Article 36 of the Court Statute did not satisfy this objection. In any case, Britain believed it would be safe to leave it to the Court to determine whether or not there existed a rule of law by which it could decide a dispute. If, contrary to Britain's belief, there were certain risks, they were worth running for the sake of 'stabilising peace'.

Britain agreed that the proposed reservation relating to BMR would not permit an indefinite suspension of disputes being sent to the Court by the League Council. (If it did have this effect it would, as the Canadians had pointed out, be 'a dangerous precedent, and one which might defeat the whole purpose of the Optional Clause'.) But it was unnecessary to have more than a temporary suspension. For Australia's view – that failure by the Council to reach a unanimous decision on a dispute involving BMR 'will inevitably involve neutrality in the case of some nations if war should break out' – was based on a misunderstanding. Because of the Kellogg pact and Article 16 of the Covenant 'we do not envisage the possibility of . . . [m]embers of the League claiming rights of neutrality when war broke out, and we should of course, be entitled to reject any such claim and to insist on the fulfilment of their duties under Article 16'.

Britain would welcome Australia's suggestion of an agreement not to take inter-imperial disputes to the PCIJ[97] – if this were acceptable to all the dominions. If that condition held, Britain would consider amplifying the reservation, although it did 'not attach great importance' to this matter. For although 'the Dominions are now Persons of International Law, the relations of the different parts of the Empire *inter se* are not governed by International Law, and in consequence their disputes inter se are not, and could not be held by the Court to be, "international disputes" '. This would hold as long as the empire/Commonwealth were united in common allegiance to the crown.

Britain was, however, willing to make a concession to Australia – one which it thought unnecessary but which might remove Australian anxieties. This was to reserve matters of domestic jurisdiction, which had not been demanded in Bruce's August telegram but had loomed large in the past and was also considered important by the India Office. In conclusion, Australia was told that the 'times require not words but deeds'. Britain hoped that its arguments would persuade the Australians to co-operate in signing the clause at the Assembly.[98]

Twisting Australia's arm, II: A London meeting

Britain's second line of persuasion was to arrange a hurriedly-convened meeting of the dominion representatives at 10 Downing Street on 27 August.[99] By now

---

[97] See above, 192 and below, 230.
[98] Draft telegram to Australia, PRO, W 8180/21/98 FO 371/14105; DBFP vi, 439, annex.
[99] The British representatives were MacDonald (in the chair), Passfield, Parmoor, Wedgwood Benn and Alexander. Cecil, Dalton, Ponsonby, Malkin and Dixon were also present. Australia was represented by Marr (honorary minister and leader of the Australian delegation to the Assembly), Sir William Harrison Moore (professor of law at the University of Melbourne and Australian delegate to League Assemblies, 1927–9) and R. G. Casey (liaison officer with the Foreign Office). New Zealand was represented by Sir James Parr (high commissioner in London, former minister for education and justice, former Postmaster-General and delegate to the Assembly); South Africa by Eales and Eric Louw (high commissioner in London, plenipotentiary-designate to the United States and delegate to

MacDonald's hesitations had vanished and he treated the Australians and New Zealanders to a 'hard-line pep talk'.[100] He was conscious that his government 'had pressed forward rather rapidly . . . [but] it was impossible to proceed any slower':

> his Government had, in his opinion, received a very definite and emphatic mandate from the electors to honour our peace pledges at the very earliest opportunity, and this opportunity was occurring at Geneva. It was for this reason that he had been compelled to put on seven-league boots. The Optional Clause presented at once the simplest and most direct issue in pursuing a policy leading up to world peace . . . . if some big country like ours were to take the lead and face squarely these peace problems the results would prove of incalculable value . . . . it would have the effect of a strong tonic on the patient of Europe who was at the moment in rather a debilitated condition.

MacDonald was most anxious to meet the views of the dominions in 'every way possible'. However, they had to consider whether, in view of the outstanding differences, the United Kingdom could sign the Optional Clause 'in complete agreement with all the Dominions, and supposing that such an agreement is found to be impossible, would the Dominions understand our motives if we signed the Clause ourselves?'[101]

In posing this question, MacDonald was doing no more than point out the consequences that were likely to follow if everyone maintained their present position. The difficulty of even arranging the meeting had shown that the dominions were in no mood to come running when Britain beckoned, and augured ill for imperial unity.[102] But Britain needed to avoid laying itself open to

---

the Assembly); and the Irish Free State by Terence Smiddy (former Free State minister to the United States who had just been appointed high commissioner to the United Kingdom): Third meeting of the sub-committee on the Optional Clause, 27 Aug. 1929, secret, PRO, OC(29) 3rd cons., CAB 27/392.
[100] W. J. Hudson *Australia and the League of Nations*, Sydney 1980, 125.
[101] OC(29) 3rd cons.
[102] Loyal India went willingly to the meeting to support the British declaration to which they had agreed and South Africa raised no problems. The Irish Free State initially refused to send anyone 'on the transparent excuse that "the subject is too complicated to brief the High Commissioner in the time available", and it was only after considerable persuasion on the part of the Dominions Office that Mr. Smiddy turned up at the last moment'. The Canadians refused to send anyone at all, even when Britain 'sank to suggesting particular personnel who might be available' (Holland, 'Commonwealth in British official mind', 149) but they were willing to talk at Geneva. 'I don't see how possible', King said. There was not enough time and '[n]o-one [?] we can send could speak with authority'. Australia and New Zealand tried to prevent any discussions at all, whether in London or Geneva. No meeting should be held, said Bruce, until the dominions had had 'ample opportunity' to consider each other's views and it should then be fixed sufficiently far in advance for the 'most distant dominions' to arrange complete instructions for their representatives. When Britain pressed that preliminary discussions were urgently needed, Bruce said that since he had neither had a reply to his 'blockade' telegram nor heard the views of South Africa, he was not in a position to put forward fresh proposals. Repeating his call to defer action and allow further time for consultations, he said his representative at the proposed meeting would restate this position. His government would only agree to a declaration at Geneva that the question of accepting the Optional Clause was being 'earnestly' considered: minutes by Mackenzie King, 22, 24 Aug. 1929, NAC, RG25 D1, vol. 762, file 274, microfilm T-1767; telegrams from Bruce to Passfield, 22, 24 Aug. 1929, PRO, W 8243/21/98 FO 371/14105 and PREM 1/72; telegram from Passfield to Bruce, 22 Aug. 1929, W 8243/21/98; telegram from Ministry of External Affairs, Irish Free State, to Passfield and British reply, 22 Aug. 1929, W 8243/21/98; minute by W. D. C. Croft (India Office), 24 Aug. 1929, London, India Office Records, L/E/9/516, E & O 6184.

accusations that it had not tried to satisfy the dominions. Whether or not agreement was possible, what mattered was to be seen to consult them. As Cecil put it later in congratulating MacDonald on his handling of the meeting, the important thing was that '[n]ow whatever happens we shall be able to sign the Optional Clause, on your terms at the Assembly without causing serious upset to the Dominions'.[103]

Having failed to prevent the meeting in London, Bruce and Ward had muzzled their representatives by ordering them to 'abstain from any discussion'. And to make things quite clear, Bruce sent a telegram repeating that Australia would only agree to a declaration that the Commonwealth was earnestly considering the Optional Clause. Agreement was possible, but only if there were time for 'complete consultation' and no member of the Commonwealth should take any action on the Clause until there had been further consultation. It was in vain that MacDonald appealed for suggestions from Harrison Moore, who was thought to be sympathetic to the British line. The latter was there only as the ear and mouthpiece of his prime minister, and said he could do no more than submit a record of the meeting to his government.[104]

MacDonald accordingly suggested that the meeting consider the consequences. Perhaps, in view of the Australian and New Zealand attitude, they should abandon altogether any hopes for a united signature of the Optional Clause and the meeting should spend its time discussing the consequences of only part of the empire adhering to the Clause? Cecil, speaking 'with great frankness . . . in the hope of clearing a very difficult situation', pointed out that the question had been under discussion for several years. The present British government's repeated declarations of its intention to sign the Clause had been noted in every chancellery in Europe and 'a considerable number of smaller European States who were watching this country with the very closest interest . . .. would definitely be guided by the action of His Majesty's Government'. The Australian formula would cause 'profound disappointment' and greatly discourage everyone at a time when it was 'highly important to recover the influence which the decision of His Majesty's Government might exercise in the broad political world'.

> The present position was that five of the seven of His Majesty's Governments desired to sign the Clause but that this signature was threatened with indefinite delay by reason of the attitude adopted by the other two. Mr. Bruce was suggesting that the whole matter should be postponed until the next Imperial Conference, which might mean a delay of at least fifteen months, and he regarded it as a very serious matter to ask the other five governments to postpone what they regarded as a matter of urgency.

At this point Passfield offered Australia and New Zealand room to manoeuvre on reservations. If they would only agree to sign the British declaration at the Assembly, they could make an accompanying announcement that certain points were still under negotiation and this might result in additional reservations being added between the time of signature and ratification.[105] MacDonald took

---

[103] Cecil to MacDonald, confidential, 28 Aug. 1929, Cecil papers, BM, Add. MS 51081; MacDonald papers, PRO 30/69/2/6.

[104] See Hudson, *Australia and the League of Nations*, 124–5 and annex to OC(29) 3rd cons. Unless otherwise indicated, the quotations in the following paragraph are from OC(29) 3rd cons.

[105] This was one of three suggestions which Passfield made for accepting the Clause on the basis of tentative agreement. The second suggestion was to accept the British draft for an initial period of

this up and urged it as the 'best way out of the difficulty'. It would 'leave the door open' for agreement and meet '[t]he great point . . . to get a block signature in the first instance, and . . . prevent . . . any idea . . . that there were points of difference between . . . the various members of the Commonwealth'. The South African, Louw, who was 'very helpful',[106] made Passfield's proposal all the more attractive by arguing that Australia and New Zealand might be left to make their own reservations – something which the Australians in particular, and the meeting as a whole, regarded as 'most undesirable'.[107]

Australia retreats (followed by New Zealand)

Two days after the meeting, Bruce capitulated. From the Pacific end of the Commonwealth, the British approach was

> doubly damned: it showed a disconcerting rashness on matters central to national security and it showed, paradoxically in a would-be radical government, a view of the British Empire which was now positively reactionary in seeing the dominions not as separate nations and League members equal with Britain but merely sub-national entities within an Empire.[108]

There was an element of intimidation, but Britain had neither given Australia an order nor made the 'novel implied threat' that the Australians perceived.[109] Britain had simply said that it going to act with or without Australia, whereas Australia was unable to contemplate doing likewise since there would have been

two years on the understanding that during this time the Commonwealth would reach agreement on a possibly modified declaration. This would allow for discussion of the Optional Clause at the 1930 imperial conference but agreement on some points might be necessary before signature took place. The third suggestion was that everyone sign a declaration embodying every reservation that any member wanted on the understanding that some of these might be withdrawn before ratification. It was clear that the list would have to be a long one if Australia and New Zealand were to be satisfied. It would also mean accepting Australia's reservation regarding disputes as to which no rule of international law existed – a course which Britain regarded 'as practically equivalent to the reservation of any matter whatsoever'. If none of these alternatives were acceptable, Passfield could only suggest accepting Bruce's idea that the Commonwealth should limit itself at the Assembly to making a declaration of intent. Each course required that an agreement be reached on inter-imperial disputes but the BMR problem could be avoided: memorandum by Passfield, 22 Aug. 1929, PRO, OC(29)14 CAB 27/392. On the basis of the minutes of this meeting Holland describes Passfield's proposals as an example of the Dominions Office's adeptness at 'technical devices which put the cosmetic touch of unity on what were really widely separated opinions', and Hudson says it was Passfield 'who explored alternatives to outright surrender either by Britain or by Australia and New Zealand': 'Commonwealth in British official mind', 149; *Australia and the League of Nations*, 125. However, Henderson had also suggested this possibility and Dalton told MacDonald that Malkin had assured him that it was perfectly possible to sign one declaration at Geneva and then ratify a different formula after further discussion: note by Henderson on the Optional Clause, PRO, W 8180/21/98; Dalton to MacDonald, 19 Aug. 1929, MacDonald papers, PRO 30/69/1/4. But cf. Dalton to Noel-Baker, private and confidential, 21 Aug. 1929, Dalton papers, BLPES, Subject File 4, Aqua passata.

106 Dalton to Henderson, 27 Aug. 1929, Dalton papers, BLPES, Subject File 4, Aqua passata.
107 Aide-memoire, conference on acceptance of the Optional Clause, 10 Downing Street, secret, 27 Aug. 1929, OC(29)19, W 8548/21/98, *DBFP* vi, 441. See also undated note by MacDonald, PRO, DO 35/75.
108 Hudson, *Australia and the League of Nations*, 123.
109 Ibid. 125.

no point in making a BMR reservation without Britain. Bruce insisted, however, that Australia's signature at the Assembly, was to be conditional on the understanding that if complete agreement was not reached on additional reservations – to safeguard BMR – there must be a written statement that further reservations were still being considered.

The New Zealand government swiftly followed the Australians, bitterly complaining at the lack of opportunity for 'the close and continuous consultation which [this] immensely important subject demands'. New Zealand was not in a position to arrive at a 'final and considered decision' and the 'introduction of a time limit' was not 'conducive to a mature consideration of questions of utmost gravity'.

> Faced, however, as we now are by the fact that abstention on our part would involve a distinct departure from Imperial unity, we have been forced to reconsider our attitude and to estimate advantages and disadvantages of following a course of action which, in the absence of this fundamental consideration, we would have had little hesitation in pursuing. It is clear that acceptance of the Clause by the United Kingdom alone . . . would, for all practical purposes, be equivalent, so far as belligerent rights at sea are concerned, to acceptance by the British Empire as a whole; no practical result would, therefore, in fact be achieved by our abstention. On the other hand, by such abstention we would be taking up an attitude which is foreign to our traditions and which we could only contemplate because, in our opinion, security of the Empire should be the first consideration.[110]

New Zealand had concluded, therefore, that although 'the effects of the form of acceptance proposed by the British government would be more or less speculative, in circumstances where certainty should be paramount',[111] it would be in 'the interests of the Empire as a whole' to sign the Clause in common with the rest of the Commonwealth. Like Bruce, Ward insisted on a declaration that certain points which were still under negotiation (i.e. the safeguarding of BMR), might have to be added before ratification, and that ratification be delayed 'pending fullest consultation in an endeavour to evolve a formula acceptable to all'.[112]

Further imperial disunity: inter-imperial disputes and international status

The lifting of the Australian and New Zealand 'blockade' by the end of August meant that the Commonwealth had agreed on signing the Optional Clause within the next three weeks but would continue negotiating at Geneva over antipodean wishes to protect BMR. But by this time a far more serious difficulty had arisen: the Irish Free State refused to reserve inter-imperial disputes.

The draft declaration of 24 July had aimed at protecting the doctrine of *inter-se* and keeping inter-imperial disputes from the purview of the PCIJ in two ways. The first of these (to which attention was drawn in the 1 August telegram) was

---

[110] Telegram from New Zealand prime minister (Ward) to MacDonald, immediate, confidential, 31 Aug. 1929, PRO, OC(29)23 CAB 27/392.
[111] Official minute quoted in Nichols to Koppel, 26 Aug. 1929, PRO, W 9505/21/98 FO 371/14106.
[112] Telegram from Ward to MacDonald, 31 Aug. 1929.

by accepting the Court's jurisdiction in 'international' disputes. The second way (which was not explained in the 1 August telegram) was by accepting the Optional Clause 'in relation to any other state' rather than using the wording of the Optional Clause, which referred to 'any other Member or State'. This could be taken to imply that the dominions were not states, an issue which Henderson's 3 July memorandum for the Cabinet had avoided by referring to the Commonwealth countries as 'autonomous units' and studiously qualifying the word 'state' by the adjective 'foreign'.

When the Irish government had replied to the Labour government's initial enquiry of 22 June, it had not mentioned the Free State's views on inter-imperial disputes. It said only that Ireland had 'always been prepared to sign the Optional Clause with as few reservations as possible'. And, while it would be 'very desirable' for the whole Commonwealth to accept the Optional Clause, the Irish government did not regard it as either advisable or in accordance with the understanding reached at the 1926 imperial conference to give the impression that a general agreement was essential before any Commonwealth country could sign.[113] However, in July, McGilligan, the minister for External Affairs, told the senate that his country would not sign the Optional Clause with a reservation that prevented the court adjudicating in inter-imperial disputes. This was because the Free State was determined to throw off the shackles of the Judicial Committee of the Privy Council, both as a court of appeal from Irish courts and as the body to which it should refer any legal dispute that might arise between the Free State and Great Britain. Although rarely used, the Judicial Committee was the court for inter-imperial disputes, and to end this role meant opening the way for such disputes to go to the PCIJ.

At one stage Hurst had been sanguine about the possibility of reaching agreement with Ireland, and Malkin had also been hopeful about the willingness of the Free State to co-operate with Britain. None the less, given Ireland's known views on the Privy Council, South Africa and Canada were privately approached in the hope of inducing them both to accept the British line on inter-imperial disputes and to get them to persuade the Free State to do likewise. Hertzog was 'remarkably helpful'. He agreed that the Court should not have jurisdiction in Commonwealth disputes and only made difficulties 'on one point and that is the point which he might have been expected to raise and to raise for the reasons which he gives'.[114] This was his objection to the inclusion of the word 'international' (in the fifth paragraph of the proposed declaration),[115] on the grounds that it implied that '*inter se* the Dominions are not international units'.[116] Australia had also queried this proposal, saying that it was not sufficiently clear-cut: it did not entirely remove the possibility of the Court asserting that it had jurisdiction in inter-imperial disputes. South Africa and Australia thought that the members of the Commonwealth should reach a specific agreement reserving inter-imperial disputes. Both were told that, although Britain did not think an agreement was important, Britain would

113 Telegram from Irish Free State, 28 June 1929, PRO, W 6320/21/98 FO 371/14104. Although at first it was thought important to enter a caveat, it was eventually decided to say nothing in response: DO 35/71.

114 Malkin to Hurst, 14 Aug. 1929, PRO, W 7931/21/98 FO 371/14104.

115 That is 'in all international disputes comprised in . . . Article 36'.

116 Telegram from Hertzog to Passfield, 19 Aug. 1929, PRO, W 7931/21/98 FO 371/14104.

welcome one if 'it were acceptable to the Governments of all the Dominions'.[117] Hertzog responded by agreeing that a 'gentleman's understanding' would be sufficient, but the Irish reply to the 1 August telegram confirmed fears that even this would be insufficient for the Free State. Thus there seemed no way of altering the declaration to satisfy both Hertzog and McGilligan.

Ireland's stand

Ireland insisted that what the British draft declaration of 24 July was trying to do was to draw an unwarranted distinction between Commonwealth and non-Commonwealth League members. Unless the words 'member or' were included, the declaration 'would not be a declaration under Article 36 at all'; the terms of the Optional Clause made it clear that any legal dispute between two Commonwealth countries would fall within the jurisdiction of the Court. The Irish objection on this point, as on the 'proviso' or 'French joker' (which suspended disputes before the League Council), was fundamental: the Free State would not agree to a draft which 'would afford a pretext to . . . the world generally for a suggestion of insincerity'.[118]

The Irish despatch was not received until 23 August, the day that the Cabinet sub-committee met to consider what to do about the Australian 'blockade'. Passfield had immediately explained to the sub-committee the Dominions Office belief that the Free State had raised important constitutional issues as to what parts of the empire were actually separate and independent. Its attitude 'might lead to a very serious situation', he said:

> It would mean, in effect, that if certain members of the British Commonwealth . . . acceded to the Optional Clause and others did not, the position, vis-a-vis arbitration, would be different in various parts of the Empire. It was quite certain that, in the unfortunate case of war arising, the British Empire must stand together and there could be no possible doubt but that foreign nations for this purpose would regard the British Commonwealth of Nations as an identic body. He felt strongly that in regard to arbitration there must be a common doctrine throughout the British Empire.[119]

Henderson's team appreciated the desirability of the Commonwealth acting as one and reserving inter-imperial disputes, but the Irish reply came at a time when they were disinclined to sympathise with the officials of the Dominions and Foreign Offices. Labour's men in the Foreign Office had been urging that imperial unity might have to be sacrificed for the sake of signing the Optional Clause, and Dalton did not understand the constitutional problem raised by the Irish. In any case, the Irish line was not dissimilar to the sort of approach which Britain was taking with Australia. As Parmoor pointed out, the real point of what the Free State was saying was that it wanted more independence than the

---

[117] Telegram from MacDonald to Bruce, No. 147, confidential 23 August 1929, PRO, PREM 1/72; DBFP vi, 439. Cf. telegram to Clifford (British representative in South Africa), drafted by Malkin and Dixon, PRO, W 7931/21/98 FO 371/14104; Malkin to Hurst, 14 Aug. 1929, W 7931/21/98.
[118] McGilligan (minister of external affairs, Irish Free State) to Passfield, 22 Aug. 1929, PRO, W 8260/21/98 FO 371/14105. See also McGilligan to Passfield, 26 Aug. 1929, secret, OC(29)20 CAB 27/392.
[119] Passfield to OC(29) 2nd cons.

other dominions. But since every dominion had 'the same independent rights as we had at Geneva', the Irish were 'technically speaking, at full liberty to do what they liked'.[120]

When the dominion representatives met in London on 27 August, Smiddy, who spoke for the Free State, did so only once, at the very end of the lengthy meeting, to point out that the Irish government's views were different from those held by the United Kingdom. He said that '[t]he Irish Free State were in effect prepared to sign without reservation'. The meeting took him to be referring only to inter-imperial disputes (whereas he might well have been warning that Ireland proposed no reservations at all). Thus the Australian, New Zealand and South African representatives repeated their objections to the way in which Britain had proposed reserving such disputes from the PCIJ. Louw of South Africa had already emphasised South Africa's objection that this implied that 'inter se the Dominions were not international units', and Harrison Moore for Australia, with the backing of Parr for New Zealand, repeated that his government was 'insistent' that disputes between Commonwealth countries must be reserved either by an explicit reservation or a 'definite agreement among the Dominions'. MacDonald soothingly dismissed the matter. '[H]e was most strongly of the opinion that any inter-imperial differences should be settled amongst ourselves', and concluded vacuously that 'it was accepted that the procedure should not be by implication'.[121]

However, there could be no solution because it was impossible to avoid or gloss over the contradictions inherent in the doctrine of inter-se. That inter-imperial disputes should not be submitted to the PCIJ was the one matter on which the Dominions Office thought agreement was necessary, either beforehand or immediately after signing the Optional Clause. An explicit reservation of inter-imperial disputes had been ruled out as it implied that Commonwealth disputes were international – which would not protect inter-se. An inter-imperial agreement – even the 'gentleman's agreement' suggested by South Africa – was unacceptable to the Irish. And the British attempt to devise a form of wording which would leave the doctrine of inter-se implicit was regarded on the one hand as insufficient, on another as a slight on the international standing of South Africa, and on a third as contrary to the Irish view that inter-imperial disputes were international. When the Commonwealth representatives gathered at Geneva, it was this problem that dominated the final steps to Britain's signature of the Optional Clause.

Geneva 1929

As soon as they arrived in Geneva, the dominions agreed to form an Optional Clause committee. The first meeting was held on Monday 2 September, and the first item on the agenda was what MacDonald was going to say about the Optional Clause when he opened the general debate the following day.[122]

---

[120] OC(29) 2nd cons.

[121] OC(29) 3rd cons.

[122] There was no secretarial assistance at the meetings and no minutes were taken. The following account is based on reports by Cecil, Hurst and the Irish delegation. The two representatives from each country included MacDonald and Cecil for Great Britain (until 5 Sept. when MacDonald left

MacDonald wanted to make a great splash and announce that not only was his country going to sign the Optional Clause but that the dominions would do likewise. Not surprisingly, the dominions were not going to concede the glory to MacDonald and they insisted that he was not in any way to speak on their behalf. The Canadians, who had rejected pressure from the British High Commissioner to send a representative to the London meeting because it was held at such short notice, were particularly firm. After a last minute modification 'to soothe Canadian susceptibilities',[123] it was agreed that the British prime minister could say that:

> I am in a position to announce to you now that my Government has decided to sign the Optional Clause. The form of our declaration is now being prepared, and will be completed and handed in during the present session of the Assembly.
> Further, my Government has consulted . . . the other members of the British Commonwealth . . . who are also Members of this League, and I believe that each of them will instruct its representatives at this Assembly to sign the Optional Clause during the present session. In accordance with their rights and their position here, however, they will make their own statements on this subject.[124]

MacDonald's announcement, for which he had prepared the press, brought a 'loud burst of cheering',[125] but most of his speech met with silence from most delegates as they sweltered in the ill-ventilated hall. MacDonald's lack of overall success with his speech was partly because the acrimony of the Hague conference on reparations had lowered his personal standing. Also, it was partly because he had once again gone to Geneva tired and without preparation so that, when he spoke, he again delivered homilies more appropriate to the Albert Hall than to the hard-boiled delegates. He also did so with a 'certain note of self-righteousness' that 'appeared to jar'.[126] Three days later, Henderson (who unlike MacDonald was a notoriously poor speaker) was far more successful. For,

> [w]hat impressed the delegates was not the form, but the matter. If a man was trying to say something, they would listen. If he really had something to say, they would listen with attention . . .. character and sincerity were always held in high respect and carried far more weight when they discarded oratorical artifices.[127]

And Henderson was not only obviously sincere but delivered 'a model of what speeches at the Assembly ought to be'.[128] During it he elaborated on MacDonald's announcement by explaining what Britain hoped to achieve by

Geneva and was replaced by Hurst); Louw (South African high commissioner in London); Dandurand (Canadian delegate) McGilligan and Costello (Irish minister of external affairs and attorney general); and the Australian, Sir William Harrison Moore. It is not clear who else attended.
123 Cecil to Henderson, 25 Sept. 1929, W 10270/21/98, *DBFP* vi, 442 (Account by Cecil). Even so, Ottawa thought Dandurand had conceded too much to MacDonald.
124 League of Nations, Records of the tenth ordinary session of the Assembly, plenary meetings, text of the debates, *LNOJ*, special supplement no. 75 (*LNA10 debs.*), third plenary, 3 Sept. 1929, 34–5.
125 *The Times*, 4 Sept. 1929.
126 *Manchester Guardian*, 4 Sept. 1929. The speech 'suggested in style and substance too much of the aggressive self-vindication which is the usual mark of our domestic political oratory': editorial, 'The Optional Clause'.
127 Harold Butler, *The lost peace: a personal impression*, London 1941, 31.
128 That is, 'a clear, straightforward statement, free from rhetorical flourishes and sentimental appeals': *Manchester Guardian*, 7 Sept. 1929.

signing the Optional Clause. 'We believe arbitration to be important on every ground', he said.

> It is important because, in any given dispute, it is more likely than any other possible method that can be devised to bring about a settlement that is wise and just; it is important because it furnishes the true alternative to war and gives a means whereby conflicts and deadlocks between nations may be resolved. But, above all, it is important because of the spirit which it can bring into the relations between the Governments of the world. A nation which relies on arbitration and is ready to accept the verdict of an impartial judge does not rely upon the use of armed force. Its national mind is turned in a new direction, and it is precisely in this new spirit which the practice of arbitration may induce that lies perhaps the most powerful single factor in bringing to the nations security from war.
>
> It is because we believe all this ... that we have decided as our first step, and I emphasise that – our first step – to sign the Optional Clause .... It is through arbitration that we shall be able to take the next step towards real security from war – the step which we shall take when we make a general Treaty of Disarmament.[129]

The British announcement on the Optional Clause was welcomed by the smaller states who emphasised their support for it and for the coming reign of law in international relations, while the French and Italians even tried to go one better than Britain. (Briand would renew France's lapsed declaration of 1924 before leaving Geneva and he was also going to do his utmost to secure ratification of the General Act. Scialoja 'went and signed for Italy, early in the morning before anyone was up'.)[130] So far as the dominions were concerned, the New Zealand representative did not take part the opening debate; the Australian representative, Marr, could say nothing definite since his government had just been defeated in parliament and had, accordingly, instructed him to make no pronouncement; and the Indian delegate simply stated that his country would sign the Optional Clause before the end of the Assembly. The Canadians and Irish, however, took the opportunity to make clear their independent policies on the matter. For the former, Dandurand (who seemed to like incendiary metaphors) emphasised that Canada had 'kept the torch burning' since 1924. He pointed out that the Canadian government had opened the Commonwealth consultations that year, and that these were in progress when the British government sent the 'welcome news' that it had decided to sign.[131] McGilligan of Ireland, who was the last speaker in the general debate, not only announced that he intended to press for acceptance of the General Act but also took the opportunity to 'remind delegates of the danger of attaching to their acceptance of Conventions reservations for which no provision has been made. Reservations ... clearly cannot be made except in so far as the

---

129 *LNA10* debs., seventh plenary, 6 Sept. 1929, 58.

130 For Briand's pronouncement see *LNA10* debs., seventh plenary, 6 Sept. 1929, 52. On Scialoja see Dalton diary entry, 1–25 September 1929, BLPES, Dalton papers, vol. 13. Italy's acceptance of the Clause was almost completely ignored by the Italian press.

131 Dandurand to the Assembly, *LNA10* debs., fifth plenary, 4 Sept. 1929, 43. Canberra protested to Ottawa at Dandurand's 'breach of confidentiality' but Mackenzie King's reply – that Dandurand had merely described Canadian policy over the years without referring to that of other governments – was not 'ingenuous': Hudson, *Australia and the League of Nations*, 127. All Dandurand had revealed was that on 1 Aug. Britain had sent a telegram announcing its intention to accept the Optional Clause at the Assembly.

Convention or Protocol expressly provides for them, and then only within the limits so provided'.[132]

Final discussions

In this way McGilligan publicly hinted at the disagreement that had quickly led to disarray and anger in the Commonwealth Optional Clause committee. Within an hour of starting to go through the draft declaration, the committee had come unstuck when the Irish representative asked the reasons for, and significance of, the words: 'I accept . . . in relation to any other state accepting the same obligation the jurisdiction of the Court as compulsory in all international disputes'. Neither Cecil nor MacDonald was able to give 'any adequate account of it'. Indeed, said Cecil, they suggested that the change from the wording of the Optional Clause had 'no particular significance'.[133] Hurst – who was not at the meeting because of a decision to exclude expert advisers – was sent for and he had no alternative but to speak relatively plainly:

> I therefore said that the word 'international' had been used because the view held in London was that relations between the different units of the Commonwealth were not international relations, and, therefore, their disputes were not international disputes. Consequently, the use of the term 'international' excluded inter-Imperial disputes. I also added that the omission of the words 'Members or' before the word 'State' was intentional, because the words 'Members or' became superfluous if inter-Imperial disputes were to be excluded. The only units which are members of the League which are not covered by the word 'states' are the various Members of the British Commonwealth of Nations. If one unit of the Commonwealth was to accept the compulsory jurisdiction of the court in relation to another Member or State accepting the same obligation, it would prejudice the interpretation of the word 'international', because the only other Member in respect of which such a unit of the Commonwealth would accept it would be another British unit. I said nothing as to the interpretation of the word 'state' and at a later stage of the meeting . . . [when asked directly] whether we regarded the units of the Commonwealth as states, I evaded a direct reply.[134]

Hurst had not denied the international standing of the dominions. But he had been forced to admit that the legal and constitutional bonds that linked the dominions with Britain – which had given rise to the doctrine of *inter-se* – did not, legally-speaking, from the British point of view, render them sovereign states on the same basis as other League members. All the dominions protested at this explanation – even Australia and New Zealand – but the Irish Free State and South Africa protested loudest. In August the British had simply told the Irish that the omission of the words 'member or' did not affect the legal validity of the declaration and was a point of 'theoretical' rather than 'practical importance'.[135] This was true enough, but did not answer the point on which Hurst had now had to come clean. Louw of South Africa was particularly

---

132 McGilligan to the Assembly, *LNA10* debs., thirteenth plenary, 11 Sept. 1929, 111.
133 Account by Cecil.
134 'Account [by Hurst] of negotiations which took place at Geneva regarding the treatment of inter-imperial disputes', 21 Sept. 1929, PRO, W 9062/21/98 FO 371/14106 (Account by Hurst).
135 MacDonald to Cosgrave, 29 Aug. 1929, PRO, OC(29)21 CAB 27/392.

aggrieved. South Africa had been most co-operative, particularly over the Australian 'blockade'. There had been only one point on which Hertzog had insisted – that the Optional Clause declaration should not compromise South Africa's international status – but Britain had not once mentioned the point raised by the Free State. Not surprisingly Louw went 'so far as to suggest that there had been something like disingenuousness in the British Government's despatches in not calling attention to the omission . . . which had evidently been made for a deliberate purpose'. In the 'confused discussion' that followed, the dominions were hopelessly divided. India, Australia and New Zealand 'definitely desired to exclude inter-Commonwealth disputes, and were ready to use whatever language was necessary for that purpose'. Canada, too, wanted to exclude such disputes from the purview of the court 'but did not wish anything to appear on the face of the declaration which would give countenance to the view that inter-Commonwealth disputes were not international'. South Africa shared Canada's view, 'only rather more strongly, and wished the exclusion of the Commonwealth disputes to be a matter of private arrangement'. The Irish Free State would not agree to any reservation on this point. It was not that Ireland was 'wedded to the Court as a Court . . . we really did not know a great deal about it'. It was 'essential from the point of view of our status, and from the point of view of our political situation at home that we should at least have the theoretic [sic] right of bringing Great Britain or any Dominion before the Court'.[136]

Nonetheless, the search for agreement continued. A sub-committee was set up and Hurst tried to persuade his colleagues – Louw, Costello (the Irish attorney general) and Harrison Moore – that they had to be prepared to recognise one another's views and find a form of wording 'that could be signed by all parties without prejudicing the principles which they held'. It appeared from their discussion that there would be 'no difficulty' and after devising a suitable wording Hurst privately discussed his drafts with Costello, Harrison Moore and Louw.[137]

At this point, with the Assembly entering its second week, Louw suddenly called a meeting of the full Commonwealth committee. He 'must have told his Government that I had said that the Dominions were not states', said Hurst, for Louw read out a telegram in which Hertzog demanded 'in peremptory terms'[138] and 'with some bluntness'[139] that Britain 'should repudiate the views which [Hurst] had enunciated'. In the ensuing acrimonious discussion Louw and Costello demanded that Britain make a fresh statement on the international position of the dominions. Cecil was able to deflect Louw by insisting that only an imperial conference could modify the work of a previous imperial conference, and by subsequently giving him a statement saying that Britain's Optional Clause declaration did not alter the 1926 agreement on the status of the dominions. But by now the chances of an inter-imperial agreement were 'getting remote'.[140]

[136] Account by Cecil; 'Optional Clause. Report on inter-Commonwealth discussions received from Saorstat [Free State] delegation', 12 Sept. 1929, NAC, RG25, vol. 3424, file 1-1929/10.
[137] Account by Hurst.
[138] Ibid.
[139] Account by Cecil.
[140] Account by Hurst. For the statement Cecil gave Louw see enclosure in Account by Cecil.

Two days later, Costello confirmed that the statement Cecil had given Louw on the status of the dominions was 'quite useless to them',[141] since the Irish Free State would definitely not enter into any agreement to withhold inter-imperial disputes from the PCIJ. On 12 September the sub-committee reported its failure to reach agreement at a lengthy meeting of all the delegations after which the Irish Free State withdrew from any further discussions. On 14 September, with discreet support from Canada and the personal support of Louw,[142] McGilligan signed the Optional Clause with the following declaration (which side-stepped the *inter-se* problem by making no mention of 'members' or 'states'):

> On behalf of the Irish Free State, I declare that I accept as compulsory *ipso facto* and without special convention the jurisdiction of the Court in conformity with Article 36 of the Statute of the Permanent Court of International Justice for a period of twenty years and on the sole condition of reciprocity. This declaration is subject to ratification.[143]

This 'dramatic, independent gesture' has been described as setting 'an example of straightforward support for the only organs of international peace which were based on international democratic equality'. And, by letting it be known that it would stand for election to the League Council, the Free State indicated its readiness 'to undertake the fullest international responsibilities'.[144] Yet, at the time, leading Irish papers made no comment; it was hardly noticed in the *Manchester Guardian*; and when *The Times* took note a few days later, the Irish government was regarded as having 'signed the Optional Clause chiefly, if not solely, because it is earnestly anxious to abolish the jurisdiction which the Judicial Committee of the Privy Council exercises . . . .. and . . . has seized upon the possibilities of the Optional Clause as a useful move in the game'.[145] Meanwhile the rest of the Commonwealth continued negotiating without shedding crocodile tears and with greater ease.

By constantly consulting the other dominion representatives and bringing them in on the drafting, Hurst was soon able to produce a reservation which explicitly excluded inter-imperial disputes and was acceptable, in substance, to all. However, since Hertzog had tied Louw's hands, and the new draft ran counter to instructions, the latter could only send it to Pretoria and await Hertzog's response. Time was running out. It was now the beginning of the third week. Henderson was due to leave Geneva on Friday and arrangements had been made to sign the Clause half an hour before the Council met on Thursday. The British representative in South Africa put pressure on Hertzog[146] who

---

[141] Account by Cecil.

[142] McGilligan in interview with Harkness: *Restless dominion*, 143.

[143] The Irish informed the other dominion delegations by letter that they were going to sign the Clause and gave them the text of their declaration immediately after it had been signed: *The Times*, 19 Sept. 1929.

[144] Harkness, *Restless dominion*, 143–4. However, the Irish had already pushed themselves forward for a seat on the Council in 1926.

[145] *The Times*, 18 Sept. 1929.

[146] Hertzog had instructed Louw that, in the absence of a Commonwealth agreement on inter-imperial disputes, he was not to agree to a declaration which reserved such disputes from the jurisdiction of the PCIJ. Clifford successfully persuaded him that the reservation was sufficiently ambiguous for each part of the Commonwealth to maintain its own position and that if he did not allow Louw to sign in the agreed form, it would have 'the most embarrassing consequences':

finally gave Louw permission just in time for him to join Henderson and Habibullah of India in signing the Clause.

Britain had now surmounted all the obstacles along the path to signature of the Optional Clause. During the discussions at Geneva several alterations had been made to the British draft in addition to that on inter-imperial disputes, but none of these were of substance. The fifteen-year time-limit had been brought down to ten years but the declaration was still to continue thereafter until denounced; a domestic jurisdiction reservation, which had been offered in London as a carrot to the Australians, was also agreed; and, finally, a twelve-month time-limit on the suspension of proceedings that were before the Council was included to satisfy the Canadian government, which had not accepted Britain's assurance that it was unnecessary. Britain's ready agreement to this addition was not surprising, but Louw only agreed to it after a personal appeal from Hurst. The British documents do not reveal any difficulties with Australia and New Zealand. This is probably because New Zealand followed Australia, and Sir Granville Ryrie, the Australian High Commissioner in London (who had quickly replaced Marr in the wake of the constitutional crisis), advised Bruce to accept the draft that had been hammered out in Geneva. Britain had, he reported, made concessions on inter-imperial disputes and domestic jurisdiction. If Bruce dragged his feet, Henderson was so eager to go ahead that he might make a declaration less favourable to Australia. The domestic turmoil might well have put Bruce in a difficult position to resist and he may have counted on amending the reservations before ratification. Whatever the reason, Bruce changed his mind. After telling the Australian delegation not to accept the Optional Clause in view of the fall of the government, he subsequently authorised Ryrie to sign the declaration that had been hammered out.

Signature

After lunch on 19 September, Henderson, Louw, Parr of New Zealand and Habibullah of India – together with the representatives of France, Czechoslovakia and Peru – signed the Optional Clause in the 'glass room' watched by a crowd of spectators and '[w]ith some attempt at ceremony, in which photographers and cinema operators played their full part'.[147] (The following day Ryrie of Australia and Dandurand, whose instructions had only just arrived, followed suit and made a declaration which was identical except in respect of the government on whose behalf they signed.) Britain's declaration was as follows:

> On behalf of His Majesty's Government in the United Kingdom and subject to ratification, I accept as compulsory *ipso facto* and without special convention on condition of reciprocity the jurisdiction of the court in conformity with Article 36, paragraph 2, of the statute of the court, for a period of ten years and thereafter until such time as notice may be given to terminate the acceptance, over all disputes arising

paraphrase telegram from Dixon (Geneva) sent to Clifford, immediate, secret, 17 Sept. 1929, PRO, PREM 1/72.

[147] *The Times*, 20 Sept. 1929.

after the ratification of the present declaration with regard to situations or facts subsequent to the said ratification, other than:–

Disputes in regard to which the parties to the dispute have agreed or shall agree to have recourse to some other method of peaceful settlement; and

Disputes with the Government of any other member of the League which is a member of the British Commonwealth of Nations, all of which disputes shall be settled in such manner as the parties have agreed or shall agree; and

Disputes with regard to questions which by international law fall exclusively within the jurisdiction of the United Kingdom.

And subject to the condition that His Majesty's Government reserve the right to require that proceedings in the court shall be suspended in respect of any dispute which has been submitted to and is under consideration by the Council of the League of Nations, provided that notice to suspend is given after the dispute has been submitted to the Council and is given within ten days of the notification of the initiation of the proceedings in the court, and provided also that such suspension shall be limited to a period of twelve months or such longer period as can be agreed by the parties to the dispute or determined by a decision of all the members of the Council other than the parties to the dispute.

Unfortunately, the show of unity was immediately marred. Immediately after signing the Optional Clause, and without forewarning the dominion delegates, Henderson read out a statement explaining the contents of the reservations. Disputes between the members of the Commonwealth were excluded by the terms of the declaration because, he said,

the members of the Commonwealth, though international units individually in the fullest sense of the term, are united by their common allegiance to the Crown. Disputes between them should, therefore, be dealt with by some other mode of settlement, and for this provision is made in the exclusion clause.[148]

Being taken aback, Louw angrily 'pencilled some hasty jottings on the back of an envelope'.[149] Then, telling Hurst that Henderson's statement was 'a great mistake', Louw proceeded to publicly assert that the Court did have jurisdiction in inter-imperial disputes but that his government preferred to settle them by other means. By a stroke of irony, Dandurand was the last Commonwealth leader to sign the clause. And when he did so, on 20 September, he accompanied his signature with a somewhat obscure and, legally-speaking, surprising statement asserting that although the reservation of Commonwealth disputes might not be considered consistent with the terms of the Optional

---

[148] PRO, W 9260/21/98 FO 371/14105. Passfield had earlier suggested that if it were not possible to find a satisfactory formula, 'the next best course' would be an explanatory declaration. This met both the South African and Australian objections and 'would also seem to constitute sufficient "notice" to the International Court'. It would also 'seem preferable to an inter-Imperial agreement . . . which would presumably only be binding as between the parts of the British Empire which had signed it and, from a juridical point of view, would not, I presume, prevent any of them being cited before the Court by any part of the Empire which had not itself signed the agreement': Passfield to Henderson, 29 Aug. 1929, Henderson papers, PRO, FO 800/280 and PREM 1/72.
[149] Manning, Policies of the British dominions, 39–40.

Clause, his government had included the reservation in accordance with its 'expressed policy'.[150]

MacDonald's wish that the tenth Assembly be remembered as the 'Optional Clause Assembly' was not fulfilled. Rather it was noted for the 'spirit of unity, of purpose, and of hope more complete than the Assembly had ever before attained or was ever destined to regain'; for the number of states represented and the quality of their delegations; and for the favourable circumstances in which it met.[151] The *Manchester Guardian* was over-optimistic in thinking that 'It is probably only a question of time, probably no long time, before membership of the League of Nations implies almost automatic acceptance of the compulsory jurisdiction of the League's Court. The acceptance of the British Empire should go a long way to bringing this about.'[152] Yet the tenth Assembly did witness a large increase in the number of signatories of the Clause. At the end of 1928 the Optional Clause was binding on sixteen states.[153] By the opening of the tenth Assembly their number had risen to eighteen.[154] During the Assembly, in addition to the seven Commonwealth signatures, another eight states signed the Clause.[155] At this time the number of countries who were parties to the Statute of the Court was forty-two. (The League's membership at this time was fifty-four.)

From signature to ratification

As the Assembly drew to a close, Dalton rejoiced in his diary: '*We succeeded, at last, in signing the Optional Clause*. Nunc dimittis!'[156] But it was not quite the end of the path, for it was necessary to ratify the signature. On 25 September the Cabinet formally approved the action that had been taken on the Optional Clause and Passfield congratulated Henderson on securing the agreement of all the dominions except the Irish Free State. However, the Admiralty was far from happy. On 19 September – the day that the Clause was signed – Alexander had joined with his colleagues on the Optional Clause sub-committee in assenting to Henderson's signing the Optional Clause in the form proposed, but he had

---

[150] Account by Hurst. '*J'ai voulu alors simplement dissocier le Canada de l'affirmation de principe faite par Monsieur Henderson, de manière à reserver l'avenir et à laisser le règlement définitif de cette question à la Conférence impériale*', explained Dandurand: Dandurand to Skelton, 15 Mar. 1930, in *Documents on Canadian external relations*, iv, *1926–1930*, ed. Alex I. Inglis, Ottawa 1971, 665.

[151] See MacDonald to the Assembly, 3 Sept., *LNA10* debs., third plenary, 35; Walters, *History of the League of Nations*, 412.

[152] Editorial, 'The Optional Clause', 4 Sept. 1929.

[153] Abyssinia, Austria, Belgium, Bulgaria, Denmark, Estonia, Finland, Germany, Haiti, Norway, the Netherlands, Portugal, Spain, Sweden, Switzerland and Uruguay. Unratified declarations had been made by the Dominican Republic, France, Hungary, Latvia, Liberia and Panama. Costa Rica, Guatemala, Luxembourg and El Salvador had signed the Clause but had not deposited a ratification of the protocol of signature of the Statute of the PCIJ.

[154] Panama ratified its 1921 declaration on 14 June and Hungary ratified its 1928 declaration on 13 Aug.

[155] These were Italy (on 9 Sept., ratified Sept. 1931), Latvia (on 10 Sept., ratified Feb. 1930), Greece (on 12 Sept., ratification not required), France (19 Sept., ratified Apr. 1931), Czechoslovakia (19 Sept., unratified), Peru (19 Sept., ratified Mar. 1932), Thailand (20 Sept., ratified 1930) and Nicaragua (24 Sept., ratification not required. It was not until Nov. 1939 that Nicaragua deposited its signature of the protocol of signature of the Statute of the PCIJ – made on 14 Sept. 1929.)

[156] Diary entry, 1–25 Sept. 1929, Dalton papers, BLPES, vol. 13.

informed both the sub-committee and the Cabinet that the Admiralty wanted its views considered before ratification took place. A memorandum expressing the Sea Lords' alarm that disputes involving BMR could be taken to the PCIJ was written by the deputy chief of naval staff, Vice-Admiral William Fisher, as soon as the Admiralty had learned the content of the final paragraph of the declaration. The Admiralty wanted the matter discussed in the Committee of Imperial Defence (CID) prior to ratification.[157]

This fear was dismissed by the Foreign Office officials on the grounds that the Admiralty had failed to take into account their argument – which had been explained at length – that if Britain loyally executed the Covenant and Pact of Paris it was hard to see 'how or by whom they could be cited before the Court'.[158] The paper itself was regarded as an ' "*Acquit de conscience*". The First Lord acquiesced in the formula adopted', said Campbell, the head of the western department, 'and I do not see how it can be altered at the time of ratification. Such a step would create the worst possible impression.' Mounsey, an assistant under secretary, agreed, as did Lindsay, the permanent under secretary. 'In view of the very careful consideration which has been given to this point before signature took place, the Admiralty cannot seriously expect that an amended declaration will be substituted on ratification', said Mounsey, 'and they should not, I think, be given any encouragement to expect this.'[159]

The Admiralty's unsuccessful rearguard action

But the Admiralty continued to press its case. Malkin, who had become the senior legal adviser on Hurst's election to the bench of the PCIJ at the tenth Assembly, was treated to an 'elaborate catechism' of technical, procedural questions arising out of the Admiralty's belief that the terms in which the Optional Clause had been accepted meant that the 'Permanent Court becomes, *in effect*, an International Court of Prize'.[160] The Foreign Office saw no point in agreeing to the Admiralty's request for an interdepartmental meeting to discuss these queries: 'The Admiralty would probably be very obdurate' and 'at this stage [it] could do little good and might easily degenerate into a fruitless rehashing up of old arguments and a waste of time'.[161] Instead Malkin replied with a lengthy memorandum in which he firmly insisted that the Admiralty's position was based on unwarranted assumptions about the nature of future wars.

When Malkin discussed his paper with Flint, the principal assistant secretary to the Admiralty, he was optimistic that 'the sailors would regard it as a

[157] See PRO, Cabinet 35(29) CAB 23/61; W 9146/21/98 FO 371/14105; 'Signature of the Optional Clause', note by the secretary, CP 255(29) CAB 24/206; W 9532/21/98 FO 371/14106; memorandum by Vice-Admiral Fisher, 18 Sept. 1929, W 9317/21/98 FO 371/14106.
[158] Minute by A. W. A. Leeper, 24 Sept. 1929, PRO, W 9317/21/98 FO 371/14106. 'It would appear that the Deputy Chief of the Naval Staff has not yet heard of the Pact of Paris', said Dalton: minute, 27 Sept. ibid.
[159] Minutes by Lindsay and Mounsey, 25, 26 Sept. 1929, ibid.
[160] Minute by Malkin, 5 Nov. 1929 on Admiralty memorandum of 4 Nov. 1929, PRO, W 10533/21/98 FO 371/14106. See also Flint to Malkin and Malkin to Flint, 16 Oct. 1929, W 10064/21/98 FO 371/14106.
[161] Minutes by C. Howard-Smith (who replaced Campbell as head of the western department in November) and Leeper, 9, 5 November 1929, PRO, W 10533/21/98.

substantial and reasonable answer to their objections', and Flint promised to try to get Madden, the First Sea Lord, into 'as receptive frame of mind as he can'. However, Flint thought it impossible to avoid a discussion at the CID. This was, firstly, because Madden would want it on the official record that the Admiralty's criticisms had been discussed and a decision taken; thus no-one could cast stones at the Admiralty in future for having let the matter go through without a final protest. Secondly, Madden might think it 'inconsistent with his responsibilities to the other chiefs of staff to let the thing disappear from the agenda'.[162]

The Admiralty had circulated memoranda to the CID in which they continued to press the case that had been lost in July. The time limit suspending proceedings before the PCIJ was said to be unsatisfactory, and the Admiralty wanted to have its July proposal – whereby disputes arising out of war measures could only be submitted to conciliation by the League Council – substituted for the final paragraph of the declaration. This was because, as Admiral Madden put it: 'The more one contemplates the implications of the optional clause as signed, the more serious they appear. There is a distinct danger, in fact almost a certainty of our sea power being restricted against a time when its exercise is vital.'[163]

Henderson rejected every assumption on which the Admiralty's views were based. In view of pressure from the opposition and the forthcoming parliamentary debate, he had Malkin and Noel-Baker draft a white paper which discussed the declaration as a whole and dealt in detail with the changes wrought in the international legal framework by the Kellogg pact and League Covenant.[164] Another memorandum, which Noel-Baker and Malkin prepared for Henderson to submit to the CID, dealt with the Admiralty's objections that neither the Covenant nor Kellogg pact could be relied on.

First of all, Henderson dealt with the possibility envisaged by the Admiralty of the whole machinery of the Kellogg pact and Covenant breaking down, either because it was impossible to determine who was an aggressor or because League members failed to apply sanctions in accordance with the Covenant. 'I invite the Committee to consider carefully what this hypothesis involves', said Henderson:

> It means that the whole machinery for the preservation of peace, so laboriously constructed since 1918, would have broken down; the Peace Pact and the Covenant would have become scraps of paper; but at the same time (and it is on this assumption that the whole of the Naval Staff's arguments rest), the one thing which remains standing in the general wreck is the Optional Clause and our commitments thereunder. This seems to me an inconceivable situation. I do not believe it would be possible for the Optional Clause alone to survive in the general ruin, and I have no

---

162 Malkin to Noel-Baker, 19 Nov. 1929, PRO, W 11074/21/98 FO 371/14107.
163 Memorandum by the First Sea Lord, 11 Nov. 1929, CID 966–B, quoted in *DBFP* vi, 444 n. 2. See also memorandum by Vice-Admiral Fisher, 18 Sept. 1929, PRO, W 9317/21/98 FO 371/14106.
164 Conversations with Noel-Baker on 27 Mar. 1974 and in June 1980. The Cabinet approved the preparation of the draft white paper on 6 November: PRO, Cabinet 45(29) CAB 23/62. It was circulated to the Cabinet on 26 Nov.: see Cabinet 50(29), PRO, CAB 23/62, CP 331(29), W 11307/21/98 FO 371/14107. A few verbal alterations were subsequently made at the request of the Dominions Office: see Dixon to Howard-Smith, 30 Nov. 1929. See also Flint to Malkin, 9 Dec. 1929, Gwyer to Malkin, 9 Dec. 1929 and Malkin to Gwyer, PRO, W 11307/21/98. It was published on 12 Dec. as *Command paper* 3452.

hesitation in saying that if such a situation presented itself, the Government of the day would be entitled . . . at once to terminate our obligations under the Optional Clause.

The other possibility envisaged by the Admiralty was that some states, possibly with the assent of the Council, would use the 1921 Assembly resolutions concerning Article 16 to avoid complying fully with their obligations to prevent an enemy being supplied through their territories. Under such circumstances, if Britain used its navy to intercept trade, it might find itself taken to the PCIJ. However, said Henderson, this would not deprive Britain of its right under Article 16 – 'which is wider than anything given by the old [prize] rules' – to intercept such trade; the only question that could arise would be whether any intercepted goods were intended for, or coming from, the enemy. The worst that could happen would be for Britain to be taken to the PCIJ and required to pay damages for having acted on the basis of a mistake of fact. It was 'difficult to treat . . . as a serious difficulty' the idea of an enemy challenging British war measures before the Court. Obviously, such a possibility could not be confined to naval action,

> and the idea that two belligerent States, while actively employing against each other all the methods of warfare at their command, should simultaneously be carrying on a litigious battle at The Hague as to the validity of each of those measures seems to me fantastic. In any case I do not think that the possibility exists as a matter of law.[165]

In short Henderson agreed with the Admiralty that the Optional Clause was meant to stop wars, not to regulate them, and that the British declaration did not endanger the defence of the empire. Rather than calling a CID meeting specifically to discuss the matter, Henderson decided to press ahead by trying to thrash out agreement with the Admiralty and taking the draft white paper to the Cabinet. By the beginning of December Henderson's argument had prevailed and Malkin had reached an agreement with the Admiralty on an interpretation of the Optional Clause declaration which satisfied the latter. It stated that:

> (i) An enemy Government cannot take this country before the Permanent Court.

> (ii) Foreign nationals must exhaust the remedies available in the British Prize Courts before appealing to their Governments to take the case to the Permanent Court.

> (iii) The Peace Pact, the Covenant of the League, and the Optional Clause are interdependent. If the Pact and Covenant fail, or members fail to carry out their obligation under either of these two, then the Optional Clause fails, and His Majesty's Government are free to terminate it at any moment.[166]

On 5 December the CID concurred in this interpretation of the Optional Clause declaration.

---

[165] Memorandum by Henderson, 19 Nov. 1929, CID 970-B, W 11458/21/98, *DBFP* vi, 444.
[166] See *DBFP* vi, 444 n. 5; Cabinet meeting, 3 Dec. 1929, PRO, Cabinet 51(29) CAB 23/62; Dalton diary entry, 5 Dec. 1929.

The parliamentary debate

It was now possible to publish the white paper and go forward with the parliamentary debate that Henderson had promised. This took the form of a resolution, introduced by Henderson on 27 January 1930, in which he asked the Commons to approve ratification of the declaration that he had made at Geneva. In the seven-hour debate, every Labour and Liberal MP who spoke was in favour of ratification. The arguments they advanced did not add to or alter the case which had been made by the representatives of these parties on numerous occasions, although they took some political pleasure in contrasting the government's policy with the 'reactionary' line of its predecessor. And it was true that Hailsham, for example, less than ten months earlier, had dismissed the proposition that the time had come to sign the Clause as 'the dream of an idealist, but . . . hardly the act of a responsible statesman'.[167]

Now, however – and very interestingly – the Conservatives did not oppose acceptance of the Optional Clause. All they wanted was an additional reservation. And, as they made clear in the amendment to Henderson's resolution, it was a reservation which Henderson had himself thought necessary in 1924. It related to 'the Laws of War on Sea . . . as being absolutely necessary to safeguard the freedom of action of the British Navy'.[168]

In putting this forward, the Conservatives were keen to point out that there was no difference 'of wide principle . . . nor of kind, but of degree' between themselves and the rest of the House.[169] But the arguments Chamberlain advanced were such that several speakers were unable to tell whether the former foreign secretary had spoken for or against the Optional Clause. The Conservatives did not accept that the Kellogg pact and Covenant had made it necessary to accept the Optional Clause or had fundamentally changed the fact that war might arise – a war in which there might be neutrals. This being so, it was vital to protect the freedom of the British navy to act as necessary. Accordingly, there must be no chance that the exercise of sea power might be referred, either directly or via the League Council, to a PCIJ which was composed of 'neutrals' who followed the continental tradition in international law (a law which was as yet too vague generally, not just in respect of BMR) and who would be bound to rule against Britain.

The difference between the Conservatives and the rest of the House was characterised by Samuel as 'almost a Debate between two centuries . . . between 1930 and 1830',[170] and by Mitchell-Thomson for the Tories as 'a dispute, not between the centuries, but between theorists and realists'.[171] The Conservative emphasis was on defence, the protection of vital interests and the lessons of the past. Their keynote was caution. But the rest of the House believed it was establishing a new world order where security would be based on law and disputes settled by reasoned argument instead of armed force. What made 'the difference between what is practical and what is not is the factor of . . . human will', said Angell.

---

[167] House of Lords debs., 1 May 1929, 308.
[168] House of Commons debs., 27 Jan. 1930, 666.
[169] Chamberlain, ibid., 668.
[170] Samuel, ibid., 684.
[171] Mitchell-Thomson (postmaster-general, 1924–9, and subsequently Lord Selsdon), ibid., 756.

[W]hen you have two courses before you and the considerations are fairly evenly balanced, the course of wisdom is to cast aside doubt and decide for the more hopeful and the more fruitful. It is that decision which will kick the beam in favour of the practicability of the more hopeful. If we believe we shall be saved; if we doubt we shall surely perish.[172]

At the end of the allotted time, the Conservative amendment was defeated by 278 to 193 votes. The Conservatives did not press a division on the resolution for it was clear that they would not win. Sir John Power, the Tory MP for Wimbledon and a member of the LNU executive, had told the whips that if they tried to do so he would lead 122 Conservatives into the lobby with the government.[173] Despite fury in the upper chamber, the government considered the approval of the Lords unnecessary and on 5 February 1930 the British and Indian ratifications of the Optional Clause were deposited in Geneva.

The Commons debate on the ratification of the Optional Clause was reported in the *Manchester Guardian* as a 'Great Step to Real Security', and a leading article hailed the ratification as

a simple executive act which may yet prove to be one of the most significant in the history of our foreign policy since the Armistice . . .. For the Optional Clause represents the farthest point yet reached in the collective effort to create a positive system of law to replace the international anarchy which prevailed before 1914.

But not everyone shared the *Guardian's* view that the opponents of the Clause supported a cause which was 'hopelessly and deservedly lost'.[174] *The Times* was one of those opponents. It had criticised both the Optional Clause and the British declaration from the Conservative point of view in September, when it intoned against '[h]asty pledges to imperil the most vital interests of great Empires and great peoples out of unreasoned devotion to . . . ideals'. 'Is it constitutional, is it right', it asked, for a minority government to 'engage in an adventure so serious?'[175] Its editorial on the Commons debate went over the same ground, arguing that Britain was depriving itself of its liberty to choose the appropriate method of settling disputes; that international law was 'hardly yet law in the strict sense of the word'; that there was leeway for 'Continental' judges to prevail in the court; and that the absence of a BMR reservation was most undesirable. 'No convincing reason has yet been given', it said, 'for the Government's haste to sign the Clause. Most of the arguments used to justify it are misleading, for they ignore the obligations we were under before we accepted the Clause.'[176] In a similar vein the journal of the Navy League protested against the danger of 'the ancient and well-known continental desire for the emasculation of sea power in war'.[177]

---

172 Angell ibid., 692-3.
173 Philip Noel-Baker said Power had told him this at the time: conversation in June 1980. During the debate Mander said that 379 MPs, many of them Conservatives, had promised in the general election to support the Optional Clause: col. 716.
174 Editorial, 'Optional Clause', 28 Jan. 1930.
175 Editorial, 'The "Optional Clause" ', 20 Sept. 1929.
176 Editorial, 'Optional Clause', 28 Jan. 1930.
177 *Navy*, Dec. 1929, cited in J. J. Underwood, 'British disarmament policy 1925-34', unpubl. MPhil diss. Leeds 1977, 55.

The LNU, in a resolution drafted by Cecil and Murray, congratulated the government on signing the Optional Clause, but its Covenant committee, by a vote of four to three, decided that the Union should not depart from its policy of objecting to all reservations.[178] Some international lawyers would have favoured a BMR reservation, although H. A. Smith and Fischer-Williams, on roughly the same grounds as the government, disagreed with Pearce Higgins's contention that the British declaration meant that the PCIJ had 'been in effect constituted an International Court of Prize'.[179] This is not the place to consider these arguments, most of which had already been discussed within Whitehall, but Lauterpacht's closely-argued examination of the legal effects of the declaration is worth noting. For he believed that the reservations had 'seriously impaired both the signature itself and, even more so, the Optional Clause as such'[180] – hardly the effect which had been so assiduously sought by Henderson and his team.

Impact

Be that as it may, there is no doubt that Britain's acceptance of the Optional Clause, together with a little diplomatic prodding, had a striking numerical effect. Firstly, Britain's ratification was quickly followed by the dominions. Britain had seen no advantage in trying to obtain a simultaneous deposit of ratifications by the Commonwealth as a whole, and studiously avoided saying anything that might imply that the dominions were not acting as independent units. Britain did, however, try to persuade them to agree to the king ratifying on their behalf, rather than by governmental action, 'in accordance not only with the importance of the instrument but also with the procedure adopted for the original ratification of the Statute'.[181] By mid-February, New Zealand and South Africa had agreed to this and their ratifications were deposited on 29 March and 7 April. By mid-June the Canadian and Australian governments had obtained parliamentary approval and, after ratification by the king, their declarations were deposited on 28 July and 18 August. The Irish Free State, however, explained that although the Statute had been ratified by the king, this was before the 1926 imperial conference, when Ireland had made clear its view that only heads of states' agreements should be ratified by the king. The Optional Clause was 'an undertaking between States Members of the League . . . and the Government would not be prepared to take any step which might cast doubt upon the scope of their acceptance of that jurisdiction as between the Irish Free State and any other member of the League, within the meaning of Article 36.'[182]

---

[178] League of Nations Union, executive committee minute 184, 17 Oct. 1929, London, BLPES, League of Nations Union papers, LNU II 9; Covenant committee minute 15, 2 Oct. 1929, LNU IV. 66.
[179] See Pearce Higgins's letter to *The Times*, 'The Optional Clause – laws of naval warfare', publ. 26 Sept. 1929 and his pamphlet, *British acceptance of compulsory arbitration under the Optional Clause and its implications*, London 1929, 9, 14–6; H. A. Smith's letter to The Times ,'The "Optional Clause": national policy and prize law', publ. 30 Sept. 1929; J. Fischer-Williams, 'The Optional Clause (the British signature and reservations)', *The British Year Book of International Law, 1930*, xi, 76–83.
[180] 'The British reservations to the Optional Clause', *Economica*, no. 29, June 1930, 137.
[181] Circular telegram, 2 Jan. 1930, PRO, W 211/18/98 FO 371/14954.
[182] Sean Murphy (department of External Affairs, Irish Free State) to Batterbee, 7 Feb. 1930, PRO, W 1660/18/98 FO 371/14954.

Accordingly, the Irish government deposited its ratification without reference to Britain on 11 July.

Secondly, a number of other states followed in the wake of Britain's decision, and it is reasonable to suppose that they might have been influenced by the British example. From the eighteen states bound by the Clause when the tenth Assembly met in September 1929, the number of declarations in force had risen to thirty-four by the end of 1930. By 1934, when there were fifty-seven League members (including Mexico, Japan and Germany whose notices of withdrawal had not become effective) and forty-nine parties to the Statute of the PCIJ, there were forty-two declarations in force. Although the number of states bound by the Clause fell from this high point, there were, none the less, thirty-eight states bound by the Clause at the outbreak of the Second World War.[183]

Thirdly, Britain's move on the Optional Clause was followed by acceptance of the General Act which provided for the peaceful settlement of all disputes, and not just those of a justiciable kind. Like the Optional Clause, this step had not been part of British policy under the previous administration. However, it was regarded as a logical consequence of the Kellogg pact and was a firm part of Labour policy. And so, on 21 May 1931 the General Act was formally accepted.[184]

This last move had been seen as a preliminary step to the disarmament conference of 1932. However, the 'outstanding feature' of 1931 was that 'men and women all over the world were seriously contemplating and frankly discussing the possibility that the Western system of Society might break down and cease to work'. The '*Annus Terribilis*', as Toynbee called it,[185] ushered in the years that wiped out the efforts of those who dreamed of building peace out of the ashes of the First World War. More specifically, the hopes placed in the system of the Optional Clause as the path to peace through law were an early casualty, and it has never recovered. Instead, after the Second World War it came to be generally accepted that obligations to resort to an international court could never play more than a very subordinate part in the achievement of international peace – if that.

---

[183] The countries that had accepted the Optional Clause by the end of 1930 were Albania, Abyssinia, Austria, Australia, Belgium, Brazil, Great Britain, Bulgaria, Canada, Denmark, Estonia, Finland, Germany, Greece, Haiti, Hungary, Norway, India, Irish Free State, Latvia, Lithuania, Luxembourg, the Netherlands, New Zealand, Panama, Portugal, South Africa, Spain, Sweden, El Salvador, Switzerland, Thailand, Uruguay and Yugoslavia. Unratified declarations had been made by Czechoslovakia, the Dominican Republic, France, Iran, Italy, Peru, and Rumania. Costa Rica, Guatemala, Liberia and Nicaragua had signed the Clause but not ratified the Statute of the PCIJ. The additional declarations in force by 1934 were those of Colombia, the Dominican Republic, Iran, Paraguay, Peru and Rumania. Poland had joined the list of states that had made an unratified declaration. The states bound by the Clause at the outbreak of the Second World War were Albania, Australia, Austria, Belgium, Bolivia, Brazil, Great Britain, Bulgaria, Canada, Colombia, Denmark, the Dominican Republic, Estonia, Finland, France, Greece, Haiti, India, Iran, Irish Free State, Latvia, Liechtenstein, Lithuania, the Netherlands, New Zealand, Nicaragua, Norway, Monaco, Panama, Peru, Portugal, Rumania, El Salvador, South Africa, Sweden, Switzerland, Thailand and Uruguay.

[184] South Africa did not adhere to the General Act but Australia, New Zealand and India ratified their accession at the same time as Britain. Canada deposited its instrument of accession on 1 July 1931. The Irish Free State acceded without reservations on 26 Sept. 1931.

[185] Arnold J. Toynbee, *Survey of international affairs, 1931*, London 1932, 1.

Conclusion

In the introduction to this book it was suggested, on the basis of one popular caricature of British politics, that the Conservative and Labour parties would respond very differently to the proposal that Britain should subject itself to the compulsory jurisdiction of an international court: the Conservatives would be quite uninterested in, not to say opposed to, the idea but the Labourites would support it enthusiastically. And on the surface, this is how things seemed to turn out in the 1920s in relation to Britain's policy towards the Optional Clause of the Permanent Court of International Justice. The Conservative government of 1922-4 hardly gave the matter a public thought, and that of 1924-9 seemed to confine itself to explaining why it was quite impossible for Britain to sign the Clause. On the other hand, the first Labour government of 1924 immediately attached importance to the development of a policy on the issue, and gave a lead in the drafting of an ill-fated treaty – the Geneva Protocol – that obliged signatories to accept the Optional Clause. And in 1929 the second Labour government actually signed the Optional Clause within a few months of obtaining office.

This book has shown, however, that the gulf between the parties on this matter was not nearly as wide as a superficial reading of events indicates, which in turn suggests that the caricature has not only exaggerated but also twisted the truth. It is true that by and large the Labour Party lived up to the expectations which were postulated. It is also true that the Conservative governments of the period had little natural sympathy for the Optional Clause, seeing it as fatuous, if not downright dangerous. But whereas the government of 1922-4 could actually ignore the Clause, that of 1924-9 found that it was a live issue in both national and international politics. And behind its façade of very polite, but slightly supercilious, disdain, the second Baldwin government was finding that its instinctive response had to undergo some adjustments, which, in the end, proved quite substantial.

These adjustments did not arise from the pressure of public opinion, whether domestic or foreign. At home, the League of Nations Union was sufficiently vocal to elicit a response, but it was not so strong, or so well placed, as to require a governmental retreat. Thus it could be given what amounted to a courteous dismissal. International public opinion as expressed at Geneva proved a bit more difficult, but in essence it received the same treatment. Britain was not going to make a major change in her policy just because of what was being said in the windy halls of the League.

From one domestic quarter, however, there emanated some small but insistent voices which, over the years, might have had an unconscious effect on governmental attitudes. For they came from within the ranks of the government and administration, and could not, therefore, be discounted as the expression of a quite different – and 'unsound' – political view. One such troublesome insider was Robert Cecil, Chancellor of the Duchy of Lancaster from November 1924 to August 1927. By 1926 he was keen on signing the Optional Clause but it is unlikely that he carried much weight. He could all too easily be seen as an eccentric, the equivalent, on a high moral level, of a court jester. His credentials were impeccable but his views were increasingly out of tune with those of his colleagues. It is not surprising that he eventually departed in frustration, and the Cabinet probably breathed a sigh of relief. But by 1926 another, much more imposing, inside figure, the foreign secretary himself – Austen Chamberlain – had also come out in favour of a limited acceptance of the Optional Clause. Unlike Cecil, he was willing to bow to the arguments of his Cabinet colleagues who opposed this step. But here, surely, was a development which might well have led to some slight mental adjustments elsewhere in the government.

Chamberlain's changed attitude to the Optional Clause can be attributed to people whose views could certainly not be dismissed – the legal advisers to the Foreign Office. As early as 1924, Cecil Hurst, the legal adviser from 1918 to 1929, had been converted to the idea that it was desirable on legal grounds to sign the Optional Clause, and from 1926 he carried his deputy, William Malkin, with him. One observer's impression of Hurst's role in the 1920s is that 'no Legal Adviser to the Foreign Office has ever had so much influence on policy', and he went on to say that when the files were opened to the public, Hurst's 'services and their effect on policy will become fully apparent'.[1] In fact the files do not show that he had any direct impact on Optional Clause policy. But like the proverbial drip of water on stone, the knowledge that so respected and experienced a civil servant was taking this line might have helped to prepare others in Whitehall for the idea that perhaps, after all, Britain could one day sign the Clause. It is, for example, surely significant that by 1929 the other senior civil servants in the Foreign Office were no longer minuting opposition to the clause, seemingly having come round to the view that signature need not threaten British interests. Accordingly, if the government decided to take that plunge, it would not be a matter for undue official concern. Clearly, the bureaucratic atmosphere was now very different from what it had been less than a decade before.

As it happened, the day when the Conservative government would have to decide whether or not to sign the Optional Clause seemed to be coming sooner rather than later. For certain international developments were hotting up the pace very sharply. They came from two directions. Firstly, the United States became indirectly involved in the matter. As a result of the negotiations leading to the Kellogg–Briand pact and regarding a new Anglo-American arbitration treaty, the government found itself faced with two surprising conclusions: that Britain's 'Monroe Doctrine' in respect of the Middle East did not necessarily stand in the way of far-reaching international commitments; and that it was possible – and compatible with the safeguarding of some of Britain's most vital interests – to contemplate the submission of disputes involving belligerent maritime rights to an international tribunal. Two apparently insurmountable obstacles along the path to signature of the Optional Clause had proved to be

---

[1] Arnold McNair, 'Sir Cecil James Barrington Hurst', *The British Year Book of International Law*, 1963, xxxviii, London 1965, 401, 406. Cf. Eric Beckett (who watched Hurst at close quarters as assistant legal adviser from 1925 to 1929), 'Sir Cecil Hurst's services to international law', *The British Year Book of International Law*, 1949, xxvi, London 1950, 3.

not insurmountable at all. This did not mean that the government would proceed along the path. But two reasons for not doing so had been shown to be vastly less weighty than had hitherto been supposed.

Then, by one of those ironies of life, the government found that the centre of the empire was being hustled along by some of its outlying parts. Britain had gone to a great deal of trouble to emphasise, when the dominions came onto the international stage, that they had to go along with Britain on important questions of policy. The Optional Clause was one such important policy issue. But now Britain found that instead of them keeping in step with her, she was having to think about keeping in step with one or two of them. For by threatening to sign the Optional Clause they were presenting a serious challenge to imperial unity. Furthermore, if they were left to themselves the nature of their acceptances of the Clause might even lead to the unseemly sight of two Commonwealth countries arguing the legal toss before a tribunal of foreigners at The Hague. Clearly, to maintain its position of leadership, Britain would have to catch up with the mavericks, and as 1929 progressed it increasingly looked as if this would mean having to sign the Optional Clause.

And why not? The Conservatives were, after all, hard-headed, and that involved knowing when to abandon a losing cause. Whether they would have signed the Clause, and what reservations they might have attached to their signature, is one of history's unknowns. But events did seem very much to be moving in that direction. Even in the 1920s, Britain could not gainsay the importance for her of good relations with the United States. And at the same time the independence of the dominions, while only just beginning, was already creating discomfort for the mother country. Both developments were to cause hugely greater discomfort over the next few decades. But in 1929 enough pressure was coming from these quarters to move the Conservative government towards a fundamental shift in its Optional Clause policy. It is a striking testimony to the ways in which a state's participation in international relations can have costs as well as benefits, and to the fact that even powerful states are not exempt from such consequences.

As it happened, of course, the Conservative government did not have to take the final decision on the matter. Its successor swept on in the direction in which the Conservatives had been edging, and even abandoned the idea of complete imperial unity for the sake of getting the Clause signed. In doing this they met no substantive opposition from officials inside the Foreign Office. It is the case that the permanent under secretary suggested that the government might move more slowly in response to antipodean anxieties. But there is no real sign of what Zilliacus called 'a stiff fight with the Foreign Office'.[2] Nor do the records justify Dalton's belief that Foreign Office personnel were trying to lead the government away from the Optional Clause[3] – a belief which has none the less been endorsed by the recent observation that the Foreign Office was 'faced with the task of holding back Labour Ministers from a policy which [it] considered dangerous'.[4] Certainly the Admiralty was opposed to what was being done, or at least some important aspects of it. But the Foreign Office went along with the government.

[2] Konni Zilliacus, *The mirror of the past: lest it reflect the future*, London 1944, 280.
[3] Ben Pimlott, *Hugh Dalton*, London 1985, 192.
[4] Robert F. Holland, 'The Commonwealth in official British mind: a study in Anglo-dominion relations 1925–1937', unpubl. DPhil diss. Oxford 1977, 140.

Of course it did so judiciously, offering advice as the occasion required. But to see it as obstructionist is more a reflection of a Labour Party myth about the Foreign Office than of what really happened in relation to the Optional Clause.

Given the support which the Labour Party had always given to the policy of signing, and its official disappointment over the failure of the Geneva Protocol, it was appropriate that a Labour government should have signed the Optional Clause on behalf of Britain. But as this book has shown, Britain would probably have signed anyway, albeit at a later date and with more reservations. For although the government was able to resist public calls, both at home and abroad, for that to be done, its ideological preferences proved less compelling than the pressure of certain international developments. Thus the Conservatives found themselves having to recognise that their instinctive trepidation about the Clause was ill-founded: signing it would present no real danger to Britain's international position. Of course, in the longer run the Conservatives could claim that it was their doubts about the value of the Clause and of the whole idea of peace through law that had been vindicated, rather than the hopes of the Labour Party. But the conclusion is inescapable that even if the Conservatives had been returned to power in 1929, Britain would almost certainly have soon been a party to the Optional Clause. For the Conservative government was finding that the path to the Optional Clause was increasingly hemmed in by external forces, permitting only one direction of travel.

APPENDICES

Biographical Notes

British politicians and public figures

(Note: The surname by which a person is referred to in the text is in capitals)

Albert Victor ALEXANDER (1885–1965) parliamentary secretary to the Board of Trade, 1924; First Lord of the Admiralty, 1929–31, 1940–5, 1945–6; Minister of Defence, 1947–50; Chancellor of the Duchy of Lancaster, 1950–1; created viscount, 1950; earl, 1963; leader of Labour peers in the House of Lords, 1955–65.

Leo AMERY (1873–1955), editorial staff of *The Times*, 1899–1909; Conservative MP, 1911–45; assistant secretary to the War Cabinet and Imperial War Cabinet, 1917; parliamentary under Secretary of State for the Colonies, 1919–21; parliamentary and financial secretary to the Admiralty, 1921–2; First Lord of the Admiralty, 1922–3; Secretary of State for the Colonies, 1924–9, for the Dominions, 1925–9; Secretary of State for India and Burma, 1940–5.

(Ralph) Norman ANGELL (Lane) (1874–1967), journalist, author, lecturer; author of *The Great Illusion* (1910) which profoundly affected the pre-war peace movement; a founder of the Union of Democratic Control; joined the Labour Party, 1920; member of Labour's advisory committee on international questions; active member of the League of Nations Union; Labour MP, 1929–31; editor of *Foreign Affairs*, 1929–31; Nobel peace prize, 1933.

Will(iam) ARNOLD-FORSTER (1886–1951), son of Balfour's Secretary of State for War; served in the Admiralty helping to direct the blockade during the war; joined Union of Democratic Control, September 1914; joined Labour Party, December 1917; member of Labour's advisory committee on international questions; served as secretary to the British delegate to League Assemblies during the first two Labour governments; organising secretary of the LNU's Optional Clause campaign; Cecil's secretary in the Foreign Office in 1929.

Stanley BALDWIN (1867–1947), Conservative MP, 1908–37; financial secretary to the Treasury, 1917–21; President of the Board of Trade, 1921–2; Prime Minister, 1923–4, 1924–9, 1935–7; Lord Privy Seal, 1932–4; Lord President of the Council, 1931–5; created earl, 1937.

Arthur James Balfour, Lord BALFOUR (1848–1930), Conservative MP, 1874–1922; parliamentary private secretary to Lord Salisbury, 1878–80; President of Local Government Board, 1885; Secretary of State for Scotland, 1886; member of the cabinet, 1886; Chief Secretary for Ireland, 1887–91; leader of the Commons and First Lord of the Treasury, 1891–2, 1895–1902; Prime Minister, 1902–5; resigned Unionist leadership, 1911; attended War Cabinet meetings, 1914–15; First Lord of the Admiralty, 1915–16; Secretary of State for

Foreign Affairs, 1916–19; Lord President of the Council, 1919–22, 1925–9; created earl, 1922.

F(rederick) E(dwin) Smith, Lord BIRKENHEAD (1874–1930), Solicitor-General, 1915; Attorney General, 1915–19; created Baron Birkenhead, 1919; viscount, 1919; earl, 1922; Lord Chancellor, 1919–22; Secretary of State for India, 1924–8.

William Clive BRIDGEMAN (1864–1935), Unionist MP, 1906–29; Lord Commissioner of the Treasury, 1915–16; assistant director of the war trade department, 1916; parliamentary secretary, Ministry of Labour, 1916; parliamentary secretary, Board of Trade, 1919–20; Secretary of Mines, 1920–2; Home Secretary, 1922–4; First Lord of the Admiralty, 1924–9; created viscount, 1929.

(Edgar) (Algernon) Robert (Gascoyne) Cecil, Lord CECIL (1864–1958), third son of third marquess of Salisbury; began career as barrister; Conservative MP, 1906–10, 1911–23; parliamentary under Secretary for Foreign Affairs, 1915–16; Minister of Blockade, 1916–18; assistant Secretary of State for Foreign Affairs, 1918; created Viscount Cecil of Chelwood, 1923; Lord Privy Seal, 1923–4; Chancellor of the Duchy of Lancaster, 1924–7; adviser on League matters and British representative to the League in second Labour government and subsequent national government; played the leading British role in drafting the League Covenant; president of the League of Nations Union, 1923–45; Nobel peace prize, 1937.

(Joseph) Austen CHAMBERLAIN (1863–1937), son of Joseph Chamberlain and elder half-brother of Neville; Conservative MP, 1892–1937; Civil Lord of the Admiralty, 1895–1900; financial secretary to the Treasury, 1900–2; Postmaster-General, 1902–3; Chancellor of the Exchequer, 1903–5, 1919–21; Secretary of State for India, 1915–17; minister without portfolio in the War Cabinet, 1918–19; Lord Privy Seal and leader of the Conservative Party in the Commons, 1921–2; Secretary of State for Foreign Affairs, 1924–9; Nobel peace prize, 1925; First Lord of the Admiralty, 1931. 'Austen always played the game and lost it', said Birkenhead who also described him as having very good judgement and generally being right on everything, except foreign affairs: A. J. P. Taylor, *English History 1914–1945*, Harmondsworth 1970, 103 n.1. A co-delegate regarded Chamberlain's knowledge of French as a national misfortune and spent much of his time in Geneva trying to prevent Chamberlain making a speech in French.

Frederic John Napier Thesiger, Lord CHELMSFORD (1868–1933), barrister, member of London School Board, 1901–4, and London County Council, 1904–5; Governor of Queensland, 1905–9; Governor of New South Wales, 1909–13; Governor-General and Viceroy of India, 1916–21; First Lord of the Admiralty, 1924.

Winston Spencer CHURCHILL (1874–1965), Conservative MP, 1900–4, 1924–64; Liberal MP, 1904–22; under secretary of State, Colonial Office, 1905–8; President of the Board of Trade, 1908–10; Home Secretary, 1910–11; First Lord of the Admiralty, 1911–15; Chancellor of the Duchy of Lancaster, 1915; commanded a batallion in France, 1915–16; Minister of Munitions, 1917–19;

Secretary of State for War (and Air), 1919–21; Secretary of State for the Colonies, 1921–2; Chancellor of the Exchequer, 1924–9; left Conservative shadow cabinet and opposed concessions to India, 1931; opposed appeasement of Hitler; First Lord of the Admiralty and member of the War Cabinet, 1939–40; Prime Minister and Minister of Defence, 1940–5; leader of the Conservative Party, 1940–55; Prime Minister, 1951–5.

(John) Robert CLYNES (1869–1949), worked in cotton factory after leaving elementary school in Oldham; president of the National Union of General and Municipal Workers, 1912–37; Labour MP, 1906–31, 1935–45; vice-chairman of the Parliamentary Labour Party, 1910–11, 1918–21; parliamentary secretary, Ministry of Food, 1917–18; Food Controller, 1918–19; chairman of the Parliamentary Labour Party, 1921–2; deputy leader of the Labour Party, 1923–31; Lord Privy Seal and deputy leader of the House of Commons, 1924; Home Secretary, 1929–31.

George Nathaniel Curzon, Lord CURZON (1859–1925), Conservative MP, 1886–98; assistant private secretary to the Prime Minister, 1885–6; under Secretary of State for India, 1891–2; parliamentary under Secretary of State for Foreign Affairs, 1895–8; created baron, 1898; Viceroy of India, 1898–1905; created earl, 1911; marquess, 1921; Lord Privy Seal, 1915–16; leader of the Conservatives in the House of Lords, 1916–25; Lord President of the Council, 1916–19; acted as Foreign Secretary for Balfour during the Paris peace conference; Secretary of State for Foreign Affairs, 1919–24; Lord President of the Council and chairman of the CID, 1924–5. Intelligent, proud and extremely hard-working, he possessed charm but bullied his subordinates dreadfully; his sudden and violent temper could only be partly excused by the chronic back pain from which he suffered.

Ronald J. McNeill, Lord CUSHENDUN (1861–1934), Unionist MP, 1911–27; parliamentary under Secretary of State for Foreign Affairs, 1922–4, 1925; financial secretary to the Treasury, 1925–7; created Baron Cushendun, 1927; Chancellor of the Duchy of Lancaster with responsibility for the League of Nations, October 1927–9; acting Secretary of State for Foreign Affairs, August–November 1928. An Ulster Tory, he achieved notoriety for throwing a book at Churchill during the Home Rule Debates before the war. But he was 'extremely dignified and conciliatory' and 'passed a large amount of time on the sofa' as if 'the propulsion of his huge [six-foot-five] frame [was] too much for his heart and muscles': Temperley, *Whispering gallery of Europe*, 80–1.

Hugh DALTON (1887–1962), son of Canon Dalton, domestic chaplain to the Royal family; served in France and Italy, 1914–19; became active in Labour Party, 1919; reader in economics, London School of Economics, 1920; Labour MP, 1924–31, 1935–59; under Secretary of State for Foreign Affairs, 1929–31; Minister of Economic Warfare, 1940–2; President of the Board of Trade, 1942–5; Chancellor of the Exchequer, 1945–7 when he resigned over leaking details of the budget; Chancellor of the Duchy of Lancaster, 1948–50; Minister of Town and Country Planning, 1950–1; Minister of Local Government and Planning, 1951; created baron, 1960. His memoirs are amongst the least reliable and a former member of the League secretariat recalled him as being the worst British delegate to the League.

(James) Eric DRUMMOND, Lord Perth (1876–1951), entered Foreign Office, 1900; private secretary to under Secretary of State for Foreign Affairs, 1906–8, 1910–11; private secretary to the Prime Minister, 1912–15; private secretary to the Foreign Secretary, 1915–19; Secretary-General of the League of Nations, 1919–33; ambassador to Italy, 1933–9; 16th earl of Perth, 1937; Chief adviser on foreign publicity, Ministry of Information, 1939–40; leader of the Liberal Party in the House of Lords, 1946–51.

(James) (Clerk) Maxwell GARNETT (1880–1958), lecturer in applied mathematics, University College London, 1903; examiner, Board of Education, 1904–12; principal of the College of Technology and dean of the faculty of technology in the University of Manchester, 1912–20; secretary of the League of Nations Union, 1920–38; chairman of the British Association's committee on post-war university education, 1941–4. Deeply religious, he had a strong personality and ran LNU headquarters with firm reins.

Richard Burdon Haldane, Lord HALDANE (1856–1928), began career as barrister; Liberal MP, 1885–1912; associated with Rosebery Group of Liberal imperialists during the Boer war; reorganised army as Secretary of State for War, 1906–12; created viscount, 1911; Lord Chancellor, 1912–15; omitted from coalition government in 1915 because of pre-war statements about the merits of German culture; joined Labour Party in 1922; Lord Chancellor, 1924.

Edward Frederick Lindley Wood, Lord HALIFAX (1881–1959), Conservative MP, 1910–25; under secretary, Colonial Office, 1921–2; President of the Board of Education, 1922–4; Minister of Agriculture, 1924–5; created Baron Irwin, 1925; Viceroy of India, 1926–31; President of the Board of Education, 1932–5; third Viscount Halifax, 1934; Secretary of State for War, 1935; Lord Privy Seal, 1935–7; leader of the House of Lords, 1935–8, 1940; Lord President of the Council, 1937–8; Secretary of State for Foreign Affairs, 1938–40; ambassador to Washington, 1941–6; created earl, 1944. He was known as 'the Holy Fox' 'because of his political acumen and his deep love of both the Church and the hunting field': John Colville, *The fringes of power: Downing Street diaries*, I: *1939–October 1941*, Sevenoaks 1986, 574.

H(enry) Wilson HARRIS (1883–1955), author and journalist; joined *The Daily News* in 1908 where he was successively news editor, leader writer and diplomatic correspondent; LNU staff and editor of *Headway*, 1923–32; editor of *The Spectator*, 1932–53; independent MP for Cambridge University, 1945–50.

Arthur HENDERSON (1863–1935), apprenticed as a moulder at the Stephenson locomotive works at the age of twelve; secretary of the Ironfounders' Union; Labour MP, 1903–18, 1919–22, 1923, 1924–31, 1933–5; secretary of the Labour Party, 1911–34; Minister in Coalition Cabinet, 1915–17; Home Secretary, 1924; Secretary of State for Foreign Affairs, 1929–31; led Labour opposition to the national government; president of the world disarmament conference, 1932–5; Nobel peace prize, 1934.

John Waller HILLS (1867–1938), solicitor and director of various companies; Conservative MP, 1906–22, 1925–38; distinguished war service as a major with the Durham Light Infantry, 1914–16, when he was invalided (a few weeks after the bells of Durham were tolled when he was mistakenly reported as killed in action); financial secretary to the Treasury, 1922–3; vice-chairman of the executive committee of the League of Nations Union. After losing his seat in the 1923 general election and failing to win a by-election, his ministerial career was over. A man of many parts who 'succeeded in combining loyalty to the Conservative Party with independent judgement'; it was said that 'a cause which could claim to have a moral basis was sure of his support'. His obituary in *The Times* is noteworthy for, unusually, beginning with the words 'We announce with deep regret': 27 December 1938.

Samuel John Gurney HOARE (1880–1959), Conservative MP, 1910–44; succeeded to baronetcy, 1915; Secretary of State for Air, 1922–4, 1924–9; Secretary of State for India, 1931–5; Secretary of State for Foreign Affairs, 1935; First Lord of the Admiralty, 1936–7; Home Secretary, 1937–9; Lord Privy Seal and member of the War Cabinet, 1939–40; Secretary of State for Air, 1940; ambassador to Spain, 1940–4; created Viscount Templewood, 1944. 'It was not without justification that he was called "Slippery Sam" . . . his intelligence was matched, or even surpassed, by his natural bent for intrigue': Colville, *Fringes of power*, 574.

Douglas McGarel HOGG, Lord HAILSHAM (1872–1950), after working for his father's sugar firm and serving in the Boer war, he was called to the bar in 1902; he made rapid progress in commercial and common law, building up a substantial practice; took silk, 1917; bencher of Lincoln's Inn and Attorney General to the Prince of Wales, 1920–2; Conservative MP, 1920–8; Attorney General, 1922–4, 1924–8; created baron, March 1928; Lord Chancellor, March 1928–9, 1935–8; created viscount, 1929; Conservative leader in the House of Lords, 1930–1; Secretary of State for War, 1931–5; leader of the House of Lords, 1931–5; Lord President of the Council, 1938.

Dame Edith LYTTLETON (?–1948), a very able, charming person of many parts; playwright and patron of the theatre; talented musician and writer of biography and travel; second wife of the universally popular Alfred Lyttleton (1857–1913 – lawyer, statesman and excellent cricketer); one of the chief movers of the War Refugees Committee, 1914–18; deputy director of the women's branch of the Ministry of Agriculture, 1917–19; worked on the Central Committee on Women's Employment, 1916–45; British substitute delegate to League Assemblies, 1923, 1926–8, 1931; member of Council for Psychical Research.

(James) Ramsay MACDONALD (1866–1937), Labour MP, 1906–18, 1922–37 (National Labour 1931–7); Secretary of Labour Representation Committee and Labour Party, 1900–12; leader of the Independent Labour Party, 1906–9; leader of the Labour Party, 1911–14, 1922–31; Treasurer of the Labour Party, 1912–29; Prime Minister and Secretary of State for Foreign Affairs, 1924; Prime Minister of Labour government, 1929–31, of national government, 1931–5; Lord President of the Council, 1935–7.

(George) Gilbert (Aimé) MURRAY (1866–1957), born in Australia he came to England in 1877; married to Lady Mary, daughter of the earl of Carlisle; father-in-law of Arnold Toynbee; professor of Greek at the University of Glasgow, 1889–99; regius professor of Greek at the University of Oxford, 1908–36;

chairman of the League of Nations Union, 1923–38; co-president of the League of Nations Union, 1938 onwards; British representative on the International Committee for Intellectual Co-operation, 1928–40; a Liberal, he had personal ties with Ramsay MacDonald through Lady Mary who helped care for MacDonald's children after their mother's death.

Philip John NOEL-BAKER (1889–1982), Olympic athlete, scholar, politician and lifelong campaigner for disarmament; chief organiser and commandant of the Friends Ambulance Unit at its inception in 1914, he spent much of the war in Italy where he was decorated for valour; assisted Cecil at the Paris peace conference, 1919; League secretariat, 1919–22; captain of British Olympic track team, 1920, 1924 and Commandant of British Olympic team, 1952; secretary to Robert Cecil, 1923–4; assisted Parmoor and Henderson at 1924 League Assembly; Sir Ernest Cassell professor of international relations at the London School of Economics, 1924–9; Labour MP, 1929–31, 1936–70; parliamentary private secretary to the Secretary of State for Foreign Affairs, 1929–31; principal assistant to the president of the world disarmament conference (Arthur Henderson), 1932–3; parliamentary secretary, Ministry of War Transport, 1942–5; Minister of State, Foreign Office, 1945–6; British delegate to the UN Preparatory Commission; Secretary of State for Air, 1946–7; Secretary of State for Commonwealth Relations, 1947–50; Minister of Fuel and Power, 1950–1; Nobel peace prize, 1959; Papal knighthood, 1977; created baron, 1977. 'His generous impulses are too much sometimes for even his intelligence', said Cadogan, 'and his personal charm makes it possible for his extreme views to prevail over saner counsels': minute for Chamberlain, 3 Nov. 1925, PRO W 9478/9478/98 FO 371/11071.

Richard William Alan Onslow, Lord ONSLOW (1876–1945), diplomatic service, 1901–15; fifth earl, 1911; distinguished army service in France, 1915–18; British war mission to Paris, 1918–19; civil Lord of the Admiralty, 1920–2; parliamentary Secretary, Board of Agriculture and Ministry of Health, 1921–3; Board of Education, 1923–4; parliamentary under secretary of State for War, 1924–8; succeeded Cushendun as head of British delegation to the 1927 League Assembly; Paymaster-General, 1928–9; deputy Speaker of the House of Lords, 1931–44.

Charles Alfred Cripps, Lord PARMOOR (1852–1941), son of a prominent lawyer who, like his father, became an authority on ecclesiastical law; his first wife, Theresa Potter, was the sister of Beatrice Webb; sometime Attorney General to the Prince of Wales (Edward VII); Conservative MP, 1895–1900, 1901–6, 1910–14; created Baron Parmoor and appointed to the judicial committee of the Privy Council, 1914; joined the Labour Party, 1921, and at this time also became a pacifist; Lord President of the Council, 1924, 1929–31; British representative on the League Council and delegate to the Assembly, 1924; leader of the House of Lords, 1929–31.

Sidney Webb, Lord PASSFIELD (1859–1947), publicist, founder of the Fabian Society, barrister, public servant; married to Beatrice Webb; War Office (lower division), 1878–9; surveyor of taxes, 1879–81; Colonial Office, 1881–91; member of London County Council, 1892–1910; Labour MP, 1922–9; President of the Board of Trade, 1924; created baron, 1929; Secretary of State for Dominion Affairs, 1929–30, and for the Colonies, 1929–31.

Walter George Frank Phillimore, Lord PHILLIMORE (1845–1929), president of the International Law Association, 1905–8; judge of the Queen's Bench division of the High Court, 1897–1913; Lord Justice of Appeal, 1913–16; chaired Phillimore committee which produced the first official British draft of the League Covenant; created baron, 1919; British member of the committee of jurists which produced the draft Statute of the Permament Court of International Justice.

Arthur Augustus William Harry PONSONBY (1871–1946), son of Queen Victoria's private secretary; diplomat and Foreign Office official, 1894–1902; Liberal MP, 1908–18, and critic of the Liberal foreign policy; a founder of the Union of Democratic Control; repudiated by his constituency because of his opposition to the war; joined the Labour Party immediately after the coupon election at which time he also became a pacifist; Labour MP, 1922–30; under Secretary of State for Foreign Affairs, 1924; parliamentary under secretary for the dominions, 1929; parliamentary secretary, Ministry of Transport, 1929–31; created baron, 1930; Chancellor of the Duchy of Lancaster, 1931; Labour leader in the House of Lords, 1931–5; resigned from Labour Party in 1935 because of Labour's support for sanctions.

James Edward Hubert Gascoyne Cecil, Lord SALISBURY (1861–1947), Conservative MP, 1885–92, 1893–1903; fourth marquess, 1903; under secretary for Foreign Affairs, 1900–3; Lord Privy Seal, 1903–5, 1924–9; President of the Board of Trade, 1905; Lord President of the Council, 1922–4; Chancellor of the Duchy of Lancaster, 1922–3; leader of the House of Lords, 1925–9.

Tom SHAW (1872–1938), secretary of the International Federation of Textile Workers, 1911–29, 1931–8; Labour MP, 1918–31; joint secretary of Labour and Socialist International, 1923–5; Minister of Labour, 1924; Secretary of State for War, 1929–31.

Philip SNOWDEN (1864–1937), son of a weaver; junior exciseman, 1886–93; became chronically crippled with an inflammation of the spinal chord, 1891; propagandist for the Independent Labour Party, 1895–1905; national chairman of the ILP, 1903–6, 1917–20; Labour MP, 1906–18, 1922–31; pacifist and champion of conscientious objectors, 1914–18; Chancellor of the Exchequer, 1924, 1929–31; Lord Privy Seal, 1931–2; resigned September 1932 over proposal for preferential tariffs; created viscount, 1932.

Helen(a) SWANWICK (1864–1939), active in the women's suffrage movement before the First World War; served on the executive of the Union of Democratic Control and a founder of the 1917 Club; associated with the Labour Party by 1918; member of the Labour Party's advisory committee on international questions; substitute delegate to League Assemblies, 1924, 1929; first president of the British section of the Women's International League.

Charles Philips TREVELYAN (1870–1958), eldest son of Sir G. O. Trevelyan; Liberal MP, 1899–1918; parliamentary secretary, the Board of Education, 1908–14; resigned from government at outbreak of war and continued to advocate peace by negotiation throughout the war; joined Labour Party, 1918;

Labour MP, 1922–31; third baronet, 1928; President of Board of Education, 1924, 1929–31; HM Lieutenant for County of Northumberland, 1930–49.

Leonard WOOLF (1880–1969), married to the writer, Virginia Woolf; Ceylon civil service, 1904–11; founded the Hogarth press, 1917; editor of *The International Review*, 1919; editor of the international section of *The Contemporary Review*, 1920–1; literary editor of *The Nation*, 1923–30; joint editor of *The Political Quarterly*, 1931–59; member of the Whitley Council for administrative and legal departments of the civil service, 1938–55; prominent Fabian and member of the Labour Party's advisory committee on international questions.

Sir (Edward) Hilton YOUNG (1879–1960), scientist, financial journalist and politician; successively Liberal, free-Liberal, Liberal, independent and Conservative MP, 1915–23, 1924–35; financial secretary to the Treasury, 1921; Liberal chief whip, 1922; joined Conservatives during the General Strike, 1926; delegate to League Assemblies, 1926–8, 1932; Minister of Health, 1931; created Lord Kennet, 1935.

Foreign and Commonwealth politicians and delegates to the League

Eduard BENEŠ (1884–1948), Czechoslovak representative at Paris peace conference, 1919; Czechoslovak Foreign Minister, 1918–35; Premier, 1921–2; President, 1935–8; left Czechoslovakia after the Munich agreement; elected President of the Czechoslovak National Committee in London, 1939; recognised by the allies as President of Czechoslovak Republic, 1940; returned to Czechoslovakia in 1945 and confirmed as President by Provisional National Assembly; elected President, 1946; resigned, 1948.

William Edgar BORAH (1865–1940), American politican; elected to the United States Senate in 1906 as a Republican; chairman of the foreign relations committee. A leading isolationist, he opposed Wilson over the League of Nations and fought against foreign entanglements of all kinds while promoting voluntary co-operation.

Léon Victor August BOURGEOIS (1851–1925), French politician; doctor of law; Prefect, 1880–95; director of local government in the Ministry of the Interior, 1895–6; member of the Chamber of Deputies, 1889–1905; president of the Chamber of Deputies, 1902–3; Minister of Foreign Affairs, 1896, 1906; Minister of Education, 1898; first French delegate to The Hague conferences of 1899 and 1907; member of the Permanent Court of Arbitration; elected senator, 1905; Minister of Work and State Insurance, 1912–13, 1917; Minister of State, 1915; president of the Senate, 1920.

Aristide BRIAND (1862–1932), eleven times Prime Minister of France and, with a brief, four-day gap in 1926, headed the Quai d'Orsay for nearly seven years, longer than any predecessor since the foundation of the Third Republic; son of an inkeeper; as a law student wrote articles for anarchist journals; founded *Humanité* with Jean Jaurès; until the age of thirty-five devoted his energies to organising labour unions; entered Chamber of Deputies as a Socialist, 1902; much involved in preparing the law for the separation of church and state and was rewarded by being made Minister of Public Instruction and Worship, 1906;

excluded from Union-Socialist party for serving in a bourgeois ministry; Minister of Justice, 1908; first French Socialist Prime Minister, 1909–2 November 1910; Prime Minister, 3 November 1910–11; Minister of Justice, 1912–13; Prime Minister and Minister of the Interior, January 1913; Prime Minister, February 1913; Minister of Justice, 1914–15; Prime Minister and Minister of Foreign Affairs, 1915; resigned and rearranged cabinet, December 1916; resigned, 1917; Prime Minister, 1921–2 when he resigned after resentment about his playing golf (of which he knew nothing) with Lloyd George (with whom he was thought to be too devotedly friendly); French delegate to the League, 1924; Foreign Minister, April–October 1925; Prime Minister and Minister of Foreign Affairs, November 1925–July 1926; Foreign Minister, 1926–9; Prime Minister and Minister of Foreign Affairs, July–October 1929; Foreign Minister, October 1929–January 1932; Nobel peace prize, 1926. Described as 'the greatest diplomatic figure of the post-war period', he was compared to Talleyrand in possessing 'the distinct qualities of the ideal Foreign Minister and the perfect diplomatist'. He was deeply devoted to peace and 'at his best, whatever he said was apposite and whatever he did was opportune': *The Times*, 8 March 1932. Witty, accessible and unassuming, he was a dextrous parliamentarian and a great orator who spoke for immediate effect.

Stanley Melbourne BRUCE (1883–1967), Australian importer, politician (first Nationalist, then United Australia), diplomat; MP, 1918–29, 1931–3; Commonwealth Treasurer, 1921–3; Australian delegate to League Assemblies, 1921, 1932–8; Prime Minister and Minister of External Affairs, 1923–9; Minister for Health, 1927–8; Minister for Territories, 1928–9; Minister for Trade and Customs, 1928; Minister without Portfolio, 1932–3; Australian minister to London, 1932–3, High Commissioner, 1933–45; Australian representative on the League Council, 1933–6; represented Australia at imperial and economic conferences, 1923, 1926, 1932, 1937; Australian representative in UK War Cabinet and Pacific War Council, 1942–5; created viscount, 1947; chairman, World Food Council, 1947–51, and Finance Corporation for Industry, 1947–57.

Joseph Gordon COATES (1878–1943), New Zealand politician; MP, 1911–43; served in France in First World War; Minister of Justice, 1919–20; Postmaster-General and Minister of Telegraphs, 1919–25; Minister of Public Works, 1920–6; Minister of Native Affairs, 1921–8; Minister of Railways, 1923–8; Prime Minister, 1925–8; Minister of External Affairs, 1928; leader of the opposition, 1928–31; Minister of Public Works, Employment and Transport, 1931–3; Minister of Finance, Customs and Transport, 1933–5; Minister without portfolio and member of War Cabinet, 1940; Minister of Armed Forces and War Co-ordination, 1942.

Raoul DANDURAND (1861–1942), French-Canadian politician; minister without portfolio and leader of the Canadian Senate during each of the Mackenzie King administrations from 1921 until his death (1921–6, 1926–30, 1935–42); delegate to League Assemblies, 1924–9, 1936–7; president of the 1925 League Assembly; Canadian representative on the League Council, 1927–30. He 'became more nearly specialist in League affairs than any other Canadian political figure' but 'only occasionally . . . made any significant attempt to influence foreign policy decisions, either in Geneva or in Ottawa': Veatch, *Canada and the League of Nations*, 19.

Desmond FITZGERALD (c. 1888–1947), Irish revolutionary and statesman; born and brought up in London, he moved to Ireland from France in 1913; joined Irish Republican Brotherhood in September 1914 and organised volunteers in Kerry; imprisoned for six months in 1915 for making a political speech; expelled from Kerry and moved to Bray; fought in Post Office in 1916 Easter rising, escaped but was arrested, court-martialled and sentenced to life imprisonment, later commuted to 20 years; *Sinn Féin* MP, 1918–22; released from prison, 1918; director of publicity *Dáil Éireann*, 1919; arrested in 1921 but released later that year when the truce was arranged; supported the Irish 'treaty'; elected to the *Dáil*, 1922–37; Minister for External Affairs, Irish provisional government, 1922; Minister for External Affairs, 1922–7; Minister for Defence, 1927–32; Senator, 1938–43; father of Garrett FitzGerald.

Sir Littleton Ernest GROOM (1867–1936), Australian barrister and politician; MP, 1901–29, 1931–6; Minister of State for Home Affairs, 1905–6; Attorney General, 1906–8, 1921–5; Minister of State for External Affairs, 1909–10; Minister for Trade and Customs, 1913–14; Vice-President of Executive Council, 1917–18; Minister of Works and Railways and acting Attorney General, 1918–21; led Australian delegation to the 1924 League Assembly; Speaker of the Federal House of Representatives, 1926–9; president of the Australian League of Nations Union.

Edouard HERRIOT (1872–1957), French radical socialist politician; Minister of Transport during First World War; Premier, 1924–5, 1926 (two days), 1932 (six months); several times president of the Chamber of Deputies which position he held in 1942 when he was taken prisoner by Vichy and the Nazis; president of the National Assembly, 1947–53, and then elected life President.

General James Barry Munnik HERTZOG (1866–1942), South African lawyer, military leader and politician; commanded Boer forces in the South African war, 1899–1902; Attorney General and Minister of Justice, Orange River colony, 1907; Minister of Justice in the first Union cabinet, 1910–12; Minister of Native Affairs, 1912 and 1924–9; leader of Nationalist Party and leader of United South African National Party from inception, 1933–9; Prime Minister, 1924–Sept. 1939; Minister of External Affairs, 1929–38.

Jan Hendrik HOFMEYR (1894–1948), South African statesman; after a meteoric academic career from which he retired in 1924, he was Administrator of the Transvaal, 1924–9; South African Party MP, 1929–48; Minister of the Interior, Public Health and Education, 1933–6; Minister of Mines, Education, Labour and Social Welfare, 1936–8; vigorously opposed the native bills in 1936 and 1938, resigning from the cabinet over the latter; Minister of Finance and Education, 1939–48; resigned from the United Party caucus in 1939 over the Asiatics bill but was persuaded not to resign over the 1943 'pegging bill' because of the war; appointed Minister of Mines and deputy Prime Minister, January 1948.

William Morris HUGHES (1864–1952), Australian politician (Labour, then Nationalist, then United Australia); born in Wales, he emigrated to Australia in

1884; trades union organiser; MP, 1901–41; Minister for External Affairs, 1904; Attorney General, 1908–9, 1910–13, 1914–21, 1939–41; Prime Minister, 1915–23; member of Imperial Cabinet and delegate to Paris peace conference; Minister for External Affairs, 1921–3, 1937–9; delegate to the 1932 League Assembly; Vice-President of Executive Council, 1934–5, 1937–8; Minister for Health and Repatriation, 1934–5, 1936–7; Minister for Territories, 1937–8; Minister for the Navy, 1940–1.

Frank Billings KELLOGG (1856–1937), American lawyer, public official and diplomat; Republican National Committeeman, 1904–12; Senator, 1916–22; ambassador to Britain, December 1923–February 1925; Secretary of State, March 1925–1929; Nobel peace prize (for the Kellogg pact), 1929; judge of the PCIJ, 1930–5.

Ernest LAPOINTE (1876–1941), barrister and Canadian Liberal politician; MP, 1919–41; minister in every Liberal cabinet from 1921 to 1941 (Minister of Marine and Fisheries, 1921; of Justice, 1924–30, 1935–41; leader of the government in the House of Commons, 1926); King's unofficial deputy, 1924–41; the 'most influential French Canadian in national political affairs' whose views on foreign policy and League matters were 'virtually identical' with those of Mackenzie King: Veatch, *Canada and the League of Nations*, 18; represented Canada at the imperial conferences of 1926 and 1937; leader of the Canadian delegation to the Geneva naval conference, 1927; keenly interested in the League of Nations, he was a member of the Canadian delegation to the 1922 Assembly and led the delegation to the 1938 Assembly; national president of the Canadian League of Nations Society from 1933 to 1935 when the Liberal Party was in opposition.

Eric Hendrik LOUW (1890–1968), South African politician; MP, 1924, 1938–68; first South African trade commissioner in the US and Canada, 1925; High Commissioner for South Africa in London, 1929; first South African Minister to the United States, 1929; Minister to Italy, 1933; first South African Minister to France and Portugal, 1934; represented South Africa at various conferences and League Assemblies 1929, 1934, 1935; represented South Africa at UN General Assemblies, 1948–9, 1956, 1958–62; Minister of Economic Affairs, 1948–54; Minister of Finance, 1955–6; Minister of Foreign Affairs, 1956–63.

William Lyon MACKENZIE KING (1874–1950), Canadian economist and Liberal politician; deputy Minister of Labour, 1900–8; MP, 1908–11, 1921–49; Minister of Labour, 1909–11; leader of the Liberal Party, 1919–48; Prime Minister, 1921–6, 1926–30, 1935–48; Minister for External Affairs, 1921–6, 1926–30, 1935–46; represented Canada at many imperial conferences and at Councils and Assemblies of the League and the UN.

Vincent MASSEY (1887–1969), Canadian statesman; lecturer in modern history, Toronto, 1913–15; on staff, military district no. 2, 1915–18; associate secretary, war committee of the cabinet, 1918; secretary, then director of government repatriation committee, 1918–19; president of Massey-Harris company, 1921–5; Minister without portfolio, 1925; attended 1926 imperial conference; Canadian minister to the United States, 1927–30; president, National Liberal Federation of Canada, 1932–5; Canadian High Commissioner in London, 1935–46; Canadian delegate to the 1936 League Assembly; chairman of Royal Commission on National Development in the Arts, Letters and Sciences, 1949–51; Governor-General of Canada, 1952–9.

Sir William Harrison MOORE, professor of law at the University of Melbourne; Australian delegate to League Assemblies, 1927–9.

Kevin Christopher O'HIGGINS (1892–1927), Irish politician; joined *Sinn Féin* movement while still a student and imprisoned for six months in 1918 for an anti-conscription speech; elected MP while still in jail; 'on the run', 1920; elected to *Dáil Éireann*, 1922; assistant minister for Local Government in Provisional government, 1919; strong advocate of the Irish 'treaty'; successively Minister for Economic Affairs, Minister for Justice and External Affairs and Vice-President of the Executive Council; took part in the imperial conference of 1926; his father was shot by Republicans in 1923 and he was shot by unknown gunmen on his way to mass in July 1927.

Sir (Christopher) James PARR (1869–1941), New Zealand politician and statesman; mayor of Aukland, 1911–15; MP, 1914–26; Minister of Public Health, 1920–3; Minister of Justice, 1923–6; Postmaster General, 1925–6; Minister of Education, 1920–6; New Zealand High Commissioner in London, 1926–9, 1934–6; leader of Legislative Council, 1931–3; New Zealand delegate to League Assemblies, 1926–9, 1934.

Joseph PAUL-BONCOUR (1873–1972), French barrister and politician; private secretary to Waldeck-Rousseau, 1899–1902, and Viviani, 1906–9; Republican Socialist deputy, 1909; Minister of Labour, 1911; president of the Foreign Affairs committee of the Chamber of Deputies and French permanent delegate to the League of Nations; resigned from the Socialist Party, 1931; War Minister, 1932; Prime Minister, December 1932–January 1933; Foreign Minister, December 1932–February 1934, March–April 1938; Minister for League of Nations affairs, January–June 1936.

Nicolas Socrates POLITIS (1872–1942), Greek diplomat and lawyer; born in Corfu, he completed his education in Paris and was successively professor of international law at the Universities of Aix, Poitiers, and Paris, 1893–14; invited by Venizelos to be secretary general of the Greek Foreign Office in 1914, he accompanied Venizelos to Salonika after the latter's breach with the king and returned with Venizelos to Athens in 1917; Foreign Minister, 1917–20, and again after the Venizelists brief return to power in 1922; represented Greece on many occasions at League Assemblies between 1920 and 1932; appointed minister in Paris, 1927; president of the League Assembly, 1932; after his third tenure of the Foreign Ministry in 1936 and a second appointment to Paris in 1938 he retired in 1940.

Oscar SKELTON (1878–1941), Canadian economist, historian and public servant; taught at Queens University, Canada, 1908–25; dean of arts and professor of political science, 1919–25; attended 1923 imperial economic conference; appointed counsellor in Department of External Affairs, 1924; under secretary of state for external affairs, 1925–41; Pickersgill, one of King's secretaries during the 1930s, said that Skelton became 'Mackenzie King's closest adviser on all public affairs, domestic as well as external' – a position which gave him even greater influence than Lapointe: J. W. Pickersgill, *The Mackenzie King record*, I: *1939–40*, Toronto 1960, 6–7. Quoted in Veatch, *Canada and the League of Nations*, 21.

Professor Timothy SMIDDY (1875–1962), envoy of *Dáil Éireann* to the United States, 1922–4; minister to the United States, 1924–9; Irish Free State commissioner to the United Kingdom, 1929–30; director, central Bank of Ireland, 1943–55.

Gustav STRESEMANN (1878–1929), born into a family of middle-class brewers, he gained his doctorate for a thesis on the development of the Berlin bottled beer trade; his early years were spent organising industrial firms into corporations and cartels; founded union of Saxon industrialists, 1902; member of the Reichstag 1907–13, 1914–29; supported an annexationist policy in the First World War; became leader of the National Liberal Party, 1917; after the war formed the German People's Party; he did not believe in the Weimar Republic and never made any secret of his attachment to the old Germany, but, realising Germany was exhausted, he supported the form of government which the majority of the people apparently wanted; Chancellor, August 1923, forming a 'Grand Coalition' cabinet of right and left; formed another cabinet and took the foreign affairs portfolio, October 1923; resigned, November 1923; Minister of Foreign Affairs in each successive government until his death, but plagued by illness after 1927; Nobel peace prize, 1926. He had a keen interest in history and profoundly admired Bismarck. A good mixer, he was popular in Geneva where he showed himself to be a tactful, astute and cheerfully patient statesman, who was ready to talk freely to journalists over an evening drink. He was ambitious from an early age, but his devotion to European pacification and restoring Germany's place in Europe went far beyond personal ambition. 'Stresemann did inestimable service to the German Republic', said *The Times*, 'his work for Europe as a whole was almost as great': editorial, 'Herr Stresemann', 4 October 1929.

Sir Joseph WARD (1856–1930), New Zealand politician; associated with W. F. Massey in national government, 1915–19; attended Imperial War Conferences and cabinets, 1917, 1918; Prime Minister, 1928–30.

British officials

(Note: The highest Foreign Office official is the permanent under secretary. In 1919 his immediate junior was the assistant under secretary. By 1922 there were three assistant under secretaries and in 1925 the senior assistant under secretary was given the title of deputy under secretary. Next in rank were the eight assistant secretaries (corresponding to the pre-war rank of senior clerk) who were known as counsellors from 1923 onwards. The western department, which handled League of Nations business, was headed by a counsellor and from 1920 to 1929 there were usually five clerks: two first secretaries (the pre-war assistant clerks) and either three second secretaries or two second secretaries and a third secretary (the pre-war junior clerks). Because these notes are intended to clarify the background of, and positions held by, officials during the period covered this book, career details are not usually given for the years after 1930.)

Harry BATTERBEE, entered Colonial Office, 1905; private secretary to Secretary of State for the Colonies, 1916–19; political secretary to vice-admiral commanding special service squadron, Empire cruise, 1923–4; assistant secretary in the Dominions Office, 1925–30 (and deputy to his brother-in-law, Harding); assistant under secretary, Dominions Office, 1930–8; high commissioner to New Zealand, 1939–45. He had close ties with the royal family and made a point of developing close personal relations with the Cabinet Office, Treasury and Foreign Office. For a description of this romantic figure, nicknamed 'the white knight', see Garner, *Commonwealth Office*, 21–2.

Alexander George Montagu CADOGAN, son of fifth Earl Cadogan; entered the diplomatic service in 1908 and served in Constantinople, London and Vienna before becoming private secretary to Harmsworth, parliamentary under secretary, 1919–20; promoted to first secretary, 1919; in 1923 Crowe, who regarded him as 'the best man in the Office' (*The Diaries of Sir Alexander Cadogan O.M. 1938–45*, ed. David Dilks, London 1971, 4), appointed him to be assistant to the British delegate to the League of Nations and adviser on the League of Nations; acting counsellor, April 1928; counsellor, September 1928; until 1933, when he became British minister in Peking, Cadogan played an invaluable and respected role in making and executing British policy at Geneva; after leaving Peking he was deputy under secretary, 1936–7, permanent under secretary, 1938–46, permanent representative to the United Nations, 1946–50; and, after retiring, he was chairman of the BBC, 1952–7.

Ronald Hugh CAMPBELL, entered Foreign Office, 1907; private secretary to the Secretary of State for Foreign Affairs, 1913–18; given the rank of second secretary while attending the Paris peace conference and later in 1919 promoted to first secretary; private secretary to Curzon, 1919–20; senior clerk in the western department, 1921–8; head of the western department in succession to Villiers, 1928–9; appointed acting counsellor, February 1928; counsellor, April 1928; appointed minister in Paris, November 1929.

Robert Leslie CRAIGIE, entered Foreign Office, 1907; secretary to various conferences and posted to Berne before the war; British representative on the inter-allied blockade committee; promoted to first secretary, 1919; posted to Sofia, 1920, and Washington, 1921; returned to London and employed as assistant director in the American section of the Department of Overseas Trade, July 1923–December 1924; clerk in the American and African department, 1925, he became the senior clerk in 1926 and in 1928 replaced Vansittart as the head of the department (on Vansittart's appointment as private secretary to the Prime Minister); counsellor, February 1928; assistant under secretary from 1935 to 1937 when he became ambassador to Tokyo.

Eyre CROWE, born in Leipzig, he came to England in 1881 at the age of seventeen; entered Foreign Office, 1885, and rapidly gained a reputation for brilliance and industry in the consular and African department; assisted in reforms of the Foreign Office, 1905–6; senior clerk and supervising head of the western department, 1906, where he became an authority on German problems and acted as principal private secretary to Sir Edward Grey; author of the famous 'Memorandum on the present state of British relations with France and Germany', 1907; secretary to the British delegation to the second Hague conference, 1907; British delegate at the London conference which drew up the abortive Declaration of London, 1908–9; British agent in the Hague arbitration between Britain and France in the *Savakar* case, 1911; assistant under secretary, 1912; minister plenipotentiary at the peace conference, 1919; permanent under secretary of the Foreign Office, 27 November 1920 until his death in April 1925. He was regarded as *the* outstanding permanent under secretary by those in a position to judge. There is a good description of him in Zara Steiner, *The Foreign Office and Foreign Policy 1898–1914*, Cambridge 1969, 108–18.

Charles DIXON, entered Colonial Office, 1911; private secretary to the permanent under secretary, 1917–19; assistant under secretary in the Dominions Office. He had 'an encyclopaedic knowledge, an unfailing memory and an infinite capacity for never overlooking the minutest detail; he became the Office constitutional expert and his advice was heavily relied upon . . .. He was regarded as so indispensable that, when he retired in 1948, he was re-employed as Constitutional adviser by successive PUSs until 1968 when he was nearly eighty': Garner, *Commonwealth Office*, 54.

Maurice Pascal Alers HANKEY, joined Royal Marine Artillery, 1895, and awarded the sword of honour at the Royal Naval College; after serving in *Ramillies*, 1899–1902, he transferred to naval intelligence and worked in the Admiralty from 1905–7 when he returned to sea as an intelligence officer; assistant secretary to the Committee of Imperial Defence, 1908, secretary, 1912–38; secretary of War Cabinet, 1916–19; cabinet secretary, 1919–38; clerk to the Privy Council, 1923–38; created baron, 1938; Minister without portfolio and member of the War Cabinet, 1939–40; Chancellor of the Duchy of Lancaster, 1940–1; Paymaster General, 1941–2.

Edward HARDING, entered the Colonial Office 1904; called to the bar, 1912; after military service in 1915–16, returned to Colonial Office; assistant secretary, 1921; deputy secretary of 1923 and 1926 imperial conferences; assistant under secretary Dominions Office, July 1925; permanent under secretary, Dominions Office, 1930 until the outbreak of the Second World War. '[I]nvariably known from his initials as E. J.', he had a cold manner, a keen eye for detail and a 'rigid sense of duty and a stern conscience' which, according to Office legend, took him back to the Office immediately after his wedding: Garner, *Commonwealth Office*, 20–1.

James Wycliffe HEADLAM-MORLEY, political historian; Fellow of Kings College, Cambridge, 1890–6; professor of Greek and ancient history, Queen's College, London, 1894–1900; staff inspector of secondary schools, Board of Education, 1902–14; historical adviser to propaganda department, 1914–17; historical adviser to the Foreign Office, 1920–8; retired December, 1928. He was 'the strongly marked product of a classical education and of the British civil service in its heyday before the First World War . . .. considerate, enlightened, rational and commonsensical, averse from every extreme, from every fanaticism, and from any emotional indulgence': E. H. Carr, *From Napoleon to Stalin and other essays*, London 1980, 166–7.

Esmé William HOWARD, entered diplomatic service, 1885; served in Rome and Berlin before resigning in 1892; assistant private secretary to the Secretary of State for Foreign Affairs, 1894–5; served in Boer war and re-entered diplomatic service, 1903; served in Rome, Washington, Hungary and Switzerland before being posted to Sweden, 1913–19; member of the British delegation to Paris peace conference; British commissioner on special inter-allied mission to Poland, February/March 1919; ambassador to Spain, 1919–24; ambassador to Washington, 1924–30; created baron, 1930. For a description of Howard and his relationship with Chamberlain, see McKercher, *Second Baldwin government*, 29–32.

Charles HOWARD-SMITH, entered Foreign Office 1912; private secretary to Cecil Harmsworth, parliamentary under Secretary of State, 1920–2; first secretary, 1922; senior clerk in the central department, 1925–9; promoted to counsellor, November 1929 when he replaced Campbell as head of the western department on the latter's posting to Paris on 29 November 1929.

Cecil James Barrington HURST, assistant legal adviser to the Foreign Office, 1902–18; legal adviser, 1918–29; member of the Permanent Court of Arbitration, 1929–50; Judge of the Permanent Court of International Justice, 1929–46; president of PCIJ, 1934–6; chairman of UN war crimes commission, 1943–4. 'There can be few during the whole [preceding] century who have done as much for international law as Hurst', wrote a subsequent legal adviser, 'and there is no one living in the United Kingdom to-day whose services can be said to have been as great': Sir Eric Beckett, 'Sir Cecil Hurst's services to international law', *The British Year Book of International Law, 1949*, xxvi, London 1950, 6. The key to his influence lay not just in the clarity of his speech and writing and his 'simple, direct and unsophisticated' mind, but also his 'downright goodness. He was the soul of honour, integrity and kindness, quite incapable of doing anything mean or petty . . . [and possessing] a high conception of duty and service': Lord McNair, 'Sir Cecil James Barrington Hurst, GCMG, KCB, QC, LLD', *The British Year Book of International Law, 1963*, xxxviii, London 1965, 400.

(Hubert) (Miles) Gladwyn JEBB, honorary attaché in Paris, 1923–4; entered Foreign Service and sent to Teheran, 1924; returned to Foreign Office, May 1927, as a clerk in the eastern department; appointed private secretary to Hugh Dalton, parliamentary under Secretary of State, June 1929; promoted to second secretary, October 1929; posted to Rome, 1931; he was subsequently acting Secretary-General of the United Nations, February 1946, and deputy under secretary in the Foreign Office, 1949–50; he succeeded Cadogan at the United Nations, 1950–4, and served as ambassador to Paris, 1954–60; created Baron Gladwyn 1960.

Ivone Augustine KIRKPATRICK, entered diplomatic service, 1910; served in Rio de Janeiro, 1919; transferred to Foreign Office, 1920; second secretary, 1920; clerk in the western department, 1921–30; first secretary October, 1928; transferred to Rome, May 1930; he subsequently became assistant under secretary in 1945 and was permanent under secretary, 1953–7.

Percy Alexander KOPPEL, called to the bar, 1900; Board of Education, 1903–5; entered news department of the Foreign Office, 1917; political intelligence department, 1918; first secretary, March 1920; counsellor, May 1925; head of the dominions information department of the Foreign Office. (The department was established in 1926 to deal with inter-imperial relations so far as they affected the Foreign Office and to deal with matters of protocol affecting the foreign relations of the dominions. After the Statute of Westminster of 1931, the department was unnecessary and it was wound up in 1933.)

(Alexander) (Wigram) Allen LEEPER, assistant, Egyptian and Assyrian department, British Museum, 1912; seconded to the foreign service and attached to the British delegation to the peace conference, remaining in Paris at the end of the conference; joined the permanent staff of the Foreign Office as second secretary, 1920; assistant private secretary to the Secretary of State for Foreign Affairs, 1920–4; first secretary, 1924; seconded for service with the government of Australia, 1924; served in Vienna, 1924–8; transferred to the Foreign Office, November 1928, where he became senior clerk in the western department.

Percivale LIESCHING, after war service entered the Colonial Office, 1920; transferred to the Dominions Office, 1925; seconded to the staff of the British High Commissioner in Canada from 1928–32 and subsequently served in South Africa and Australia before becoming assistant under secretary in the Dominions Office in 1939; after working in the Board of Trade in the Second World War he became permanent under secretary of the Comonwealth Relations Office, 1949–55, and British High Commissioner in South Africa, 1955–8.

Ronald Charles LINDSAY, entered foreign service, 1899; served in St Petersburg, Teheran, Washington and Paris; assistant private secretary to Sir Edward Grey; transferred to The Hague and promoted to first secretary, 1911; seconded to the Egyptian government, 1913; returned to diplomatic service, 1919; served in Washington as counsellor, 1919–20, and Paris as minister, 1920; assistant under secretary in the Foreign Office, 1921; representative and then ambassador in Istanbul, 1924–5; transferred to Berlin, 1926; permanent under secretary in succession to Tyrrell, July 1928; appointed ambassador to Washington in succession to Howard, March 1930.

(Herbert) William MALKIN, entered Foreign Office, 1911; assistant legal adviser, 1914–25; second legal adviser, 1925–9; legal adviser, 1929–45. He stayed on two years after the retiring age to play a major role in planning the UN and ICJ and was killed when the plane on which he was returning from the San Francisco conference went missing. Tolerant and kind, detached and calm, he rarely wasted effort on unnecessary things. He had a 'clear, logical mind . . . tremendous common sense and a (partly intuitive) good judgment . . .. He seldom tendered advice until it was asked for, but it was almost always sought': Sir Eric Beckett, Malkin's successor as legal adviser, The Times, 19 July 1945.

George Augustus MOUNSEY, entered foreign service, 1903, and served in The Hague, Berlin, Constantinople and Rome; first secretary, 1915; transferred to the Foreign Office, 1919; head of the treaty department, 1922; counsellor, 1924;

head of the far eastern department, 1926–9; assistant under secretary, 1929; deputy under secretary, September 1930.

Charles William ORDE, entered Foreign Office, 1909; first secretary, January 1920; senior clerk in the western department, 1923–6; by 1 January 1927 he was the senior clerk in the northern department; in 1928 he was (the only) clerk in the dominions information department while Maxse was on a one-year secondment to the College of Imperial Defence; head of the far eastern department, January 1929; counsellor, July 1929.

Orme Garton ('Moley') SARGENT, entered Foreign Office, 1906; served in Berne, 1917–19; first secretary, 1919; attached to Peace delegation in Paris, 1919, where he remained for the work of the Conference of Ambassadors; transferred to Foreign Office, 1925; counsellor in central department, 1926–33. He subsequently became assistant under secretary, 1933–9, deputy under secretary, 1939–46, and permanent under secretary 1946–9.

Walford Harmood Montague SELBY, entered Foreign Office, 1904; served in Berlin, The Hague and London before acting as private secretary to Grey, 1911–15; private secretary to Robert Cecil, 1917–18; on active service in the army, August–November 1918; acting head of northern department, 1919; first secretary in Cairo, 1919; returned to Foreign Office, 1922, and was senior clerk in the central department; counsellor, February 1924, and private secretary to the Secretary of State in succession to Vansittart, 1924–September 1932.

Terence Allen SHONE, entered diplomatic service, 1919, and appointed to Lisbon; transferred to the Foreign Office, 1921, where he was a clerk in the western department until December 1927 when he was promoted to first secretary and transferred to Oslo; transferred to Washington, 1928.

Gerald Sydney SPICER, entered Foreign Office, 1894, and served in Vienna and Athens; private secretary to the permanent under secretary, 1903; senior clerk, 1912; given the rank of counsellor while at the Paris peace conference, 1919; assistant secretary in the Foreign Office, April 1919; seconded to the cabinet secretariat in October 1920 to take charge of the League of Nations branch; resigned from the Foreign Office, January 1922 and joined staff of the League of Nations Union.

Charles Henry TUFTON, appointed attaché in 1900 and served in Paris before being transferred to the Foreign Office; private secretary to parliamentary under secretary, 1908–10; assistant clerk, 1911; senior clerk, 1918; given rank of counsellor of embassy at Paris peace conference; assistant secretary in the Foreign Office, 1920; head of the western department until the end of 1920 when he became head of the central department; died in Geneva after a short illness in September 1923.

William George TYRRELL, entered Foreign Office, 1889; private secretary to permanent under secretary, 1896; assistant clerk, 1903; acting second secretary in Rome, 1904; précis-writer and then private secretary to Sir Edward Grey, 1905–15; senior clerk, 1907; head of political intelligence department, 1918; assistant under secretary, 1920–5; succeeded Crowe as permanent under secretary in May 1925, a position he held until July 1928 when he was appointed ambassador to Paris. (His request for a post abroad prompted Chamberlain to complain that 'You have given me stomach-ache indeed!': Ashton-Gwatkin in *Dictionary of National Biography 1941–50*, London 1959, 894.); created baron, 1929; retired from Paris in 1934 at the age of sixty-eight, a record for British diplomatists of the period. He had a 'nervous, sensitive and affectionate nature' (ibid.) which may in part explain why his brilliant career was twice interrupted by a period of breakdown when he resorted to the bottle: See Edward G. Corp, 'Sir William Tyrrell: the eminence grise of the British Foreign Office 1912–15', *Historical Journal* xxv (1982).

Robert Gilbert ('Van') VANSITTART, entered diplomatic service, 1902, and served in Paris, Teheran, Cairo, Stockholm; secretary to Curzon, 1920–4; assistant under secretary and principal private secretary to the Prime Minister, February 1928–30; permanent under secretary in succession to Lindsay, January 1930–7; chief diplomatic adviser to the government, 1938–41; created baron, 1941.

Gerald Hyde VILLIERS, entered Foreign Office, 1902; private secretary to parliamentary under secretary, 1913; assistant clerk, 1913; senior clerk in the western department, 1920; counsellor, 1921; succeeded Tufton as head of the western department, December 1920; head of the northern department, 1928; resigned April 1929.

Victor Alexander Augustus Henry WELLESLEY, entered Foreign Office, 1899; posted to Rome, 1905–6; commercial attaché, 1908; assistant clerk, 1910; senior clerk, 1913; controller of commercial and consular affairs, 1916; assistant secretary, 1919; head of the far eastern department, 1920–5; promoted to deputy under secretary, May 1925.

Statute of the Permanent Court of International Justice, Article 36

The jurisdiction of the Court comprises all cases which the parties refer to it and all matters specially provided for in treaties and conventions in force.

The Members of the League of Nations and the States mentioned in the Annex to the Covenant may, either when signing or ratifying the Protocol to which the present Statute is adjoined, or at a later moment, declare that they recognize as compulsory *ipso facto* and without special agreement, in relation to any other Member or State accepting the same obligation, the jurisdiction of the Court in all or any of the classes of legal disputes concerning:

(a) the interpretation of a treaty;

(b) any question of international law;

(c) the existence of any fact which, if established, would constitute a breach of an international obligation;

(d) the nature and extent of the reparation to be made for the breach of an international obligation.

The declaration referred to above may be made unconditionally or on condition of reciprocity on the part of several or certain Members or States, or for a certain time.

In the event of a dispute as to whether the Court has jurisdiction, the matter shall be settled by the decision of the Court.

The Optional Clause

The undersigned, being duly authorised thereto, further declare, on behalf of their Government, that, from this date, they accept as compulsory *ipso facto* and without special Convention the jurisdiction of the Court in conformity with Article 36, paragraph 2, of the Statute of the Court, under the following conditions:

League of Nations Covenant, Articles 10–16

(Note: Emphasis added to the amendments which were made to take account of the establishment of the Permanent Court of International Justice and which came into force on 26 September 1924.)

Article 10

The Members of the League undertake to respect and preserve as against any external aggression the territorial integrity and existing political independence of all Members of the League. In case of any such aggression or in case of any threat or danger of such aggression the Council shall advise upon the means by which this obligation shall be fulfilled.

Article 11

1. Any war or threat of war, whether immediately affecting any of the Members of the League or not, is hereby declared a matter of concern to the whole League, and the League shall take any action that may be deemed wise and effectual to safeguard the peace of nations. In case any such emergency should arise the Secretary-General shall on the request of any Member of the League forthwith summon a meeting of the Council.

2. It is also declared to be the friendly right of each Member of the League to bring to the attention of the Assembly or of the Council any circumstance whatever affecting international relations which threatens to disturb international peace or the good understanding between nations upon which peace depends.

Article 12

1. The Members of the League agree that if there should arise between them any dispute likely to lead to a rupture they will submit the matter either to arbitration *or judicial settlement* or to inquiry by the Council, and they agree in no case to resort to war until three months after the award by the arbitrators *or the judicial decision* or the report by the Council.

2. In any case under this Article the award of the arbitrators *or the judicial decision* shall be made within a reasonable time, and the report of the Council shall be made within six months after the submission of the dispute.

Article 13

1. The Members of the League agree that whenever any dispute shall arise between them which they recognise to be suitable for submission to arbitration *or judicial settlement*, and which cannot be satisfactorily settled by diplomacy, they will submit the whole subject-matter to arbitration *or judicial settlement*.

2. Disputes as to the interpretation of a treaty, as to any question of international law, as to the existence of any fact which if established would constitute a breach of any international obligation, or as to the extent and nature of the reparation to be made for any such breach, are declared to be among those which are generally suitable for submission to arbitration *or judicial settlement*.

3. *For the consideration of any such dispute, the court to which the case is referred shall be the Permanent Court of International Justice, established in accordance with Article 14, or any tribunal agreed on by the parties to the dispute or stipulated in any convention existing between them.*

4. The Members of the League agree that they will carry out in full good faith any award *or decision* that may be rendered, and that they will not resort to war against a Member of the League which complies therewith. In the event of any failure to carry out such an award *or decision*, the Council shall propose what steps should be taken to give effect thereto.

Article 14

The Council shall formulate and submit to the Members of the League for adoption plans for the establishment of a Permanent Court of International Justice. The Court shall be competent to hear and determine any dispute of an international character which the parties thereto submit to it. The Court may also give an advisory opinion upon any dispute or question referred to it by the Council or by the Assembly.

Article 15

1. If there should arise between Members of the League any dispute likely to lead to a rupture, which is not submitted to arbitration *or judicial settlement* in accordance with Article 13, the Members of the League agree that they will submit the matter to the Council. Any party to the dispute may effect such submission by giving notice of the existence of the dispute to the Secretary-General, who will make all necessary arrangements for a full investigation and consideration thereof.

2. For this purpose the parties to the dispute will communicate to the Secretary-General, as promptly as possible, statements of their case with all the relevant facts and papers, and the Council may forthwith direct the publication thereof.

3. The Council shall endeavour to effect a settlement of the dispute, and if such efforts are successful, a statement shall be made public giving such facts and explanations regarding the dispute and the terms of settlement thereof as the Council may deem appropriate.

4. If the dispute is not thus settled, the Council, either unanimously or by a majority vote, shall make and publish a report containing a statement of the facts of the dispute and the recommendations which are deemed just and proper in regard thereto.

5. Any Member of the League represented on the Council may make public a statement of the facts of the dispute and of its conclusions regarding the same.

6. If a report by the Council is unanimously agreed to by the members thereof other than the Representatives of one or more of the parties to the dispute, the Members of the League agree that they will not go to war with any party to the dispute which complies with the recommendations of the report.

7. If the Council fails to reach a report which is unanimously agreed to by the members thereof, other than the Representatives of one or more of the Parties to the dispute, the Members of the League reserve to themselves the right to take such action as they shall consider necessary for the maintenance of right and justice.

8. If the dispute between the parties is claimed by one of them, and is found by the Council, to arise out of a matter which by international law is solely within the domestic jurisdiction of that party, the Council shall so report, and shall make no recommendation as to its settlement.

9. The Council may in any case under this Article refer the dispute to the Assembly. The dispute shall be so referred at the request of either party to the dispute, provided that such request be made within fourteen days after the submission of the dispute to the Council.

10. In any case referred to the Assembly, all the provisions of this Article and of Article 12 relating to the action and powers of the Council shall apply to the action and powers of the Assembly, provided that a report made by the Assembly, if concurred in by the Representatives of those Members of the League represented on the Council and of a majority of the other Members of the League, exclusive in each case of the Representatives of the parties to the dispute, shall have the same force as a report by the Council concurred in by all the members thereof other than the Representatives of one or more of the parties to the dispute.

Article 16

1. Should any Member of the League resort to war in disregard of its covenants under Articles 12, 13 or 15, it shall *ipso facto* be deemed to have committed an act of war against all other Members of the League, which hereby undertake

immediately to subject it to the severance of all trade or financial relations, the prohibition of all intercourse between their nationals and the nationals of the covenant-breaking State, and the prevention of all financial, commercial or personal intercourse between the nationals of the covenant-breaking State and the nationals of any other State, whether a Member of the League or not.

2. It shall be the duty of the Council in such case to recommend to the several Governments concerned what effective military, naval or air force the Members of the League shall severally contribute to the armed forces to be used to protect the covenants of the League.

3. The Members of the League agree, further, that they will mutually support one another in the financial and economic measures which are taken under this Article, in order to minimise the loss and inconvenience resulting from the above measures, and that they will mutually support one another in resisting any special measures aimed at one of their number by the covenant-breaking State, and that they will take the necessary steps to afford passage through their territory to the forces of any of the Members of the League which are co-operating to protect the covenants of the League.

4. Any Member of the League which has violated any covenant of the League may be declared to be no longer a Member of the League by a vote of the Council concurred in by the Representatives of all the other Members of the League represented thereon.

Protocol for the Pacific Settlement of International Disputes 1924 (The Geneva Protocol), Articles 3, 4, 5, 10, 11

Article 3

The signatory States undertake to recognize as compulsory, *ipso facto* and without special agreement, the jurisdiction of the Permanent Court of International Justice in the cases covered by paragraph 2 of Article 36 of the Statute of the Court, but without prejudice to the right of any State, when acceding to the special protocol provided for in the said Article and opened for signature on December 16, 1920, to make reservations compatible with the said clause.

Accession to this special protocol, opened for signature on December 16, 1920, must be given within the month following the coming into force of the present Protocol.

States which accede to the present Protocol, after its coming into force, must carry out the above obligation within the month following their accession.

Article 4

With a view to render more complete the provisions of paragraphs 4, 5, 6, and 7 of Article 15 of the Covenant, the signatory States agree to comply with the following procedure:–

(1) If the dispute submitted to the Council is not settled by it as provided in paragraph 3 of the said Article 15, the Council shall endeavour to persuade the parties to submit the dispute to juridical settlement or arbitration.

(2) (a) If the parties cannot agree to do so, there shall, at the request of at least one of the parties, be constituted a Committee of Arbitrators. The Committee shall so far as possible be constituted by agreement between the parties.

(b) If within the period fixed by the Council the parties have failed to agree, in whole or in part, upon the number, the names and the powers of the arbitrators and upon the procedure, the Council shall settle the points remaining in suspense. It shall with the utmost possible despatch select in consultation with the parties the arbitrators and their President from among persons who by their nationality, their personal character and their experience, appear to it to furnish the highest guarantees of competence and impartiality.

(c) After the claims of the parties have been formulated, the Committee of Arbitrators, on the request of any party, shall through the medium of the Council request an advisory opinion upon any points of law in dispute from the Permanent Court of International Justice, which in such case shall meet with the utmost possible despatch.

(3) If none of the parties asks for arbitration, the Council shall again take the dispute under consideration. If the Council reaches a report which is unanimously agreed to by the members thereof other than the representatives of any of the parties to the dispute, the signatory States agree to comply with the recommendations therein.

(4) If the Council fails to reach a report which is concurred in by all its members, other than the representatives of any of the parties to the dispute, it shall submit the dispute to arbitration. It shall itself determine the composition, the powers and the procedure of the Committee of Arbitrators and, in the choice of the arbitrators, shall bear in mind the guarantees of competence and impartiality referred to in paragraph 2(b) above.

(5) In no case may a solution, upon which there has already been a unanimous recommendation of the Council accepted by one of the parties concerned, be again called into question.

(6) The signatory States undertake that they will carry out in full good faith any judicial sentence or arbitral award that may be rendered and that they will comply, as provided in paragraph 3 above, with the solutions recommended by the Council. In the event of a state failing to carry out the above undertakings, the Council shall exert all its influence to secure compliance therewith. If it fails therein, it shall propose what steps should be taken to give effect thereto, in accordance with the provision contained at the end of Article 13 of the Covenant. Should a State in disregard of the above undertakings resort to war, the sanctions provided for by Article 16 of the Covenant, interpreted in the manner indicated in the present Protocol, shall immediately become applicable to it.

(7) The provisions of the present article do not apply to the settlement of disputes which arise as a result of measures of war taken by one or more signatory States in agreement with the Council or the Assembly.

Article 5

The provisions of paragraph 8 of Article 15 of the Covenant shall continue to apply in proceedings before the Council.

If in the course of an arbitration, such as is contemplated by Article 4 above, one of the parties claims that the dispute, or part thereof, arises out of a matter which by international law is solely within the domestic jurisdiction of that party, the arbitrators shall on this point take the advice of the Permanent Court of International Justice through the medium of the Council. The opinion of the Court shall be binding upon the arbitrators, who, if the opinion is affirmative, shall confine themselves to so declaring in their award.

If the question is held by the Court or by the Council to be a matter solely within the domestic jurisdiction of the State, this decision shall not prevent consideration of the situation by the Council or by the Assembly under Article 11 of the Covenant.

Article 10

Every State which resorts to war in violation of the undertakings contained in the Covenant or in the present Protocol is an aggressor. Violation of the rules laid down for a demilitarized zone shall be held equivalent to resort to war.

In the event of hostilities having broken out, any State shall be presumed to be an aggressor, unless a decision of the Council, which must be taken unanimously, shall otherwise declare:

(1) If it has refused to submit the dispute to the procedure of pacific settlement provided by Articles 13 and 15 of the Covenant as amplified by the present Protocol, or to comply with a judicial sentence or arbitral award or with a unanimous recommendation of the Council, or has disregarded a unanimous report of the Council, a judicial sentence or an arbitral award recognizing that the dispute between it and the other belligerent State arises out of a matter which by international law is solely within the domestic jurisdiction of the latter State; nevertheless, in the last case the State shall only be presumed to be an aggressor if it has not previously submitted the question to the Council or the Assembly, in accordance with Article 11 of the Covenant.

(2) If it has violated provisional measures enjoined by the Council for the period while the proceedings are in progress as contemplated by Article 7 of the present Protocol.

Apart from the cases dealt with in paragraphs 1 and 2 of the present Article, if the Council does not at once succeed in determining the aggressor, it shall be bound to enjoin upon the belligerents an armistice, and shall fix the terms, acting, if need be, by a two-thirds majority and shall supervise its execution.

Any belligerent which has refused to accept the armistice or has violated its terms shall be deemed an aggressor.

The Council shall call upon the signatory States to apply forthwith against the aggressor the sanctions provided by Article 11 of the present Protocol, and any signatory State thus called upon shall thereupon be entitled to exercise the rights of a belligerent.

Article 11

As soon as the Council has called upon the signatory States to apply sanctions, as provided in the last paragraph of Article 10 of the present Protocol, the obligations of the said States, with regard to the sanctions of all kinds mentioned in paragraphs 1 and 2 of Article 16 of the Covenant, will immediately become operative in order that such sanctions may forthwith be employed against the aggressor.

Those obligations shall be interpreted as obliging each of the signatory States to co-operate loyally and effectively in support of the Covenant of the League of Nations, and in resistance to any act of aggression, in the degree which its geographical position and its particular situation as regards armaments allow.

In accordance with paragraph 3 of Article 16 of the Covenant the signatory States give a joint and several undertaking to come to the assistance of the State attacked or threatened, and to give each other mutual support by means of facilities and reciprocal exchanges as regards the provision of raw materials and supplies of every kind, openings of credits, transport and transit, and for this purpose to take all measures in their power to preserve the safety of communications by land and by sea of the attacked or threatened State.

If both parties to the dispute are aggressors within the meaning of Article 10, the economic and financial sanctions shall be applied to both of them.

APPENDIX 5

United Kingdom declaration accepting the Optional Clause, signed by Arthur Henderson, 19 September 1929

On behalf of His Majesty's Government in the United Kingdom and subject to ratification, I accept as compulsory *ipso facto* and without special convention, on condition of reciprocity, the jurisdiction of the court in conformity with article 36, paragraph 2, of the statute of the court, for a period of ten years and thereafter until such time as notice may be given to terminate the acceptance, over all disputes arising after the ratification of the present declaration with regard to situations or facts subsequent to the said ratification, other than:-

Disputes in regard to which the parties to the dispute have agreed or shall agree to have recourse to some other method of peaceful settlement; and

Disputes with the Government of any other member of the League which is a member of the British Commonwealth of Nations, all of which disputes shall be settled in such manner as the parties have agreed or shall agree; and

Disputes with regard to questions which by international law fall exclusively within the jurisdiction of the United Kingdom.

And subject to the condition that His Majesty's Government reserve the right to require that proceedings in the court shall be suspended in respect of any dispute which has been submitted to and is under consideration by the Council of the League of Nations, provided that notice to suspend is given after the dispute has been submitted to the Council and is given within ten days of the notification of the initiation of proceedings in the court, and provided also that such suspension shall be limited to a period of twelve months or such longer period as can be agreed by the parties to the dispute or determined by a decision of all the members of the Council other than the parties to the dispute.

*Explanatory statement made by Arthur Henderson
on behalf of the United Kingdom at time of
signature of the Optional Clause*

The 'optional clause', which His Majesty's Government in the United Kingdom are now accepting, gives the Permanent Court of International Justice at The Hague jurisdiction over juridical disputes with other parties accepting the like obligation without the necessity for framing in respect of each dispute a special agreement for its submission to the court.

The formula which I have just signed on behalf of the United Kingdom, and copies of which are, I believe, available, follows the usual practice in being subject to reciprocity and in including a time-limit. This is fixed at ten years, but the acceptance continues in force after the expiration of the period, unless notice is given to terminate it. The signature is also subject to ratification. This will enable the question to be raised in Parliament, if so desired, before the acceptance of the compulsory jurisdiction comes into operation.

The declaration accepting the jurisdiction covers only disputes which may arise in future. Past disputes and disputes relating to past events will continue to be submitted to the court under a special agreement concluded in each case.

Three classes of disputes are excluded from the operation of the declaration of acceptance. These are disputes for the submission of which some other method of peaceful settlement provision is made by existing or future agreements, disputes with some other members of the British Commonwealth of Nations, and disputes about matters which fall within what is called the domestic jurisdiction of a State. Commercial treaties and conventions dealing with special subjects, such as reparations, or with technical matters, such as copyright, very often contain provisions setting up special tribunals to deal with disputes which may arise as to the meaning or application of their terms. When that is the case, the dispute will be dealt with as provided in the agreement and will not be submitted to the court at The Hague. This is the effect of the exclusion of the first class of disputes.

Disputes with other members of the British Commonwealth of Nations are excluded because the members of the Commonwealth, though international units individually in the fullest sense of the term, are united by their common allegiance to the Crown. Disputes between them should, therefore, be dealt with by some other mode of settlement, and for this provision is made in the exclusion clause.

On certain matters international law recognizes that the authority of the State is supreme. When once it is determined that the subject-matter of the dispute falls within the category of cases where this is so, there is no scope for the exercise of the jurisdiction of an international tribunal.

At the end of the formula comes a proviso which enables disputes to be referred to the Council of the League before they are dealt with by the court. This is to cover disputes which are really political in character though juridical in appearance. Disputes of this kind can be dealt with more satisfactorily by the Council, so that the conciliatory powers of that body may be exercised with a view to arriving at a friendly settlement of the dispute. This formula places the United Kingdom in much the same position as a State which has agreed to a treaty of arbitration and conciliation providing for the reference of all disputes to a conciliation commission before they are submitted to judicial settlement. The formula is wide in character because the extent to which it operates depends on the Council itself. It would cease to operate from the moment when the Council decided that it was better that the question should be submitted to the court, and therefore declined to keep the dispute under consideration. Within these limits, however, the proviso would apply to any justiciable dispute, whatever its origin. It would extend, for instance, to disputes arising out of cases where it had been necessary for the United Kingdom to take action at the instance of the Council in pursuance of its obligations as a member of the League.

Dominion statements and Irish declaration on the Optional Clause, September 1929

Explanatory statement made by Eric Louw on behalf of South Africa at time of signature of the Optional Clause

With regard to the reservation as to disputes between Members of the British Commonwealth of Nations, I wish to state that although in the view of my Government, such disputes are justiciable by the International Court of Justice, my Government prefers to settle them by other means – hence the reservation.

Explanatory statement made by Raoul Dandurand on behalf of Canada at time of signature of the Optional Clause

The Dominion of Canada has excluded from the purview of the Court legal disputes with other members of the British Commonwealth for the sole reason that it is its expressed policy to settle these matters by some other method, and it has deemed opportune to include its will as a reservation, although a doubt may exist as to such reservation being consistent with Article 36 of the Statute of the Court.

Irish Free State declaration accepting the Optional Clause, signed by Patrick McGilligan on 14 September 1929

On behalf of the Irish Free State, I declare that I accept as compulsory *ipso facto* and without special convention the jurisdiction of the Court in conformity with Article 36 of the Statute of the Permanent Court of International Justice for a period of twenty years and on the sole condition of reciprocity. This declaration is subject to ratification.

Bibliography

Unpublished primary sources

Great Britain, Public Record Office

Prime Minister's office
PREM I Correspondence and papers

Cabinet Office papers
CAB 2 Minutes of the Committee of Imperial Defence
CAB 4 CID memoranda
CAB 16 CID sub-committees
CAB 21 Registered files
CAB 23 Cabinet minutes
CAB 24 Cabinet memoranda
CAB 27 Cabinet committees
CAB 32 Imperial conferences
CAB 63 Hankey files

Foreign Office papers
(i) FO 371 Political correspondence
The War, Miscellaneous general (1919–20)
W 98 Western, League of Nations (1920–31)
A 45 America, selected files (1928–9)

(ii) FO 372 Treaty department
T 317 Tunis Nationality Decrees (1922, 1923)
T 383 Arbitration agreements (1926)

(iii) FO 411 League of Nations, confidential prints

(iv) FO 412 Geneva conference for the limitation of armaments

(v) FO 426 Inter-imperial relations, confidential prints, 1926–8, 1930

(vi) FO 800 Private collections
Arthur Balfour, first Earl of Balfour; Austen Chamberlain; Eyre Crowe; George Nathaniel Curzon, Marquess Curzon of Kedleston; Baron Cushendun (Ronald McNeill); Eric Drummond, Earl of Perth; Arthur Henderson; James Ramsay MacDonald; Philip Noel-Baker, Baron Noel-Baker of Derby; Arthur Ponsonby; Godfrey Locker-Lampson.

(vii) PRO 30/69 James Ramsay MacDonald papers

(viii) FO 899 Cabinet papers

Dominions Office papers
DO 35 Correspondence (1928–30)

India Office records
L/E/9 Economic and overseas department (1929)

Unpublished documents and collections of private papers

Birmingham University Library: Austen Chamberlain
Cambridge University Library: Stanley Baldwin, first Earl Baldwin of Bewdley
Churchill College Archives Centre, Cambridge: Philip Noel-Baker, Baron Noel-Baker of Derby; Alexander Cadogan; Maurice Hankey, Baron Hankey
Beaverbrook Library, London: Andrew Bonar Law; J. C. C. Davidson
Bodleian Library, Oxford: W.H. Dickinson; Gilbert Murray
British Library, London: Arthur Balfour, first Earl of Balfour; Robert Cecil, Viscount Cecil of Chelwood
British Library of Political and Economic Science, London: Hugh Dalton, Baron Dalton; League of Nations Union; Sidney Webb, Lord Passfield; Beatrice Webb

National Archives of Canada, Ottawa

RG25 Department of External Affairs
RG25 D1 Department of External Affairs, office of under secretary of state
MG26 J William Lyon Mackenzie King papers
MG27 Raoul Dandurand papers
MG27 III B10 Ernest Lapointe papers
MG30 D33 Oscar Skelton papers

United States National Archives, Department of State

Political relations with Great Britain
711.4112 Arbitration treaty between the United States and Great Britain 1927, 1928, 1929
711.4112A Arbitration treaty between the United States and Great Britain; negotiations for a treaty renouncing war 1928

Published primary sources

Canada:

Documents on Canadian external relations, iii: *1919–1925*, ed. Lovell C. Clark, Ottawa 1970
Documents on Canadian external relations, iv: *1926–1930*, ed. Alex I. Inglis, Ottawa 1971
Documents on Canadian foreign policy, 1917–1939, ed. Walter A. Riddell, Toronto 1962

Great Britain:

British general election manifestos, 1918–1966, ed. F. W. S. Clark, Chichester 1970
Documents on British foreign policy, 1919–1939, ed. W. N. Douglas Dakin, and M. E. Lambert, ser. 1A, i–vi, London 1966–75
Independent Labour Party, *Report of the annual conference* (annual), 1925–30
Labour Party, *Report of the annual conference* (annual), 1917–31
Labour yearbook, 1919, 1924, Brighton 1972, 1973
The Parliamentary debates, House of Commons, official report, fifth series
The Parliamentary debates, House of Lords, official report, fifth series

Parliamentary papers

Fifth Assembly. *Report of the British delegates relating to the Protocol for the Peaceful Settlement of International Disputes*, Misc. no. 21 (Command paper 2289), 1924
Protocol for the Pacific Settlement of International Disputes. *Correspondence relating to the attitudes of the dominions* (Command paper 2458), 1925
Sixth Assembly. *Report of the British delegates to the secretary of state for foreign affairs. London, November 26, 1925*, Misc. No. 1 (Command paper 2576), 1926

BIBLIOGRAPHY

Imperial conference 1926. *Summary of proceedings* (*Command paper* 2768), 1926

Seventh Assembly. *Report of the British delegates to the Secretary of State for Foreign Affairs. London, November 19, 1926*, Misc. no. 12 (*Command paper* 2780), 1926

Eighth Assembly. *Report of the British delegates to the Secretary of State for Foreign Affairs, London, November 25, 1927*, Misc. no. 1 (*Command paper* 3008), 1928.

Correspondence with the United States ambassador respecting the United States proposal for the renunciation of war (United States no. 1) (*Command paper* 3109), 1928

Further correspondence with the government of the United States respecting the United States proposal for the renunciation of war (United States no. 2), (*Command paper* 3153), 1928

Ninth Assembly. *Report of the British delegates to the Secretary of State for Foreign Affairs, London, November 21, 1928*, Misc. no. 8 (*Command paper* 3242), 1928

Memorandum on the signature by His Majesty's Government in the United Kingdom of the Optional Clause of the Statute of the Permanent Court of International Justice, Misc. no. 12 (*Command paper* 3452), 1929

Tenth Assembly. *Report of the British delegates to the Secretary of State for Foreign Affairs. London, November 15, 1929*, Misc. no. 13 (*Command paper* 3458), 1929

United States:

Department of State, *Papers relating to the foreign relations of the United States*, 1927, ii; 1928, i, ii, Washington, DC 1942, 1943

League of Nations:

Assembly

The records of the first Assembly. Plenary meetings, Geneva, 1920

The records of the second Assembly. Plenary meetings, Geneva, 1921

The records of the third Assembly. Plenary meetings, I: Text of the debates. Geneva, 1922

The records of the fourth Assembly. Plenary meetings. Text of the debates. *Official Journal*, special supplement no. 13, 1923

Records of the fifth Assembly. Plenary meetings. Text of the debates. *Official Journal*, special supplement no. 23, 1924

Resolutions and recommendations adopted by the Assembly during its fifth session. *Official Journal*, special supplement no. 21, October 1924

Records of the sixth Assembly. Plenary meetings. Text of the debates. *Official Journal*, special supplement no. 33, 1925

Resolutions and recommendations adopted by the Assembly during its sixth session. *Official Journal*, special supplement no. 32, October 1925

Records of the seventh ordinary session of the Assembly. Plenary meetings. Text of the debates. *Official Journal*, special supplement no. 44, 1926

Resolutions and recommendations adopted by the Assembly during its seventh ordinary session. *Official Journal*, special supplement no. 43, October 1926

Records of the eighth ordinary session of the Assembly. Plenary meetings. Text of the debates. *Official Journal*, special supplement no. 54, 1927

Resolutions and recommendations adopted by the Assembly during its eighth ordinary session. *Official Journal*, special supplement no. 53, October 1927

Records of the ninth ordinary session of the Assembly. Plenary meetings. Text of the debates. *Official Journal*, special supplement no. 64, 1928

Resolutions and recommendations adopted by the Assembly during its ninth ordinary session. *Official Journal*, special supplement no. 63, October 1928

Records of the tenth ordinary session of the Assembly. Plenary meetings. Text of the debates. *Official Journal*, special supplement no. 75, 1929

289

Records of the eleventh ordinary session of the Assembly. Plenary meetings. Text of the debates. *Official Journal*, special supplement no. 84, 1930
Records of the twelfth ordinary session of the Assembly. Plenary meetings. Text of the debates. *Official Journal*, special supplement no. 93, 1931

Committees of the Assembly

Records of the first Assembly: meetings of the committees, i, Geneva 1920
Records of the second Assembly: meetings of the committees, i, Geneva 1921
Minutes of the first committee (constitutional questions), *Official Journal*, special supplement no. 24, 1924
Minutes of the third committee (reduction of armaments), *Official Journal*, special supplement no. 26, 1924
Minutes of the first committee (constitutional and legal questions), *Official Journal*, special supplement no. 34, 1925
Minutes of the first committee (constitutional and legal questions), *Official Journal*, special supplement no. 45, 1926
Minutes of the first committee (constitutional and legal questions), *Official Journal*, special supplement no. 55, 1927
Minutes of the third committee (reduction of armaments), *Official Journal*, special supplement no. 57, 1927
Minutes of the first committee (constitutional and legal questions), *Official Journal*, special supplement no. 65, 1928
Minutes of the third committee (reduction of armaments), *Official Journal*, special supplement no. 67, 1928

Council

Procès-verbal of the second session of the Council, London, February 1920, *Official Journal*, March 1920
Procès-verbal of the third session of the Council, Paris, March 1920, *Official Journal*, March 1920
Procès-verbal of the fourth session of the Council, Paris, April 1920, *Official Journal*, April–May 1920
Procès-verbal of the fifth session of the Council, Rome, May 1920, *Official Journal*, June 1920
Procès-verbal of the sixth session of the Council, London, June 1920, *Official Journal*, July–August 1920
Procès-verbal of the seventh session of the Council, London, July 1920, *Official Journal*, July–August 1920
Procès-verbal of the eighth session of the Council, San Sebastian, July–August 1920, *Official Journal*, September 1920
Procès-verbal of the tenth session of the Council, Brussels, October 1920, *Official Journal*, November–December 1920
Procès-verbal of the eleventh session of the Council, Geneva, November–December 1920, *Official Journal*, January–February 1921
Procès-verbal of the thirteenth session of the Council, Geneva, June 1921, *Official Journal*, September 1921
Procès-verbal of the fourteenth session of the Council, Geneva, August–October 1921, *Official Journal*, December 1921
Procès-verbal of the forty-sixth session of the Council, Geneva, September 1927, *Official Journal*, October 1927
Procès-verbal of the forty-seventh session of the Council, Geneva, September 1927, *Official Journal*, December 1927

BIBLIOGRAPHY

Permanent Court of International Justice

Advisory Committee of Jurists, *Documents presented to the Committee relating to existing plans for the establishment of a Permanent Court of International Justice*, London 1920

Advisory Committee of Jurists, *Procès-verbaux of the proceedings of the Committee*, The Hague, June 16–July 24, 1920, London 1920

Advisory Committee of Jurists, *Draft scheme of the Committee with reports to the Council of the League of Nations and resolutions by the Council relating to it*, London 1920

Documents concerning the action taken by the Council of the League of Nations under Article 14 of the Covenant and the adoption by the Assembly of the Statute of the Permanent Court, London 1920

Arbitration and security: the Geneva Protocol and the General Act

General report submitted to the fifth Assembly on behalf of the first and third committees by M. Politis (Greece), rapporteur for the first committee, and M. Beneš (Czechoslovakia), rapporteur for the third committee, 1924, [A.135.1924]

Extracts from the debates of the fifth Assembly including those of the first and third committees. Reports and resolutions adopted by the Assembly and the Council, 1924, [C.708.1924.IX] <C.C.0.1>

Arbitration, security and reduction of armaments. Documents and proceedings of the fifth Assembly. September 1924, (Prepared by the information section), 1924

Protocol for the Pacific Settlement of International Disputes. Adopted by the fifth Assembly of the League of Nations on October 2, 1924, June 1925, [A.25.1925.IX]

Arbitration and security. Exposé of the proposals, declarations and suggestions made at the sixth Assembly, with a view to the pacific settlement of international disputes, Presented by the legal section of the secretariat in view of the Council resolution of December 12 1925, February 1926, [C.33.M.75.1926.V]

Arbitration and security. Systematic survey of the arbitration conventions and treaties of mutual security deposited with the League of Nations, Lausanne, 1926, [C.34.M.74.1926.V.] (Also second edition, revised and augmented, containing all treaties deposited before 15 December 1927, Geneva, 1927, [C.653.M.216.1927.V].)

Minutes of the fourth session of the Preparatory Commission for the Disarmament Conference and of the first session of the Committee on Arbitration and Security, 1928, [C.667.M.225.1927.IX] <C.P.D.1.(d).> (1928.IX.2)

Preparatory Commission for the Disarmament Conference. Committee on Arbitration and Security. Memoranda on arbitration, security and the articles of the Covenant with annexes containing documents submitted to the Committee for consideration at its second session, <C.A.S.10.> (1928.IX.3.)

Minutes of the second session of the Committee on Arbitration and Security and of the fifth session of the Preparatory Commission for the Disarmament Conference, 1928, [C.165.M.50.1928.IX] <C.P.D.1.(e).> (1928.IX.6.)

Documents of the Preparatory Commission for the Disarmament Conference. Committee on Arbitration and Security. Report of the Committee on Arbitration and Security on the work of its second session, 1928, [C.P.D.108 (C.A.S.39)]

Minutes of the third session of the Committee on Arbitration and Security, 1928, [C.358.M.112.1928.IX.] <C.P.D.1.(f).> (1928.IX.8)

Preparatory Commission for the Disarmament Conference. Committee on Arbitration and Security, Report of the Committee on Arbitration and Security on the work of its third session held at Geneva from June 27 to July 4 1928, 1928, [C.342.M.100.1928.IX] <C.P.D.123> <C.A.S.75.> (1928.IX.9)

Pacific settlement of international disputes, non-aggression and mutual assistance, 1928, [C.536.M.163.1928.IX.] (1928.IX.13.)

Pacific settlement of international disputes. Model bilateral conventions for conciliation, arbitration and judicial settlement, 1928, [C.539.M.166.1928.IX]

Newspapers and periodicals

Headway (Monthly journal of the League of Nations Union)
Manchester Guardian
The Times

Memoirs, biographies, diaries and collections of private papers

Amery, Leo, *The Leo Amery diaries*, i: *1896–1929*, ed. John Barnes and David Nicholson, London 1980

Angell, Norman, *After all*, London 1951

Bartlett, Vernon, *This is my life*, London 1941

Brockway, Fenner, *Inside the left: thirty years of platform, press, prison and parliament*, London 1942

Butler, Harold, *The lost peace*, London 1941

Cecil of Chelwood, Viscount, Robert, *A great experiment: an autobiography*, London 1941
—— *All the way*, London 1949

Chamberlain, J. Austen, *Politics from the inside: 1906–1914*, London 1936
—— *Down the years*, London 1935

Chatfield, Admiral of the Fleet, Lord, *It might happen again*, ii: *The navy and defence*, London 1947

Clynes, J. R., *Memoirs*, 2 vols, London 1937, 1938

Craig, Gordon A. and Felix Gilbert (eds), *The diplomats, 1919–1939*, 2 vols, New York 1972 (first publ. 1953)

Dalton, Hugh, *Call back yesterday: memoirs 1887–1931*, London 1953

Edwards, Cecil, *Bruce of Melbourne: man of two worlds*, London 1965

Gladwyn, Lord (Gladwyn Jebb), *The memoirs of Lord Gladwyn*, London 1972

Haldane, Richard Burdon, *An autobiography*, London 1929

Halpern, Paul G. (ed.), *The Keyes papers: selections from the private and official correspondence of Admiral of the Fleet Baron Keyes of Zeebrugge*, London 1980

Hamelin, Marcel (ed.), *Les mémoires du Sénateur Raoul Dandurand, 1861–1942*, Québec 1967

Hamilton, Mary Agnes, *Arthur Henderson*, London 1938
—— *Remembering my good friends*, London 1944

Herriot, Edouard, *Jadis*, II: *D'une guerre à l'autre, 1914–1936*, Paris 1952

Howard of Penrith, Esmé, Baron, *Theatre of life: life seen from the stalls, 1905–1936*, London 1936

Hutchison, W. Bruce, *Mackenzie King: the incredible Canadian*, Toronto 1952

Hyde, H. Montgomery, *Baldwin – the unexpected prime minister*, London 1973

James, Robert Rhodes (ed.), *Memoirs of a Conservative. J.C.C. Davidson's memoirs and papers, 1910–1937*, London 1969

Jones, Thomas, *Whitehall diary*, 2 vols, London 1969

Kenworthy, J. M., *Sailors, statesmen – and others*, London 1933

Liddell Hart, Basil, *The memoirs of Captain Liddell Hart*, i, London 1965

The Mackenzie King diaries, Toronto 1973

de Madariaga, Salvador, *Morning without noon: memoirs*, Farnborough 1973

Mander, Geoffrey, *We were not all wrong*, London 1944

Marquand, David, *Ramsay MacDonald*, London 1977

Massey, Vincent, *What's past is prologue*, London 1963

Maurice, Major-General Sir Frederick, *Haldane: the life of Viscount Haldane of Cloan*, London 1939

Middlemas, Keith and John Barnes, *Baldwin: a biography*, London 1969

Morris, A. J. A., *C. P. Trevelyan 1870–1958: portrait of a radical*, Belfast 1977

Murray, Gilbert, *An unfinished autobiography with contributions from his friends*, ed. Jean Smith and Arnold Toynbee, London 1960

Neatby, H. Blair, *William Lyon Mackenzie King*, ii: *The lonely heights*, London 1963

Nicolson, Sir Harold, *Curzon: the last phase 1919–1925: a study in post-war diplomacy*, London 1934

—— *King George the fifth: his life and reign*, London 1952

Noel-Baker, Philip, *The first world disarmament conference 1932–1933 and why it failed*, Oxford 1979

Page, Sir Earle, *Truant surgeon: the inside story of forty years of Australian political life*, Sydney 1963

Parmoor, Lord, *A retrospect: looking back on a life of more than eighty years*, London 1936

Paul-Boncour, J., *Entre deux guerres: souvenirs sur la IIIe République: les lendemains de la victoire 1919–34*, Paris 1945

Petrie, Sir Charles, *The life and letters of the Rt. Hon. Sir A. Chamberlain*, ii, London 1940

Pimlott, Ben, *Hugh Dalton*, London 1985

Rose, Kenneth, *King George V*, London 1983

Roskill, Stephen, *Hankey, man of secrets*, ii: *1919–1931*, London 1972

—— *Admiral of the Fleet Earl Beatty: The last naval hero: an intimate biography*, London 1980

Samuel, Viscount (Herbert), *Memoirs*, London 1945

Selby, Sir Walford, *Diplomatic twilight 1930–1940*, London 1953

Snowden, Viscount (Philip), *An autobiography*, ii, London 1934

Sommer, Dudley, *Haldane of Cloan: his life and times 1856–1928*, London 1960

Suarez, Georges, *Herriot, 1924–32*, Paris 1932

Swanwick, H. M., *I have been young*, London 1935

Temperley, Major-General A. C., *The whispering gallery of Europe*, London 1938

Thomas, J. H., *My story*, London 1937

Thurtle, Ernest, *Time's winged chariot*, London 1945

Webb, Beatrice, *Beatrice Webb's diaries*, ed. Margaret Cole, 2 vols, London 1952, 1956

Wedgewood, Josiah, *Memoirs of a fighting life*, London 1940

West, Francis, *Gilbert Murray: a life*, Beckenham 1984

Wilson, Duncan, *Gilbert Murray OM 1866–1957*, Oxford 1988

Wilson, Trevor (ed.), *The political diaries of C. P. Scott*, London 1970

Wilson-Harris, H., *Life so far*, London 1954

Woolf, Leonard, *An autobiography*, 2 vols, London 1980 (first publ. in six vols. 1960–9)

Young, G. M., *Stanley Baldwin*, London 1952

Secondary sources

Books

Birn, Donald S., *The League of Nations Union 1918–1945*, Oxford 1981

Brand, Carl F., *The British Labour Party: a short history*, London 1965

Burton, Margaret E., *The Assembly of the League of Nations*, New York 1974 (first publ. 1941)

Butler, David & Sloman, Anne, *British political facts 1900–1979*, 5th edn, London 1980

Carlton, David, *MacDonald versus Henderson: the foreign policy of the second Labour government*, London 1969

Carr, E. H., *The twenty years' crisis*, 2nd edn, London 1946

Carter, Gwendolen, *The British Commonwealth and international security: the role of the dominions 1919–1939*, Westport, Conn. 1971 (first publ. 1947)

Ceadel, Martin, *Pacifism in Britain 1914–1945: the defining of a faith*, Oxford 1980

Cecil, Viscount, *The way of peace: essays and addresses*, London 1928

Chubb, Basil, *The government and politics of Ireland*, London 1970

Cline, Catherine Ann, *Recruits to Labour: the British Labour Party 1914–1931*, New York 1963

Cowling, Maurice, *The impact of Labour 1920–1924*, Cambridge 1971

Cross, J. A., *Whitehall and the Commonwealth: British departmental organisation for Commonwealth relations 1900–1966*, London 1967

Dalton, Hugh, *Towards the peace of nations: a study in international politics*, London 1928

Drummond, Ian M., *Imperial economic policy 1917–1939: studies in expansion and protection*, London 1974

Fachiri, Alexander P., *The Permanent Court of International Justice: its constitution, procedure and work*, London 1925

Fawcett, J. E. S., *The British Commonwealth and international law*, London 1963

Ferrell, Robert H., *Peace in their time: the origins of the Kellogg-Briand pact*, New Haven 1952

Garner, Joe, *The Commonwealth Office 1925–1968*, London 1978

Gordon, Michael R., *Conflict and consensus in Labour's foreign policy 1914–1965*, Stanford 1969

Great Britain and the dominions (Harris Foundation Lectures 1927), Chicago 1928

Hancock, W. K., *Survey of British Commonwealth affairs*, I: *Problems of nationality 1918–1936*; II: *Problems of economic policy 1918–1939*, London 1937, 1940

Harkness, D. W., *The restless dominion: the Irish Free State and the British Commonwealth of nations 1921–1931*, London 1969

Headlam-Morley, J., *Studies in diplomatic history*, London 1930

Hilliker, John, *Canada's department of External Affairs*, I: *The early years, 1909–1946*, Montreal-Kingston-London-Buffalo 1990

Hudson, Manley O., *The Permanent Court of International Justice, 1920–1942: a treatise*, New York 1943

Hudson, W.J., *Australia and the League of Nations*, Sydney 1980

Jones, S. Shepard, *The Scandinavian states and the League of Nations*, Princeton, NJ 1939

Jordan, W. M., *Great Britain, France and the German problem 1918–1939: a study of Anglo-French relations in the making and maintenance of the Versailles settlement*, London 1943

Keatinge, Patrick, *The formulation of Irish foreign policy*, Dublin 1973

Kimmich, Christoph M., *Germany and the League of Nations*, Chicago 1976

Lauterpacht, H., *The function of law in the international community*, Hamden, Conn. 1966 (first publ. 1933)

League of Nations secretariat, *Ten years of world co-operation*, Geneva 1930

Lyman, Richard, *The first Labour government 1924*, London 1957

MacCartney, C. M. and others, *Survey of international affairs 1925*, ii, London 1928

McKercher, B. J. C., *The second Baldwin government and the United States, 1924–1929: attitudes and diplomacy*, Cambridge 1984

Maddox, William P., *Foreign relations in British Labour politics*, Cambridge 1934

Manning, C. A. W., *The policies of the British dominions in the League of Nations*, London 1932

Mansergh, Nicholas, *The Commonwealth experience*, ii: *From British to multiracial Commonwealth*, 2nd edn, London 1982

Marks, Sally, *The illusion of peace: international relations in Europe 1918–1933*, London 1976

Miller, David Hunter, *The Geneva Protocol*, New York 1925

—— *The Peace Pact of Paris: a study of the Briand-Kellogg treaty*, London 1928

Miller, J. D. B., *Britain and the old dominions*, London 1966

Murray, Gilbert, *From the League to the UN*, London 1948

Noel-Baker, P. J., *The Geneva Protocol for the Pacific Settlement of International Disputes*, London 1925

—— *The present juridical status of the British dominions in international law*, London 1929

Northedge, F. S., *The troubled giant: Britain among the great powers 1916–1939*, London 1966

—— *The League of Nations, its life and times*, Leicester 1986

Orde, Anne, *Great Britain and international security 1920–1926*, London 1978

Politis, N., *The new aspects of international law*, Washington 1928

Problems of peace (Lectures delivered at the meeting of the Geneva Institute of International Relations) 1st–4th ser., London 1926–30; 7th ser., London 1933

Rappard, W. E., *International relations as viewed from Geneva*, New Haven 1925

—— *The Geneva experiment*, London 1931

—— *The quest for peace*, Cambridge 1940

Richardson, Dick, *The evolution of British disarmament policy in the 1920s*, London 1989

Roskill, Stephen, *Naval policy between the wars*, 2 vols, London 1968, 1976

Shotwell, James, *War as an instrument of national policy and its renunciation in the Pact of Paris*, London 1929

Stacey, C. P., *Canada and the age of conflict*, ii: *The Mackenzie King era*, Toronto–Buffalo–London 1981

Taylor, A. J. P., *The trouble makers: dissent over foreign policy 1792–1939*, London 1957

—— *English history 1914–1945*, Harmondsworth 1970 (first publ. 1965)

Tilley, Sir John and Stephen Gaselee, *The Foreign Office*, London 1933

Toynbee, Arnold J., *The conduct of British empire foreign relations since the peace settlement*, London 1928

—— *Survey of international affairs 1920–1923, 1924, i, 1925, 1926, 1927*; (asst by V. M. Boulter) *1928, 1929, 1930, 1931*, London 1925–32

Tucker, W. R., *The attitude of the British Labour Party towards European and collective security problems*, PhD diss. Geneva 1950

Veatch, Richard, *Canada and the League of Nations*, Toronto–Buffalo 1975

Walters, F. P., *A history of the League of Nations*, London 1969 (first publ. in 2 vols, 1952)

Watt, D. C., *Personalities and politics: studies in the formulation of British foreign policy in the twentieth century*, London 1965

Webster, C. K. and S. Herbert, *The League of Nations in theory and practice*, London 1933

Wheare, K. C., *The constitutional structure of the Commonwealth*, Oxford 1960

Wheeler-Bennett, J. W. and Maurice Fanshawe, *Information on the world court 1918–1928*, London 1929

Williams, John Fisher, *Some aspects of the Covenant of the League of Nations*, London 1934

Winkler, H. R., *The League of Nations movement in Great Britain 1914–1919*, New Brunswick 1952

Winter, J. M., *Socialism and the challenge of war: ideas and politics in Britain 1912–1918*, London 1974

Wolfers, Arnold, *Britain and France between two wars*, New Haven 1940

Woolf, Leonard, *International government*, London 1916

Wooton, Graham, *Pressure groups in Britain 1720–1970*, London 1975

Zilliacus, Konni [Roth Williams], *The League of Nations today, its growth, record and relation to British foreign policy*, London 1923

—— *The League, the Protocol and the empire*, London 1925

—— *The mirror of the past: lest it reflect the future*, London 1944

Zimmern, Alfred, *The League of Nations and the rule of law 1918–1935*, 2nd edn, London 1939

Articles and chapters in books

Arnold-Forster, W., 'Arbitration: the government's record', *Socialist Review*, January 1929

(Noel-)Baker, Philip, 'The Permanent Court of International Justice', in H. W. V. Temperley (ed.), *A history of the peace conference of Paris*, vi, London 1924

—— 'The making of the Covenant from the British point of view', in P. Munch (ed.), *Les origines et l'oeuvre de la Société des Nations*, ii, Copenhagen 1924

—— 'The obligatory jurisdiction of the Permanent Court of International Justice', *The British Year Book of International Law, 1925*, vi, London 1925

Barcroft, Stephen, 'Irish foreign policy at the League of Nations 1929–1936', *Irish Studies in International Affairs* i (1979)

Beckett, Sir Eric, 'Sir Cecil Hurst's services to international law', *The British Year Book of International Law, 1949*, xxvi, London 1950

Beneš, E, 'Ten years of the League', *Foreign Affairs* viii (1930)

—— 'The League of Nations. Successes and failures', *Foreign Affairs* xi (1932)

Boyce, G., 'From war to neutrality: Anglo-Irish relations, 1921–50', *British Journal of International Studies (Review of International Studies)* v (1979)

Bramsted, Ernest, 'Apostles of collective security: the League of Nations Union and its functions', *Australian Journal of Politics and History* xiii (1967)

Brierly, J. L., 'Matters of domestic jurisdiction', *The British Year Book of International Law, 1925*, vi, London 1925

—— 'The judicial settlement of international disputes', *International Affairs* iv (1925)

—— 'The General Act of Geneva', *The British Year Book of International Law, 1930*, xi, London 1930

Butler, Sir J. R. M., 'The League of Nations', in H. W. V. Temperley (ed.), *A history of the peace conference at Paris*, iii, London 1920

Carlton, David, 'Great Britain and the League Council crisis of 1926', *The Historical Journal* xi (1968)

—— 'Disarmament with guarantees: Lord Cecil 1922–1927', *Disarmament and Arms Control* iii (1965)

—— 'Great Britain and the Coolidge naval disarmament conference of 1927', *Political Science Quarterly* lxxxiii (1968)

Cecil, Viscount and Arnold-Forster W., 'The freedom of the seas', *International Affairs* viii (1929)

Cecil, Hugh, 'Lord Robert Cecil and the League of Nations', *History Today* xxv (1975)

Crowe, Sibyl, 'Sir Eyre Crowe and the Locarno pact', *English Historical Review* lxxxvii (1972)

Cushendun, Lord, 'Disarmament', *International Affairs* vii (1928)

Dalton, Hugh, 'British foreign policy, 1929–31', *Political Quarterly* ii (1931)

—— and M. Hamilton, 'The eleventh Assembly of the League of Nations', *International Affairs* ix (1930)

'Diplomatic relations within the empire', *International Affairs* ix (1930) (Record of a discussion by members of the British empire delegations)

Duroselle, J. B., 'Reconsiderations – the spirit of Locarno: illusions of pactomania', *Foreign Affairs* l (1972)

Grün, G., 'Locarno, idea and reality', *International Affairs* xxxi (1955)

Hammarskjöld, A., 'The Permanent Court of International Justice and its place in international relations', *International Affairs* ix (1930)

—— 'Sidelights on the Court', *International Conciliation*, no. 232, Sept. 1927

—— 'Extension de l'arbitrage obligatoire et compétence obligatoire de la Cour Permanente de Justice Internationale', *Revue de Droit Internationale et de Législation Comparée* ix (1928)

Headlam-Morley, James, 'Treaties of guarantee', *Cambridge Historical Journal* ii (1926–8)

Hill, N. L., 'British arbitration policies', *International Conciliation*, No. 257, February 1930

Hudson, Manley O., 'The Permanent Court of International Justice', *Harvard Law Review* xxv (1922)

—— 'Ten years of the World Court', *Foreign Affairs* xi (1932)

Johnson, Douglas, 'Austen Chamberlain and the Locarno agreements', *University of Birmingham Historical Journal* viii (1961)

Keane, John, 'The Irish Free State and the British Empire', *International Affairs* v (1926)

Keatinge, Patrick, 'Ireland and the League of Nations', *Studies* lix (1970)

Lauterpacht, H., 'The British reservations on the Optional Clause', *Economica*, June 1930

—— 'The absence of an international legislature and the compulsory jurisdiction of international tribunals', *The British Year Book of International Law, 1930*, xi, London 1930

—— 'The so-called Anglo-American and continental schools of thought in international law', *The British Year Book of International Law, 1931*, xii, London 1931

Law Times, 'Hague Court: Optional Clause', 28 September 1929, vol. 168, no. 4513.

Lloyd, Lorna, ' "A springboard for the future": a historical examination of Britain's role in shaping the Optional Clause of the Permanent Court of International Justice', *The American Journal of International Law* lxxix (1985)

—— 'Le Sénateur Dandurand, pionnier du règlement pacifique des différends', *Études Internationales* xxiii (1992)

—— 'Philip Noel-Baker and peace through law' in David Long and Peter Wilson (eds.), *Thinkers of the twenty years' crisis. Inter-war idealism reassessed*, Oxford 1995

—— ' "Equality means freedom to differ": Canada, Britain and the world court in the 1920s', *Diplomacy and Statecraft*, vi (1996)

—— and James, Alan, 'The external representation of the dominions 1919–1948: its role in the unravelling of the British empire', *The British Year Book of International Law, 1996*, xlv, Oxford 1997

Loder, B. C. J., 'The Permanent Court of International Justice and compulsory jurisdiction', *The British Year Book of International Law, 1921-2*, ii, London 1921

MacDonald, J. Ramsay, 'Protocol or pact', *International Conciliation*, No. 212, September 1925

McNair, Lord, 'Sir Cecil James Barrington Hurst', *The British Year Book of International Law, 1962*, xxxviii, London 1964

MacQueen, Norman, 'Eamonn de Valera, the Irish Free State and the League of Nations, 1919–1946', *Eire-Ireland* xii (1982)

Manning, C. A. W., 'The "failure" of the League of Nations', *Agenda* i (1942)

Merrills, J. G., 'The International Court of Justice and the General Act of 1928', *Cambridge Law Journal* xxxix (1980)

—— 'The Optional Clause today', *The British Year Book of International Law, 1979*, l, Oxford 1981

Miller, J. B., 'The decline of inter-se', *International Journal* xxiv (1969)

Moore, Professor Sir William Harrison, 'The dominions of the British Commonwealth in the League of Nations', *International Affairs* x (1931)

Murray, Gilbert, 'The inevitable League', *Agenda* i (1942)

—— 'A League of Nations: the first experiment' in Joel Larus (ed.), *From collective security to preventive diplomacy*, London 1965

Nyholm, D. G., 'La Cour Permanente de Justice Internationale' in P. Munch (ed.), *Les origines et l'oeuvre de la Société des Nations*, ii, Copenhagen 1924

Page, Donald, 'The Institute's "popular arm": the League of Nations Society in Canada', *International Journal* xxxiii (1977-8)

Pollock, Sir Ernest, 'The International Court of the League of Nations', *The Cambridge Law Journal* i (1921)

Pollock, Sir Frederick, 'The Permanent Court of International Justice', *The British Year Book of International Law, 1926*, vii, London 1926

Polson Newman, Major E. W., 'The League of Nations Union', *English Review*, May 1929

Ponsonby, Arthur, 'Disarmament by example', *International Affairs* vii (1928)

Raffo, Peter, 'The League of Nations philosophy of Lord Robert Cecil', *Australian Journal of Politics and History* xx (1974)

Rappard, William E., 'Small states in the League of Nations', *Political Science Quarterly* xlix (1934)

Reynolds, P., 'The League of Nations', in *The New Cambridge modern history*, rev. edn, XII: *The shifting balance of world forces*, Cambridge 1968

Richards, Sir Erle, 'British prize courts and the war', *The British Year Book of International Law, 1920–1*, i, London 1921

—— 'The jurisdiction of the Permanent Court of International Justice', *The British Year Book of International Law, 1921–2*, ii, London 1921

Rolin, H., 'L'arbitrage obligatoire: une panacée illusoire', *Varia Juris Gentium*, Liber Amicorum, JPA, Français, 1959

Root, E., 'The constitution of an international court of justice', *The American Journal of International Law* xxv (1921)

Ross, A., 'Reluctant daughter or dutiful dominion? New Zealand in the inter-war years', *Journal of Commonwealth Political Studies* x (1972)

Scott, James Brown, 'Origins and draft scheme for a Permanent Court of International Justice with review', *International Conciliation* clvii (1920)

Sharp, Alan J., 'The Foreign Office in eclipse 1919–22', *History* lxi (1976)

Stambrook, F. G., 'The foreign secretary and foreign policy: the experiences of Austen Chamberlain in 1925 and 1927', *International Review of History and Political Science* vi (1969)

Steiner, Zara and M. L. Dockrill 'The Foreign Office reforms 1920–21', *The Historical Journal* xvii (1974)

Toynbee, Arnold, 'The trend of international affairs since the war', *International Affairs* x (1931)

Verzijl, J. H. W., 'The system of the Optional Clause', *International Relations* i (1959)

Waldock, C. H. M., 'The decline of the Optional Clause', *The British Year Book of International Law, 1955–6*, xxxii, London 1957

Williams, Sir John Fischer, 'The Geneva Protocol of 1924 for the Pacific Settlement of International Disputes', *International Affairs* iii (1924)

—— 'Model treaties for the pacific settlement of disputes', *International Affairs* vii (1928)

—— 'The place of law in international affairs', *International Affairs* vii (1928)

—— 'The Optional Clause. (The British signature and reservations)', *The British Year Book of International Law, 1930*, xi, London 1930

Winkler, H. R., 'The development of the League of Nations idea in Great Britain, 1914–19', *Journal of Modern History* xx (1948)

—— 'The emergence of a Labour foreign policy in Great Britain, 1918–1929', *Journal of Modern History* xxviii (1956)

Wright, Quincy, 'The General Act for the Pacific Settlement of International Disputes', *American Journal of International Law* xxiv (1930)

Young, Rt. Hon. Sir Hilton, 'The work of the eighth Assembly of the League of Nations', *International Affairs* vi (1927)

Zimmern, A. E., 'Is there an empire foreign policy?', *International Affairs* xiii (1934)

Pamphlets

Arnold-Forster, W., *Victory of reason, a pamphlet on arbitration*, London 1926

Chamberlain, Sir Austen, *The League of Nations*, Glasgow 1926

Fawcett, J. E. S., *The inter-se doctrine of Commonwealth relations*, London 1958

Henderson, A., *Labour and the Geneva Protocol*, London 1925

Higgins, A. Pearce, *British acceptance of compulsory arbitration under the Optional Clause and its implications*, London 1930

Johnson, D. H. N., *The English tradition in international law*, London 1961

Keen, F. H. N., *The Permanent Court of International Justice*, London 1922

League of Nations Union, *The Covenant and the Geneva Protocol with a brief explanatory introduction* (pamphlet 165), London 1924

—— *The Optional Clause* (pamphlet 240), London 1928, 1929

—— *Some questions on the Geneva Protocol* (pamphlet 166), London 1924

MacDonald, J. Ramsay, *Labour and the League of Nations*, London 1923

—— *Protocol or pact? The alternative to war*, Labour Party 1925

Murray, Gilbert, *The future of the British empire in relation to the League of Nations*, Sheffield 1928

—— *The League of Nations movement: some recollections of the early days*, London 1955

Rappard, W. E., *The British Empire as seen from Geneva*, London ?1930–31

—— *The quest for peace yesterday and today*, London 1954

Smith, Herbert A., *The British dominions and foreign relations*, McGill 1926

Unpublished works

Bargman, A., 'The role of the Assembly of the League of Nations in the pacific settlement of disputes', unpubl. PhD diss. 1952

Holland, Robert F., 'The Commonwealth in the British official mind: a study in Anglo-dominion relations 1925–1937', unpubl. DPhil diss. Oxford 1977

Manning, C. A. W., 'The policies of the British dominions in the League of Nations' (draft manuscript)

Page, Donald, 'Canadians and the League of Nations before the Manchurian crisis', unpubl. PhD diss. Toronto 1972

Raffo, P. S., 'Lord Robert Cecil and the League of Nations', unpubl. PhD diss. Liverpool 1967–8

Underwood, J. J., 'British disarmament policy 1925–34' unpubl. MPhil diss. Leeds 1977

Wigley, Philip George, 'The end of imperial unity: British-Canadian relations 1917–1926', unpubl. PhD diss. Cambridge 1971

Yearwood, Peter J., 'The Foreign Office and the guarantee of peace through the League of Nations, 1916–1925', unpubl. DPhil diss. Sussex 1980

Index